MD A

THE DISCOVERY OF BRITAIN

Also by Graham Robb

IN ENGLISH

Balzac
Victor Hugo
Rimbaud
Unlocking Mallarmé
Strangers: Homosexual Love in the Nineteenth Century
The Discovery of France
Parisians: An Adventure History of Paris
The Ancient Paths
Cols and Passes of the British Isles
The Debatable Land
France: An Adventure History

IN FRENCH

Baudelaire Lecteur de Balzac
La Poésie de Baudelaire et la Poésie Française

GRAHAM ROBB

THE DISCOVERY OF BRITAIN

An Accidental History
From 500 Million BC to the Next Election

PICADOR

First published 2025 by Picador
an imprint of Pan Macmillan
The Smithson, 6 Briset Street, London EC1M 5NR
EU representative: Macmillan Publishers Ireland Ltd, 1st Floor,
The Liffey Trust Centre, 117–126 Sheriff Street Upper,
Dublin 1 D01 YC43
Associated companies throughout the world

ISBN 978-1-0350-2611-1 HB
ISBN 978-1-0350-2612-8 TPB

Maps artwork by ML Design, redrawn from originals by Graham Robb.

Grateful acknowledgement is made for permission to reprint the following material:
Lines from 'MCMXIV', by Philip Larkin, from *The Whitsun Weddings*. Copyright © 1964 by
Philip Larkin. Reprinted by permission of Faber and Faber Limited. Lines from
'Di Great Insohreckshan' © Linton Kwesi Johnson, reproduced
by kind permission of LKJ Music Publishers Ltd.

3 5 7 9 8 6 4 2

A CIP catalogue record for this book is available from the British Library.

Typeset by Palimpsest Book Production Ltd, Falkirk, Stirlingshire
Printed and bound in the UK using 100% Renewable Electricity by CPI Group (UK) Ltd

To

Starling Lawrence

and

Peter Straus

Contents

List of Illustrations

1. 'Vikings Heading for Land', by Francis Bernard Dicksee (1873).
2. Excavations of a prehistoric site at Heathrow Terminal 5 and one of the Franco-British supersonic Concorde airliners, in service from 1976 to 2003. © *Framework Archaeology*.
3. Robinson Crusoe's island in Daniel Defoe's *Serious Reflections During the Life and Surprising Adventures of Robinson Crusoe* (1720).
4. The 'Saxon Shore' forts of south-east England in the late Roman Empire, from a list in the *Notitia dignitatum* compiled c. AD 420, illustrated by Peronet Lamy at Basel in 1436. The forts, from top left, are Othona (Bradwell), Dubris (Dover), Lemannis (Lympne), Branodunum (Brancaster), Gariannum (Burgh Castle near Great Yarmouth), Regulbium (Reculver), Rutupiae (Richborough), Anderida (Pevensey) and Portus Adurni (Portchester). © *The Bodleian Libraries, University of Oxford, Bodleian Library MS. Canon. Misc. 378, fol. 153v.*
5. Tombstone of a Roman cavalry officer of the Germanic Treveri tribe serving at Lancaster in c. AD 80. The trampled body and severed head are those of a Briton, probably of the local Brigantes tribe. © *Lancashire County Council.*
6. The compass-drawn design which produced the face on the Celtic funerary urn known as the Aylesford Bucket (c. 50 BC) and the solstice bearings of the British map of southern England based on a 4:3 grid, superimposed on a modern map. Author's drawing.
7. A figure from the early-fourth-century Roman mosaic discovered at Hinton St Mary (Dorset) in 1963. © *The Trustees of the British Museum.*
8. The British Museum's reconstruction of a helmet from the ship burial excavated in 1939 at Sutton Hoo (Suffolk) by the river

Deben, believed to be the resting place of Rædwald, King of East Anglia (r. c. 599 – c. 624). © *The Trustees of the British Museum.*

9. Powick and environs on the Ordnance Survey One-Inch map. Sheet 199, surveyed 1882–6, revised 1907, published 1909.
10. Midland shires in the 'Victory' jigsaw puzzle of industries in England and Wales (Bournemouth: G. J. Hayter, early 1970s). Author's photograph.
11. The Bayeux Tapestry (1070s), showing the completion of the new Westminster Abbey in 1065 and the funeral of King Edward the Confessor in January 1066, nine months before the Battle of Hastings. *Details of the Official digital representation of the Bayeux Tapestry – 11th century. City of Bayeux, DRAC Normandie, University of Caen Normandie, CNRS, Ensicaen, Photos: 2017 – La Fabrique de patrimoines en Normandie.*
12. Hills Tower near Dumfries, a bastle (fortified farmhouse) built c. 1530 for the Maxwell family. The windowed house was added in 1721. *Courtesy of HES (John Fleming Collection).*
13. The Tabard Inn in Southwark, demolished in 1873. 'In Southwerk at the Tabard as I lay / Redy to wenden on my pilgrimage / To Caunterbury with ful devout corage, / At night was come in-to that hostelrye / Wel nyne and twenty in a companye, / Of sondry folk' (General Prologue to Chaucer's *Canterbury Tales*). © *Print Collector/Contributor/Getty Images.*
14. The English actor John Philip Kemble as Shakespeare's Macbeth, c. 1800. From The New York Public Library. https://digitalcollections.nypl.org/items/510d47e4-4ffd-a3d9-e040-e00a18064a99
15. Hessle Road at the corner of Madeley Street, St Andrews Ward, Kingston upon Hull, May 2024. The mural commemorates Hull's 'fishing heritage'. Author's photograph.
16. Cheviot sheep near the source of Liddel Water, Scottish Borders, October 2021. Author's photograph.
17. Janet (Jenny) Geddes hurling her stool at the Dean of St Giles' Cathedral in Edinburgh on the day when the Book of Common Prayer authorized by Charles I was introduced in Scotland (23 July 1637). © *19th era/Alamy Stock Photo*

30. World War Two Fighter Planes Flying over the Forth Rail Bridge and the Firth of Forth, Scotland. © *Chris Hellier/Alamy Stock Photo.*
31. Tarsem Singh Sandhu boarding a London bus at the Chiswick bus depot on 17 June 1968. © *Keystone Press/Alamy Stock Photo.*
32. Aneurin Bevan, Minister of Health, on the first day of the National Health Service (5 July 1948), at Park Hospital (now Trafford General Hospital), Davyhulme, Greater Manchester. © *University of Liverpool Faculty of Health & Life Sciences.*
33. Engraving by Simon J. Phillips (1957–83), given to the author in 1975. The anthropophage pig was inspired by George Harrison's 'Piggies' on the Beatles' 'White Album'.
34. Old Sarum near Salisbury, May 2022, the site of an Iron Age hillfort, Roman and Saxon towns, and a Norman castle and cathedral. The town of Old Sarum was derelict and deserted by 1540. Author's photograph.

List of Maps

1

Off Course

'Vikings Heading for Land'.

IN THE AUTUMN of 2018, my wife Margaret and I returned from a French cycling expedition to find one half of Great Britain cut off from the other. We had taken the Scotland-bound train from London Euston. It was still running to time when the first signs of devastation appeared shortly after the Watford Gap. This is the nearly invisible pass in the middle of England where the Grand Union Canal, the London & North Western Railway, a Roman road and the M1 motorway converge. Sheep stood numbly in flooded fields; trees were teetering or horizontal. In the 'quiet coach', an over-amplified metallic screaming reached us from a distant part of the train: someone seemed to be shouting at us from an exposed footplate next to a fireman shovelling coal. We and our fellow passengers hazarded an interpretation of the noise: the card-reader was broken and only cash would be accepted at the on-board shop. Then came a second, barely audible announcement informing us that we would be lucky to reach Preston.

An Atlantic hurricane named Ali by the Irish Meteorological Service had closed motorways, snapped overhead cables, precipitated landslides, killed someone in Cheshire and caused all train services between Preston and Scotland to be cancelled. A gale was still blowing and high-sided trucks were still being toppled.

The ease with which the island of Great Britain can be cut in half was noted by the Nazi invasion planners in 1940:

> The only two lines between England and Scotland pass through [Carlisle and Newcastle]. It is no exaggeration to say that destruction of these two stations would interrupt all rail traffic between Scotland and England.

Later that day, as the sun rushed to bed in a distant place behind the battlements of a medieval castle, having no light by which to read, I had the idea for this book. I imagined a social, geographical and political history of the British Isles based on the evidence of natives, nomads, invaders and immigrants, the mighty and the impotent, the blindingly famous and the utterly obscure. The narrator would refer to his own self-inflicted or unavoidable experience as a child and young adult. He would recall the muddled mystery of events but, having what he had apparently called 'a good rememberer', he would not feel the need to reminisce.

No creature or nation lives life in chronological order, and so there would be room for the surprising contractions, dilations and reversals of time. Just as a naturalist would never refer to only one era when describing a landscape, the ages of this four-dimensional history would not begin on a certain day and then, when they ended, end for ever.

On that day of devastation and delay, it struck me that our most rewarding adventures and uprootings had been the result of accidents – the collapse of a canal path on a transnational cycle route, a dead body on a railway line, the geological events which placed a mountain pass in one place rather than another and all the other mishaps and strokes of luck produced by the two-wheeled time machine which has been our sole means of private locomotion for the last forty years.

*

At the Victorian railway station of Preston in the county of Lancashire, passengers had been 'detraining' since early afternoon. It looked like the mass evacuation scene in a war film. Women were dictating shopping lists and simple recipes into mobile phones. No replacement buses were running and none would have taken bicycles anyway. The next train for Scotland would not leave until breakfast the following day.

Preston is the mill town which Charles Dickens used as a model for 'Coketown' in his novel of social and industrial misery, *Hard Times*. 'It was a town of red brick, or of brick that would have been red if the smoke and ashes had allowed it.' Margaret and I both knew something of Preston and did not want to spend the night in it. We found a member of the platform staff and told her that we had to reach Carlisle in time to cycle the eighteen miles to our home on the Anglo-Scottish border where a night without a moon means total darkness.

The staff member told us in confidence of a rumour: twenty-five miles up the line at Lancaster a train driver was preparing to attempt the crossing of Shap, the wind-scourged gateway to the Carlisle Plain and Scotland. If we could get to Lancaster in, say, two and a half hours, we might be home in time for tea . . . I left the bikes with Margaret, ran up the exit ramp and down Fishergate in search of an efficient bookshop.

'Maps?' 'Upstairs.' I grabbed a rudimentary road atlas and tore out the relevant sheets while my card payment was accepted. Plotting a rapid but safe route through an unfamiliar region normally takes at least a day. I ran back to the glutted station. In urban footage of the early 1900s a running pedestrian never turns heads; now, the thump of feet on concrete suggests emergency or crime. From a far platform, I waved the map sheets reassuringly at Margaret.

We pushed the bikes up the exit ramp into a barrage of police officers. 'Which way is north?' The constable pointed without hesitation to a cloud-streaked sky beyond a parapet. People stared and smiled: a helpful bobby, two slim touring bikes lightly packed, a crumpled map and a compass direction – these were the elements of a children's adventure book, Chapter One.

*

The plan was to reach Lancaster as quickly as possible without being killed. We zigzagged through the Industrial Revolution terraces of Plungington then Fulwood, in and out of the single-minded primary-school rush-hour traffic and out onto the A6. The surging circulation was siphoned off by the Preston Bypass. This was the first stretch of motorway to be built in Britain (1958). On trips north with my parents, the name 'Preston' had rarely been uttered without the sound of a deflating tyre on the 'P'. Tailbacks and accidents usually forced us onto the old trunk road to Garstang and the North. I recognized the wide grassy verges and the now-deserted pavements of 1930s road building. The mesmeric cat's-eyes were scuffed and bruised but still viable in their rubber-and-metal skulls.

In the absence of information on traffic flows and local attitudes, it is usually advisable to head for the past. Near Catterall, we branched off onto the turnpike road. The swerving undulations of these eighteenth-century stage-coach express routes can be frustrating to modern motorists. I spent a few precious seconds photographing a turnpike milestone with its proud flourish of curlicues: 'To Garstang ¾ Mile | To Preston 10 Miles.' Immediately after the milestone came a double bend and a fast descent to the river Wyre.

A month later, I found the exact same spot in an account written by Thomas De Quincey, the 'English opium-eater'. He was travelling to Lancaster in a mail coach at the speed of a bicycle in 1817 or 1818:

> About ten miles from Preston, it came about that I found myself left in charge of his Majesty's London and Glasgow mail, then running at the least twelve miles an hour.

The night was deep and peaceful, the road smooth, the lamps agleam. Coachman and guard had fallen asleep; the horses raced along on the right (i.e. the wrong) side of the road, finding the sandy surface softer on their hooves. In opium-induced slow motion, De Quincey saw the pony and trap of a young man and his lady frantically manoeuvring as the coach bore down, and then the splintering collision. The post horses dutifully thundered on. Mail coaches were under no legal obligation to stop.

> I rose in horror, to gaze upon the ruins we might have caused . . . The young man trembled not, nor shivered. He sat like a rock. But his was the steadiness of agitation frozen into rest by horror . . . The turn of the road carried the scene out of my eyes in an instant, and swept it into my dreams for ever.

Journeying into the past in a post-industrial conveyance can create serious practical problems. Beyond Garstang, the road narrowed on the approach to a humpbacked canal bridge. This was forty years before the railway and twenty years before De Quincey's accident. I heard a car making up its mind, too late, to squeeze past before the bridge. As we reached the bottleneck, it juddered to a halt beside me. After a purely telepathic conversation, I invited the driver to proceed. She sidled onto the bridge just as another car came blindly from the other side.

This farcical situation is easy to explain. The Lancaster Canal, opened in 1797, was an artery of the new mass-transit nationwide system which connected Lancaster to almost every part of England. Canal barges had precedence over road traffic, and so the bridges were built at right angles to the roads, regardless of inconvenience to drivers. The simple geometry of these arrangements is still inscribed on the landscape.

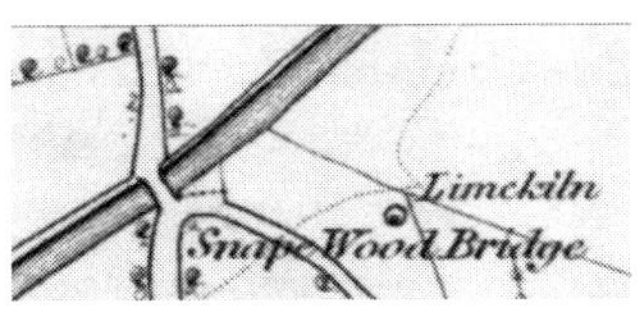

Ordnance Survey Six-Inch map, sheet xxxix (1847).

The region we now entered was a rolling plain of miry heaths and lanes which led to small farmhouses or perhaps nowhere but the sea. Each landscape has its own repertoire of skies: these were grey and endless, a planetarium projection of coastal cloud forms. A smudge on the western horizon was the ruin of a twelfth-century monastery – Cockersand, 'standing veri blekely and object to all wynddes', according to the travelling antiquary John Leland, who passed that way in 1538. I knew nothing of it, nor of the land we were crossing. The name of the region – Amounderness – rang a faint bell.

In nearly faceless but unforgettable country like this, it is hard to escape a feeling of being lost even when you know where you are. The squiggly lines of the field boundaries indicated ancient countryside; the erratic lanes which cut across them are more ancient still. Amounderness was one of the Viking divisions of the eminently invadable west coast of Engla-land. It was the headland ('ness') of Agmundr, which is either the name of a tenth-century Norse chieftain or a figment of etymology. The Norman Domesday Book (1086) classified most of 'Agemundrenesse' as 'waste'.

The route we were piecing together had begun to coincide with a Roman road. Typically Roman, the road proceeded, not in a single straight line, but in a sequence of knight's moves on a triangulated chessboard. Beyond Cockerham, it changed direction. This was disconcerting: the new bearing would take us more than a mile to the west of Roman Lancaster, the *castrum* on the river Lune.

Outside the old smugglers' inn at Conder Green, a rare inhabitant of Amounderness had been watching our approach. He assured us that the side-lane which seemed to end at the sandflats of the river Lune would eventually take us into Lancaster. Daylight was drooping; the waves of the tidal Lune flopped onto the muddy shore; the last edible supplies had been consumed. I felt cold, jittery and optimistic. This was intellectually familiar territory. Two years before, I had discovered the simple grids which make sense of the eerily accurate British maps digitally preserved by Ptolemy in the second century AD (ch. 6). I knew that the city on the Lune had been an inland port of the Brigantes tribe and that we were now in the Celtic Iron Age on our way to the town called Vinnovium. The estuary route had existed before the Romans: from then until the early 1800s, Lancaster had been one of the busiest Atlantic trading ports in Britain. A route which survives for that length of time never disappears entirely unless the sea engulfs it.

Five miles later, we were hauling ourselves up a street lined with stone houses. The battlements of Lancaster Castle came into view at the same moment as a hedge-obscured lane. It led down to the left, then to the right and straight onto the northbound platform of Lancaster Station where, as foretold, a train was waiting.

The platform manager stared at the bicycles. 'Where have you just come from?' Apparently, we were the first stranded passengers to make it through from Preston. As I answered his question, I realized that we had ridden an accidentally coherent route backward through two thousand years of British history. This book was conceived at that moment and at first it seemed a matter of secondary importance that the train was going nowhere until tomorrow.

2

'Crap Country'

Heathrow Terminal 5.

We reached home that evening because a bus driver wanted to test his nerve on the dying storm and its spent munitions. He threw our bikes into the hold, wrestled his bus over the debris-strewn roads of the Lake District and delivered us to the seemingly gaslit, semi-derelict or, according to the local Member of Parliament, 'dynamic' city of Carlisle. A taxi resembling an ambulance stripped of its medical equipment took us eighteen miles north and dropped us on a nameless road at the entrance to a wood which drivers from other parts of the country fear to enter.

Remote-controlled by memory, we tiptoed over the cattle grid and the cow-cropped track bed of the long-defunct North British Railway. A steam train once sped past on its way from Edinburgh to London. In the drawing-room carriage, Queen Victoria clutched the fittings and scribbled a note 'requesting reduced speed for the rest of the journey'. On being handed this surprising complaint at Carlisle Station, the driver would promise 'the utmost steadiness' and the Queen would arrive safely at Windsor Palace on the morning of 6 November 1886.

Some other source of illumination must have been operating – probably the airglow of ions in the upper atmosphere familiar to all earthly creatures until the Industrial Revolution. Everything seemed to be normal. A tall oak born on the steep sliding bank of the ravine at the time of the Battle of Waterloo had been felled by the wind like all its ancestors. Its tree-top thicket now blocked the lonning.* Animals which had crossed from the Continent on a swampy land bridge at the end of the last ice age had colonized the garden. A light in the house showed one roe deer, then three, then four, looking up from their flower-bed buffet.

At dawn, we inspected our kingdom for the usual unexpected changes. As though by the gravitational force of re-entry, the centuries now lapsed in accelerated reverse order. I had recently begun to split the stones brought by melting glaciers and which the river arranges on its shifting beds of shingle. Those stony 'dungeons of the soul' (V. Hugo) contain archival evidence of sedimentations and eruptions. Cracked by the hammer, some gnarly black lumps released powerful smells of sulphur from a four-hundred-and-fifty-million-year-old Cumbrian eruption. Since time is the medium of history, I thought that the book should acknowledge the enormous weight of years on which we walk.

Even in the exceptionally unwooded island of Great Britain, time is measured by a bewildering variety of clocks. The pendulum cycles of the river move its pebble beaches to midstream then back to the shore between one series of floods and the next. Willow-pattern crockery sherds datable to c. 1900 began to reach us in 2020 from the nearest habitation by a clogged rivulet formerly used as a rubbish chute, indicating a conveyance speed of about eight feet a year. The concentric calendars of tree rings comprise accurate records of

* Or 'loaning' (Scots): a track along which livestock and certain people are allowed to pass.

weather and local events – years of drought or deluge, summers long and short, half-centuries of overshadowing and crowding abruptly ended by earthflow, death or felling by hand and tool.

*

'Protohistoric' is the word applied to periods which predate deliberate records other than the testimony of outsiders. I felt the need for a term other than pre- or proto-historic – perhaps 'non-human historic' would do.

One day, near the mouth of the burn on the edge of our land where the torrent has exposed a cliff face, I realized that I was looking at frozen footage of an event which took place around three hundred million BC in the early Carboniferous Period.

A close-knit population of mussel-like brachiopods had been feeding in warm shallow waters south of the Equator. A storm had come and created a mudflow in which they perished all at once. There they still were, turned into knobs of calcite in flaky shale, having long since migrated tectonically to the future Anglo-Scottish border.

The brachiopods had shared those primeval waters with millions of dainty, flower-like creatures which first appeared five hundred million years ago. The frondy arms and tubular feet of the crinoids trapped plankton, transferring it to the mouth, which was adjacent to the anus. Beautiful even in fossilized disintegration, many a crinoid is still accompanied in its lithic photograph by the air-breathing gastropod which supped at its anal vent.

Natural selection equipped these complex beings with water vessels, nerves and muscles, a digestive tract and a reproductive system. They possessed a head or 'calyx' of coiled and radiant nerves. I have one in front of me now – a clutch of neat polygonal plates the size of a cupped palm. This ancestor of a brain lived through the micro-events and catastrophes of all sentient creatures. It had no emotions or morality and was not subject to the random brain-wiring events which prevent us from becoming clones of our parents. Some crinoids 'learned' to crawl or swim, which enabled them to refine their diet by specializing in particular kinds of plankton, but never in five hundred million years of evolution did they experience the need to develop the notion of 'history'.

*

The first hominins known to have walked on land which is now British appeared less than one million years ago. In a landscape of conifers, grass and mud, a group of five adults and children left their footprints by the banks of the ancestral river Thames. The site, recently submerged, is on the Norfolk coast. For the next eight thousand centuries, at least four distinct species of *Homo* came and went, as did ice sheets and shorelines. Average temperatures rose and fell. In 450,000 BC, a gigantic lake burst its banks and created the English Channel.

At periods in its long history of damming and release, the Channel was less of an obstacle than a snagging swamp. Log boats and coracles of hide-bound hazel and willow are presumed to have existed. Yet in all the years from 180,000 to 60,000 BC, when Britain was once again joined to the Continent by the marshes of 'Doggerland' (named after a sandbank in the North Sea), five thousand generations of bison, reindeer, cave bear and woolly rhinoceros roamed the chilly tundra on the edge of the habitable world without ever having to deal with humans.

In other parts of Europe towards the end of that period, gods came into being, as did the realities and concepts of spare time, art, cosmetics, sport and humour, which existed long before 'Wise Guy' *Homo sapiens sapiens* arrived (after *Homo sapiens neanderthalensis*) on the south coast of Britain around 40,000 BC.

Geography and climate are not just matters of comfort or complaint: they determine patterns of settlement, architecture, clothing, outlook and, in the long term, physical attributes. They create communities like the one in which I live, where humans from different parts of Britain and, in one case, the world behave like members of a distinct tribe.

Twenty years ago, I knew a man from 'Down Under' – a term semantically similar to 'Dumnonia', the Celtic 'underworld' of Britain's South West Peninsula. He had come from the red dust deserts of Western Australia to England, where until the late Middle Ages the Earth was also called 'the Mould' or just 'Mould': 'Our time is three score yeare and ten, that we do live on mould.' He missed the unwitnessed day-and-night-long bike rides across the deserts and his native population density of one human per square kilometre. Here, he had to share his square kilometre with two hundred and seventy-eight other people. When something went wrong, even if it was his own fault – boarding the wrong train or closing the front door and then remembering the key – he blamed this sodden, self-aggrandizing island outpost of humanity: 'I'll tell you what the problem is – the problem is, this is a crap country.'

For the purposes of human beings, Britain remained a 'crap country' until c. 9700 BC when the Gulf Stream began to warm these fortunate isles. From then on, there would always be a human presence in Britain. Much of it became what most people would call liveable or even pleasant. Brain-accelerated evolution enhanced the sapient primate's puny jaws, hands and, to a lesser extent, legs. (Wheels did not reach Britain until c. 1300 BC and the revolutionary wheelbarrow not until the Middle Ages.) The people of the Neolithic or New Stone Age fished and hunted, worked wood, wore beads, warmed themselves at fires, used cooking stones and ate deer, elk, boar and shellfish under thatched roofs. They formed relationships with dogs. They buried their dead and communicated with beings wiser and more powerful than themselves.

They did not stay long in one place, which reduced the need for maintenance and improvement. For four years, we lived on the edge of Oxford under a recently made thatched roof which, by the time we left, was sagging, green and rodent-ridden. Here, we use willow and alder to firm up muddy stretches of woodland path. In the burn, there are flat 'bakestones' but we venture to use them only as decoration.

Agriculture in non-competitive, kitchen-garden forms came from the Continent in c. 4000 BC. Only then were permanent settlements established on British soil. The earliest known proto-villages – one in the far south, others in the far north – date from c. 3700, which means that, in the history of civilization, the British Isles come later than the Americas and Australia.

*

THE INCONGRUOUSLY DECOROUS village of Horton ('dirty farm' in Old English) lies in the environs of a sand-and-gravel quarry between Windsor Castle and Heathrow Airport Terminal 5. John Milton lived at Horton in the 1630s and evoked its prettiness in his poetry – its 'aged oaks' and smoky cottages, the lawns and fallows 'where the nibbling flocks do stray', and the 'enclosure green' of Eden in *Paradise Lost*, set off from the 'hairie' wilderness 'with thicket overgrown, grottesque and wilde'. To Horton's first permanent residents, it was a place where crops and children could be raised, a home on the wide Mould to which tribal memories would be attached.

In 2013, when topsoil was stripped away for gravel extraction, archaeologists discovered the ground plans of four rectangular houses. Thatched sheds made of oak planks and posts stood there some time between 3800 and 3600 BC. The largest house was partitioned into two rooms and probably had a mezzanine floor. It measured 1,132 square feet, making it slightly more spacious than the average detached house in Britain today. The occupants of this Neolithic housing development were not hand-to-mouth hunter-gatherers but settled inhabitants of a fertile floodplain. They made flint tools and arrowheads; they ground corn and used cooking pots. They had answers to the problems of rainwater and rubbish. Floor-sweepings were found at what had evidently been a front door.

These proto-Hortonians were connected to the filaments of a basic trading economy. They owned one of the must-have commodities of the fourth millennium BC – a polished greenstone axe from a cone-shaped mountain in the inaccessible heart of the Lake District two hundred and fifty miles to the north. Langdale axes have been found all over England and southern Scotland, with heavy concentrations in low-lying areas. For tree felling, flint was more effective, but the axes were beautiful to touch and behold. The polished greenstone might have brought good luck from the high fabled places which glimmered in its metamorphic sheen.

I was startled to discover by a simple calculation that we live within mind's-eye distance of these outermost suburbs of British civilization. The Psalms of the fifth century BC posited seventy years as the standard length of a human life. By this measure, we of the Fossil Fuel Age are separated by only eighty-one lifetimes from the Neolithic colonists of Horton. Writing was invented in Mesopotamia three hundred years after their houses were built. There were cities in the Near East that were already a thousand years old.

From here on, we are dealing with relatively short periods. The entire span of documented British history covers no more than thirty lifetimes, which is why we are able to live in several ages at once without being disturbed by the anachronism.

*

THOUGH IT BELONGED to the same period (c. 3700 BC), the first Neolithic dwelling I knew was quite unlike the detached sheds of Horton. It lay, partially intact, in the far north of Scotland in the county of Sutherland – so named by early-medieval settlers from the Northland. In central and eastern Sutherland, there are thousands of stone 'hut-circles' on platforms cut into sloping ground for drainage and the view. These circles mark the sites of roundhouses. Some are surrounded by miniature fields, identifiable by alignments of boulders or cairns that were heaped up when the land was cleared of stones.

In the wandering glens and hummocky hills of eastern Sutherland, there are also mounds of stone which cover passages leading to a sunken chamber. Some of these dwellings of the dead, dated to 3700–3000 BC, were entered directly from an adjoining hut. Life changed so little that many remained in use well into the Ages of Bronze and Iron.

One 'passage grave' in Strath Brora was probably abandoned in prehistory. Five thousand winters and countless generations of browsing, burrowing and transhumant animals came and went, yet the tomb retained a palpable structural coherence. Even now, it was only half hidden by turf and heather.

In the summer of AD 1971, after befriending a free-range cow and then finding nothing else to do, my sister Alison and I, aged fourteen and thirteen, decided to investigate the bulges that were clearly visible in slanting sunlight all over the rough pasture around our rented hovel in Strath Brora. Excavating by hand, we uncovered a cavity which seemed to open into a narrow tunnel. 'Treasure' was unlikely but there was a good chance of a bone or preferably skull to take home as a holiday souvenir.

Having some experience of stonemasonry, our father recognized the work of human hands. He proposed a visit to the seaside town of Dornoch, seventeen miles down the coast. At Dornoch public library, the council archaeologist listened politely to our description and then, to my surprise, informed us that we were describing a 'chambered tomb'. These prehistoric structures, she told us, were extremely common in the area. In fact, they were so numerous, and funding was so scarce, that only a tiny fraction had been investigated.

That night in the cottage, my mother, unusually for her, was visited by a nightmare. The local population of prehistoric living dead had clawed and crawled its way out of its chambered graves and come to peer glumly through the rain-streaked windows of our bleak and helpless abode. In the morning, though there was still another day or two to run on the lease, we left the moorland mortuary and migrated in our rented Dormobile to a vast encampment of semi-nomadic travellers and holidaymakers two miles from Dornoch on the edge of the North Sea.

Archaeologists in a distant future may struggle to explain this caravan metropolis. Arriving from the Neolithic Age, we found its version of modernity hysterically funny. The name of the encampment was displayed in giant letters on the gable end of an old stone cottage: 'GRANNIE'S HEILAN' HAME'.

The eponymous grandmother had died and many of her clan relatives had left the shores of ancient Caledonia and migrated to Massachusetts. The 'highland home' alluded to a popular song of the 1920s for voice and accordion. To the plangent compressions and expansions of that lung-like instrument, the voice from 'ower the sea' recalled 'those days of long ago' in the heathery highlands – 'and it seems it was just yesterday'.

3
The Size of Britain

Robinson Crusoe's island.

A GIRL AT MY third and last primary school lived in a tall pink house on a quiet back road to the next village. She had cheeks like Worcester Pearmain apples and a Christian name to match. Her surname was the name of a star sign. The house stood alone at the top of a rise where the lane twists itself around a blind corner. Whenever my friend Simon and I walked or pedalled along that stretch of hedge-shrouded lane, we looked up at her bedroom window and thought of an ocean pushing into the heart of the countryside, lapping at the limits of our landlocked rustic world.

Her seemingly risible claim that she could see the sea from her bedroom window struck us as a yokelish delusion or even as a lie since she refused to allow a verification committee to come and inspect the enchanted casement. And yet, because she was a modest girl who rarely drew attention to herself, a doubt remained. We loiteringly plotted break-ins that would have involved diversions, disguises and grappling-hooks. Planning a burglary must be one of the best means of fixing topographical details in the mind: the scene was still vivid when, two years ago, I happened upon a digital 'visibility cloak' and was able to test her claim without breaking the law.

Early on a school day in spring – the cartographic 'cloak' revealed – the rosy-cheeked visionary might have spotted the pearly sheen of dawn drawing a convincing maritime horizon along the Cotswold escarpment twenty-five miles to the south-east where a Georgian folly called Broadway Tower stands on the Worcestershire–Oxfordshire border. The view over the hedgerows is impressive enough to have satisfied the needs of a child's imagination. As a literal-minded adult, I found it slightly disappointing. Then the visibility app suggested moving to higher ground across the lane and placed its crosshairs on an inconspicuous knoll which I must have seen a hundred times from my own bedroom window half a mile to the south-east.

The summit of the grandly named 'Bush Hill' is only forty-two feet higher than the casement, yet the view is vast. From that bump in the landscape, she may indeed have caught the glint of annual floodwaters laying siege to Tewkesbury and the fields of Gloucestershire washed and scoured by the incoming tide of the Severn Sea.

*

Seeing the sea from far inland is supposed to evoke an exhilarating, dreamlike apprehension of unanticipated distance – which is why J. R. R. Tolkien's homebody hobbits, who 'liked to have books filled with things that they already knew', have not the slightest desire to discover the view from the tallest of the elf-towers:

> [They] said that you could see the Sea from the top of that tower, but no hobbit had ever been known to climb it. They did not go in much for towers.

The elf-tower is believed to have been modelled on Broadway Tower, in which case the elves would have enjoyed a very similar view of the Severn floodplain or, in their universe, the shores of the Great Sea of Belegaer.

These inland visions show how small the island is. Few high clouds over central England are not simultaneously observable from a ship at sea. In Britain, it is impossible to be more than seventy miles from the coast. All counties in Scotland, all but one in Wales, and twenty-nine of the thirty-nine English shires boast one or several hilltops with a view of the open sea, an estuary or of mountains on an opposite shore.

In the North Pennines at rare moments of clarity, eagle-eyed walkers can reputedly make out two oceans from the summit of Cross Fell. When it roars and tumbles past my house on the Anglo-Scottish border, Liddel Water is barely fifteen miles from the Solway Firth. Follow it upstream for twenty miles to the point where the river disappears into a forest, and there, on the peaty sponge of Peel Fell, a binocular-assisted eye can make out the headland where the Tweed enters the North Sea.

Admiring the view of the North Sea from the top of the Cheviot in 1726, Daniel Defoe was surprised to be told by his guide that if he turned around, he might catch sight of the Irish Sea. Defoe was right to be sceptical and perhaps disinclined in any case to see both oceans almost at once, having previously experienced in his mind the shrivelling effect of realizing that one is stuck on an island:

> I travelled for discovery up to the top of that hill, where, after I had with great labour and difficulty got to the top, I saw my fates to my great affliction, viz. that I was in an island environed every way with the sea.*

*

As THOUGH TO make up for the exiguity of the island, there is a long tradition of overestimating the length of Great Britain. The Romans bragged of conquering a land which overstepped the bounds of civilization. Caesar was told by traders or by the people of Cantium (Kent) that the side of Britain facing Germany ran north for eight hundred miles. This was a good enough estimate for the Venerable

* *Robinson Crusoe*, chapter 4.

Bede in 731 and also for the thirteenth-century hagiographer of a Midland saint:

> Vif kinges þer were þulke tyme   in Engelond ido
> For Engelond was god and long   & somdel brod þerto
> Aboute eiȝte hondred mile   Engelond long is
> Fram þe souþ into þe norþ   and to hondred brod iwis
> Fram þe est into þe west*

By 'England', he probably meant Britain, which is about three hundred miles at its widest and six hundred at its longest. My parents, natives of that reputedly rain-sodden realm of 'wild and waterless mountains and desolate and swampy plains' (Cassius Dio), often encountered similar conceptions of British geometry. Friends of my mother had a mental image of Britain which an ancient Roman might have recognized but which most medieval cartographers would have known to be false.

Our annual holiday to Scotland was deemed an appallingly long and spartan expedition. Why not take the children to Devon and Cornwall like everyone else? One year, my mother gave in. That July, as we sat in the sweltering holiday traffic squeezing into the lobster-pot peninsula, she looked forward to thanking her friends in no uncertain terms. From our home in Stafford, it was one hundred and ninety-four miles to Ilfracombe in Devon, where it rained all the time, but twenty miles less to Gretna Green, where it rained only some of the time.

This sub-insular misperception of remoteness survived the advent of turnpike roads, railways and even the first stretches of motorway. It had the power to defy mathematical and legal evidence. In 1676, a highwayman who had robbed a sailor at four o'clock one morning at Gads Hill in Kent was tried and acquitted because he was able to prove that he had been in York before sunset on the same day. The

* 'Five kings there were in England then, / For England was good and long and also somewhat wide. / About eight hundred miles long is England / From south to north, and, forsooth, two hundred wide / From east to west.'

Lord Mayor of York himself testified in court. It was obvious to the jury that the accused could not have been in two such different parts of the kingdom on the same day. Gads Hill lay south of the Thames and twenty-six miles east of London, whereas York was quite definitely in the North.

The Gravesend ferry, the back roads and downs as far as Huntingdon, two stops for food, fodder, rest and sleep, then the Great North Road, and there was time aplenty to freshen up and change before going out and engaging the mayor in conversation at a bowls match. The amazing thing about William Nevison's ride is the jury's credulity. Nutmeg the mare averaged an impressive but not preposterous seventeen-and-a-half miles an hour over two hundred and twenty miles. In 1745, a Mr Cooper Thornhill rode almost the same distance over some of the same terrain, from Stilton to London and back, averaging almost twenty miles an hour. These days, the entire island, from Land's End to John o'Groats, can be bisected by a human-powered vehicle in less than two days.

*

SEVENTEEN HUNDRED YEARS after Romans sailed around the top of Caledonia in pursuit of pirates and proved to themselves that Britannia is an island, the longest domestic expedition in the history of British science gave an irrefutable measure of the island's extent.

Since before the time of Edward III (r. 1227–77), who replaced the wood stacks with pitch pots, and probably before the Saxon settlements, it had been known that vast areas could be covered by a telecommunications network of beácen-fýres lit on standing platforms. 'The ghastly war-flame' of the beacons could spread at the speed of light and a watchman's torch. In 'The Armada' (1832), Macaulay, who was later made Secretary at War, pictured the scintillant web of intelligence which electrified a sleepless population:

> Far on the deep the Spaniard saw, along each southern
>   shire,
> Cape beyond cape, in endless range, those twinkling points
>   of fire.
> . . .

Southward from Surrey's pleasant hills flew those bright
couriers forth;
High on bleak Hampstead's swarthy moor they started for
the north;
. . .
Till twelve fair counties saw the blaze on Malvern's lonely
height,
Till streamed in crimson on the wind the Wrekin's crest of
light,
. . .
Till Skiddaw saw the fire that burned on Gaunt's embattled
pile,*
And the red glare on Skiddaw roused the burghers of
Carlisle.

The triangulation of the United Kingdom by the Board of Ordnance (1783–1858) incidentally revealed the remarkably small number of vantage points required to span the entire island. Macaulay was right to believe that 'twelve fair counties' can be seen from the Worcestershire Beacon, the culmination of the Malvern Hills. Living only thirty fields from the summit, the girl in the pink house was just one blink away from a trans-national chain of signals.

The map of principal triangulation stations (1856) makes it fairly simple to devise two optical highways – or eyeways – crossing Britain at its longest and widest extent using the smallest possible number of points. The trajectories shown here (map 1) run from Carn Llidi to Lowestoft and from Start Point to Cape Wrath. The two lines intersect at the Worcestershire Beacon. This vast invisible marvel of Victorian science also embraces a vast length of time. Elizabethan beacons had blazed from some of the triangulation stations. Others were served by upland Roman roads. Almost all had been occupied by Iron Age hillforts or prehistoric burial mounds.

Heading east from Pembrokeshire to the Norfolk coast, the distances between the triangulation points are separated by ever

* Lancaster Castle.

shorter distances and require the occasional assistance of a tower. But from south to north, the ground is covered in great glancing leaps. In ideal conditions, thirteen pairs of eyes are all it would take to see from one end of Britain to the other.

4

Sea-Fearing Nation

The 'Saxon Shore' forts of the late Roman Empire.

THE SEA CHOMPS away at this gangly island from head to toe, tearing off lumps of cliff and headland, slobbering over farmland and leaving its mess behind. 'Nowhere is the sea's dominion wider', wrote the Roman historian Tacitus. He owed this cinematic description of the shredded shores of Caledonia to his father-in-law, who commanded the fleet-led invasion of northern Britain in AD 79–84:

> The many currents of the sea are carried hither and thither, and their swellings and swallowings are not limited to the coast: they go swirling and rushing deep inland, pushing in amongst the hills and even the mountains as though in their own domain.

On the coasts of north-west England, windy harbours are engulfed by mud, silt, sand and shingle delivered by the sea or dumped by angry rivers. Winds, tides and dyke-builders create such complex processes of accretion and erosion and such ambiguous zones of floodplain and watery field that no two maps show an identical coastline.

On the eastern seaboard and the Channel coast, garden sheds and swimming pools teetering on the briny brink or lying slumped and shattered on a beach are now a common news item. At least as far back as records exist, there were tales of flourishing towns whose houses and histories had been stolen by the sea. Sometimes, only a name survived. The port of Dunwich in Suffolk, once the commercial capital of East Anglia, sank out of sight in the fourteenth century. Winchelsea in Sussex had a seasonal population of Gascon wine merchants and pilgrims bound for Compostela. It was swamped by storm surges in 1287 and was last shown on a map in 1610 as a circular blot on the sea labelled '*Old Winchelsey Drowned*'.

More than twenty of these sandcastle towns and villages are listed in the Domesday Book of 1086. Even then, Dunewic was contemplating its day of doom: 'Formerly two carucates of ploughland, now only one. The other was carried off by the sea.' At Wrangle in Lincolnshire, Guy de Craon, a knight from Anjou, found himself lord and master of seven households and land that was 'waste on account of the sea's overflowing' – probably in the sector now marked on Ordnance Survey maps as '*Danger Area*' and '*Mud & Sand*'. In Norfolk, the harbour town of Scepedane (Shipden) – the name means 'valley of the sheep' – has completely disappeared. It was last heard of in 1888, when a paddle steamer taking day-trippers from Great Yarmouth to Cromer impaled itself on a submerged flinty formation one hundred and fifty yards off the end of Cromer pier. Local fishermen were able to identify the obstruction as the tower of Shipden parish church.

*

According to a reasonable assumption, this island nation has always been a nation of sea-farers. When a mini-armada of French or Icelandic trawlers seems to threaten the maritime integrity of Britain, a government minister will hoist the ensign which bears the legend, 'a proud sea-faring nation'. (The expression is also commonly applied to Norway, Denmark, the Netherlands, Latvia, Oman and several other small countries which are not islands.)

'Sea-*fearing* nation' would be more appropriate. In 1740, when two Scottish poets composed the patriotic hymn, 'Rule, Britannia', Britons may have ruled the waves and looked forward to never ever ever being slaves, but for more than one and a half millennia, from the twilight of pre-Roman independence to the last successful invasion from the Continent (1688), the sea was not the theatre of global dominance: it was the 'wall' of a 'fortress built by nature' or 'a moat defensive to a house' (Shakespeare, *Richard II*). For James Stuart, the first King of Great Britain, whose supporters staged *Richard II* in London in 1603, the 'fortress' was 'a little world within itself', with 'but one common limit or rather guard of the Ocean sea'.

A trident-brandishing Britannia riding a wave-lapped throne has figured on British coins since her reintroduction by Charles II in 1672. She was a remodelling of the allegorical figure on coins minted under Emperor Hadrian. The genteel Lady Britannia of the second century AD symbolized the watchfulness of an imperial outpost whose barbarian inhabitants had been enslaved and walled off from even more barbaric neighbours north of the Tyne. The Britannia of 1672 wore a trembling negligee and waved a hopeful olive branch. The intention was to inspire the populace with confidence in the navy, which was suffering regular humiliations at the hands of the Dutch, and so she was depicted on halfpennies and farthings – the coins most likely to be handled by common people.

Then, as in days long past, the rivers which were the veins and arteries of a trading nation seemed to be the conduits by which the whole body would be destroyed. To Samuel Pepys, a high-ranking naval administrator under Charles II, the navy was a joke – recklessly underfunded and mismanaged by braggarts, liars and fools. Its warships were manned by freshwater sailors and landlubbers illegally press-ganged and 'wholly unfit for sea'.

The noise of sea battles was heard far inland. Twenty miles from the coast at his vicarage in the Colne Valley, the Reverend Ralph Josselin was roused one morning in 1653

> to heare the thumping, thundering Cannon, which filled into country houses, and our beds with the dreadfull noise, I have not ever heard the like shooting in my life, its no question a terrible sea fight neare our doores between the Hollander and us.

News of later Anglo-Dutch battles was transmitted to Londoners by the Thames. The guns were once plainly heard in the streets of Bethnal Green two miles from St Paul's Cathedral. On 4 June 1666, hundreds of people gathered in Kensington and St James's Park to listen to the booming sound of English ships being sunk by the Dutch navy.

The sea was to pre-eighteenth-century Britain what the sky was to wartime London, Liverpool, Hull and Glasgow in 1940–45. London itself, the key to Fortress Britain since Queen Boudica's revolt against the Romans, was vulnerable to attack through the tidal gashes of the Thames and the Medway. An unwieldy iron chain was stretched across the Medway between wooden posts at Gillingham Reach. In June 1667, with the aid of English pilots, the Dutch disposed of the Medway defences and made off with the flagship of the English fleet, the *Royal Charles*. Having been assured that 'all is safe as to the great ships against any assault', Pepys was devastated to learn the news on returning home:

> . . . all our hearts do now ake; for the news is true, that the Dutch have broke the Chain and burned our ships . . . And the truth is, I do fear so much that the whole kingdom is undone.

*

FAR FROM THE boom of cannon and the dismaying spectacle of smoke rising over incinerated dockyards, a river-faring nation went about its perilous and unheroic business.

I came across this neglected waterborne population when interviewing a medieval English sailor in the company of my sister Alison, my friend Simon and the Robb family dog. The telecommunications apparatus consisted of twenty-six Scrabble tiles and a small upturned water-glass. Connection was signalled by a twitching of the glass and a queasy growl.

The interviewee had been born in the fifteenth century under Henry VI. He had lived in a house of wattle and daub in the town of Droitwich (spelled in its modern form), which is ten miles from Worcester on the road to Birmingham. He had earned his living as a sailor. Death had occurred, unsurprisingly, as a result of drowning. We speculated that his ship had been holed by a French or Spanish cannonball, seized by pirates or even smashed by a whale. Where exactly had he died, we wondered. The answer came again: D R O I T W I C H.

Droitwich, we ventured to observe, is a long way from the sea . . . The glass swerved, as though tetchily, across the table, nudging each letter in turn. It was the last message we received from the unfathomable depths: I N A P O N D.

*

THIS FIGMENT OF three self-hypnotized minds now seems quite credible. I have found no record of a sailor drowned in Droitwich, but I did discover that in the thirteenth century a boy from 'Dirtewychy' had been 'miraculously' saved from drowning. A deputation including the boy's mother had gone to Worcester to have his salvation certified as a miracle.

With no coordinated flood management or agricultural safety inspectors, inland drownings were run-of-the-mill events – especially at mills. Even in our safety-conscious age, two or more farm workers a year drown in their animals' waste by falling into a slurry tank. In the fifteenth century, Droitwich, noted for its ancient salt springs, was also famous for flooding, as it still is. Since most Saxon place names could be understood without recourse to an etymological dictionary, Dirtewychy ('dirty town') and its river, the Salwarpe ('dark sediment'), were as good as warning signs.

Under Henry VI, before the parasitic 'sea dogs' employed by the Crown challenged the dominance of Portugal and Spain by preying on the predators and snatching their booty on the high seas, England was also a nation of boatmen and bargees. It rowed, towed, punted and paddled. Even when global trade routes opened up in the late sixteenth century, the most popular tales of British naval heroes still had an earthy inland flavour: Francis Drake playing bowls on a lawn at Plymouth Hoe; a pipe-smoking Walter Raleigh doused in his armchair with a bucket of water; the same man draping his precious cloak over a puddle so that Elizabeth I could traverse 'a plashy place'.

*

Now that the seaside is associated with certain notionally pleasant destinations, it is hard to recapture the sea's pervasive presence in daily life. A mast and a square sail floating across open fields would look to us like a hallucination. Sea-going vessels reached Worcester and York on tidal rivers. Like a twisting, unfinished Panama Canal, the Thames almost bisected the island. Two hundred miles from its mouth, woven cloth and wine from France, Germany and the Low Countries were unloaded at Lechlade and could then be carted less than thirty miles to the navigable Severn at Gloucester, where a lugger serving Channel ports could take on a load of salt delivered by a sailor from Droitwich who plied the Salwarpe and the Severn.

A dozen towns along the central axis of Britain were inland ports, some of them sheltering beneath the Malverns, the Chilterns and the Cotswolds or, even more incongruously, in Pennine valleys. There were docks at Corbridge on Hadrian's Wall, at the wool and mining centres of Wakefield, Sheffield, Derby and Nottingham, at the Midland markets of Shrewsbury, Worcester, Stratford and Oxford. The docks at Gloucester are still an impressive sight. This mutating internal trade network of more than two thousand miles had been in use since Roman and pre-Roman times. Thirty-seven of the sixty-one towns on the decoded maps of Iron Age Britain (ch. 6) are ports, of which sixteen are coastal and twenty-one inland.

Long before the canal-building boom of the late eighteenth and early nineteenth centuries, longships recognizable from the Bayeux Tapestry and logboats of a type first used in the Bronze Age transported textiles and pottery, lead and iron, coal and peat, building stone and timber, wine and cheese, fresh fish, livestock on the hoof and human beings. In the fourteenth century, it cost a shilling or more a mile to move a ton of grain by road, but only seven pence by river. Even a logboat could carry half a ton of merchandise.

Given a certain vigour and imperviousness in the workforce, and legal purges of obstructions such as 'weirs, mills, stanks, stakes and kiddles' (outlawed in clause 23 of the Magna Carta), the inroads of the ravenous sea were one of Britain's main commercial assets. More than nine-tenths of medieval England and Wales lay within fifteen miles of navigable water. (See map 3.) The farthest point in Britain from the coast is Coton in the Elms in Derbyshire, but that most landlocked of English villages is only forty-five miles from the nearest high tide at Cromwell Lock on the river Trent, and a mere four miles by road from Burton-upon-Trent, where cargo vessels out of sea ports on the Humber and the Wash tied up at the wharves.

*

EVEN LANDLUBBERS WERE expected to be waterproof. Until the mid-nineteenth century, most road journeys of more than a few miles included a ford or a ferry, a flood or its aftermath, and, in the swathes of eastern England that will be under water by the end of this century, a stretch of river or navigable ditch.

Fleeing the wrath of Henry II in the rainy autumn of 1164, Thomas Becket left the road at Lincoln and 'wended his way by water forty miles to the hermitage of Sempringham'. From there, he was rowed and punted another twenty miles by interconnected rivers and channels to Haverholme. Even without his mitre, the Archbishop of Canterbury was a recognizable figure, and so he fled mainly by night. With the glint of moonlight on water, and without a bone-shaking cart and a hungry horse, he could travel more swiftly than on a road.

This was not a tale of steady progress. On the rivers of Britain, time seems to stop and then run backwards before another onward surge. Four centuries after Becket's flight to France, the fluvial network developed by the Britons, the Romans, the Saxons and the medieval English was in a clogged and dilapidated state. In 1623, the proselytizing 'water-poet', John Taylor of Gloucester, a half-lame bookseller and vintner, urged his contemporaries to consider the sources of their island's prosperity:

> You shall find that in the whole dominion of England, there is not any one Town or City which hath a Navigable River at it that is poor.

As Taylor recounted in *A Very Merry Wherry-Ferry Voyage* (1622), he sailed from London to York, hugging the coast and entering the river system from the Wash. He covered fifty miles on the first day, negotiated the derelict Roman Fossdyke which joined the Witham to the Trent – an eight-mile-long 'ditch of weeds and mud' – and rowed triumphantly into York without '[coming] in sight of Sea again'.

The following year, he thrust his sea-going wherry up the congested, undredged Wiltshire Avon. In 1372, Edward III had ordered that a barge 'be made at Salisbury' (forty-one miles by river from the Channel coast) 'to resist the malice of his enemies of France'. The cathedral city had since become a backwater. Like an explorer in a ruined empire or the hero of a late-Roman epic poem, Taylor reached the centre of Salisbury guided by swans which 'swam in the deepest places before me, and showed me the way'.

*

BETWEEN THE EVACUATION of the Roman legions to the end of the Middle Ages, Britain might look like a typically insular island – busily engaged within, fearful of the world without, forever weighing up the advantages and the perils of trading with foreigners. As late as the seventeenth century, a mental state of siege could affect whole communities.

Buffeted by the 'rolling billows' of a high sea off the Norfolk coast on his voyage to York in 1622, the water-poet and his crew decided to make for land. In failing light, they rowed and dragged their wherry onto the beach at Cromer, 'supposing all was safe and well'. Nothing too outlandish was likely to reach seventeenth-century Cromer from the hinterland, but the sea was still the habitat of wild invaders:

> . . . some women, and some children there
> That saw us land, were all possessed with fear:
> And much amaz'd, ran crying up and down,
> That enemies were come to take the town.

Word spread through the hinterland: Cromer was under attack from pirates, thieves or Catholics. The pikestaffs of forty local defence volunteers in varying states of panic and inebriation bristled on the shore. Taylor and his crew were placed under arrest, the wherry was rendered unseaworthy by the tearing up of a hull plank and sentries stood guard over the town until three o'clock the following afternoon when two magistrates were found who happened to have read some of the water-poet's productions and invited him to spend a few days of cheerful recuperation at the country estate of Sir Austin Palgrave, J.P.

Suspicion of the sea was an only slightly hysterical response to a historical reality. A political journalist has recently recorded seventy-three significant invasions of British soil since the Norman Conquest – by Danes, French, Spanish and Dutch, and, later, by Scots, Americans and Germans. (Several hundred minor raids and invasions in Wales and the South-West are omitted from the total.) The sea was not considered picturesque and healthful until invention of the deck-chair and the bathing hut in the nineteenth century. The jagged coast and all other natural impediments and threats were the work of the Devil or a capricious God – as a character in Chaucer's *Franklin's Tale* complains: 'these grisly feendly rokkes blake', 'this werk unresonable': 'It dooth no good, to my wit, but anoyeth.'

Echoes of this landlubberly trepidation can be heard in the nightly lullaby broadcast on BBC Radio 4. The incantatory shipping forecast issued by the Meteorological Office draws three verbal loops around the Isles – the far-flung sea areas with their 'warnings of gales', then the coastal stations keeping watch on the sea-swept frontiers, and finally the more familiar-sounding inshore waters. When the third circumnavigation is complete, the whole archipelago has been tucked up for the night and can fall asleep to the muted trumpets and drum rolls of the national anthem followed by the hypnotic Greenwich Time Signal which anchors Great Britain on the prime meridian to which all the world defers.

*

Island nations are not predestined to be insular. Anthropologists have found that island societies tend to be open to trade and immigration, whereas coastal societies with extensive hinterlands can be more insular than islands. Some maritime states had trading empires

(Venice, Genoa or the Veneti tribe of Atlantic Gaul); others, like medieval Brittany and eastern Provence, turned their backs on the sea. For long periods, France was more inward-looking than England and often aspired in times of crisis to the status of an island, taking comfort in its natural frontiers and reinforcing them with citadels.

National self-perceptions are a subtle, subatomic force compared to the Newtonian physics of civil and military engineering, but their effects are more profound. Rivers and gorges can be bridged; entire countries can be reimagined. In every age and generation, there is another Britain to rediscover.

The unmoored appearance of the British Isles first entered common consciousness in the early twentieth century. World maps on school-room walls showed Britain as an ungeometric jumble, almost impossible to draw from memory. This was not the double axe-head or triangle pictured by the Romans nor the 'middle earth' of the Anglo-Saxons* suspended between sky and netherworld. It looked like nothing at all until the 1950s, when the British School of Motoring popularized the indelible image of Great Britain as a giraffe-necked car driver, with the accelerator pedal at Land's End, the steering wheel at Anglesey and a cigarette in the mouth of the Clyde.

The British world map improved this geological accident by placing it on the line of zero longitude at the centre of the Earth. The spider brain of the Empire was attached to every continent by the shipping lines of international commerce. Territories in states of dependence, subjection or revolt were uniformly coloured red or (for the legibility of captions) pink. As the cosmetic hue of empire faded, Britain would again look like the defiant but friable little nation floating off the edge of a continent which was itself an appendix of Asia.

At 10 Downing Street in June 1997, the new prime minister, Tony

* The Angles were a Germanic tribe from Angeln in the northernmost part of modern Germany; the Saxons came from Saxony. The name 'Anglo-Saxon' is first recorded in 1602. After 1678, it was used to refer to the Old English language. In Britain, 'Anglo-Saxon' usually means the post-Roman, pre-Norman, non-Celtic people of England and south-eastern Scotland. In France, 'les Anglo-Saxons' are the modern English.

Blair, urged his press secretary and his chief of staff to ponder the disturbing cartographic evidence. Britain was about to hand its richest remaining colony, Hong Kong, back to China. The map on the wall spoke to the leader of New Labour like the anxious guardian spirit of an ailing kingdom:

> 'We shouldn't lose any more territory . . . Britain's not big enough. . . . Britain needs to be bigger. I mean, look at the map. Look at it! Britain is so small!'

The Prime Minister's perception of geopolitical titchiness foreshadowed another brief and calamitous period of skimpily justified imperialism (the Iraq War), which, in turn, heralded another celebration of indignant but cosy detachment. Such is the amphibious nature of Britain and its constituent kingdoms that while some of its citizens asserted their national identity and felt 'a little bit more English' after the Brexit Referendum, others, north of the border, longed for a time when their own independent nation-within-a-nation would become a political island in its own right.

5

'Barbarians Beyond the Ocean'

A Roman cavalry officer and the body of a Briton.

Far back in time – but not so long ago in geographical history – this spindly, sea-wracked island was part of a vast commercial empire of the ocean. Once the last reedy islets and mudflats of 'Doggerland' had been covered by the North Sea, long-distance travel to south and east had become faster, cheaper and probably less dangerous than on land. A thousand years before the Roman conquest, the largest of the Pretannic Isles was a well-connected landmass on the inshore highways of the Western Ocean.

Traces of this Atlantic–North Sea trading zone can still be detected in archaeological digs and human genes. Amber, glass, jet and especially copper and tin (for bronze) were the main drivers of trade. When iron, more locally available than copper and tin, replaced bronze as the metal of choice for weapons and tools in the sixth century BC, the international trade routes continued to flourish. A *lingua celtica* began to evolve in lands that would become known as Iberia, Armorica, Hibernia and Britannia.

By the time the Massalian merchant-explorer Pytheas set off from the Mediterranean coast of Gaul in c. 325 BC, it was possible to travel from the Pillars of Hercules to the far north of Caledonia without having to employ a translator. Pytheas apparently had no difficulty in obtaining local information as he 'traversed all of Britain on foot'. He was not bludgeoned to death by natives or turned back by immigration officers.

To Roman geographers, this Greek- and (probably) Celtic-speaking adventurer, with his precise observations and accident-free tour of the hyperborean land of monsters and sub-humans, was either a fantasist or a fraud. Nearly three centuries later, at Gesoriacum (Boulogne) in AD 43, the flappable Roman soldiers looked over at the white cliffs of Nearer Britain and refused to venture 'beyond the limits of the known world'. The Emperor's director of communications had to shame them into action with a rousingly insulting speech.

When the tribes of Cantium (Kent) had been subdued 'without battle or bloodshed', Emperor Claudius followed on with a troop of war elephants to impress the savages and proceeded in triumph to the royal city of Camulodunum (Colchester).

For a barbarian settlement at the ends of the Earth, Camulodunum was strangely civilized. The capital of the Trinovantes tribe was a busy inland port with a temple and burial grounds, warehouses and factories, tidy fields and paddocks, and fifteen miles of earth dykes topped with towering palisades. When this rural-industrial complex became the first capital of Roman Britain, it had been minting its own gold coins for more than a century. The replica native *oppidum* constructed for the celebration of Claudius's 'Conquest of Britain' in the Campus Martius later that year is unlikely to have been realistic. The inscription on the new Arch of Claudius made the Britons' signing of treaties sound like a grovelling surrender:

> Tiberius Claudius Caesar Augustus Germanicus [etc.] received the submission of eleven British kings defeated without loss and

was the first to subject the barbarians beyond the Ocean to the rule of the Roman people.

*

ONE OF THOSE eleven kings was said to have travelled to Camulodunum from distant 'islands in the Ocean on the farther side of Britain' (the Orkneys). This epic voyage to pay tribute to the Emperor might have been a self-flattering Roman fantasy but it is now thought to be consistent with the material and historical evidence. News would have reached the stone brochs of the Orcadian court by the shipping lanes and the king would have sailed down to Camulodunum in about three days to hail the Emperor, conclude a trade deal and see the elephants.

The significant difference between Claudius and the Orcadian king is the fact that the King of the Orkneys knew exactly where he was in the world. He had sailed the length of Britain and was familiar with the long-established trade routes which account for the surprising genetic diversity of the Orkneys. Over half the islands' non-British, pre-Roman population had ancestral roots in France and Belgium.

The Romans' seriously skew-whiff conception of European geography is hard to visualize. More than thirty years after Claudius came to Britain, the Roman general Agricola, equipped with the latest measuring devices and the accumulated knowledge of Roman geographers, believed that if he sailed from Caledonia to Hibernia, crossed to the other side of 'Winterland' and kept heading west, he would make land on the shores of sunny Spain.

*

ORIENTATION, OR THE sense of knowing where you are in the world, is culturally determined and subsequently reinforced by habit. The first photograph of Earth taken from space was printed upside down by picture editors so that Africa would be the right way up. A home approached from an unusual direction can assume an entirely different demeanour. On 'oriented' medieval maps with east at the top, Britain has a clownish appearance, stubbing its Cornish toe and falling on its rugged Highland face.

In a Roman mind's eye, the world was in stationary orbit around Rome. Everything on the *orbis* was defined by its distance from the *urbs*. Consequently, southern Britain was named Britannia Superior and northern Britain Britannia Inferior. Both epithets were as ambiguous as they are today. The southern half of Britain was higher up and better than the northern half.

An inferior North looming beyond the Watford Gap and Watling Street is one of the longest-lived of all socio-geographical prejudices. (Map 7.) It still influences central government policies, and it makes it harder for modern Britons to find their bearings in the Iron Age.

The mental compass of the British mind, if it has one, is normally oriented north–south, like almost every map since the invention of the magnetic compass. Growing up in the Midlands, I naturally thought of London as a city which lay 'down south'. When I left Worcester for Oxford, then Oxford for London and thence to the hoverports of Dover and Calais, I continued to imagine myself southbound. Seeing this nearly straight line drawn on a map, I still feel that it points in the wrong direction. On that trajectory, it would reach the Southern Hemisphere only when it was off the coast of New Guinea and well on its way to New Britain.

Before I found it expedient to be aware of the cardinal points when cycling off the map or negotiating the streets of a city on a cloudy day, the sense of living on a north–south axis exerted a stronger influence than geographical fact. Hitching to London in 1975 with my best friend from school, and concerned that on this, his maiden trip, Geraldo would become disheartened by the inconveniences of that mode of transport – the interminable wait, the fume-laden wind, the cruel accelerations of cackling motorists – I accepted a ride to Bristol. This was not ideal, but since Bristol lay to the south, we would at least, I thought, be closer to the capital.

Oddly, having been dropped off on the outer limits of Bristol, where we half-slept in a frozen moonlit graveyard next to a medieval pub, we were five miles farther from London than when we started out.

I suspected that something of the sort had happened when, an hour before dawn, we crumpled onto the tarmac of a deserted Earl's Court Road in London, having lost the use of our legs after a horrendously long ride from Bristol on the back of a speeding Land Rover with no seats or roof.

A few years later, uncured of the north–south prejudice, while punting and mostly drifting along the darkening Thames with a fellow undergraduate, I had the distinct physical impression of going *down* and therefore south to London.* The 'plan' or, more accurately, stupid idea was to enact Rimbaud's poem 'The Drunken Boat' ('As I descended the impassive rivers, suddenly I felt the tow-ropes slacken . . .') and to arrive at Putney Bridge, where the Oxford–Cambridge Boat Race begins, in time for breakfast and perhaps our photographs in the *Evening Standard*. As the sun rose over the Thames Valley, it would have been dazzlingly obvious that we were punting our frail bark east, not south.

*

THIS THEORETICALLY EFFORTLESS itinerary, dictated by the river and requiring no map, is one of the oldest known routes and frontiers in Britain. When Caesar forded the Tamesis in 54 BC, he knew that he was entering the territory of a different tribe. Six centuries later, the nearly transinsular Thames separated two Anglo-Saxon kingdoms and formed an uninterrupted border between seven shires which exists to this day.

Along that river to the west and on either side of the main watershed of southern England, the Roman legions under Claudius advanced deep into the peninsulas of the western tribes, pursuing the British king Caratacus – or being lured by him – from the mouth of the Thames to the mountains of Wales. 'With the considerable difficulties posed by its terrain', the German invasion planners noted in 1940, Wales 'is an ideal region in which to mount a persistent defence.'

Many years before, immigrants from the Continent had followed the same route. According to Caesar's Gaulish informants, Belgic

* The correct expression used to be '*up* to London'. It is often associated with the 'up train' (outbound to London), but it predates the railways by at least three hundred years. Like the French equivalent, 'monter à Paris', it referred to the pre-eminence of the metropolis.

tribes whose ancestors came from east of the Rhine had crossed the Channel in great numbers and settled in Cantium (Kent). They had since spread west as though in fulfilment of an ancient prophecy.

Caesar's intelligence-gathering somehow escaped the attention of the University of Oxford's 'People of the British Isles' researchers. In 2015, they were astonished to find high concentrations of northern French and Belgic DNA in southern and far south-western Britain. This westward migration was confirmed three years later by the restored Iron Age map of Britain which shows the Belgae inhabiting the promontory fort of Tintagel in Cornwall.

Mass movements to east and west are typical of Celtic tribal migrations. The fabled founder of Gaul, Ogmios, drove his stolen cattle along the path of the rising sun towards the Alps. An epic, well-planned exodus of Gaulish tribes to the east in the fourth century BC is mentioned by seven Roman historians. In more recent times, the tribes of Helvetia had uprooted themselves, setting fire to their own towns and villages to prevent backsliding, and were trekking due west on the path of the equinoctial sun to new lands on the Atlantic seaboard when they were intercepted and massacred by Caesar in 58 BC.

Orientation (or occidentation) in its literal sense was already an ancient tradition when the Belgae moved west across the Channel. One easterly migration has recently been sighted in the very dimmest corner of protohistory. Isotopic analyses showed that many of the people who were buried at Stonehenge in its infancy (c. 3000 BC) had come from the Preseli Hills of Pembrokeshire, where some of the Stonehenge bluestones had been quarried.

Those stones, which an early British legend claimed had been magically transported from Ireland, were found to have stood in a stone circle by a col in the Preseli Hills where the river Gwaun begins its short journey to the Irish Sea port of Fishguard. Both Stonehenge and the Preseli circle were oriented on the solstice sun. It appeared that the ancient Welsh had taken with them on their journey east not only their household effects but also part of their henge.

6

The Iron Age Atlas of the British Isles

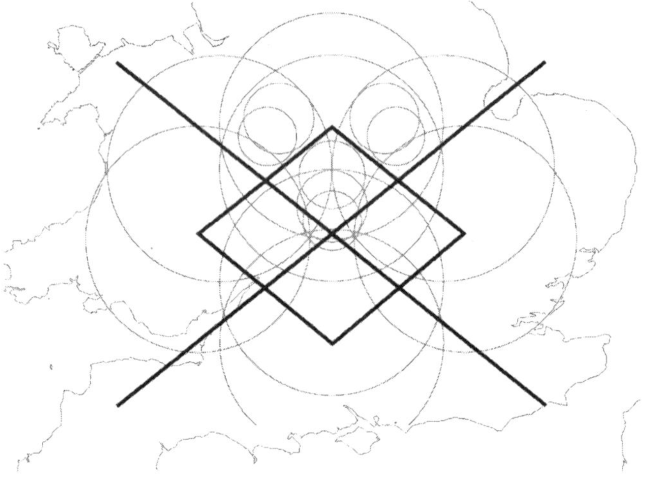

The geometry of the Aylesford Bucket and a Celtic map.

COMBING THROUGH THE Great Library of Alexandria in c. AD 150 on the trail of an earlier cartographer, the Greek-Egyptian scholar Klaudios Ptolemaios (Ptolemy) amassed a huge and miscellaneous collection of sailors' logbooks, merchants' diaries, travellers' itineraries and even some 'precise maps' drawn or etched on tablets. The material had come from all corners of the Roman Empire and beyond.

He then digitized the data by attaching latitude and longitude coordinates to all the towns, ports, rivers, estuaries, headlands, mountain ranges, islands and seas. Each inhabited place was listed under the name of the local tribe. The result was a world atlas in numerical form. A purchaser of Ptolemy's data lists could plot the points on a sheet of parchment, a paved courtyard or a smooth wall and thus acquire a set of maps without spending a fortune on postage.

The map of Roman Gaul was based on the latest scientific measurements, which was unfortunate because, although the science was theoretically correct, the instruments lacked precision. As a result, the Gaulish map was a hopeless mess: it could only have served as decoration. The British and Hibernian map, plotted on the eleven-by-twenty grid recommended by Ptolemy (because it produced a map of convenient size and shape), looks similarly chaotic. Its cockeyed appearance seems to match the traditional image of bumbling ancient Britons purveyed by Dickens in his *Child's History of England*: 'clever in basket-work', capable of producing 'some very bad earthenware', otherwise profoundly ignorant.

Six years before finding a way into this abandoned cartographic cavern, I discovered that the Celts of Gaul and Britannia had each devised a standard solstice angle which they applied to every kind of structure – long-distance roads and field systems, urban street grids, the floor plans of temples and houses, the designs of metalwork and jewellery. The 'Four Royal Roads' of Britain, for example, reputed to predate the Romans and known to the Saxons as the Fosse Way, Watling Street, Ermine Street and the Icknield Way, all observe this efficient Celtic convention.

Simple equations invisibly governing complex structures are typical of Celtic art and science. I knew, therefore, that if the original map had been created by native Britons, there was a good chance that it was more accurate than it seemed.

As an experiment, I took two places whose locations are known – Camulodunum and Londinium – and amended the 11:20 grid until they were correctly positioned in relation to one another. If all the other known places then occupied the correct positions, the *unknown* places could be identified. More importantly, it would show that this 'Roman' map was a British wonder of the ancient world . . .

With that adjustment, the strangely well-oiled doors of a new Old World opened up. (Map 4.) Instead of Ptolemy's 11:20 grid, the restored map used a simpler and more significant ratio of 4:3. This is the ratio derived from the angle of the rising sun of the summer solstice in southern England and which also produces a perfect

Pythagorean triangle. In the flood of fresh information, I failed to notice at first that this was the same national British ratio I had deduced from the written and material evidence for the southern half of England.

For the next thirty days, the sun rose and set on something new. Every map of 'Roman Britain' would have to be comprehensively revised. Tribal territories had been misdrawn and towns placed in the wrong region and even on the wrong coast. Several 'Roman' sites with visitor centres were operating under false names.

*

THE 'MAP' TURNED out to be an atlas comprising five distinct maps, each with its own grid and significant ratio. These zones of coherence imply the existence of five large cultural and political divisions: Dumnonia (Devon and Cornwall), Wales and the rest of England south of the Dee and the Humber, the north of England up to the Solway, Caledonia and Hibernia. This was the wide-scale organization of 'barbarian' Britain which facilitated the Roman Conquest.

The accuracy of all five maps is astonishing, but the dazzling gem of the collection is the map of that maligned half of England, 'the North'. Friends and acquaintances were amused or delighted, depending on regional loyalties, to learn that by far the finest map in the ancient world had been made 'oop North'. Who would have guessed that Carlisle and Ilkley were once at the cutting edge of Western science and technology? It covers the lands of the Brigantes and their client states from coast to coast and from Chester to Carlisle – an area of about seven thousand square miles. Distances and directions are so precise that no comparable map would be created until the Renaissance thirteen centuries later.

These maps are undoubtedly products of British science and technology. The names of the towns are Celtic rather than Roman. Solstice bearings were used on occasion by Roman surveyors and architects but never with such consistency. The northern England map is aligned on the rising sun of Beltane, the Celtic festival which marked the beginning of summer. It shares this unusual orientation with the map of Hibernia, where the Brigantes were also present. This is the surest sign of native origins: no Roman army ever set foot in Hibernia; no Roman roads have been found there, and no Roman merchant would have had the ability, the funding or the need to undertake the kind of over-arching survey required to create such cartographic gems.

An over-arching survey . . . Only generations of professional training and inter-tribal cooperation on a grand scale could have enabled Iron Age cartographers to perform the feat of drawing straight survey lines across the barrier of the Pennines. Some of these maps may have been on public display like the lost *mappa mundi* at the Druid University of Augustodunum in Gaul. The map of southern England – unique in the history of cartography – functions like a viewing platform. Directions to places as far away as south-west Wales are impressively precise, but only if the user of the map is presumed to be in Londinium. Perhaps the sketch or engraving which found its way to the Library of Alexandria was a copy made by a curious Roman visitor. The map shows only the principal places, but for such accuracy to exist, there would have to have been far more detailed maps showing all the other places in between.

Perhaps the only Roman who would not have found this technical excellence incredible was Julius Caesar. In his annual report to the Senate in 53 BC, he described the Druidic syllabus (law, science, medicine, religion), which demanded up to twenty years of study. Since his best friend in Gaul was a leading member of the caste of priestly intellectuals and diplomats, Caesar could write with some authority:

> This body of knowledge [*disciplina*] is considered to have been devised and developed in Britain and subsequently brought over to Gaul. And so now most of those who desire a deeper acquaintance with the subject travel to Britain in order to study it.

Caesar was informing the Senate that Iron Age Britain was home to one of Europe's great centres of learning. An analogous situation would curiously recur in the sixth and seventh centuries when Hibernian and Caledonian missionary saints, also called 'druids', reintroduced Christianity to a Continent overrun by pagans.

*

This was the largely unknown land which Emperor Claudius claimed for Rome in AD 43. The politically dangerous international Druid institution, which Claudius banned, was reimagined as an evil sect of religious maniacs. Such was the potency of this propaganda that it survived the fall of the Empire. Not even the most jingoistic British historians have ever quoted Caesar's report as evidence of Celtic Britannia's world-beating brilliance.

> The ancient Britons, being divided into as many as thirty or forty tribes, each commanded by its own little king, were constantly fighting with one another, as savage people usually do.

Thus Charles Dickens in 1852 primed Victorian children for life in the impudent British Empire. The view expressed in *The Oxford Illustrated History of Britain* in 2021 is basically similar: 'The Celts were characterized by quarrelsomeness, both within the tribe and in their indulgence (*sic*) in inter-tribal warfare.' They lacked self-discipline and had 'little or no "national" sentiment'. 'Why are we not starting this *History of Britain* before the Romans?' asks the contributor. Because only the Romans had 'literacy' and 'the rule of law'.

When I published parts of the atlas in *The Debatable Land*, the Scottish historian and broadcaster Andrew Marr wrote that the decipherment of the first British map ought to be front-page news at home and abroad. This would have surprised me. For the English in particular, the national tale of grubby Britons enlightened and cleaned up by civilized invaders with underfloor heating and flush toilets carries almost Biblical authority.

Colonialist conceptions of our ancestors are more Roman than the Romans. The Romans generally referred to the tribes of Gaul and Britannia as *nationes* or *civitates*. They knew that the Celts were not a single race but an ethnically diverse group of societies with a shared cultural and religious heritage, compatible systems of government with elected senators and magistrates, a meritocratic education system, a common language and the political wherewithal to form wide-ranging military alliances and monetary unions.

Some Iron Age Britons were residents of Rome. Caesar's 'greatly respected' friend Diviciacus the Druid – a diplomat, orator and authority on *physiologia* (the study of nature) – was a house-guest of Cicero on the Palatine Hill. He once cried on Caesar's shoulder. As a Druid scholar, Diviciacus would have studied in Britain, quite possibly at Camulodunum or, more likely, on Mona (Anglesey). His namesake and perhaps relative had ruled a cross-Channel, Gallo-British kingdom. He had been invited to address the Roman Senate. This rare honour was later granted to Caratacus, the defeated king of the Catuvellauni, who lived as a free man with his family in Rome.

With a yet-to-be-invented trans-epochal video link, Diviciacus could just as usefully address the House of Commons. He could present Members of Parliament with a copy of the pre-Roman atlas of Britain and reveal to them the meaning of their country's name – the 'Pritani' or 'Prettani' were not the 'painted', woad-smeared Picts of a later age but the 'makers' or 'craftsmen' who produced some of the micro-engineered marvels on permanent display in Room 50 of the British Museum.

I hope this virtual visit never happens. The hypothetical Diviciacus might have read *The Oxford History of Britain*. Raising a manicured eyebrow, he might have skimmed Prime Minister Johnson's book on the Roman Empire, in which barbarian foreigners disastrously spurn the gift of civilization. As a statesman who had enjoyed the benefits of a Gaulish monetary union, he might interpret the shunning of a European confederation as an unaccountable act of self-conquest. He might also notice that the politicians who habitually quote snippets of classical Latin are also those most likely to express condescending or openly insulting views of the modern 'Celtic' nations.

*

THE TIRELESS TROWELS of archaeologists have prevented the body of early British History from seizing up altogether. Field systems, farmsteads and roads of the late pre-Roman Iron Age are now frequently discovered and described.

In 2010, a section of Roman road at Sharpstone Hill near Shrewsbury was shown to have been laid on top of a road which was reliably dated to the second and first centuries BC. The Iron Age highway had been metalled, kerbed and cambered. Heavy goods vehicles had used it and it had been regularly maintained, which suggests a highways department with a pothole-repairing budget funded, as in Gaul, by tolls and taxes.

Having witnessed British cavalry racing highly manoeuvrable chariots along 'the well-known roads and byways' of the Thames Valley, Caesar would have taken the Sharpstone road for granted. The farmland on either side of the native carriageway appeared to have been reorganized on a grid system. A senior academic from a nearby institute was interviewed by the BBC.

> He accepted that dating results had put the road in the Iron Age period but said he just did not believe structured roads would have happened in that period. 'If it is an Iron Age road, what is it doing? . . . I just can't see where it fits in with everything we know about the Iron Age,' he said. 'My instinct is that it is Roman.'

While the academic shared the insights of 'instinct', a team of archaeologists from the University of Reading was uncovering a large British town in and around the quiet village of Silchester in Hampshire. The Romans knew the town as the capital of the Belgic Atrebates tribe. The oldest streets of Calleva had been laid out in a grid pattern. They were oriented, according to Druidic practice, on the local summer solstice. Later, when Calleva became a Roman town of seven thousand people, its streets were remodelled on a north–south grid.

To the citizens of British Calleva, their town was not pre-Roman. It was a modern, Belgic-style *oppidum* with a gigantic timber hall and its own mint an hour's walk from the river Thames. Caesar never saw Calleva, but he did discover another Belgic *oppidum* thirty miles to the east and judged it an 'outstandingly good' marriage of terrain and engineering. To him, this was further evidence of the highly successful Belgic diaspora: 'Their buildings are exceedingly numerous and just like those of the Gauls.'

From the top of Silchester's flint walls with their battlements of bramble and nettle, there is little to see but tall grass waving in the wind instead of busy urban streets and, in the other direction, a view to the east and the lingering lane called the Devil's Highway which was once the road from Calleva to Londinium and which formed the shire boundary of Berkshire and Hampshire.

This dynamic age is a backwater of British history only because we know so little of it. Tribes which had migrated from northern France and the Low Countries retained and developed their commercial and cultural links with the Continent. They transformed the landscapes of southern England and their agricultural and administrative innovations would survive the traumatic downsizing of the Roman Empire.

Callevans will have heard of Emperor Claudius's arrival at Camulodunum in AD 43. Writing implements have been found at Calleva and so they might have read about it too and recorded it in writing. Some of the earliest British legends refer to long-lost documents which told of a golden age of independence when the roads and tribal boundaries of Britain were first laid down.

News of the invasion would reach them by the same efficient arteries that brought luxury tableware and speciality food from the Mediterranean. Glass bowls, dinner plates and a miniature pet dog from the Continent suggest an enviably smooth delivery service. It would be an insult to our ancestors to picture them lounging in their neatly planned *oppidum* drinking Gaulish wine with a side dish of Italian olives, waiting for a superior civilization to come and build the roads and show them on a map exactly where they lived.

7

'Yon Outrageous Romans'

From the Roman mosaic at Hinton St Mary.

IT TOOK LIVING in America for four years (1982–6) to make me realize I was British in certain psycho-historical respects. My new friend Margaret had given me a road atlas of the United States, prophetically inscribed 'for the long journey'. We drove from Nashville, Tennessee to the California coast by way of Death Valley. At night, above the fenced-off desert, the cosmos was as described in Rimbaud's 'Drunken Boat': 'Starry archipelagos and islands whose delirious skies lie open to the rover.'

Down on Earth, near the meeting point of four states, a small monolith in the 'lone and level sands' proved to be a derelict toilet shack. In the unmysterious emptiness of the desert, half a continent and an ocean away from Britain, I discovered an unfamiliar yearning for hobbity holes and Narnian nooks, for the rustlings of riverbanks or the teeming bio-metropolis of a hedgerow.

The nocturnal punting expedition down the Thames struck me in retrospect as a characteristically Old World adventure. Its setting was not the Victorian or Edwardian Oxford which the impressive American Rhodes scholars expensively recreated to the abashment of the native English, but the grubby and secretive, impenetrably allusive world of Anglo-Saxon England in which, according to them, we still lived.

To those of us who had sampled life beyond school and university, Oxford seemed an extraordinarily navel-gazing institution. I did not know that one of the oldest surviving Celtic legends identified Oxford as the mathematical *omphalos* or navel of the island of Great Britain (p. 59), nor that a place so wrapped and armoured in its own history can induce its inhabitants to behave like sleepwalking actors in an ancient drama.

Gliding past the drooping willows of Iffley village and under the thunderous ring road bridge, we entered the domain of plopping water voles and irritated swans. We felt for the plunging river bed with the dripping pole and used the paddle to turn the punt around. The clinging cold of a Thames Valley night had stripped the expedition of its magic. Besides which, we had run out of matches.

My companion was a native of deepest Gloucestershire who was reading mathematics at Magdalen College. Strangers thought him shy but he was capable of startling acts of studious recklessness. At his suggestion, on the way back to college, we pulled up alongside a houseboat. He knocked at the window and asked politely for a light. Unfazed by the vision of a long, gaunt face bobbing up and down in the dark, the river-dweller extended a silent arm and a dazzling flame shot up as though this sort of thing happened all the time.

*

In the self-fictionalizing world of Oxford, it was natural to assume that whatever went on in its hidey-holes and micro-habitats was appropriate for that place and time. 'In the usual way' was the unsettling phrase routinely used in instructions from tutors, librarians and college administrators. We moored at the Magdalen College punting station near the mouth of the Cherwell and, observing a custom of our own, clambered into the cloistered citadel over the wrought-iron gates on Addison's Walk. Most of the older colleges had scalable gates or, as at my college, Exeter, a drainpipe and a helpfully eroded limestone wall. Even if we had remembered to cadge a 'late key' from a college porter, it seemed appropriate to make re-entry into the fortress dependent on the solving of a puzzle.

Beyond the Cloister, the great Tower loomed, palely floodlit and caged with scaffolding. Signs marked 'Do Not Climb' suggested a realistic possibility. A hundred feet up, we left the face of the tower and, entering the barn-like belfry, saw wooden ladders pointing the way to the top.

A red bicycle light was coasting up the arc of the High Street towards Carfax. The dark mass to the west was Cumnor Hill; in the other direction, Shotover Hill and the old road to London; beneath us, as in Milton's *Paradise Lost*, 'some renowned metropolis / With glistering spires and pinnacles adorn'd'. It was easy to pick out each college in the honeycomb. They looked like tiny walled principalities. A bell in a nearby college began to strike the midnight hour, and then, as though each college existed in its own local time zone, chimes rang out from all quarters of Oxford for at least five minutes.

At that hour, 'the learnèd air that breathes from the grassy quadrangles' was concentrated in gleaming panes suggestive of an essay crisis or some other form of devout orgy. From a darkened window to the south, an eye and something more powerful than an eye had been observing our ascent.

Late next morning, in his pigeonhole at the Porter's Lodge, my companion found a sealed envelope. It was marked with the college shield and contained a handwritten note from the Junior Dean. Mr H— had been spotted after midnight on the north face of the tower with an unidentified gentleman and was hereby informed that the appropriate fine would be added to his battels account to be settled by the usual date.

*

Like other panoramas of unbombed British cities, the twenty-square-mile vista from Magdalen Tower gives a dizzying impression of historical density – the streets and alleys with their Anglo-Saxon names, the wood and stone carvings decaying or anciently restored, the treasures displayed in museums or awaiting rediscovery under chapel floors and college lawns.

In the late 1970s, with its single-sex colleges and a majority of students from a small number of private schools, Oxford lent itself to the Elizabethan or Victorian conception of an English identity begotten in a remote past or thriving as a perennial flowering of the land itself. It evoked the beautiful and fallacious image of an immemorial English (rather than British) culture which had been adding growth rings to itself since the days when that hybrid 'race' from Germany and the Low Countries, the Anglo-Saxons, arrived to take over from the Romans.

We had all absorbed the basic elements of the story. The Romans had brought discipline, justice and security, city life and public services, taxation and access to European markets. When the legions sailed away in AD 410, never to return, the province lapsed into autarky. The tesserae of unrepaired mosaic floors in temples and villas were incorporated into the tilth of vegetable plots. A few mosaics were preserved as boundary markers like the 'fágan flór' (multicoloured floor) near the river Evenlode north of Oxford. As a foreign innovation, towns were left to crumble and the population spread out over the countryside like abandoned livestock. Here and there, a petty warlord offered brief protection against marauding Saxons, Picts and Irish. Later, there would be Danes and Vikings, incorrectly presumed to be pagan.

This tale of alien power and native impotence was developed in the nineteenth century. Missing links were supplied: the tale had to be compatible with ethnic nationalism. If Britons reverted to near-savagery when left to their own devices, how did Britain ever become a great imperial nation? The French could point to the continuity of tribal identities in the political and religious organization of Gaul: France was the child of imperial Rome *and* of the Gauls who gloriously opposed its tyranny. In England, the date at which the national spirit asserted itself had to be pushed forward a few centuries to the age of the Anglo-Saxon kingdoms and the demise of the last pagan kings of England in the late seventh century.

The story continued . . . Their fibre stiffened by Germanic blood from Saxony and Schleswig-Holstein, the English took control of their 'destiny'. The Danes who occupied half of England were defeated by King Alfred. Meanwhile, the aboriginal British, a swarthy race, presumed inferior in intellect and stature, scurried away to the hilly extremities – Cornwall and Devon, Wales, Cumbria and Scotland. These craggy survivors of prehistory with their incomprehensible tongue would be lumped together under the increasingly derogatory denomination, 'Celts'.

*

THE KEYSTONE OF this tale of destiny is the Roman Empire. Ironically, the earliest objection to the view that Romans brought unity to Britain was expressed by Calgacus, leader of the allied tribes of Caledonia, in a pre-battle speech probably invented by Tacitus but based on General Agricola's first-hand account:

> Yon outrageous Romans . . . gie spurious names tae thair *modi operandi*. Stealin', killin' and plunderin', this thay ca' 'empire'. Whin thay create a wasteland, thay ca' it 'peace'.

In the usual way of conquerors, the Romans deliberately destabilized native society. They concluded trade deals with friendly tribes and disrupted long-standing coalitions. With bribes and butchery, they turned one tribe against another. Yet the long campaigns fought by Caratacus, Boudica and Calgacus between AD 43 and 84 imply an ability to organize on a grand scale, and the rapid advance of the Romans in quiescent parts of the island suggests that domestic political structures were sufficiently robust for peace treaties to be effective.

The greatest British resistance movement was said by the chronicler Cassius Dio to be 'the biggest war' fought anywhere in the Roman Empire in the late second century. A coordinated attack in the North was launched by allied British land and sea forces. Towns in the far south of England were hurriedly fortified and when the last battle had been fought, the rebellion was 'ruthlessly put down'.

This anti-Roman uprising was led by the man of mystery and medieval bestsellers who subsequently floated through several centuries of Scottish, Welsh and English history like a Dark Age Doctor Who, materializing in the Caledonian highlands, the mountains of Snowdonia, at Glastonbury and Tintagel, and ultimately at the non-existent court of Camelot with the knights of the fictitious Round Table.

The only solid evidence of a general called 'Arthur' is a list of twelve battles in the *Historia Brittonum* (c. 828). The writer seems to have discovered in his monastery a rhyming list of battles in a much earlier Brittonic poem and adapted it so that it would appear to refer to the recent Saxon invasions.

Early Brittonic texts were usually factual rather than mythical. The problem confronting Arthurian scholars as well as nationalists or regionalists wanting to claim Arthur as their own is that many of the battle sites in the list were unidentifiable. The restored Iron Age atlas now makes it possible to identify them. It also shows that they were listed in a geographically logical order. The original poem described a coherent military campaign spanning the territories of at least six tribes on both sides of the Pennines from southern Scotland to the Roman legionary headquarters of Chester and York. This campaign matches the brief but devastating war of resistance recorded by Cassius Dio.

This is the very earliest example of a historical event recorded from a British point of view. The original Arthur, named 'leader of battles' (probably a translation of the Celtic 'Cadwalader'), can now be divested of his medieval frippery and celebrated along with Caratacus, Boudica and Calgacus as one of the would-be saviours of Britannia. The Scottish or northern English hero of British resistance should be given a state-funded statue – ideally on the banks of the Thames in London near the equestrian group of Boudica and her daughters which stands in front of Portcullis House at the Parliament end of Westminster Bridge.

*

At no point was the Roman province entirely at peace. It was vulnerable to the coups d'état of empire-building governors (195–7 and 287–96) and to galloping armies of Brittunculi ('little Brits' – a snooty term used in a document found on Hadrian's Wall). It suffered from economic downturns and from Frankish and Saxon sea-robbers. In the 'Barbarian Conspiracy' of the late 300s, Londinium itself came under attack.

The Romanized rather than militarized zone never accounted for more than one-quarter of the island of Great Britain. If villas are a benchmark of civilization, Rome colonized less than one-third of the island. Over ninety-six per cent of known Roman villas and all Roman mosaics lie on or south of the Humber. On the western side of Britain, there are no villas north of the Mersey and only sixteen in all of Wales and Dumnonia (the South-West Peninsula). Most were owned by farming members of the British elite who had served as military officers or administrators.

In the last century of Roman rule, beyond the monumental towns and a small number of exceptionally wealthy estates, Britain was still a rural Iron Age country. As the empire shrivelled, the island was once again an outpost at the ends of the Earth. A twenty-minute chariot or bicycle ride from our house on the Anglo-Scottish border, the Iron Age atlas shows an inland port and *oppidum* called, in ancient Celtic, Curia ('tribal centre' or 'meeting place'). It stood on the edge of a buffer zone between three tribes later known as the Batable or Debatable Land.

When Arthur's army passed that way in the late second century, Curia was a military fort called Castra Exploratorum ('Scouts' Camp'). The exploratores patrolled the pirate-infested Cumbrian coast. The native British had learned to spot the Romans' camouflaged spy ships, which they called pictae or 'painted' vessels. Smugglers and rebels scanning the sea from a cove on the Solway Firth would catch sight of a ship materializing against the sky like a faded fresco, its sails, ropes, timbers and even the black pitch painted sea-blue, with a silent crew dressed in uniforms of the same colour, protecting a convoy carrying lead or iron from mines in the Southern Uplands of Caledonia and defending the devastation they called 'peace'.

8
Invisible Invaders

A helmet from the Sutton Hoo ship burial.

WITH THE DEPARTURE of the Romans in the early 400s, a dense sea-fog seems to settle over Britain. Evidence is either lacking or uninterpretable. Coins were no longer minted; Continental imports were scarce. There were no imperial taxes to pay and consequently no national defence budget. Migrants continued to arrive by the North Sea from Saxony, Anglia, Frisia and Jutland. The towns fell into disrepair: many were abandoned or used by local chiefs as centres of operation.

The earliest British sources talk of a heathen invasion spearheaded by 'fierce and impious' Saxon mercenaries who had been invited 'like wolves into a sheepfold' to repel marauding tribes from north of Hadrian's Wall – the Picts from Caledonia and the Scots from Ireland. The resulting Saxonization of Old Britain once seemed to be confirmed by the rapid dominance of Anglo-Saxon dialects and the eradication of the ancient British language except in the 'Celtic fringe'. In England today, astonishingly few inhabited places have names of Celtic origin. East of a line drawn from Cumbria to Dorset, there are no more than eighty. There was a similar linguistic takeover in Romanized Gaul, where Gaulish or Continental Celtic was ousted by Latin. By the early sixth century, Gaulish was spoken only in the remotest rural districts.

Extinctions and flourishings of languages are hard to explain but they are not unusual. Even without migration or invasion, the dominant language of a region can change from one generation to the next. My uncle Dod, a cattle-farmer in Aberdeenshire, spoke only the Doric or Buchan dialect, which, as a six-year-old, I took to be a deliberately incomprehensible made-up language, especially since his grown-up children spoke only standard Scots English. These language 'barriers' can be discombobulating to monolingual English-speakers but they are easily overcome. With my father translating, I discovered that the nonsensical 'wee caffie in the field' was not a café but a calf. I soon found it possible to conduct a simple bilingual conversation: 'Fit like, loon?' 'I'm very well, thank you, Uncle Dod. How are you?' 'Ach, aye chavin awa.'

The Saxon invasions used to be the one thing we knew for certain about this deepest night of the Dark Ages. They now appear never to have taken place. Archaeologists have found no trace of a flood of foreigners or of an immigrant military elite. Geneticists estimate that Anglo-Saxons in the parts of England closest to Germany may have accounted for no more than ten per cent of the population.

Some sort of breakdown must have occurred. The militant Christian monk Gildas who wrote *On the Ruin and Conquest of Britain* in c. 530 mentions famine and a 'famous plague' which left 'the foolish populace' too short-handed to bury the dead. Poorly connected societies are prone to economic collapse. Starvation, pestilence or emigration could easily account for the steep decline in population between the end of Roman rule and the Norman Conquest.

The theory that Germanic tribes overwhelmed the hapless aboriginal Britons was falling out of favour anyway, based as it was on an almost exclusively male conception of the formation of complex societies by brief, calamitous periods of burning, killing, raping and enslaving. Faced with the genetic evidence that Anglo-Saxons were an ethnic minority, historians of the Victorian Age would have been shocked to find science so completely at odds with established history.

*

COMPARED TO MUCH later English villages with their pampered greens and stolid church towers, the settlements of post-Roman or 'sub-Roman' England look like traumatized witnesses to social ruin. To a modern eye, a dispersed habitat can appear shapeless and unkempt, with no clear position in the hierarchy of cities, towns and villages.

For the last fifteen years, we have lived in a non-nucleated settlement. The first element of its name is Brittonic: Penton, pronounced, like Penrith, with the emphasis on the second syllable. The Ordnance Survey locates its geographical centre in a typical claggy patch of rough grassland between a 'chalybeate spring' and a 'sheep dip'.

The area is officially designated 'severely disadvantaged', which means an area in which 'the natural characteristics (geology, altitude, climate, etc.) make it difficult for farmers to compete'. Arable fields are almost absent; corn is grown only as animal feed. The main products are sheep, dairy cattle, grass for the cows and slurry to feed the grass. A common local term for this type of agricultural enterprise is 'shit farm'.

It is easy to reach Penton without noticing it. Drivers from far away as well as from neighbouring parts of Cumbria, having wandered into a zone of mobile phone deafness, will often ask an outdoor native, 'I'm trying to get to Penton: do you know where it is?', to which the answer would be '*Circumspice*' or 'You're in it' or, more helpfully, 'Who are you looking for?'

The unfindability of this literal utopia or 'no place' on the edge of England has a disorienting effect on outsiders. The closest town is Longtown or Langtoon eight miles to the south near the site of Castra Exploratorum. Even this impoverished but intensely social place of three thousand people is considered by most Cumbrians to lie beyond the pale. 'How safe do you feel in Longtown?' was the leading question asked by a recent Conservative Party survey produced in the city of Carlisle, the former western command centre of Hadrian's Wall. A place which lies *beyond* Longtown is a sinister concept to some descendants of the 'timorous chickens' of *The Ruin and Conquest of Britain* who begged the Romans to come and save them from the northern barbarians.

The population of Penton (372) is spread over fourteen square miles. This makes it only four square miles smaller than the city of Oxford, which has a population of 152,000. The roads are unlit; ospreys are a more common sight than police cars. In the nineteenth century, sub-hamlets of four or five miscellaneous dwellings coalesced around a smithy, a dame school, a small church on a cross-border corpse road and along the North British Railway, but the general physiognomy is still strikingly sub-Roman and even Iron Age.

Each of the small steep hills of the miniature massif is occupied by a farmhouse surrounded by its outbuildings like a family hillfort. The names of the hills are Brittonic, Anglo-Saxon and Norse. Most are visible to one or several other farms. They once belonged to a wider network of lookout hills named 'Beacon', 'Watch', 'Ward' and 'Wakey'.

The stone walls of barns and bastle houses from the days of the cattle-rustling reivers four centuries ago give the modern structures a temporary air, just as the timber buildings raised among the ruins of Roman villas suggest post-apocalyptic squatters rather than settled tillers of the soil. The medieval walls are so massive that some farmers find it easier to work around them or allow them to fall apart in their own good time.

To incomers, the dispersed settlement shows no sign of harbouring a real community. Speculative landowners blundering into this Dark Age environment might be oblivious to the community until they cause offence. A scattered population can be more passionately cohesive than a juxtaposition of individuals in a town. Community spirit in out-of-the-way places is often attributed to genetic inheritance, but many of the common 'surnames' or clans of the area came here in the sixteenth and seventeenth centuries from Yorkshire and Lowland Scotland and even further afield.

By the late sixth century, the Angles, Saxons, Jutes, Scandinavians and Gauls living in Britain were similarly intermingled. Archaeologists find it hard to tell them apart. The ethnic groups of the Celtic regions were already muddled by time and marriage. They were not a residual subspecies retreating into its natural rocky habitat but a collection of pastoral societies that would suffer the contempt and hostility of agrarian communities.

That oldest division of humanity would remain an active fault line – the transhumant and the rooted, the people of the hills and the people of the plain, the thistle-munchers and the Sassenachs ('Saxons'), the troublesome Celtic Cains and the stalwart English Abels.

*

FROM THE TOP of Magdalen Tower, we looked down on one of the oldest international frontiers in Britain. According to an early British legend recorded in the Welsh *Mabinogion*, a king of Britain with the name of the Celtic god Lludd had ordered a great measuring of the length and breadth of the island. By mystical calculations probably based on the Roman or pre-Roman road system, the exact centre was found to be Rhydychen ('ford' + 'oxen').

As a swampy but strategically valuable place at a confluence of rivers, Oxford may have served as a neutral territory like the Debatable Land between Scotland and England. I plotted on a map all the locations at which Celtic coins have been discovered in south-central England. It shows 'Rhydychen' standing very obviously at the intersection of three tribal territories. On this evidence, in pre-Roman Oxford, a merchant could have paid for a new barge or repairs to his punt in Atrebatian, Catuvellaunian or Dobunnian currency.

In the 570s, the lands along the upper Thames and below the Chiltern ridge had been joined to the kingdom of the West Saxons (Wessex). A generation later, Wessex was overpowered by the Midland kingdom of Mercia. In the mid-600s, the hills of Cumnor and Wytham belonged to a Mercian sub-king called Dida of Eynsham. His daughter Frithuswith or Frideswide was a Christian convert. She became the patron saint of Oxford.

The terms 'sub-kingdom' and 'petty king' conjure up visions of a protoplasmic state of near-anarchy tempered by local despots from which a recognizable Englelonde would emerge in the southern half of Bretenlond. In reality, even before nucleated settlements became the norm, the existence of sub-kingdoms indicates a complex hierarchy of political divisions which civil wars, feuds, invasions and untimely deaths would fail to erase.

As students at the fabled centre of early England, we were unaware of these ancient partitions. To us, Wessex was the romantic West Country world of Thomas Hardy's novels; Mercia was the name of a television company and the West Midlands police constabulary. However, we did know that until 1974, the county town of Oxford had occupied an eccentric position on the border of two shires, Oxfordshire and Berkshire.

Oxford still had something of a border city. In the local vernacular, we heard the familiar furry *arrs* and boingy diphthongs of rural Gloucestershire and Worcestershire, but in the speech of young Oxford natives, there was already the grunty urban glottal stop of London: its rapid spread from the south-east would soon be as noticeable as the increasing traffic.

The South seemed to us to end just after Oxford, not forty miles north at the Watford Gap. There was a similar but more fluid division in student perceptions of cultural geography – in dress, musical tastes, drinking haunts and habits, disposable income, treatment of the opposite sex and the categorization of each other's accents as 'posh', 'regional' or, in rare cases, 'working class'.

*

Like long-term weather systems, these cultural divisions seem to arise at random. They are virtually impossible to analyse in detail, but like the 'strange attractors' of chaos theory, they are instantly perceptible as coherent patterns. Their longevity is astonishing. The monastic annals known collectively as the Anglo-Saxon Chronicle and the boundary charters of the seventh to eleventh centuries frequently describe local and inter-regional boundaries as 'well known' or 'ancient'. They seem always to have been old.

Three hundred yards up the High Street on a staircase in Queen's College and later in the bowels of the Ashmolean Library, I sometimes exchanged a wordless greeting with a luminous historian of Anglo-Saxon Oxfordshire. I see now that at that time, near the end of the last century, he was pondering this 'great unsolved problem in early English history': a 'startlingly comprehensive system of dividing up the countryside' which 'apparently existed by the mid-seventh century'.

The new Anglo-Saxon overlords and their courts may have thrilled to the bone-splintering exploits of warrior-heroes like Beowulf, yet they seem to have fitted quite smoothly into pre-existing networks of local government. When had this mysteriously solid foundation of the later state come into being, and where in that literally uncivilized, largely townless land had it taken root? Was it a spontaneous or a deliberate creation? 'Whatever the answer,' said the historian, 'it remains an oddly stable substratum in an unstable political world.'

Mysteries are so common in this sparsely documented period that they appear to have been an inherent feature of Anglo-Saxon culture. Grendel, the 'grim ghost' of *Beowulf*, pops up at the turn of a path in some otherwise humdrum Anglo-Saxon boundary charters, usually associated with a watery place or a pit. The charters mention Stone Age dykes and tumuli preserved as precious landmarks. A grant of 931 begins the circumambulation of the estate with a prehistoric 'stone castle' and a barrow on Inkpen Hill by the Wiltshire–Berkshire border:

> . . . Then [go] north over the hill and westward to the mossy bank, and down to the fence on the boundary of Beowa's place [perhaps related to Beowulf], then east to the blackberry thicket and on to the black pit, whence north by the headland of the field to the short dyke (excepting one acre) to the fowl's pond and the path to the otter's ford and along that path to the wood mere, then the rough hedge and after that the long meadow and Grendel's mere and the hidden gate.

To the Anglo-Saxons, this was a land of ancient living history. The apprehension of solvable mysteries is not necessarily anachronistic. A sense of unearthliness is quite in keeping with the period. Recently, while tracing the boundaries of the shires (Chapter 10), I saw the depths at which some of those creations of pre-urban England had existed, and it was like looking down from a tower at something I was not supposed to have seen.

9

'When Is This?'

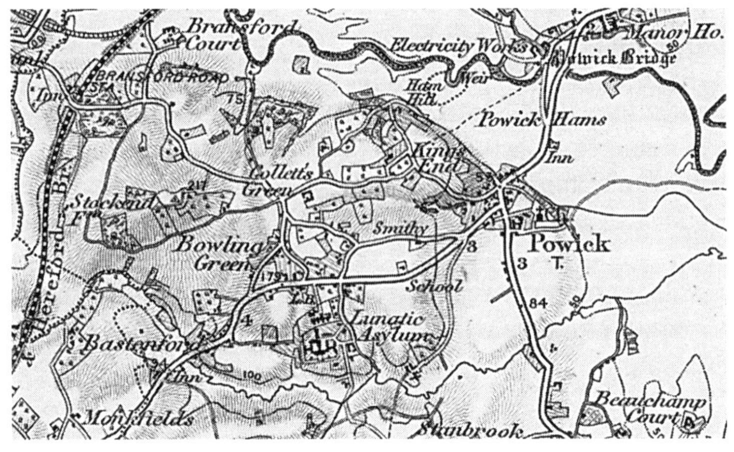

Powick and environs.

IN 1968, THE Robbs and their only surviving ancestor (my mother's mother) moved south from Staffordshire to Worcestershire, where people looked different, spoke a different kind of English and, according to my parents, belonged to a different century. I knew Worcestershire as the most awkwardly knobbly piece in the 'Counties of England and Wales' jigsaw puzzle. It was depicted as a land of apples, pears, hops, gloves, tin cans and Worcestershire Sauce. After the move, I learnt from my parents that it was 'feudal' and even less like Scotland than the previous county.

My father had been appointed Chief Probation Officer of Worcestershire. This was somewhat unexpected. He had worked in Manchester and the Black Country and had an impressive record: none of the 'juvenile delinquents' under his care had ever re-offended.

However, because of the war, he lacked a university degree, and his unmuted belief that criminals ought to be befriended rather than punished was not to the taste of the deeply conservative worthies of Worcestershire. He found it amusing that he owed his appointment to the energetic advocacy of a lady magistrate who belonged to 'the landed gentry' and lived in a 'feudal' mansion.

The institution of the magistracy was still functioning much as it had done in the eighteenth century, when Justices of the Peace, unbribably wealthy and familiar with the ways of the shire, had replaced the commands of central government with the authority of their own opinions. The other early sign of institutional anachronism, which my father found less amusing, was the obligation – despite having bought the house – to pay an annual rent of several shillings to a shadowy moneybags calling himself the Earl of Coventry. If I found a gold nugget when digging in the garden – and there *had* once been a gold-mine in the Malvern Hills – I would have to hand it over to his Earlship.

*

Our new home was a long bungalow which backed onto open fields halfway between the Victorian spa town of Malvern and the county town of Worcester. The nearest village was Powick and our telephone number was Powick 328. There were half a dozen overcrowded council houses, some mouldering cottages and five pubs within a mile of our house.

The house had been a compromise. My father pined in his spare time for the mountains and 'the waste howling wilderness'; my mother, born and raised in Glasgow, did not want her children to grow up as friendless rural anomalies. She had learned that a middle-class housing estate was about to be built in the fields at the front of the house. In the meantime, she rediscovered an interest in social history which had been sparked by Walter Scott, the English Romantics and the historians she had read after the war at the Institute of Almoners in London.

Every weekday morning, an assortment of rural types left the pages of Anglo-Saxon and medieval English history and processed along the road. A wiry, sun-blackened man leading a pony on a rope headed for

Lord's Wood, where he was believed to have business with badgers. Beyond the wood ran the turbulent river Teme, where a leathery man had lived for many years in a 'house' made of willow branches. Our next-door neighbour, bare-chested even in winter, marched by on his way to shoot pigeons for a farmer. Elderly twins in agricultural smocks disappeared in the same direction before turning (as I discovered on a reconnaissance mission) down the unpaved Cabbage Lane – a name used locally but never recorded on a map. It wandered for miles through uninhabited countryside towards the Malvern Hills.

From her vantage point at the kitchen sink, my mother mentally captioned the historical apparitions with verses memorized at school. At certain times of year, as the sun went down, a ploughman actually did homeward plod his weary way. The re-enactment was ridiculously true to past life. One day that winter, she saw a fox fleeing across the stubbly field at the back of the house. Seconds later, she heard the toot of a hunting horn and the baying of a pack of hounds. Shrieking with laughter at the perfect implausibility of the scene, she watched as the Madresfield Hunt with its red jackets and sherry-inflamed faces went crashing through the hedges, wrecking the farmer's drainage channels in pursuit of the inedible fox.

In our first year there, an arthritic old woman would plant herself on a bench in the morning sun under an ancient oak by the Three Nuns pub. She seemed oblivious to the wider world. Before the year was out, she was buried and the oak was felled as a danger to life and limb. My mother wondered whether this had once been the green, where, as in Oliver Goldsmith's 'The Deserted Village', 'all the village train, from labour free, / Led up their sports beneath the spreading tree.' There was no focus to the place; the school, the butcher's shop and the church were all a mile away in Powick village. She asked a neighbour, 'Where *is* this?' 'Well now,' said the neighbour, 'that there's Bowling Green where the Nuns is, and down there [two hundred yards away] is Collett's Green, and you'm somewhere in between.'

*

My mother could just as well have asked, '*When* is this?' The place and its inhabitants had fallen off the cart of history and been left at the side of a road which no longer existed. Only in the most cliché-ridden fiction did peasants still touch their forelocks to their supposed superiors. The gesture of servility was performed as a matter of course by labourers and tradesmen. The female equivalent was a bowed head and repeated expressions of gratitude for the honour of being spoken to. This might sound incredible, and so it seemed at the time. Talking to a local woman, my mother was appalled to see her shrivel up with humility at the idea that she might ever set foot in the 'big house' which towered over the village. Captain S— and his wife, who lived there, were not and never pretended to be aristocrats, but their 'manor house', their charitable activities and their accent qualified them as members of the nobility.

To a Scot, these rigid relations between social classes were acutely embarrassing. One of the few history books on our shelves – G. M. Trevelyan's *English Social History* (1944) – may have suffered from the old 'dour' and 'thrifty' Scots prejudice and conflated Highlands and Lowlands, but it did accurately observe the power of this cultural distinction:

> The peculiar spirit of Scottish society, feudal in the personal loyalty of the vassal to his lord, but equalitarian in the human intercourse between classes, was utterly unintelligible to the English mind until Sir Walter Scott's novels retrospectively afforded the key.

The territory or *pays* in which these historical scenes were acted out was small enough to be covered in a morning by an unmotorized postman and the butcher's boy on a bicycle. My father had known teenagers in post-war Manchester who had never seen the countryside until he took them rock-climbing in the Lake District. Here, there were grown-up people who had never been to Malvern or to Worcester, which could be reached on foot in fifty minutes or on the 144 bus from Birmingham. Several years later, when my sister and I were under-age drinking in the Three Nuns with a friend from primary school, a man we had never seen before came in, downed half a pint and left. 'Who was that?' we asked our friend. 'Im? Oi dunno. E'm just a stranger passin' through.'

*

The many 'Greens' of the area – Collett's, Bowling, Broadmore, Castle, Coles, Smith End, etc. – belonged to the pioneer period of Anglo-Saxon settlement starting in the seventh century when woodland pasture on the edge of the Malvern 'wilderness' was brought into cultivation. Iron ploughs with deeply gouging mouldboards broke up the weighty clods of clay which my parents and their infant serfs stabbed and flung about at the weekend. The clay was so pure and solid that a fist-sized lump could be washed under the tap of the water butt and fashioned into an unfired bowl that might have passed for the work of an unskilled Stone Age potter.

The landscape was a miscellany of hamlets, farms, tracks and field systems. No two fields had the same configuration; straight lines were rare and the width of each lane varied from one bend to the next. These were not the methodical enclosures imposed by Acts of Parliament in the late eighteenth and nineteenth centuries. They were part of the Anglo-Saxon and early-medieval puzzle of piecemeal enclosure and coexisted with ridge-and-furrow vestiges of the older 'open-field' system of the late ninth century when villages coalesced and the arable land was divided into unfenced strips to be shared among the villagers.

The unenclosed system created an entanglement of innumerable paths. These were now the quiet cul-de-sacs and escape routes which lent themselves to the sub-criminal adventures of a probation officer's children. Many survived as ghostly tracks which cut through the later roads and boundaries and seemed to lead nowhere.

A few yards from our bungalow, at the entrance to Cabbage Lane, six spidery tracks converged as though Collett's Green had once been a place of importance. As we lurked along that lane, we were following the remnant of a road which, before it was barred by the railway in 1861, had led to a small ruined castle at the now roadless Castle Green before joining a lane which a boundary charter of 972 called the *ealdan straet*. 'Old street' was the usual Anglo-Saxon term for a Roman road, which, in this case, could only refer to the long road from South Wales to Worcester. In those days, 'strangers passin' through' would have been a common sight.

The landscape not only implied a certain way of life, I now realize that it had the power to mould a human being into the semblance of a contemporary native. Among the oldest survivors were the hedges. Within a year of moving to Collett's Green, I had colonized the area with three dens and drawn a secret map. One was in a hedge so wide that a low corridor had formed inside it. The corridor provided cover from both the field and the road but made it hard to spy on passers-by. The second was less secure but more convenient. An old elm had made room for itself and one person in the hedge. This den unfortunately had to be decommissioned after a dog-walking woman spotted me among the foliage and asked, as though smiling into a pram, 'Are you hiding?' Evidently I wasn't.

The master den was in a deceptively spacious hedgerow on top of a steep bank overhanging the hollow way which leads to the hamlet of King's End. The bank could be scaled and the hedge entered several yards up the lane, leaving the grassy earth below the thorn-clad fortress undisturbed. There was enough room to hide a bicycle and yet, to anyone passing on the lane, the hedge was just a hedge.

Before mechanical diggers and herbicides, hedges in tricky terrain were almost impossible to eradicate. Many of those hiding-hedges can be dated by boundary charters and the diversity of species to a period before the Norman Conquest. When the leafy lanes of Powick stymied the Roundhead cavalry in the Battle of Powick Bridge (1642) and sheltered the Royalist soldiers of Charles II, they were already ancient.

We passed that way in the spring of 2022 on an unplanned cycle trip. I doubt I would have been able to identify anyone I had known at Powick primary school, but old hedges age so slowly that, even at a distance, the physiognomy of the master den was instantly recognizable after more than half a century.

*

Even places that seem set apart or left behind are full of clues to the wider world. The time-muddled landscape of the Worcestershire far west is a typical frontier zone. It has features of all three English 'landscape provinces' defined by naturalist-historians: 'ancient countryside' (isolated farms, winding paths and hedges and a proliferation of woods, heaths and ponds); 'planned countryside' (open-field farming and extensive evidence of clearance); and a 'Highland zone', represented by the dramatic eruption of the Malvern Hills.

I knew nothing of these vast orderings of Nature and human intervention. My naturalist knowledge was confined to tree spotting, flower pressing and butterfly chasing, each with an upper limit of fifty species set by the picture-card series which came free with packets of PG Tips tea. But I did know that we were living in a borderland.

To most of the Powick locals, the spa town of Great Malvern four miles across the fields was the last leery outpost of Worcestershire. It had genteel guest houses, lacy tea rooms, high-class boarding schools and middle-class hippies as well as their lower-class cousins, the grebos. A visit to that cultural enclave, let alone a camping trip beyond the hills to Wales, was likely to produce the semi-jocular query, 'What the bloody 'ell d'you want to go there fur?'

Beyond the Malverns and over the *yates* ('gateways' or passes), which cut through some of the oldest rocks in England, lay the land of the setting sun. The 'English Alps' marked an unofficial international frontier. To the east, the Worcestershire Plain encompasses the Severn Valley and the Birmingham conurbation; to the west, signs of industry and human habitation are scarce and the horizon is blocked by the barrier of the Black Mountains. Officially known as Herefordshire, this trans-Malvernian realm was considered in Powick to be effectively Welsh.

'Erruh-furd-sheer' was the local pronunciation. In Powick, 'shire' – the administrative division – was still the Anglo-Saxon *scir*, pronounced 'sheer', rather than the modern 'shy-uh' or, as a suffix, 'shuh'. On this subject, conceptually as well as phonetically, a person from the early Middle Ages would have been closer to a Powick native than a speaker of standard English. 'Herefordscir in Walia' was the term used by scribes in the reigns of Henry II and Richard the Lionheart.

Along with other 'sinister usages and customs', the Welsh language was banned for official purposes in 1535, though it could still be heard in the streets of Hereford under Elizabeth I, and several parishes in Herefordshire and Shropshire were Welsh-speaking in the 1690s. In Worcestershire, Welsh was probably extinct before the Norman Conquest. No Welsh translators were used by the compilers of the Worcestershire section of the Domesday Book in 1086. Yet there are traces of Old Welsh in the Powick boundary charter of 972 and, a thousand years later, in the normal but unrecorded local pronunciation of 'Powick' as *pow-ick* (like 'Powys', the early Welsh kingdom).

Was the insistence on not being Welsh the echo of some ancient insecurity in the matter of tribal identity? Or was it the enduring effect of the administrative anachronism which placed the county of Worcestershire under the jurisdiction of the Council of Wales and the Marches until 1689? The stone bridge at Worcester – which is still the only road bridge – was often assumed to mark the border between England and Wales, thus placing Powick and Collett's Green in a foreign country.

In 1885, when the woman who sat under the old oak at Collett's Green was a babe in arms, an internationally respected anthropologist from Bewdley, fifteen miles up the Severn, confirmed the foreignness of the Trans-severnian natives. His research showed that the river was 'a distinct ethnological frontier' with 'extremely striking' differences from one bank to the other in faces, eyes, hair and skulls. The population of this Anglo-Welsh buffer zone was distinguished by a conspicuously high degree of 'nigrescence' (blackness).

Here in darkest Worcestershire, according to Professor Beddoe, a phrenologically Welsh population preserved the racial memory of the Celto-British tribes which had been pushed west by the Anglian invaders. Less than a century later, he might have added to his documentation a hedge-dwelling boy of Celtic descent and a half-naked, sun-burnt man inhabiting a house of willow by the banks of the Teme.

10

The Shires

Midland shires.

EVEN THE PEOPLE of that small *pays* who never went to Malvern or Worcester felt an attachment to the shire. Towns and villages some distance from Powick but within the shire boundaries were recognized as belonging to Worcestershire while others, closer to home but across the border, were metaphorically and physically beyond the pale, even if they weren't Welsh.

The Anglo-Saxon 'shire', rather than its Norman equivalent, 'county', had been associated since the sixteenth century with rural parts of England where the metropolitan gentry went to hunt foxes and patronize the peasants. To go 'down to the shires' was to leave the southern counties whose 'shire'-less names are those of Anglo-Saxon kingdoms (Surrey, Sussex, Kent and Essex) and visit the Midlands – especially Northamptonshire and Leicestershire. Anthony Trollope noted in 1882:

> A man will be almost ashamed to confess that he hunts in Essex or Sussex, because the proper thing is to go down to the Shires.

Shire names can still refer to sub-populations believed to share certain characteristics, as in the versatile couplet, 'Cheshire born, Cheshire bred' (as I first heard it), 'Strong in the arm, thick in the head'. At the time of writing, this tribal adage is applied almost exclusively to counties north of the Humber, especially Derbyshire and Yorkshire as well as the city of Liverpool, and to the entire south-west region of 'rhoticity' – including Herefordshire and Worcestershire. This is where local dialects retain the reputedly rustic postvocalic /r/ which speakers of standard English have lost, sometimes on purpose, and which lives on in modern American English. Dialectically, the durrty shit-farrms of Woostersheer are a fah cry from the pahks and gahdens of the Home Kine-tees (the counties closest to London).

*

When a sweeping reorganization of local government in England took effect on 1 April 1974, personal attachment to a shire seemed to have become a largely historical phenomenon. The grand government plan was to create a uniform pattern of counties and districts and to solve the intractable problem of apportioning grants fairly to local authorities. Suggestions made in frustration by the previous, Conservative administration had included sending the Environment Minister to 'fly over the country in a helicopter, dropping bags with the appropriate amount of [grant] money on local authorities as he passed'. Another proposal was to 'sacrifice a goat before programming the Department of the Environment computer'.

Though the adjacent counties were practically untouched, the border between Herefordshire and Worcestershire was abolished. After much head-scratching, 'Malvernshire' was rejected and the new county was named 'Hereford and Worcester', pronounced as one word.

Foisting on the made-up county the name of two cities was unsatisfying to say the least. The 'Counties of England' jigsaw puzzle and the address embosser we had inherited from the previous owners of the house became instantly obsolete. On the other hand, I was pleased to note that, as Chief Probation Officer of 'Herefordnworcester', my father now held sway over the entire population of convicted delinquents between the Avon and the Wye and from the Cotswolds to the Black Mountains.

This bureaucratic monkeying with the ancient shires proved lastingly unpopular. The Whitehall monkeys were irked and baffled by what the official inquiry called the 'depth of feeling'. In 1986, government commissioners belatedly discovered what half an hour in the Three Nuns would have taught them: 'Hereford looked west rather than east.' 'Surveys of shopping patterns showed that Hereford residents tended to travel to Gloucester or Cardiff rather than to Worcester or Birmingham.' There was 'little community of interest' between rural Herefordshire and rural Worcestershire. Undaunted, the commission disagreed with its own findings and decided that the case for restoring the old shires was based on 'an emotional attachment'. This was hard to quantify and could therefore be ignored.

The hybrid pseudo-shire lasted only another twelve years. A full and honest consultation was held in 1994 and found that only two per cent of the population wanted to retain the new system. It was ditched in 1998.

Such was the efficacy and rootedness of the shiring of England that any tampering with the system invariably made it worse. Even with television and modern transport, the old shires still enfolded an area which a human mind could comfortably perceive as home territory.

Until the Industrial Revolution, some shire boundaries determined the choice of marriage partners. Studies of nineteenth-century Leicestershire and of the Cambridgeshire–Huntingdonshire border from 1580 to 1850 show the surnames changing from one shire to the next. But was this personal identification with the shire a post-medieval development? Were the shires a bureaucratic innovation of the late-Anglo-Saxon period, or do their mazy boundaries trace the limits of even older communities?

*

The English shire system is usually said to have come into existence after the Anglo-Saxon kingdoms were united under King Æthelstan of Wessex in 927. But some kind of shire identity was already active in the ninth century. The men of Wessex who fought

Viking invaders were called up by scīr (shire) or as the sǣtan (the 'sitting' or 'settled' inhabitants) of a shire: the Wilsǣte in 802, the Sumorsǣte and Dornsǣte in 848, Hamtunscīr (first attested in 755) and Berrocscīr in 860.

On the evidence of a historian-monk at Worcester Cathedral Priory in the late 1100s, some historians attributed the bewilderingly intricate shire system to a single high-ranking official called Eadric. His nickname was Streona ('the Grabber'). As ealdorman or under-king of Mercia from 1007 to 1017, Eadric served King Æthelred the Unready (the 'ill-advised') before defecting to the buoyant Danish king Cnut. The Grabber allegedly amalgamated 'at will' the old 'counties' or 'provinces', expropriating estates and muddling the time-honoured divisions of the land and its people.

Did this thieving, 'smooth-tongued' defector really manage to redraw the complex ancient boundaries while war was raging? This simple tale is sometimes taken as the literal truth, though the Worcester monk gave only one example, referring to his own diocese: the merging of the tiny shire or sub-shire of Winchcombe with Gloucestershire. Yet there were countless other sub-divisions – ferdings or farthings, rural *vills* or *tuns*, manorial estates, wapentakes and hundreds – and over this multiplicity of plots, properties and regions, the old folk territories with their ancient British names prevailed.

Large administrative units abruptly imposed by an aggressive central power rarely command the long-term loyalty of a population. Even after two and a half centuries, the French *départements* of 1789 still look culturally artificial compared to the former *pays* and *provinces*. Few people ever identified themselves as Pas-de-Calaisiens or Bouches-du-Rhôniens.

The shires of England are at least eight centuries older. They were an agglomeration of earlier territories rather than a centralized partitioning of a huge unmapped landmass. Their snaky boundaries have the intimacy of intensely local arrangements – a trickling, intermittent stream noticeable only as a line of alders and willows, a 'blind road' visible from afar but not up close, or a minor watershed betrayed only by the squelch of a boot or the gurgling of hidden springs.

These were the traces of societies rooted in the land. Most were *folclande* (known by ancient repute) rather than *boclande* (recorded in documents). Many would have been lost to farming and industry if the foot-slogging mapmakers of the nineteenth-century Ordnance Survey had not obtained the knowledge of their windings from the mouths of local people.

Hardly an inch of land was unrecorded in memory. In 1740, the rector of Kirkandrews on the Anglo-Scottish border decided to trace the limits of his parish. On reaching the rambling river Sark, he learned that the boundary and thus the frontier of Scotland and England had been misdrawn. Though centuries of flooding, silting and erupting bogs had repeatedly forced the river to find a new bed, the local people on both sides of the border had preserved the memory of its original course.

This feat of time-defying exactitude suggests a minimum lifespan for oral records of five hundred years. In fact, the boundary is at least twice as old. This is also the western edge of the Debatable Land. When it was conquered and divided between Scotland and England in 1552, it had remained uninhabited, by ancestral agreement, for well over a thousand years.

*

When the nation was under partial house arrest and the future looked as cloudy as it always is in reality, I set out – without leaving the house – to explore the entire system of shire boundaries. Using the first Ordnance Survey maps, Anglo-Saxon and medieval charters and chronicles, tithe and estate maps, county maps, place-name studies and the findings of academic shirology, I traced the earliest known outlines on a virtual pedometer.

Some weeks later, I transferred the several thousand miles' worth of digitized meanderings to an image file and coloured every part of the network according to the physical nature of the boundary – road, track or path; river or stream; watershed line with or without a track; edge of field or woodland.

The endless hieroglyphic scrawl of an anonymous, undated message from the past filled the screen. A broad distinction was perceptible between counties lying north and south of the Thames. The farther north, the more likely the boundary was to be wet. In the south, the kingdoms of Wessex showed a significant preference for dry land and prehistoric paths.

The boundaries of Worcestershire showed a similar sleepwalking adherence to ancient divisions. At Collett's Green, we were living on the edge of the territory of the Celtic Dobunni, whose prancing-horse coins are suddenly less prevalent west of Worcester. In the late 500s, this was part of the kingdom of a people called the Hwicce, who occupied much the same area as the Dobunni. Their Brittonic name – unrelated to the neo-pagan Wicce – is variously interpreted as 'the People of the Ark', 'the Excellent Ones' or 'the Cowards'. After 577, the 'Hwiccan province' became a tributary state of Mercia and then, after the official adoption of Christianity, one of the five Mercian dioceses.

For about three hundred miles, the Hwiccan borders coincide with those of eight shires, which means that when Eadric the Grabber appeared on the scene, the boundaries, if not the shires themselves, were already more than three centuries old.

Here, the road to the past petered out. In search of signposts, I studied the list drawn up for King Offa of Mercia in the late 700s. It records the old British names of thirty-three 'provinces' or tribal territories, including the Hwicce. These are suggestive of embryonic shires though the list gives only a vague idea of location. Then I mapped every datable battle and treaty from the end of Roman rule to the tenth century. These, too, hinted at the existence of shire boundaries as far back as the fifth century.

There seemed to be nothing else to add to the pixelated palimpsest. I thought of the poet William Langland who had attended my school in Worcester, which was founded in the 680s by the first Bishop of the Hwicce. His *Vision of Piers Plowman* (c. 1377), written in Worcestershire English, opens on a summer's day 'on Malverne hulles' and thus on the Herefordshire–Worcestershire border. Given that location, above the Malvern wilderness and the Worcestershire Plain, his analogy for an impossible task seemed appropriate:

> Thow myghtest better meten myst on Malveren hylles.*

* 'You might be better off measuring the mist on the Malvern Hills.'

It was appropriate, too, that the narrator of Langland's state-of-the-nation allegory was resting, not by the serene Severn or the tumbling Teme, but beside a nameless brook.

> And as I lay and leaned and looked on its waters,
> So merry was its sound that I slumbered and slept.
> And then a marvellous dream I began to dream:
> I was in a wilderness, I knew not where . . .

In tracing the shires' outlines, I had been struck by the incongruous importance of trifling tributaries. South of the Mersey and the Humber, the only big rivers which serve as frontiers for more than a few miles are in the old Saxon kingdoms and at the southern end of the Welsh border. The boundaries often dither along tadpoley brooks even when a nearby river offers an obvious alternative. Many of those shire-dividing streams have untranslatable Brittonic names which were probably already too old to be understood in the seventh century.*

Why had such insignificant riverlets so often been used as shire boundaries? A boundary that could be crossed on foot or without noticing was clearly not defensive. As an experiment, I made a map of the principal rivers of England and superimposed it on the shire map.

Like dark dust settling on invisible ink, a magnificent, well-ordered kingdom shimmered onto the screen (map 5). It showed eleven thousand square miles of the shired land in which we still live, comprising all of Mercia and its sphere of influence. The Dark Age Midland empire had been organized as though some pagan countenance divine had shone forth upon those misty wolds and clouded hills and tastefully rearranged the jumbled results of geological chance.

All the Mercian shires south of the Mersey and north of the Thames were bisected by their largest internal river. Each river was

* The Mercian saint Guthlac (674–714) was said by his eighth-century biographer to have understood the 'stridulent speech' of the British demons who talked to him only because he had spent time among the Britons (i.e. in Wales).

like the spinal column of an organism drawing life from its circulatory system of tributaries. Natural settlement patterns would never have produced such regularity, and cartographic triangulation was not rediscovered until the sixteenth century. Yet the pattern is strikingly coherent and visibly distinct from the configuration of the Saxon and northern shires.

Apart from the fact itself, there is no record of this epic feat of political landscaping. Viking armies annihilated nearly all of Mercian art, architecture and writing and left a gap of four centuries in the history of central England. A Midland Renaissance had married pagan and Christian, Celtic and Anglo-Saxon traditions and techniques, but of this, we knew next to nothing until 2009, when a hoard of thirteen hundred exquisitely patterned gold, silver and garnet-inlaid artefacts of the sixth and seventh centuries was unearthed near Lichfield in the heartland of Mercia.

Like the elegant system of bisecting rivers, the visual riddles of ancient Celtic metalwork and the multifaceted metaphors of Anglo-Saxon poetry, the designs of these Mercian treasures have an insidious logic which draws the eye into a crepuscular forest of unending paths and glinting zoomorphic faces. Their geometric language has not been deciphered and their origins are unknown. Were they taken in battle, obtained by trade in Britain or abroad, or manufactured in Mercia itself?

A folded strip of gold was found bearing a Latin inscription from the Vulgate Old Testament. It was the prayer offered up by Moses whenever the Ark of the Covenant was to be moved. It might have sounded a trumpet note of triumph or defiance to stiffen the resolve of a Mercian warrior. In the naked light of hindsight, it looks like a plea to be spared the inevitable annihilation:

> Rise up, Lord, and let Thine enemies be scattered; and let them that hate Thee flee before Thee.

*

The Staffordshire Hoard had been buried between 650 and 675 on high ground near the top of a ridge within sight of Watling Street, one of the two great diagonals of the British Roman road network.

The fact had no particular connection with the subject of shires, but it gave me the idea of marking on the shire map all the roads, tracks and paths which follow Roman roads. (Lockdown had given potentially fruitless but finite tasks a special charm.)

The boundaries of Anglo-Saxon estates and parishes often follow Roman roads, sometimes for great distances.* The Anglo-Saxons tended to leave the 'old roads' to wild animals and the weather, settling instead in valleys and open country. Akeman Street, the Fosse Way and many other long-distance Roman *viae* are still remarkably unsociable, running for many miles without passing through any human settlement.

Since the shires are known to be older than the parishes, it is widely believed that their boundaries, too, often adhere to Roman roads. I was startled to see the map disagree so emphatically. When I repeated the search, the result was the same: Roman roads almost never coincide with shire boundaries.

This seemed to defy reason. The ealden straete made useful corridors through no-man's-land. With their raised banks and metalled surfaces, they would have been a more visible presence in the Anglo-Saxon landscape than at the later date when the parishes were founded. The other surprise was that, despite clear regional differences in the type of boundary, the same cold-shouldering of Roman roads was evident in all the kingdoms of England.

Two exceptions stood out, enormously long by comparison and impossible to miss on the map. One is the boundary of Warwickshire and Leicestershire, formed by Watling Street. The other is the Fosse Way, split into three sections, separating Gloucestershire from Wiltshire. Together, they cover thirty-two miles, which is well over half the total length of shire boundaries on Roman roads.

* As a test, I took four hundred miles of nine Roman roads from the Welsh border to the North Sea and from Derbyshire to the south coast. Parish boundaries account for thirty-nine per cent of their total length. To make the survey as comprehensive as possible, I included those 'Roman roads' that were probably Iron Age, alignments produced by later rationalizations and sections short enough for the coincidence of boundary and road to be accidental.

This was the observable fact: the shire boundaries, unlike the later parish boundaries, systematically ignore Roman roads. The only workable hypothesis was that the shire boundaries, like those of the inter-tribal Debatable Land, came into being in an age when there were no Roman roads in Britain. A partial explanation presented itself a few days later.

*

IN 878, THE Great Heathen Army of Vikings which had blazed through Northumbria, East Anglia and Mercia was ravaging the south-western shires. King Ælfred ('elf-counselled') of Wessex had retreated into the woods and wetlands of the Somerset Levels and billeted himself on a cowherd and his wife. He busied himself with 'making bows and arrows and other instruments of war' but neglecting other basic logistical measures such as remembering to turn the *panes* in the oven before they burned to a crisp on one side.

Re-armed and with a fresh supply of Somerset flatbreads, Alfred and his army marched from 'Egbert's Stone' – at or near the meeting point of Wiltshire, Somerset and Dorset – to Edington in Wiltshire, where he defeated the Danish king Guthrum or Gudormr, whose name means 'battle-snake'. After the battle, a treaty was signed which set the frontier between Wessex and the Danelaw (the area where Scandinavian laws and customs were in force):

> First as to the boundaries between us: [they shall run] up the Thames, and then up the Lea, and along the Lea to its source, and from its source by the direct route to Bedford, and thence up the [Great] Ouse to Watling Street.

This would account for the twenty-two-mile stretch of Watling Street on the Warwickshire–Leicestershire border. Ancient boundaries formed of streams and field edges did not lend themselves to military treaties dealing with vast areas. Ignoring the ancient complexities, the diplomats of Wessex and the Danelaw reduced the border to the smallest possible number of elements: two rivers, a 'direct route' (or 'straight line'), another river and the unmistakable Roman Watling Street.

The Fosse Way sections on the Gloucestershire–Wiltshire and Hwiccan border probably have a similar origin. At the northern end is Cirencester, where the Mercian king Penda defeated the West Saxons in 628 and 'agreed terms', according to the Anglo-Saxon Chronicle. The treaty has not survived, except perhaps in the form of this anomalous boundary which brought the five-hundred-year-old Fosse Way back into use as a military frontier.

These treaty lines have remained as battle scars on the face of England. They cut through the pre-Roman, Iron Age network like motorways or Victorian railways. A border devised by a war committee, the A5 Watling Street trunk road is the least traveller-friendly of shire boundaries. On a two-wheeled chariot or on foot, it is all too easy to visualize it as a military stop-line. As a B road, the Fosse Way is marginally safer, but as the signs on the Warwickshire border warn, this too is a 'High Risk Crash Route'.

*

EVEN IN THESE exceptional cases, the shire network showed remarkable resilience. Slicing blindly through the fields, the Roman Fosse Way had created awkward shapes and unploughable corners: this is the usual proof that a field system is older than the road that bisects it. As it approaches Tetbury, however, the boundary depicted on the first Ordnance Survey maps leaves the straight road and goes tripping off along the old field boundaries to Wor Well, the source of the Little Avon.

One of the great centres of learning in early-medieval Europe lies two miles east of the road. The monks of Malmesbury Abbey and the families who farmed the land seem to have preserved the memory of the pre-Mercian landscape. In 680, fifty-two years after Penda's victory, the abbey petitioned King Æthelred of Mercia claiming a bulge of land west of the Fosse Way which includes the Wor Well and another, larger area to the south-west.

The petition was granted and the ancient boundary was restored, which is why pre-1930 maps show the straight line of the Roman road between Gloucestershire and Wiltshire interrupted by the older, sinuous line of fields, paths and streams. This is no longer the case. In 1930, an administrator decided that military rigour was preferable to folkland and returned the boundary to its seventh-century position, where it still is today.

The Watling Street boundary has endured without change. This could be a lasting effect of the Alfred–Guthrum treaty, which banned cross-border migration except for trade and then only if hostages were provided as surety. Curiously, although the Roman road boundary survived, the distribution of Scandinavian place names (map 6) shows an Anglo-Danish population spilling over onto the 'wrong' side of the treaty line to occupy the already ancient shires of Bedford, Northampton and Warwick.

The shire network is one of the cultural treasures of Europe. It was a masterpiece of administration, but it also seemed to offer a more intimate reassurance that the countless tiny places that make up a country can be interwoven with human desire to form what the London-born Welsh poet Edward Thomas in 1914 called 'a system of vast circumferences circling round the minute neighbouring points of home.' It survived the greatest trauma in British history, when other descendants of Danish Vikings sailed across the Channel from Normandy to conquer most of the conveniently shired country. Even ten centuries later, when aftershocks of the Norman Conquest were still being felt, it aroused a passionate conservatism in the borderlands of the Malvern Hills.

11
Conquered

Westminster Abbey on the Bayeux Tapestry.

I LEARNED ABOUT THE literal disaster (from *astrum*, 'star') at a primary school in the village of Walton-on-the-Hill between Stafford and Cannock Chase. This was exactly nine hundred years after the 'long-haired' comet appeared at Easter in the skies over England and the young kingdom which had been united under Æthelstan in 927 became a vassal state of a few hundred scions of Frankish Vikings. There are places named 'Walton' in two-thirds of English counties, many of them on poor land near a larger settlement of Anglo-Saxon or Roman date. 'Wal' comes from the Anglo-Saxon 'wealh', which referred to the native British or 'Welsh'. After 1066, it meant 'serf' or 'slave'.

Walton-on-the-Hill was the hub of several former hamlets – Baswich or Berkswich, Milford, Weeping Cross and, latterly, 'The Village'. The

Victorian school received about a hundred pupils aged between five and eleven. A girl in my class walked to school every day from the dairy next door. At the top of the hill was a blacksmith whose clanging hammers and pyrotechnic displays attracted an appreciative juvenile audience.

We lived a mile from the school on a cul-de-sac (literally, 'bag end') called Glastonbury Close. The name had no direct connection with Arthur or King Alfred; it commemorated only the developers' use of a list of West Country place names for the new streets which were laid out on the former Wildwood estate. The 'wood' in question had never been 'wild'. The Anglo-Saxon word was 'weald', meaning rough, sometimes treeless country of the kind favoured by the hunting-mad Norman overlords. It had once formed the western edge of Cannock Chase, where distant relatives of the fallow deer and rabbits imported by the Normans prevent trees from growing back. The poachers are now equipped with guns, lamps and four-wheel drives and are still hunted down and brought to justice.

An Anglo-Norman historian described the change more than sixty years after the Conquest:

> All the English were reduced to servitude and sorrow, so that it was a disgrace even to be called an Englishman . . . If anyone should kill a stag or a boar, his eyes were plucked out and never was heard a murmur of protest. William [the Conqueror] loved beasts of chase as though they were his children, and so he gave them a home in the hunting ground called New Forest [in Hampshire] and caused churches and villages to be destroyed and the people driven out.

*

As a whole (which it wasn't), Walton resembled the multi-period Lego village depicted on the back of the Cornflakes packet – comfortingly Olde Worlde but on the fringes of Lego-like modernity. There was a field of barley near the house and a pub called the Barley Mow. Just beyond the canal and the railway bridge, the English Electric Company employed thousands of workers in a brutalist factory confiscated from its German owners shortly before the First World

War. The Barley Mow's neighbour was a Wimpy Bar – a burger chain that was moribund in its native America but thriving in Britain. A tribe of alarmingly coiffed, comb-wielding chain-smokers hung about outside. My mother identified them as 'Teddy Boys', which struck me as a cruel collision of two worlds.

The ambiguous nature of the rural-urban environment was reflected in the playground of Berkswich Primary School. A spirit of mirthful wiliness prevailed compared to which Powick School would seem unsophisticated. Passers-by on Weeping Cross Road could see girls and boys playing traditional games of Anglo-Saxon, Tudor and Victorian vintage – conkers, hopscotch, tag and, when the time came, dancing round the maypole. They heard the rhymes of Merrie England by which skipping infants unconsciously memorialized major outrages and disasters in British history – the Black Death, the Dissolution of the Monasteries, the Catholic plot to blow up Parliament.

They also heard snippets of pop songs like the wailed chant of 'Come Bonnie Love' by the Beatles (I took this to be a Scottish ballad) and barrack-room songs which fathers had picked up during the war. The war itself was present in the scream of dive-bombers and the rattle of machine-gun fire. A child sporting an unreturned gas-mask was not an unusual sight.

Nostalgia is the Alzheimer's of history. It can contemplate war and destruction with a blank face and a blissful smile. The Norman Conquest as a concept is now well into its second childhood. The Bayeux 'Tapestry' – which is not woven but darned with wool like an old teddy – depicts events which affected the entire population, but it now looks more like a comic strip than the propaganda of an absolute monarchy emerging from its early kleptocratic phase. Its embroidered half-truths and scenes of gloating savagery seem endearingly simplistic. It was not until we had spent a few years in Powick that I realized how raw that humiliation still was.

*

Glee at the discomfiture of an enemy or a despised ally is one of the motive forces of war and politics. In classrooms stalked by the spectre of boredom, a high value was attached, not just to bartering goods such as picture cards and marbles but to anything that might baffle, disturb or dismay: a glob of white paper stuck by mysterious means to a vaulted classroom ceiling; the maypole ribbons twisted into a hopeless entanglement; a pound note screwed up and smoothed out again into a ridiculous dwarf replica of itself; or the sudden inexplicable collapse of school furniture.

These ludic refinements seemed to give the daily imposition of school an educational purpose. Most pranks were victimless and the perpetrators' anonymity was usually respected. Guile was the key ingredient because then the trick was played for everyone's benefit. To arrive at school expecting to impress other children with a private possession unavailable for trade was always an ill-starred enterprise.

In 1966, the GPO (General Post Office) made history by breaking with tradition in two respects at once. Requiring postmen and postwomen to exchange their uniforms for bell-bottom trousers and mini-skirts would have been only slightly more revolutionary. The idea, first mooted by a 'Celebrations Council' set up in Hastings in 1961, was to mark the anniversary of the Norman Conquest with a special issue of stamps.

Four years of campaigning and bickering ensued. The matter was debated more than once in Parliament. Special stamp issues were supposed to commemorate royal and postal anniversaries and important current or recent events such as the opening of the Forth Road Bridge or the holding of the European Postal & Telecommunications Conference in Torquay.

After dismissing the Hastings event as too 'local', the Post Office was persuaded to proceed, only to face 'very strong' objections voiced by the Member of Parliament for Bournemouth West – a place which, though it lies on the same coast as Hastings, had been passed over by William the Conqueror because it did not then exist. The GPO 'should not be seen to commemorate an English defeat', said the MP. Only victories 'in English history' (*sic*) deserved to be stuck on envelopes and sent all over the world.

The Battle of Hastings won the day. The Bayeux Tapestry lent itself splendidly to the philatelic medium. Moreover, it had been made by English nuns (probably) in the earldom of Kent, which William the Conqueror had bestowed on his half-brother Odo, Bishop of Bayeux. For the first time, the GPO produced a 'se-tenant' (unsevered) strip of six fourpenny stamps, as well as two longer stamps worth sixpence and one shilling and threepence. Also for the first time, the Queen's head was depicted in gold, but not beside the head of William, despite the urging of the Society of the Descendants of William I – a group which in genealogical reality would include the Queen and approximately five million other people.

At Berkswich Primary, word soon spread that a boy had brought to school a set of stamps which reproduced the entire Bayeux Tapestry. This would have required a perforated strip thirteen feet long. The reality was slightly disappointing, but the miniature realism was compelling. Even the two self-appointed school bullies were eager to inspect the treasure.

The six se-tenant fourpenny stamps showed tumbling horses, lopped limbs, a naked corpse being stripped of its chainmail, King Harold with a psychedelic shield and a handlebar moustache, the arrow stuck in his eye and his bottom resting on the rear end of a horse.

One of the two longer stamps depicted a Viking longship in Day-Glo blue and green. Two Norman archers had been reversed by the stamp artist so that they appeared to be fighting on the English side. The intention might have been to hint at the future glory of Agincourt. The original tapestry shows only one English archer – a cringing man of low status with a puny little bow. Perhaps the Member for Bournemouth West was right: a once-proud nation was presenting itself to the world as the butt of Norman jokes.

The owner of the stamp strip warned us with the pedantry of a collector that it would lose its value if it came to be torn. It was not inevitable that this would happen. The stamps were printed on damp-resistant paper strong enough to withstand the rough and tumble of letter boxes and offices, yet somehow as they passed from hand to hand the stamps began to separate. First one, then another perforation failed. At lunchtime, the fluttering line still held, but only just. When it was restored that afternoon to its haggard owner, each of the six stamps was hanging, as though a malign fate had been at work, by a single perforation tooth.

*

The Bayeux Tapestry itself was damaged, either torn off or cut away at its nether end. As a result, the final scenes are missing. The cloth chronicle might have ended with William I's coronation at Westminster Abbey on Christmas Day 1066 when Norman soldiers started a fire which burned down the neighbouring houses,* but the ragged edges make a fitting conclusion. Unarmoured soldiers, one with an arrow in his eye (perhaps a conventional image of death in battle), flee into the tattered void while a quaking churl ludicrously tries to hide in skimpy vegetation from two flail-wielding Normans.

The scale of the disaster is apparent from the great survey of all the wealth of England. The Book of Winchester, later known as the Domesday Book, was completed twenty years after the Battle of Hastings when rebellions had been crushed, castles built, homes and livelihoods destroyed and native landowners expelled. Their underlings and serfs stayed behind in England.

The upper-class English diaspora spread to Lothian (the English-speaking part of Scotland), Scandinavia and Constantinople. Almost the entire Anglo-Saxon aristocracy was replaced by a small foreign elite. From the Welsh Marches to the Scottish border – but not Carlisle, which was then in Scotland – the lands of more than four thousand English lords were gifted to fewer than two hundred French and Norman barons. Only six per cent of the estates recorded in the Domesday Book had an English lord, but their land was poor and many would be bought out or forced to leave.

Walton-on-the-Hill and Berkswich were retained by the new Norman Bishop of Chester. His portfolio included ninety-three other holdings from Nottinghamshire to the Welsh Marches. Powick remained under the aegis of Westminster Abbey, which held estates in sixteen other shires. Since all land in the feudal state was in the hands of the King, these clerical overlords were tenants-in-chief

* The English chronicler Orderic Vitalis (b. 1075) stated that the soldiers outside the Abbey heard the newly crowned King being acclaimed in English as well as French, presumed that 'treachery was afoot' and, in a panic, set fire to some buildings. This sounds like the deliberate creation of an exclusion zone by soldiers who were well practised in scorched-earth tactics.

rather than landowners. Beneath them were the sub-tenant *domini* (lords or barons) who paid rent in tax and services.

Every layer of what remained of Anglo-Saxon society is represented in the Domesday Book. In the large parish of Powick, there were seventeen *villani* (villagers and freemen who farmed a sizeable chunk of land with their own pair of oxen), forty-five *bordarii* and *cotarii* (smallholders and cottagers who owned five acres on average and had a share of the village plough team), one *presbyter* (a priest), twenty-three *servi* (serfs) and one *ancilla* (a female serf). The *ancilla* of Powick would have been an unmarried woman or a widow. Most of the common people recorded in the survey are male, nameless and listed without children or other dependants.

*

> Be the winter never so stark, I dare not hide myself at home for fear of my lord . . . I have a boy driving the oxen with a goad-iron who is hoarse with cold and shouting . . . It is mighty hard work, for I am not free.

This is the traditional image of the post-Conquest English peasant. I 'knew' this wretched servitude to be true from history lessons and an old book in red leather which had been passed down through a line of ancient aunts to end up on our spartan bookshelves. In *Little Arthur's History of England* (first edition, 1835), a happy nation of freedom-loving Christian farming folk had fallen prey to Norman bullies who trampled on their 'witenagemot' or 'council of wise men', 'spoilt their gardens' and made all householders put their fires out and go to bed at eight o'clock every evening.

As I later discovered, given a certain lapse of time, all history is wrong, including the histories which correct the erroneous histories. The above quotation comes from a schoolboys' Latin primer which gives examples of everyday conversations in Latin and Anglo-Saxon. It was written by an English abbot at Eynsham in Oxfordshire sixty years *before* the Norman Conquest.

The Domesday deluge of data gives a misleading impression of cataclysmic change. For the country-dwelling ninety per cent of the population, once the rebellions and massacres were over, life went on much as before. The main differences were a sense of belonging to a defeated people and the fact that most peasants now worked for a single lord who spoke a foreign language and rarely or never showed his face. King William himself paid only occasional visits to England after 1072.

Before the Conquest, Powickians in the north-east of the parish had farmed the lands of men called Æthelward, Alwin, Brictmer and Sæwulf. Now, they served a minor *seigneur* from a village near the mouth of the Seine who had come over with the Conqueror and earned himself or was perhaps even baptized with the unusual name of 'Bear'.

The dynasty of Urse d'Abetot is known to modern inhabitants of Powick and Malvern under the name of Urse's son-in-law, William de Beauchamp (pronounced 'Beechum'). There are Beauchamp streets, pubs, a manor house, three hamlets within nine miles of Powick, a mineral spring and various local clubs and institutions. Urse the former soldier of fortune was made sheriff ('shire-reeve') of Worcester and built a castle, the graceless earthen motte of which stood next to the cathedral until 1830.

In the early 1100s, it was reported that '[Urse d'Abetot] shoved [this castle] down the monks' throats, as one might say, by having its ditch cut through part of their cemetery.' Ealdred, the Saxon Bishop of Worcester, who was briefly tolerated because he had crowned William and then his wife Matilda at Westminster, claimed to have stood up to the Norman vandal, prodding his bearship with a pointed Saxon pun: 'Hattest þu Urs, haue þu Godes kurs' ('Your name is Urse, on you be God's curse'). This is incidentally interesting because it implies that, unlike most of his compatriots, Urse had a smattering of English. It also suggests that Anglo-Saxon – a term now euphemistically applied to vulgar language – was already the idiom of the defiant and downtrodden.

*

The Norman Conquest was not a population movement but a takeover of the richest and most stable large nation in Europe. The house had been set in order and made ready for the robbers. The old Viking menace had been neutralized by King Harold nineteen days before Hastings at the Battle of Stamford Bridge. He and his soldiers had covered nearly a thousand miles that spring and summer, which implies a well-maintained network of drovers' roads and *herepaths* (military roads). The area of English land under the plough was only one-fifth smaller than the total arable acreage in 1914. With its transport infrastructure, productive fields and long-established shires, England was a prize of greater transferable value than the war-racked territories ruled by Norman knights in southern Italy.

William had to secure the loyalty of the knights who helped him to defend and enlarge the Dukedom of Normandy. England's charted estates could swiftly be parcelled out as gifts, and because the holdings of each major landowner were scattered and not contiguous, it would be hard for an ambitious Norman baron to create a rival sub-kingdom of the kind that made France an unmanageable embroilment of principalities, fiefdoms and self-governing enclaves until the 1789 Revolution.

The parasitic nature of the Conquest is spelled out in the toponymic landscape of England. The names of towns, villages, hamlets and farms are overwhelmingly Anglo-Saxon: Poiwic and Waletone are still Powick and Walton; the Old English cnocc (hill) is audible in the hunting ground of Cannock, modified by Norman speech in the same way that Cnut became Canute. Only three per cent of inhabited places in England have Celtic names. In the Danelaw, which accounted for about three-fifths of England, nearly one-quarter of place names are Danish. But the proportion of names from Old French is negligible – about half a per cent. Many, like the 'Beauchamps' of Worcestershire, were simply tacked on to the Saxon name like badges of ownership.

*

IT IS IMPOSSIBLE to know whether England would have developed differently if an English or Anglo-Danish royal dynasty had prevailed. It was out of local practices and the partially codified laws of Alfred and his successors that the Normans evolved their centralized legal system. Primogeniture – inheritance by the eldest legitimate male heir – shifted power from the many-membered clan to a single thin branch of a family. The family's surname (another Norman innovation) would be the name of its estate or manor, sometimes its castle and often the ancestors' domain or village in Normandy. The practice of taking the name from a place rather than an attribute such as 'Forkbeard' or 'Swan-neck' would spread downwards in the feudal hierarchy, which is why novelists can always find convincing names for their characters by poring over a map of the British Isles.

The Norman Conquest is not fertile ground for 'what if?' historians. The real and alternative futures might be too convergent. The English monarchy was already part Norman. King Æthelred's mother-in-law was Gunnora, Duchess of Normandy. Her daughter, Emma of Normandy, married King Cnut. One of her sons was Edward the Confessor, who spent much of his life in exile, probably in Normandy, and built the first Norman Romanesque church in England, Westminster Abbey.

The 'Lingua Romana' of Normandy and the Île-de-France was already enriching the English language and creating a superior form of diction useful for pontification and obfuscation. It was not just because of a small Norman elite that English with its wealth of synonyms came to be such a register of social division. Even if Harold had driven William's army into the English Channel, ox, boar, calf, sheep, deer, fowl and swine would have been served on one table and beef, brawn, veal, mutton, venison, poultry and pork on another, just as petits pois au gratin and cheesy peas are today. However, the changes were accelerated and some features of British society are clearly the result of sudden invasion rather than gradual evolution.

On the Bayeux Tapestry, the disembodied hand of a Christian God hangs from a small brown cloud and blesses Edward's new Westminster Abbey to which the finishing touches are being made. This sacred emblem of cross-Channel continuity is not entirely fallacious, but it relates only to the highest level of the Anglo-Norman hierarchy. In this uniquely bamboozling needlework chronicle, historical events take place in a realistic chaos of mysteries and accidents.

Oblivious to the hand of God, one of the unidentifiable long-necked birds of the upper margin speculatively pecks at the cross on top of the abbey's lantern tower while a terrified workman teeters on a ladder, clutching a turret as he tries to attach a silly-looking cockerel to the east end of the church. A counterpoise to the hand of God on the other side of the tower, this fickle weathercock will spin whichever way the wind happens to blow.

12

'High Or Lowly'

A bastle house near Dumfries.

Thus did England come into the hands of Normandy,
And since the Normans could speak no language but their own,
They spoke French as at home and taught their children too,
Wherefore the high-born of this land who are of the same blood
All speak the tongue that they learnt from their kin,
For unless a man know French, he is held in poor esteem.
Yet lowly men stick to English and their own way of speaking.

This description of a monolingual elite placing its bit between the teeth of English-speakers was written more than two hundred years after the Norman Conquest by a monk known as Robert of Gloucester. He chose English rather than Latin or French for his verse chronicle because English was understood by 'learned' and 'lewed' alike.

The rude health of the English tongue was evident in its several dialects (West Saxon, Kentish, East and West Mercian, Northumbrian, none of which bore any social stigma) and in the rapidity of its evolution. A day's ride north of Gloucester, another thirteenth-century scholar, named the Tremulous Hand of Worcester because of a neurological disorder which imparted an occasional seismographic flickering to his careful script, studied texts in Old English and tried to elucidate the increasingly obscure and antiquated tongue in marginal notes.

A generation later, when one French royal dynasty (the Kings of Valois) was at war with another (the Plantagenêts), the prestige of the conquerors' language was on the wane. Twenty-five years before Chaucer began his *Canterbury Tales*, the Statute of Pleading (1362) made English the language of the law courts. King Edward III had been alerted to 'the great Mischiefs that have befallen divers subjects of the Realm':

> '[Due to] common ignorance of the *lange Franceois*, the People . . . have neither understanding nor knowledge of that which is said for them or against them by their Serjeants and other Pleaders.'

The new English language, which we call Middle English, had been associated with national self-assertion since the end of the thirteenth century. In 1295, Edward I warned that the French were preparing an invasion that would 'utterly expunge the English language from the Earth'. The same rousing claim was made by Edward III in the 1340s. (The text was written, as legal custom still demanded, in Norman French.) King Philippe VI 'and certain grandees of France and Normandy' had issued the order 'a destruire & anientier tote la Nation & la Lange Engleys.'

*

As the Tremulous Hand of Worcester knew from his work of decipherment, the language promoted by Edwards I and III as a defining mark of Englishness had already suffered a partial annihilation. Old English was now a vast abandoned cemetery of words. Lícbeorg (cemetery) was lost; word survived. Wer (man) lived on only in werewulf. Except in the remotest parts of the kingdom where 'lowly men [stuck] to English and their own way of speaking', about eighty-five per cent of Anglo-Saxon vocabulary was dead and forgotten. To Middle English speakers, the Anglo-Saxon tale of Beowulf had become moulderingly obscure.

Linguistics may lack the blood and thunder of military and political history but the revolutions it records are as consequential as battles and assassinations. English retained fewer than thirty Celtic words, most of which are of dubious or indirect origin. The contributions of Old Norse, though more numerous and more commonly used (get, give, take, want, etc.), are remarkably meagre in view of the long years of Danish settlement and rule. But these migrant vocabularies were outnumbered by the great linguistic armada which crossed the English Channel. The tunge or spræc of Alfred and Æthelstan had been transformed and reorganized by the foreign *langaige* of England's conquerors and closest enemies. The changes were profound: they affected not only vocabulary but also word formation, word order, spelling, prosody and pronunciation.

About one-third of the words in *The Canterbury Tales* and more than a quarter of *Piers Plowman* and the romance of *Sir Gawain and the Green Knight* – all written in the late 1300s – come from Norman or Parisian French. A speaker of Old English would have found Chaucer very hard going, whereas a modern anglophone can follow, albeit limpingly, the tales of the Canterbury pilgrims with the help of a small glossary. A speaker of Scots or a practitioner of West Country dialects can recite them quite convincingly.

The fact that this powerful hybrid vehicle owes its superabundance and versatility to French is not just an amusing irony. The sounds of Old England would descend to the scullery and mingle with the lowing of cattle and the grunting of pigs, while in the halls and bedchambers of the gentry, the conquerors' imperious articulations were embedded in the bone and muscle of spoken and written English.

*

English is still the language of the law courts, but not every English-speaker understands it in its official forms. Lawyers and members of other high-status professional bodies commonly use 'big words' (literally) of French origin and, consciously or not, de-Saxonize their speech. My father heard a barrister announce to the court in Worcester that his 'client' was 'currently exploring alternative avenues of employment'. The defendant requested elucidation: 'What's 'e saying?' The magistrate translated the idiom of the ruling class into an older and lower register: 'He's saying that you're on the dole.'

Academic discourse still armours itself with Anglo-Norman constructions and vocables. A normally affable professor of French who was trying to write a biography told me of his bitter struggles with an editor. The editor's bold mission was to spare the reader the needless lexical display of professional authority. 'Impecunious', for instance (a word of French and Latin origin): could he not just say 'penniless' or 'hard up' or even 'skint'? Why did it have to be 'impecunious'? The professor was not inconsiderably irate and expressed his wrath in 'Anglo-Saxon'.

The language of conquered Engelterre with its 'four-letter words' (in contrast to the long, compound words of French origin) became the voice of social inferiority and native resistance almost a thousand years ago. A thirteenth-century life of the East Anglian outlaw Hereward the Wake, written in Latin and based on a text of the early 1100s and the eyewitness accounts of his ageing comrades, describes him returning home to the Fens after 1066 to find the main gate of his father's house decorated with his brother's severed head and a horde of fornicating French-speakers celebrating the conquest:

> A jester was insulting the English in song, leaping about the room in a lubberly fashion in taunting imitation of English dancing.

Disguised as 'a rustic who had no idea what [the Normans] were saying', Hereward was able to gather intelligence of a Norman military operation. The original lost text had been written in Old English. This would have given it a potency it lacks in Latin. The later text has a supposedly happy ending: Hereward is reinstated in his father's lands and 'faithfully serves King William' – which makes this a historically accurate tale of an English thegn absorbed and neutralized by a colonial power. The legendary Robin Hood and the real Eadric the Wild ended in similar states of subjection.*

Reading the *Gesta Herewardi* with its haughty Normans poking fun at vernacular-speaking natives, I thought of other such scenes from recent times. Filiations of cause and effect can be as hard to trace as the tributary waters of a great river, but the river's flood will reveal the fellings of forests, the landslides and the drainings of peat bogs which took place far upstream. Some historic upheavals were so violent that the wreckage is still reaching us today.

*

AT WALTON IN suburban Staffordshire in the late 1960s, the classroom idiom was standard infant English: we were all more or less mutually comprehensible. Fifty miles south in the former territory of Urse d'Abetot with its allegedly 'feudal' population, I discovered that, like the son of foreign invaders, I was 'posh' and therefore rich, only slightly redeemed by vestigial Scottish 'r's and, crucially, short 'a's in 'grass', 'path' or 'laugh'.

I had been taught that language was like the times table: everything was either right or wrong. In Powick, even the most basic constructions were patently incorrect or, according to a family friend who taught English to hospitalized children, 'lazy'. The verb 'to be' had been simplified as though for simpletons: 'I'm', 'you'm', ''e'm', 'we'm', 'you'm', 'they'm', but, for some reason (a terminal consonant), ''er's' ('her is'). ''Er' was the female subject pronoun, as in ''er's gone down the pub'.

Of the underlying complexities, I was entirely ignorant. The 'we'm, you'm' conjugation was a relatively recent introduction to western Worcestershire. 'I be' (or 'bin'), ''er be', 'us be', etc., attested in 1898, were still in occasional use, reflecting Powick's transitional location between the dialect regions of the West Country and the industrial Black Country.

* Eadric Salvage or Silvaticus was a wealthy Shropshire contemporary of Hereward who led a guerrilla campaign against the Conqueror and then fought for him in Scotland.

In our early days in Powick, my mother encountered a peculiarity which occurs in very few of the world's languages but which maps of English dialects record from Land's End and the Solent to an area ending about ten miles north of Powick. The light was failing and the window cleaner had been forced to call it a day. 'D'you moind if oi leave 'im 'ere?', he asked. My mother fleetingly imagined a dog or child in need of overnight accommodation, then realized that the masculine pronoun referred to the window cleaner's ladder.

Thomas Hardy's friend, the folklorist Edward Clodd, seems to have been thinking of this remnant of the gendered pronouns of Old and early Middle English when he told Hardy in December 1890, 'Your Dorset peasants [represent] the persistence of the barbaric idea which confuses persons and things.'

At that time, nearly all 'educated' conceptions of dialect belonged to one of two camps: the 'ignorant' and the 'vestigial' or 'primitive'. Only a scholar who was immune to the prejudices of post-Conquest England would know that mere ignorance would never spawn such coherent and lively forms of English. Significantly, the first scientific classification of English dialects was produced in 1875 by an explorer of the English shires who had grown up in Italy. By a fluke of fate, he was born four miles from Worcester in 1813. His father had been captured on his way to the United States by the Royal Navy and placed under house arrest at Thorngrove Hall because his brother was Napoleon Bonaparte.

*

THE ONE THING my sister and I knew for certain about the Worcestershire vernacular was that any child who spoke it was likely to be poor. At Walton, signs of poverty had been comparatively rare – a few lice-ridden scalps and rotten black teeth and one case of rickets. At Powick, the contrast between the scrawny rural and plumper middle-class pupils was unmistakable, though perhaps not as statistically stark as in 2019–20, when thirty per cent of households with children in Worcester were judged to be living in 'absolute poverty'.

Even before the new housing estate upset the delicate social balance, an air of unhappiness hung about some of the leafy corners and dead-end lanes. The villages we had seen while house-hunting in

Worcestershire lacked the private funding that would soon render them unaffordable to local people. Some tied cottages owned by the big estates were the sagging refuges of paupers with authentic medieval inconveniences such as mouldy thatch and head-splintering beams and – a later luxury – septic tanks.

At morning assembly, in keeping with the village setting, we sang the Irish Anglican children's hymn, 'All Things Bright and Beautiful', written in 1848 during the Irish Famine. It included the verse which most hymn-books now omit. Its vignette of ageless rural inequality had an appealing air of social realism. It sounded like a hymn that might have been sung in cold stone churches by Norman knights and their shivering Saxon serfs.

> The rich man in his castle,
>   The poor man at his gate,
> God made them, high or lowly,
>   And ordered their estate.

Rereading the hymn, I now realize that the pauper didn't even have a gate. 'His' in both cases refers to the rich man, the gate being the place where alms were traditionally doled out to the needy.

Poor children did in fact come to our gate. A little girl from up the road was invited to meet my sister's life-size doll. Despite the horrific facial mutilations the doll had suffered by falling into the fire, the girl was love-struck. Later, we discovered that she had stolen the doll's panties for her younger sister. Having worked in the tenements of industrial Glasgow, my mother was surprised but not repelled by the reek of stale urine on the girl's clothes. What shocked her was the total ignorance of nursery rhymes. 'The poor wee thing' was thrilled to be introduced to Little Miss Muffet and her spider and the four-and-twenty blackbirds served up to a King, and went happily home to share her treasures.

13

Servants of History

The Tabard Inn in Southwark.

FOUR MILES FROM a modern city centre, we were living in two ages at once. The Conqueror's parcelling out of land to a small elite and its oldest sons was evident in the big estates which covered much of Worcestershire. In no other large country is land so unequally distributed. At least thirty per cent of England and perhaps nearly half still belongs to the gentry and the nobility. The exact boundaries of the estates are usually known only to the landowners themselves, but clues can be found on walls and gates, on woodland edges and posts driven into festering ponds: 'Keep Out', 'No Dumping', 'Trespassers Will Be Prosecuted'.

A thirty-minute walk from Collett's Green, the 'Private Property' signs of Madresfield Court led irresistibly to a maze of tall yew hedges in which we trespassed after dark with a torch and refreshments.

Madresfield and its owners were the inspiration for the stately home in Evelyn's Waugh's *Brideshead Revisited*. When the Malvern area was being prepared as an emergency seat of government in 1938, Madresfield had been earmarked as a boltholе for members of the Royal Family in case Hitler took London. If the Germans broke through the Malvern stop-lines, the Princesses Elizabeth and Margaret would be whisked up to Liverpool and from there to the Dominion of Canada.

We crept across the lawns, watching the lighted windows of the moated mansion and calculating the movements of a patrol dog from its bark. Madresfield was still the seat of Baron Beauchamp of Powyke, the descendant of Urse d'Abetot. Urse had come from Normandy with an ancestor of Beauchamp's fellow Knight of the Garter, Gerald Grosvenor, the 6th Duke of Westminster, one of the richest landowners in Britain. When asked by the *Financial Times* if he had advice for ambitious young entrepreneurs, the Duke replied, '[They should] make sure they have an ancestor who was a very close friend of William the Conqueror.'

The forelock-tugging which embarrassed my mother seemed to indicate a misplaced sense of historical identity, as did the contrary equivalent in the younger generation – a resentful servility which, at the age of ten, I found pointless and sad. There was a collaborationist us-and-them mentality in the school playground which had been absent from Walton. The village children kept a sharp eye out for any rule-breaking and then, predicting dire consequences – 'Shouldn't do that! Oi'm tellin' of you!' – denounced offenders to the headmaster.

Tragically, the authority they invoked was not on their side. Only the village children were ever caned – sometimes on both hands, palm and back, in front of the class. The worst I received by way of punishment was a cursory slap on the thigh administered in private at the behest of the headmaster by Mrs M—, who had friends in common with my parents.

At Powick, the nominally democratic primary-school system coexisted with a form of educational apartheid. In the final year, the pupils who were expected to pass the eleven-plus examination* were

* In Worcester, those who passed the eleven-plus (less than a quarter of all pupils) were admitted to one of the two state grammar schools; those

placed at the 'top table' near the headmaster's desk. The so-called 'cream' – some of whom would fail the examination – were almost exclusively middle class. Most of the bound-to-fail group was characterized by Worcestershire accents, parents on low wages or unemployed, and by the cheaper, less durable version of the supposedly uniform school uniform. They might be assigned a non-speaking role in the Nativity play, but they would never be allowed to hold or pay homage to the child that was born in a stable. In the end-of-term dramatic production of 1969, the indigent couple who lived with tear-jerking fortitude on stale bread and water and were evicted from their hovel by a cruel landlord were played by the Chief Probation Officer's son and a girl who lived in a large mock-Tudor house with its own grounds.

*

THERE WAS NOTHING fundamentally exotic about these arrangements. The well-meaning Welsh headmaster, Mr Vaughan, was something of an anachronism, but so in many respects was the nation that employed him, with its ancient shire system, its poorer 'Celtic' siblings, its north–south divide, medieval Christian rituals, anti-Semitism, lopsided land ownership and undevolved central government.

Recent studies by an economist and a historian have revealed an 'underlying social physics surprisingly immune to government intervention'. Analysing the prevalence of Norman surnames from 1170 to 2012, they found an eerily persistent trend: not only was social mobility in twenty-first-century England 'little greater than in pre-industrial times', the most reliable indicator of status, longevity and the likelihood of being admitted to Oxford or Cambridge Universities was possession of a Norman surname.

Peasants are commonly depicted as the unconscious guardians of tradition, while the middle and upper classes are supposed to have been able, on occasion, to escape the clutches of the past. Yet we too were faithful servants of history. Our speech contained the usual

---

who failed went to a secondary modern school. The former were expected to progress to higher education, the latter to leave school at sixteen.

percentage of words of French origin. Our families exemplified the inequalities which still distinguish Britain from its Western European neighbours. Our surnames were not specifically Norman, but the diversity of their origins (London, Devon, East Anglia, Yorkshire, Northumberland and Aberdeenshire) reflected the social mobility of the middle class. The surnames of the village children were nearly all local and Anglo-Saxon.

What I took to be pointless antagonism was a sign of frustration and defeat. Aggression was justified by bigotry and its retinue of bug-eyed beliefs. Boys deemed to be 'poofters' were chased and insulted. An ungirlish girl was likely to be ostracized as a 'lezzy'. Presumed 'gippoes' (Gypsies or Roma, the largest minority ethnic group in Worcestershire) were accused of spreading the virulent non-existent disease called 'the lurgy', which the *Oxford English Dictionary* records only in a 'humorous' or 'ironic' sense.

Sexual and sub-racial prejudices were endemic in British society but they were usually expressed passively or in euphemisms. In Powick, they frequently took a physical form. My mother was talking to an elderly woman on her doorstep one day about the plan for a children's playing field. A toddler tried to squeeze past his grandmother's legs to see who was at the door. A savage kick sent him squealing back inside. At my mother's cry of protest, the woman explained, as though to set her mind at rest, 'E'm a bastard.'

*

THERE HAD BEEN a time when the people of Collett's Green and Powick rose up against their oppressors. Between 1760 and 1820, the aristocracy and the Church made several attempts to enclose the common fields and 'wastes' of Powick. This was one of countless obscure episodes in the longest-running drama in British history. By placing every last acre of England in the hands of the King, the Norman Conquest had cleared the way for the confiscation and, as agricultural practices changed, the enclosing of common land. (Ch. 22)

The crofters and small stock breeders of Collett's Green, Bowling Green, Leigh and Piddlefield by the river Teme on the far side of Lord's Wood were outraged and alarmed at the fencing-off of the waterside meadows which had always been treated as a communal resource. They petitioned the lords of the manor (Beauchamp and the Earl of Coventry), protesting at the 'great and unreasonable encroachments [which] have been made to gratify the avaricious and selfish designs of individuals'. Then, as the piecemeal conquest of common land continued,

> With their faces blackened and being otherwise disguised, and armed with guns and other offensive weapons, [they] in the most daring manner did cut down, burn, and entirely destroy all the posts, gates and rails.

These ancestors of my classmates were in the unusual position of being able to support their claims with documents: court records from the early 1500s specified the common rights attached to each cottage. Even so, the great estates would prevail. 'Since ancient times' and other such phrases in the old Anglo-Saxon charters were like prayers whispered to extinct gods compared to the powerful spells of well-paid lawyers. By the 1870s, all the old common rights had been lost – pasturing, gleaning, wood-collecting and fishing. A century later, the only representative commoner of pre-Conquest Powick was the man who dwelt in a house of willows by the Teme.

Now, at the end of the 1960s, the 'great and unreasonable encroachments' took the form of a hundred modern family homes for middle-income earners. Soon after Mr Vaughan's pupils went their separate ways, to grammar school and to secondary modern, work began on the Collett's Green 'village' development. The land had been acquired from – but in certain lucrative respects still belonged to – the Earl of Coventry. The population of Powick would increase by a third and middle-class immigrants might soon outnumber the natives. Newcomers would find the grocery-shack unhygienic and lacking in essentials. They would turn their noses up at the friendly fug of Mr and Mrs Samuels' roadside Bijou Café (locally pronounced 'Buy Jew'), noted for its bread-and-butter pudding and the hospitality it offered to patients from the nearby Powick Mental Hospital, previously known as the Worcester County and City Pauper Lunatic Asylum.

*

The first houses had been built on 'The Orchard' and 'The Drive', and some families had already moved in when the last sputtering of village resistance broke out. On the site of the next stage of development, two mountains of earth and rubble had risen, and it was already hard to remember what had been there before.

Coming home late one afternoon from the Worcester Royal Grammar School, I noticed that some boys I had known at primary school had gathered on one of the earth mounds along with other children from the neighbouring hamlet of Callow End. A bonfire had been lit. The occupying force was shouting abuse at anyone who happened to come within earshot.

I recognized a boy whose family had once farmed the land on which the 'loony bin' had been built more than a century before. N— and I had been on good-to-neutral terms at primary school. Since then, he and his cronies had become deliberately obnoxious. Finding him alone one day, I asked him why he now hated me. He answered with grudgeful sincerity, 'Cos you've got a droiveway.' In Powick, a driveway was a social barrier as flagrant as the spiked Cutteslowe Walls which divided a council estate in North Oxford from the middle-class houses on the same street between 1934 and 1959 (p. 276).

Along with some of the new estate children and a few anxious adults, we clambered to the top of the opposite mound to see what was going on. The bonfire was blazing and there was a smell of burning rubbish. When the first missiles reached us, we realized that, like Britons defending a claggy hillfort, the 'peasants' – as we had taken to calling them – had a stockpile of ammunition. As playground convention demanded, we responded in kind, but the stones were coming at us now in nearly straight lines as though shot from catapults. A boy's bloodied head was the signal for retreat. We left as nonchalantly as we could under a barrage of stones and insults. The parents hurried home to phone the police.

*

A thousand years after Hereward the Wake saw his nation's folklore and language ridiculed by Normans, 'rustic' forms of English were still considered amusing. Standard English had evolved from the merging of London English and the dialect of the prosperous East Midlands. Dialects of the South-West, despite the cultural eminence of early-medieval Worcester, were among the 'barbarous', 'rude' or 'babbling' idioms which English scholars tried to eradicate.

Television and popular music are thought to have had a levelling effect on the class system. At that time, they seemed to be ushering in a new age of cultural stereotyping. On the 'goggle-box' which was now the flickering hearth of sitting rooms, the natives of rural Worcestershire heard and saw themselves through the eyes and ears of a wider society.

For a short spell in 1976, West Country English was all the rage thanks to a pop group called the Wurzels. Their surprise hit was 'The Combine Harvester' ('Oi got a brand-new combine 'arvesterr'), sung to a backing chorus of 'ooh arr, ooh arr'. The band members came from Somerset but sounded like middle-class people mimicking a generic West Country accent. The lead singer acted a scrumpy-befuddled yokel with half his mind on his new-fangled acquisition and the other on traditional pursuits: 'Oi drove moi tracturr thru' yur 'aystack last noight . . .' It was the best-selling single in Britain for two weeks. I heard it performed at an open-air concert in Malvern where it was a favourite with the middle-class hippies and public-school alumni.

By that time, having turned into the semblance of an adult, I was able to go with my sister to the only place where inter-tribal relations flourished – not that any other middle-class offspring went there unless we dragged them along with us. The Three Nuns was one of nine pubs in the parish of Powick – one pub for every two hundred and fifty-eight adult inhabitants, which was nearly three times the national average. At legal closing time, the Nuns would lock its doors in case 'Drinky', the local police constable, decided to pay a visit. Then the customers or 'guests' would get stuck in to the several hours' worth of pre-bought pints lined up on the bar.

The custom of arriving at the pub with a wheelbarrow on one's birthday so as to be taken home after the binge was observed as a matter of course. The wheelbarrow came to Britain about three hundred years after the Norman Conquest, but the ritual of the 'mead-cup' – a cup with a rounded bottom so that it could be put down only when empty – was already an ancient tradition in the days of Hereward the Wake.

A friend from the council houses up the road assured us that this festive leglessness was nothing compared to olden days. At harvest time, his grandfather would set off for fields a mile away with a satchel of bread and cheese and a heavy jug of homemade cider. An hour later, his wife would arrive with a fresh jug, take the empty home, refill it and return to the field, by which time he would be ready for the next one. This went on all day. His son never touched a drop; his grandson imposed a strict nightly limit on himself of eight pints of beer.

According to a historian of Anglo-Saxon England, bingeing 'seemed to stabilize society and foster group-cohesion'. This was at least partly true of the Nuns. Temporarily relieved of the weight of our inherited social status and coming from a house a few doors down the road in which Scots was like a family language, we revelled in the multilingual ambiance. With some former pupils of Powick School, we discussed various historical and socio-economic interferences with normal human relations: 'Oi pays tax so you c'n read all them books; I moight as well buy you a pint while oi'm at it.' This was one eternally pregnant topic of conversation. And so, in the shadow of the hills where the vision of Piers Plowman began not so many centuries ago, we wenten quite ofte to the taverne ful of folk that highte the Thre Nonnes, there to jangle and jape and jugge, with the wercmen and the wastours seyinge 'Gwaan 'ave anutherr!' and 'Get it down yur neck!', and longe after the sonne goyng doune we fedde us with thicke ale and seten so till we hadde yglubbed a gallon and a gill.

14

'A tale tauld bi an idjot'

J. P. Kemble as Shakespeare's Macbeth.

FROM TIME TO time, my mother would take soundings of the depths of English obliviousness by asking what Alison and I were studying in History at our respective schools. Had we done the Wars of Scottish Independence (1296–1341)? (Not that I had noticed.) Surely there had been at least a passing reference to the nation-building exploits of William Wallace and the thrilling comeback tale of Robert the Bruce? (Nope.) On the other hand, we knew that Edward I of England (r. 1272–1307) was 'the Hammer of Scots' but not that the 'hammering' had had the accidental effect of beating an iron-hard Scottish nation into shape.

The Battle of Bannockburn (1314) may have been omitted from the curriculum because it was a humiliation for the English. But we also hadn't 'done' Flodden Field (1513), when the Scots invaded

England to distract Henry VIII from his war with Scotland's French allies. We touched on Culloden (1746), which put paid to the Jacobite uprising and sent Bonnie Prince Charlie fleeing 'over the sea to Skye' dressed as an Irish maid, but not the ensuing repression of Highland clans by the British army and the relief of many Lowland Scots when the old Highland threat was neutralized.

To fill the gaps and lend some colour to the mist-obliterated places we passed through or were stuck in on holiday, my parents would recall their own history lessons. With his sunny Edinburghian disposition, my father had a fondness for tales of bleak and hapless misery. Shakespeare's twice-removed-from-reality Macbeth and his 'tale tauld bi an idjot'* (more impressive in fighting Scots than actorly English) was a frequent quotation as was, when setting off up another mountain,

> 'Lay on, Macduff,
> And damn'd be him that first cries "Hold! Enough!".'

Scottish history seemed to be rich in tales of murder and betrayal, typically involving foul weather and morale-sapping terrain. Somewhere in the boggy remotenesses of Glencoe in 1692, the Campbells in cahoots with the English had massacred my maternal ancestors the Macdonalds to whom I owed my middle name. On the far side of Gretna Green near a settlement of caravans and grey pebble-dash bungalows, we visited the dank cave where King Robert the Bruce, after stabbing to death his rival for the throne of Scotland at the altar of a church in Dumfries in 1306, was said to have hidden from the soldiers of his former ally, Edward I of England. There, he had watched a spider spinning, repairing and re-repairing its web in a howling gale, and was inspired to have another go at the English.

* From Robin Lorimer's Scots translation of *Macbeth* (1992), of which he gave me a copy at his Strathtummel home after a traditional meal of roadkill. He was also the editor of his father's Scots translation of the New Testament, in which the only words in standard English are spoken by the Devil: '"If you are the Son of God, tell these stones to turn into loaves." Jesus answert, "It says i the Buik: Man sanna live on breid alane."'

During that visit, I acquired as a cheap souvenir in a jam jar a possible descendant of the auspicious spider. Two weeks later, I released it onto my bedroom window sill in Powick. It skedaddled in the direction of the Malvern Highlands, probably hunting for English flies.

*

Bruce's spider belongs to a long-legged line of Scottish legends. The cave at Kirkpatrick Fleming is just one of several candidates. The tale was popularized in 1827 by the Romantic rationalist Walter Scott to whom most English readers owed their knowledge of Scottish history. In an earlier version of the legend, the spider-watcher in the cave or cabin was one of Bruce's generals, but I wonder now whether the folkloric elements indicate much older origins in a Celtic parable of perseverance or the art of divination by the threads of Fate.

Scottish nationalism promotes the image of a proud, culturally coherent race of non-English Britons battling to free itself from the cruel and condescending Auld Enemy. In reality, few neighbouring nations in Europe enjoyed such long and mutually profitable periods of stability and cooperation. After Edward I, most invasions by English or Scottish armies were raids intended to maintain the borderlands as a buffer zone of devastation. The worst offender was Henry VIII with his 'Rough Wooing' of Scotland. This was a vicious attempt to win by 'fyre and sworde' the hand of the baby Mary Stuart for his son Edward. But even with a psychopathic commander-in-chief, it was hard to start a proper war.

When Border disputes were at their height, officers on both sides reported foot soldiers chatting politely with the enemy on the battlefield. These men of the Borders considered themselves neither Scottish nor English – a concept which, I was interested to discover, has remained controversial and inflammatory. These independent Border mercenaries sometimes pretended to have been captured and went off for a meal. If they noticed an officer watching, they pranced about harmlessly like popinjays in a fencing school.

There are many such flies in the pure nationalist ointment. Scotland was governed for several centuries by transnational elites. Malcolm 'Canmore' III, the nemesis of Macbeth whose descendants ruled Scotland for two hundred years, was married to the Hungarian-born Margaret of Wessex (later Saint Margaret of Scotland). Her great-uncle was Edward the Confessor; her brother was the Anglo-Saxon heir to the English throne. Most of Malcolm's successors had foreign wives: three French, three Norman, four English. Medieval Scottish history contains a wealth of fiendish quiz questions: 'In which European nation were the following women Queens Consort in the thirteenth century – Ermengarde de Beaumont, Joan of England, Marie de Coucy, Margaret of England and Yolande de Dreux?'

*

The stirring name 'Wars of Scottish Independence' (independence from England) is anachronistic: it was not used until after the American War of Independence of 1776. Most of these 'wars' were fought in the medieval fashion with sword and dagger by rival British dynasties and their allies. Both the Bruce and the Balliol claimants to the throne owned estates in England. The first British de Brus had come over from Normandy in 1100 and helped Henry I to consolidate the Norman colonization of Yorkshire, of which he was granted a large portion.

Robert the Bruce owned English estates as far away as Middlesex and Essex. His father was born in Essex, either at Writtle by Chelmsford or at Hatfield Broad Oak near Stansted Airport. 'Bruce Castle' is a sixteenth-century brick manor house built on land once held by Robert the Bruce two streets from the stadium of Tottenham Hotspur Football Club in North London.

In 2022, millions of people saw two Tottenham players conversing chummily on the pitch after a hard-fought World Cup quarter-final. Some England fans booed at their unseemly behaviour. One of the players was the centre-forward Harry Kane, captain of the defeated English, the other was his Tottenham teammate, the goalkeeper Hugo Lloris, captain of the victorious French.

National affiliations always coexist with other loyalties. On the field of Bannockburn in 1314, on the morning after the Scottish side had won by a margin of seven hundred knights to not very many, an elderly English knight called Marmaduke Thweng wriggled out of his hiding place in a 'busk' (thicket), then picked his way across the crow-pecked carnage. On his shield, he sported the three heraldic parrots of the House of Thweng. On reaching the English side, he surrendered politely to Robert the Bruce, who 'tret him curteusly' and invited him to a post-battle breakfast along with Marmaduke's comrade in arms, Ralph de Monthemer.

Marmaduke's mother Lucy was one of the Yorkshire Bruces; his father had been a vassal of Bruce's father. Ralph de Monthemer had known Robert at the English court. He had warned him of King Edward's intention to arrest him, causing Robert to flee to Scotland. After Bannockburn, Marmaduke 'dwelt lang in [Bruce's] cumpany' and returned to England with no ransom on his head, nicely dressed by his host and laden with 'gret giftis'.

At Bannockburn, Bruce behaved in the correct chivalric fashion. The Paisley Tartan Army – the 'Sons of Scotland' who celebrate Scottish history and culture, pin-up girls in kilts and, despite repeated humiliations, the national football team – would have booed him off the field.

*

THE SCOTLAND RULED by King Robert the Bruce was not a northern equivalent of England. No part of Caledonia had been Romanized. No overseas invaders had conquered it as thoroughly as the Normans conquered England. Scotland's agriculture and ways of life were predominantly pastoral. Its *burghs* were founded much later than the *burhs* of Alfred the Great and its system of sheriffdoms or shires was not complete until the seventeenth century.

Early medieval Scotland was the land of Picts, Gaels, Galwegians (in Galloway), Scots (from Ireland), Scandinavians and Manx (on the Isle of Man), Anglo-Saxons and Anglo-Normans, each with their own language, laws and traditions. As a political and geographical label, 'Scotia' or 'Scotland' was ambiguous until the late Middle Ages. It originally referred to Ireland – it was used in this sense by Robert the Bruce – and then to the Gaelic lands north of the river Forth.

The piecing together of the country now called Scotland was slow and intermittent. Alexander III, the son of an English Plantagenet and husband of a Frenchwoman, acquired the Hebrides and the Isle of

Man in 1266 from the King of Norway for a lump sum and an annual payment. Orkney and Shetland would be added two centuries later when the penniless King of Denmark and Norway pawned them to Scotland without telling his own parliament. (The pawnbroker shut up shop and the pledge has never been redeemed.) By then, the Anglo-Scottish border had been known in precise detail for many centuries. It was reconfirmed in 1245 when twelve knights – six Scottish and six English – then twenty-four, then forty-eight (the Scots were being difficult) squelched along several miles of the 'true and ancient marches and divisions between the two kingdoms'.

Last of all came the only part of Great Britain that had remained truly independent – the fifty-square-mile autarkic enclave of the Debatable Land, which belonged to neither country. A Scottish Act of Parliament in 1587 defined its inhabitants as primitive clans who 'delight in all mischiefs'. These 'clans' had descended into anarchy largely because of a law passed fifty years before with the aim of destabilizing and destroying Border society:

> All Inglichemene annde Scottesmene . . . shalbe fre to rube, burne, spoyll, slaye, murder annd destrewe, all annd every suche person or persons, ther bodys, heldynges, goodes annd cattalles, as dothe remayne or shall inhabyde upon any partt of the sayde Debatable lannde, witheowtt any redresse to be mayde for the sayme.

Thus Scotland acquired its modern size and shape.

*

One sunny morning in the Border badlands, I met the BBC's Scotland correspondent for an on-the-bike interview on the subject of cols and passes. We cycled out of the small town of Langholm and up Ewesdale on the A7 to a narrow pass through the hills: Sorbie Hass, once known as 'the Gates of Eden'. To the west lay the almost deserted valley of the Esk whose natives had migrated long ago to the English side of the border half a day's walk to the south. Two hours later, back in Langholm, where Colin had left his company car, I noted the absence of any BBC insignia. He stared at me in disbelief:

'God no! The car wouldn't still be here . . . If it *was* still here, it would have been smashed to bits. I'd have been lucky to get out alive!'

Attacks on the free press in the name of political freedom had been frequent before the 2014 referendum on Scottish independence. The referendum had been fate-temptingly held exactly seven hundred years after the army of Robert the Bruce slaughtered the army of Edward II at Bannockburn. Losing the independence vote was all the more bitter. It was easy to share the frustration with 'Westminster' and the pudgy-faced Old Etonian chancer (Prime Minister Cameron) who had humoured the Scots with a vote (specifically, adults of any nationality resident in Scotland). In the two regions adjacent to England, 'Yes' voters had been outnumbered by two to one, but there, too, many people who voted 'No' to independence did so with gritted teeth.

In some parts, the bitterness had a flavour of living history. With the rise of Scottish nationalism in the 1960s, the old antagonism between Gaelic-speaking Highland *teuchters* and English-speaking Lowland Sassenachs had mutated into a stand-off of proletariat and bourgeoisie. In 2014, there were serious discussions about the desirability of reclassifying 'posh' southern Scots as English – especially those with Morningside (Edinburgh) or Kelvinside (Glasgow) accents. The trappings of claymore-wielding Highlanders were snatched from the jumbled wardrobe of Jacobite propaganda, Romantic fiction and Victorian tourism and sported by tartan-clad city-dwellers. Little was said publicly about the related divide between Protestant and Catholic, of which few English people south of the Humber are aware. Sectarian divisions muted by the independence campaign were proclaimed as usual on the football terraces.

In the years leading up to the 2014 referendum, some academics, perhaps influenced by funding bodies, ignored or distorted well-documented realities of Scottish history. One scholar, employing a key concept of nationalist rhetoric, dismissed the copious evidence of cross-border marriages as 'scaremongering'. Like sixteenth-century Scottish and English officials confronted with the non-aligned

Debatable Land, they were irritated by the fact that a cross-border society had survived for centuries without feeling the need for a national identity.

*

English ignorance of Scotland also played a role: it seemed to exemplify the obliviousness of Westminster. I was unaware of the extent of this ignorance until we moved to the border in 2010. Some of our visitors shared their amazement at discovering that Hadrian's Wall is not the national border and that Carlisle is an English city. They were surprised to learn that the wife of Walter Scott was an Anglican and that the couple spent the night before their wedding at the Crown and Mitre next door to Carlisle Cathedral.

On the other hand, some Scots who have the means to explore Scotland bemoan the ignorance of their compatriots. In the geologically complex and socially diverse British Isles, some degree of ignorance is inevitable. A country which has no secrets from its own population would scarcely be worth discovering in any case.

The novelist John Buchan, who was born in Perth and grew up in Fife and Tweeddale, saw far more of Scotland than most of his contemporaries. On foot and by bicycle, he discovered a three-thousand-square-mile peninsula of which many Scots have only a hazy notion though it accounts for one-seventh of mainland Scotland. It was in this hiding place the size of a small country that Robert the Bruce relaunched his military campaign in 1307.

When Buchan wrote *The Thirty-Nine Steps* (1915), he knew that readers both north and south of the border would be excited by a non-fictional Highlands situated seventy miles south of Glasgow and which his fugitive hero would reach on the 7.10 a.m. from St Pancras and the slow train from Dumfries, arriving late in the afternoon of the same day.

> I got out an atlas and looked at a big map of the British Isles [probably *The Queen's Jubilee Atlas of the British Empire*]. My notion was to get off to some wild district . . . I considered that Scotland would be best, for my people were Scotch and I could pass anywhere as an ordinary Scotsman . . . I fixed on Galloway

as the best place to go to. It was the nearest wild part of Scotland, so far as I could figure it out, and from the look of the map was not overthick with population.

Galloway lost what remained of its independence in the Scottish Wars of Independence. Culturally and economically, it belonged to a Norse-Gaelic 'Mediterranean' which included the Hebrides, the Isle of Man, the kingdom of Dublin and the Norse-settled parts of north-western England. In 2014, it elected by a very large majority to remain in the kingdom of Great Britain and Northern Ireland.

This neglected region is the largest part of the council area commonly referred to as 'Dumgal' (Dumfries and Galloway). It has no motorways. West of Dumfries and the river Nith, there are only twenty miles of functioning railway and one station. Its language, Galwegian Gaelic, was extinct by 1800 and is now only partly decipherable. The passes leading west from Dalbeattie then north across the upland moors are still of use to smugglers. They bear names that would suit an adventure tale for young adults. A sample east–west route might run from the Nick of Whirstone and the Nick of Knock, over the Corse of Slakes, past the hill formerly known as Noggin, to the Deep Nick of Dromore, the Nick of Curleywee, the Neive of the Spit, and finally to the shores of the Hibernian Sea.

*

I TALKED ABOUT the Debatable Land in Glasgow on a rainy night three and a half years after the referendum. Glasgow was one of the few council areas in which a majority voted for independence. In the bowels of the Mitchell Library, a red-faced man glowered at me as I spoke. His wife appeared to be egging him on to do something. When the time came for questions, I pointed him out to the chair, and then the pent-up question burst forth: 'Where *is* this "Debatable Land" . . .?'

I began the minute description of its well-charted bounds, but this empurpled the man even more. 'I'm not answering your question, am I . . .?' 'Well,' he shouted triumphantly, '*I*'ve never heard of it! And I was *born* in Dumfries!'

In normal circumstances, it would have been a mystifying remark.

The man had never heard of the land twenty miles from his place of birth which had been a major foreign policy issue for English and Scottish parliaments for more than a century and which appeared to have made a mockery of the very idea of nationhood. Therefore, he denied its existence. There were solid arguments for independence as a remedy to regional inequalities, but nationalism had fostered a state of heroic indignation in which only certain truths were deemed worthy of being true.

I walked back along the river, past the few hulking remnants of the Clyde shipyards which, as my mother liked to point out in her battles with English ignorance, had been one of the powerhouses of the British Empire. Rising in the Southern Uplands, the Clyde rolls through the industrial heartland, sullen and majestic, and meets the Irish Sea at the Highland Boundary Fault. Its hundred miles could form the leitmotif of a chronicle describing the diversity of Scotland's geography and people from the days of Robert the Bruce to the present.

It was still early in the evening. At certain times, Glasgow can appear to be recovering from various hangovers – physiological or historical – but the bars were looking lively and hospitable. I knew it as a city of unexpected encounters, some real, like a friend on a bicycle materializing in the mist, others imaginary but too satisfying not to be real. As a young girl, confined to an isolation ward in Glasgow with scarlet fever, my mother had encountered a woman from the Gorbals who had seen 'wi' ma ain een' the Devil walking down the Broomielaw and disappearing into the Clyde: 'He wis wearin' a top hat 'n' tails!' No one was surprised to learn that the Devil was an Englishman.

15

'Al was hethynesse som tyme Engelond and Walis'

St Andrews Ward, Kingston upon Hull.

While Britons high and lowly had been making the best of their earthly existence, in another dimension, events of a cataclysmic or merely mind-boggling nature had been taking place for no known reason. That they *had* occurred was beyond doubt: weird and other-worldly phenomena had been witnessed from one end of Britain to the other, but the meaning of those 'tokens' or messages was never firmly established. Nor was it clear that human affairs had been foretold or influenced in any way by heavenly doings.

Early-medieval chroniclers could be remarkably noncommittal. During the first week of Lent in 1106, 'an unusual star' was seen for several nights in a row. It was reported to be 'small' and 'dark' and accompanied by a long beam of light which streamed out to the north-east. 'But', wrote the monk of Peterborough Abbey who was responsible for updating the Anglo-Saxon Chronicle, 'we do not write more fully about it, because we saw it not ourselves'.

Mysteries were the stuff of history and therefore had to be recorded. That year, on the night before the Mass of the Lord's Supper, two full moons hung in the dawn sky, one in the east, the other in the west. The following year, the Moon's radiance appeared to 'wax and wane in a manner contrary to nature'.

Only a few historians would now present their readers with uninterpreted chronological coincidences. For twelfth-century chroniclers living under fathomless skies which mirrored the vast ignorance they perceived in themselves, this was standard scholarly practice. Cistercian monks at Melrose Abbey translated the old Saxon and Norman chronicles into Latin and produced their own authoritative compilation. They gave more weight to Scottish history but preserved the conceptual simplicity of the original texts. These are the last bald items listed under 1066:

> William the Bastard [the Conqueror] fought to gain England and won, and was consecrated king at Westminster by Aldred, Archbishop of York.
>
> A comet was seen.

*

In this early Age of Reason with its continent-wide network of monastic schools and scriptoria, observation and experiment coexisted with Christian observance. The orthodox view was that Pope Gregory's envoy, Augustine, had converted the Angles to Christianity in 597 and ended the barbaric age when 'England and Wales were entirely heathen'.

In reality, pagans and Christians continued to cohabit peacefully for centuries.

The early Saxon kings Æthelbert of Kent, Rædwald of East Anglia, Edwin of Northumbria and Peada of Mercia (son of Penda) publicly converted to Christianity without feeling the need to convert or murder heathens. Penda of Mercia remained a pagan but 'did not forbid the preaching of the Word even among his people' according to the Venerable Bede. Tales of cruelly persecuted British martyrs, virtually none of which can be substantiated, belong to the Reformation rather than the Dark Ages. All the reliably recorded martyrs of Britain were martyred by other Christians (p. 145).

Pagan scholarship was a respectable field of study. In the early eleventh century, Eilmer, a monk of Malmesbury Abbey, crossed the Channel and delved into the priceless collection of pre-Christian and Muslim texts held in the library of Reims Cathedral. Back at Malmesbury, he applied his new scientific knowledge and successfully – apart from two broken legs – flew through the air from the abbey tower for a distance of one furlong (six hundred and sixty feet).

Five centuries into the future, time seems to have been ticking past in the wrong direction. The first Catholic priest trained on the Continent was executed at Launceston in 1577. By then, Nature was more likely to be studied in the blinding light of ideology. In the same year, Raphael Holinshed published his compilation of chronicles, *An Historicall Description of the Islande of Britayne* (1577). It began with the creation of the world and the age when giants walked the Earth. The voice of Renaissance humanism introduced a note of scepticism in the matter of popular superstition, but strange or spectacular occurrences such as earthquakes, astronomical anomalies, biological aberrations and mass hallucinations were still likely to be interpreted as signs of God's wrath or as evidence of sorcery. 'Blasing starres' like the comet of 1066 were 'a prediction of mischéefe imminent', 'for they never appeare but as prognosticats of afterclaps'.

This cultish mode of false reasoning in which logic was the slave of dogma thrived in the age of the Tudors. It was in the sixteenth century that sorcery was made punishable by death, first by Henry VIII and then by his daughter Elizabeth. The 'swimming' or 'ducking' of witches – innocent if submerged, guilty if buoyant – had its heyday in the sixteenth and seventeenth centuries. To audiences of Shakespeare's *Macbeth* (1606), the storm-raising 'weird sisters' on the 'blasted heath' were recognizable as a recent news item, some of their ilk having been convicted of summoning a tempest to sink the ship that brought Elizabeth's successor, King James VI and I, back to Scotland. The King himself reproduced this 'Newes from Scotland' in his studiously credulous *Daemonologie* (1597; reprinted 1603).

As late as 1712, a Hertfordshire widow, Jane Wenham of Walkern, was denounced as a witch by three local clergymen, all graduates of Cambridge University, and accused of foul acts such as communing with a cat, failing to bleed when pins were pushed into her arm and causing a sheep to stand on its head. The jury found her guilty of witchcraft but she was reprieved by the judge – a man of modern views, who informed Widow Wenham and the court that she was free to pursue her alleged nocturnal activities, there being 'no law against flying'.

*

At the Church of England primary school in Powick, those of us who thought about such things believed that we were living in a post-Christian age. Once upon a time, everyone had been pagan, which meant fearfully ignorant and a danger to themselves and other people. Then came Christianity and the obligation to attend church. Now that we had reached the age of television and modern conveniences, religion could be dispensed with altogether.

Religion at Powick School was manifest only in morning assembly and in the soul-withering tedium of the vicar's half-hour or, more to the point, one-thousand-eight-hundred-second-long homilies. The calendar was a mixture of sacred and profane: Christmas, Easter, Whitsun (the unexplained name of a half-term holiday), the hard-to-remember days of the four patron saints and the more important Pancake Day, Poppy Day, Sports Day, Last Day of Term, Next-to-Last Day of Term, etc. Lent was never mentioned, let alone observed. Much later in life, my secular French friends were amazed by my ignorance of the liturgical calendar.

As a Welshman, the headmaster was perhaps not especially keen on Anglican ritual. Instead, he enjoyed telling us about the muddle of competing traditions. 'Eostre' and 'Yuletide' were pagan festivals, respectively Anglo-Saxon and Norse. The rubicund deliverer of presents, though unmentioned in the Bible, was technically Christian. According to Mr Vaughan, who conducted the experiment, if all the class mumbled 'Saint Nicholas' repeatedly, the mashed sounds would turn into 'Santa Claus' (the Flemish 'Sinterklaas' must have escaped him). The days of the week commemorated Viking and other gods, while the months had been named by the Romans until they ran out of gods and used numbers instead, for some reason counting months nine to twelve from *septem* to *decem*.

Some of the village children professed a belief in a punitive deity. Anyone who used the words 'God', 'Jesus', 'hell' or 'bloody' in a profane context would go to Hell; pending that, they would be delivered up to the headmaster. 'Blimey', 'cor', 'crikey' and 'struth' were permissible because the blasphemy was no longer evident.

Only old people and a few village worthies willingly attended church. In that ancient parish on the western edge of the Hwiccan kingdom, the spirit world communicated with human beings and demons dragged their victims down to Hell only at the creepy Victorian hospital up the road. The question, 'Do you believe in God?' belonged to the same category as 'Do you like pop or classical music?' In our eyes, the village police constable was a figure of far greater authority than the meddlesome man in the dog collar.

The playground attitude to religion was one of ignorant mockery or blank indifference. Some of the hymns sung in morning assembly, especially Christmas carols, had been subjected to sly alterations: shepherds washed their socks by night; 'Good King Wences last looked out' of his Mini Minor before skidding round a double bend and ending up in China. I found out much later that this orally transmitted corpus of poetic manglings was known throughout Britain, with local variations. I assumed it to be the work of some forgotten sarcastic genius who had left the school without committing his devilish inventions to paper.

*

Disrespect belongs to a very old tradition of resistance to established religion. The earliest evidence is in Bede's life of St Cuthbert (c. 700). At the mouth of the Tyne, Cuthbert stood on the riverbank in 'an intemperate crowd of common people'. A group of monks had rafted down to Tynemouth to fetch a load of building timber for their abbey. As they floated by, a violent gust pushed them out to sea. Rescue boats were launched from the nearby monastery but the tide was too strong. To Cuthbert's disgust, the rustic crowd, noticing the monks' predicament, cackled and jeered. When Cuthbert reproached them, they retorted that they hoped to see the monks drown because they had 'taken away the old customs, and no one knows how the new ones are supposed to be observed'.

The God-and-Hell-fearing peasant is a post-medieval invention. In March 1208, when John Lackland, the seventh post-Conquest King of England, disputed Pope Innocent III's appointment of a new Archbishop of Canterbury, the Pope placed an interdict on England and Wales. For the next six years, churches were locked and parishioners were denied the sacraments of marriage, burial and Communion. King John himself was excommunicated in 1209. 'People must have been upset' is a common remark. Historians of the period disagree: in the six years of interdiction 'there was hardly a murmur of public protest'; 'neither was there an upsurge of interest in alternative religions'.

Was this the sign of what some historians call a 'premature Reformation', or was it simply normal practice? Long before Martin Luther nailed his theses to the church doors in Wittenberg in 1517, most antagonism was a reaction to ecclesiastical corruption. The wandering clerics known as Goliards were able to make a healthy living out of blasphemy with apparent impunity. Educated but unemployed, they begged and minstrelled their way through western Europe from the eleventh to fourteenth centuries, singing parodies of hymns and liturgical texts.

Now at the dawning of the day To God as suppliants we pray.	Now at the dawning of the day We must start drinking straight away.
That from our daily round he may All harmful beings keep away.	Let's drink now till the drink's all gone And have another later on.
(Latin hymn, 6th century)	(Goliard parody, 12th century)

The Goliardic tradition was not inherently childish. It was not even particularly outrageous. In the late 1300s, the Bible was no longer the magic fortune-telling grimoire which only a priest could understand. Even before it was translated for the 'unlettred', the Gospels, rather than their anecdotal representation in folk tales and mystery plays, were becoming a popular topic of conversation.

'As you know', says Chaucer's narrator to his fellow pilgrims, each Evangelist gives a different account of Christ's Passion, 'yet everything they teach is true.' The notion seemed to imply that the Gospels were the work of several fallible individuals rather than a divine revelation. A similarly pointed question is posed by a character in Langland's *Piers Plowman*: if Mary and Joseph were penniless, why were they looking for a room at the *diversorium* (inn or lodging house) in Bethlehem? True scholarship wore a smile not a frown. Modern Bible scholars have detected a similar discrepancy between text and tradition: the original Greek suggests that Mary chose the privacy of a stable, not because 'there was no room at the inn' but because the crowded caravanserai was 'no place to have a baby'.

Questioning of any kind was a threat to civil as well as ecclesiastical authority. Peasant rebellions were common throughout Europe in the fourteen and fifteenth centuries. The greatest of these was the Peasants' Revolt of 1381, when an army of labourers and artisans descended on London to protest against the shilling poll tax, imposed indiscriminately on rich and poor.

The spiritual and intellectual leader of the Peasants' Revolt was an Essex priest who used the codename 'Piers Plowman'. To John Ball, Langland's tinkering with holy writ sounded like a call to arms. One of his characters claimed that the gifts brought by the Magi were not luxury items but 'ertheliche honeste thynges' ('down-to-earth, decent things') – gold meant justice, myrrh was 'mercy' and 'frankincense' was 'common sense'.

John Ball's radical message was that the Bible said nothing of a primordial distinction between master and serf. All men were created equal. No one should pay a tithe to someone richer than himself and especially not to a priest who lives a more sinful life than his parishioners. This was also the opinion of Chaucer's poor parson: a priest should always remember what a shameful thing it is to have 'a shiten shepherde and a clene sheep'.

*

Chaucer was writing for an increasingly self-confident and literate audience. The Black Death had killed at least one-third of Britons between 1348 and 1350. The pandemic caused a severe labour shortage and dealt a blow to feudalism by creating a larger landowning or land-leasing middle class and a peasantry aware of its social and economic worth.

The children of the plague survivors were the first generation to hear the words of Christ and the apostles in their own language. From 1381 to 1395, the Latin Bible was translated into English for the first time in its entirety by the Oxford theologian John Wycliffe and his collaborators. In its final version (1395), the Wycliffe Bible beautifully echoed the unsophisticated Greek of the Gospels.

> And sche bare hir first borun sone, and wlappide hym in clothis, and leide hym in a cratche, for ther was no place to hym in no chaumbir.
>
> And scheepherdis weren in the same cuntre, wakynge and kepynge the watchis of the nyyt on her flok.
>
> And lo! the sterre, that thei siyen in the eest, wente bifore hem, til it cam, and stood aboue, where the child was.
>
> And thei siyen the sterre, and ioyeden with a ful greet ioye.

The hand-printed texts, recopied and excerpted, reached a wide readership. Perhaps as many as one in seven lay people in towns and cities could read English by the end of the fourteenth century. Secondary literacy was obviously more widespread: a single reader could reveal the contents of a book to a household, a neighbourhood or a whole village, and then each turning of the page was the opening of a door.

The General Prologue urged 'Cristen men and wymmen, olde and yonge' to study the New Testament, 'for it is of ful autorite, and opyn to undirstonding of simple men'. This direct appeal to the people smelled of heresy. The Archbishop of Canterbury, William Courtenay, persuaded the young king Richard II to order the Wycliffites to be hunted down and locked up. He convened a synod at the Blackfriars monastery in London on 21 May 1382 to discuss ways of combating Wycliffe and his followers, soon to be known as Lollards ('mumblers' or 'mutterers').

The synod was a disaster. During the afternoon session, the monastery walls began to tremble. Outside, chimneys and steeples were crashing to the ground. The cross of St Paul's Cathedral suffered terminal damage. The Dover Straits earthquake was one of the most destructive to hit the British Isles in the last thousand years. It was followed by two major aftershocks and a 'waterquake' which had ships at harbour yawing and swaying.

When the earthquake abated, the Archbishop announced that it signified or actually was the violent expulsion of noxious heretical spirits from the bowels of the Earth. On returning to Canterbury, he would have to explain why God's purging operation had also destroyed the bell-tower of Canterbury Cathedral.

Wycliffe's own explanation, which he claimed 'decent men' preferred, was that God, who had not been invited to the synod, had asked the Earth to speak in his stead, 'as it did at the time of Christ's Passion when He was condemned to bodily death'.

It would be some time before the State joined the Church in declaring all-out war on English heretics. Wycliffe died peacefully in the quiet rectory at Lutterworth in Leicestershire in 1384. Forty-four years after his death, as though in accordance with some spiteful pagan ritual, the Church had his body exhumed from the graveyard of St Mary's parish church. The body was incinerated; then the ashes were carried to the little river Swift, five miles from its confluence with the river Avon, and thrown in. This, too, has a ritualistic air. In other religions, it might have symbolized the dissemination of the spirit. Four or five weeks later, via the Avon and the Severn, John Wycliffe's ashes would have reached the open sea.

*

Religious scholars draw a useful distinction between 'world religions' such as Christianity which set out to save the heathen soul with book, sword or bribe, and 'indigenous religions', which mind their own traditional business and become militant only when their beliefs and practices come under attack. This is what St Cuthbert had witnessed at Tynemouth. Most indigenous religions are scriptureless and unsanctioned by a state.

Only when the Church became punitive was it generally remarked that indigenous religion continued to flourish under the skirts of the Church of England and that practically everyone was heretical in some way. In a land of saint-worshippers and fondlers of relics, orthodoxy was the exception.

The expression 'poor (or hungry) as a church mouse' derives from the obligation on Protestant as well as Catholic priests to ensure that no visible crumb of the Eucharist, conceived as the body of Christ, is left to be swept or vacuumed up. Equally, any unused or contaminated Communion wine must not be poured down a drain connected to a sewer. I learned this after surprising the rector of Nicholforest one morning lurking among the trees behind the parish church.

Dressed in his cassock, the rector was pouring the contents of a bottle of strong red wine into the earth at the foot of an oak as though enacting a pagan ceremony. Having recently arrived from Australia, he was unaware that the tree was an English oak and that his libation was consistent with traditions predating Christianity. He was simply following diocesan guidance.

This heathenish performance was quite in keeping with this lonely parish on the edge of England. In the 1560s and 70s, Reverend Bernard Gilpin, the 'Apostle of the North', had ventured into the godless borderlands where he found abandoned churches with 'neither bell nor book' or nothing but a mouldering psalter from an earlier age. Half a century later, the Lord's Prayer was still widely unknown in North Cumberland and Northumbria. Burials were haphazard. The only regular sacraments involved magic wells, fairies and ghosts.

Under Elizabeth I, papist 'superstition' was conflated with paganism. The wild people of the Borders were presumed to be unreformed Catholics. The Protestant Reformation had passed through the region like the wind in the high trees, and so, it seemed, had the Christianization of Britain in the sixth century. When Walter Scott first entered the valley of the Liddel in 1792, he realized that the people could barely be called religious in a conventional sense. They only appeared to have remained attached to the Romish religion because of 'total indifference on the subject'.

The previous rector of Nicholforest had come from an inner-city parish. He found the muddle of indigenous traditions unsettling. The annual blessing of the sheep who accompany the hymns with their bleating and the blessing of a new pedestrian suspension bridge to prevent its use by the Devil struck him as theologically suspect. He upbraided his human flock for treating Holy Communion as an intermission allowing a few moments of chitter-chatter. Another important rite is conducted at the other end of the church after the final blessing. This is the sharing out of tea, coffee and home-baked biscuits. To refuse this feeding of the few is a social sin. The crumb-fed church mice at Nicholforest are a contradiction of the saying. Removing their martyrized bodies from the traps is one of the duties of the volunteer church cleaners.

16
Uplonders

Cheviot sheep near the source of the Liddel.

A GENERATION AGO, AT the Oxford college where the anti-Wycliffite Archbishop of Canterbury studied in the 1360s, it was customary to allow guests at High Table to soliloquize on any subject for as long as they wished. 'Talking shop' was frowned upon among the Fellows, and since the plates and the 'guest night' wine would be whisked away by a college servant as soon as the Rector had finished his meal, it was vital not to become trapped in a conversation. Evasive pedantry was the usual ploy. If, for instance, a guest asked a History fellow about the Peasants' Revolt, the response might be either 'Which one?', or 'It depends what you mean by "peasant".'

When Wycliffe was a junior fellow at Merton College in 1355, it was the poor quality of the wine served at a nearby Oxford tavern that caused a major riot between 'townies' (thirty dead) and students (sixty-three dead). Riots – either town v. gown or college v. college – were frequent and nearly annual. One of the last traditional Jesus v. Exeter riots took place in 1978 in what seemed at first a spirit of jovial rivalry. It was Exeter's turn that year to have its fortress stormed. As flour bombs and college crockery rained down on the heads in Turl Street, a heaving mass of Exeter 'gentlemen' tried to prevent the gates from being breached. Compressed against the iron-studded oak, I had the impression of having accidentally joined an interminable game, now in its six-hundredth year, most of whose participants were long dead and buried.

*

THE EXACT CAUSES and motives of medieval riots and rebellions can be hard to determine. Along with the burning, thievery and killing, there was often an air of festivity and the observance of old traditions. Like pilgrimages and fairs, protest marches were one way in which normally sedentary populations discovered the world beyond the sound of the parish bell. From Yorkshire to Somerset, through much of East Anglia and into the south-eastern supply zone of the capital, both before and after the 1381 revolt and even before the Black Death (1348–50), 'peasant' campaigns of resistance displayed a complete rainbow of common men and women – artisans, tradesmen, disaffected minor clergy, soldiers back from France and Flanders or deserters who had taken the King's money but never sailed, as well as 'landmen' or 'uplonders',* both prosperous and poor, free and unfree.

The spirit of post-Black Death rebellions was angry self-confidence rather than chronic despair. They were inspired by specific demands rather than generalized rancour. Some campaigns against local lords were fought in the courts. Petitions were drawn up against taxes, statutory wage control and restrictions on movement. In the summer of 1377, 'rebellious villeins' in forty villages from Sussex to Devon purchased legally certified excerpts from the Domesday Book in order to assert their right to withhold tithes and services.

* A peasant or countryman. 'Uplond' was country as opposed to town ('in London and opelond') or hinterland as opposed to sea, not necessarily high ground.

The ineffective but infuriating Statute of Labourers (1351) had outlawed any non-essential internal migration and imposed a penalty of three days in the stocks or the nearest jail. Simply leaving one's *vill* could be an act of rebellion. Rural labourers, whether freemen or hereditary serfs, were obliged by law – though rarely compelled – to take a twice-yearly oath by which they promised not to go wandering off in search of more lucrative employment. An exception was made for the rough, intractable parts of Lancashire, Yorkshire, Derbyshire, Staffordshire and the Welsh and Scottish Marches, but only in August (for reaping and threshing).

The Peasants' Revolt of 1381 was not unique but it made a lasting impression: it showed on an epic scale that distinctions between lord and commoner, educated and ignorant, rural and urban were increasingly archaic. A new kind of society might soon be established and perhaps already existed. The surest sign of visceral change is the fact that, after 1381, court records and chronicles more frequently mentioned women as instigators of rebellion.

*

THE WORLD IN which the Peasants' Revolt took place seemed to lack the critical mass required to topple a national government. Change would be slow enough for governments to adapt or repress. More than four-fifths of the population still lived on the land. This is now the proportion of people in the United Kingdom who live in urban areas. In the thirteenth century, England's population had probably reached four million, giving an average of thirteen acres per person. Modern Algeria has the same population density.

In 1377, only nine English towns had more than six thousand inhabitants.* London was overwhelmingly the most populous (about seventy thousand after the Black Death). Inner-city anonymity was barely a concept. Seventy-eight thousand people now live in the city of Carlisle and no one who lives there or in its North Cumbrian hinterland can walk about its streets for an hour without seeing a familiar face.

* London, York, Bristol, Coventry, Norwich, Lincoln, Salisbury, King's Lynn and Colchester.

The peasant army which gathered in 1381 on the windy wastes of Blackheath Common four miles east of Tower Hill struck contemporaries as an utterly extraordinary sight: most accounts talk of tens of thousands of people. Figures in the lower thousands are not implausible given the organizational thoroughness of the rebels. Marching through Essex and Kent, they recruited 'men of divers villages and sundry countries', and then, on reaching their goal, their numbers were swollen by 'the perfidious commoners' of London, according to the official record. An eyewitness saw sixty thousand rebels arrive at Southwark to tear down the Marshalsea debtors' prison. After one of the leaders, Wat Tyler, was fatally slashed in self-defence by the Lord Mayor of London at Smithfield, 'about ten thousand, it is believed, suddenly fled and disappeared'.

*

THE 'UPLOND' INTO which the peasant army disappeared began less than thirty minutes on foot from the centre of London. Even the largest towns were a discreet presence in the landscape. A twenty-first-century visitor to a medieval town would probably classify about a third of the urban space as rural with its vegetable plots, orchards and paddocks. Beyond the stinking tanneries and the town ditch or wall, there was nothing but countryside.

'Countryside' was not the vaguely comforting concept which sociological surveys sometimes include under the heading 'leisure activities'. The third of England in which the open-field system prevailed was characterized by untidy expanses of mostly hedgeless fields dotted with diminutive livestock and human beasts of burden. The more familiar patchwork of fields and copses accounted for about another third, and the rest was 'highland'. Each type of landscape had complex local variations.

Medieval writers found that the island of Great Britain could easily be divided into 'highland' (moor and mountain) and 'lowland' (field and farm), but when they tried to describe each county as a coherent whole, they soon became bogged down in exceptions. Many settled for a simple bipartite division of a shire, often into farmable, flat 'champaign' and more intricate areas of woodland, dells, downs and wastes.

Following a visually coherent long-distance route through England is possible only by teetering along a geological corridor like the oolitic Limestone Belt or by taking a northbound train from London. Assuming clean windows, this journey presents a simple transition from arable to pasture with interludes of industrial conurbation. Corn gives way to cows, then the pasture deteriorates and the cows disappear into ever-larger cowsheds to be replaced by sheep, first munching in fields, then hoof-anchored on precipitous slopes.

Beyond Lancashire, as the geologically determined direction of travel changes to east–west – the Pennine passes and Hadrian's Wall – the sequence breaks down and tourists who were looking out for signs of guidebook Scotland are subjected to a series of thrills and disappointments. After the brief but spectacular Lune Gorge, the Carlisle Plain and the mudflats of Gretna Green come the cloud-draped pine forests of the thousand-foot-high Beattock Pass and the descent to Carstairs Junction. Here the train slows to a crawl and sometimes stops altogether for no apparent reason. The tourists can then inspect at their leisure the pigsties, the sewage works and the high-security psychiatric State Hospital on the muddy banks of the Clyde.

For the purposes of tourism, Britain is a poorly organized country. It will be another fifty miles before they reach the Highland Boundary Fault. If they change trains at Edinburgh for Aberdeen and the North, they will eventually find themselves in a low-lying region of prime farmland reminiscent of the Home Counties four hundred miles to the south. Here, the days are sunnier, the rain less frequent and the winds lighter than in most of England. Only the English were surprised when, in 1962, tropical plants flowered 'miraculously' at the spiritual community of Findhorn on the Moray Firth.

*

THE INHABITANTS OF all these muddled micro-habitats were traditionally seen as products of their immediate natural environment like the local livestock and vegetation. Each *pays* had its own 'breed' of human, distinguished by appearance, language and behaviour. If the land was recalcitrant and thorny, then so was its human population. This crude form of social geography now seems to verge on domestic racism, but it reflected the isolation in which most communities existed.

Even places close to large towns in what looked like innocuous terrain could be cut off for long periods in any season. As late as 1794, according to an official report, it was 'extremely dangerous and frequently impracticable [in winter] to ride on horseback along the main roads' in Kent. For motor-free travellers, this is still the case. Barred from major roads, walkers and cyclists are signposted onto the claggy 'Pilgrims' Way' which slithers unpredictably across the North Downs to Rochester and Canterbury. The entire route from Canterbury to Gravesend involves a staggering assortment of surfaces – chalky limestone, flinty clay, grit and gravel, brick and rubble, pebbles, sand, greensward, woodland floor, alluvial flood channel and asphalt.

Local conditions required remedies which struck many city-dwellers as primitive or outlandish. In John Clare's Lincolnshire in the 1820s, the striding shepherd with his long hooked pole 'Progs oft to ford the sloughs that nearly meet / Across the lands.' In *The Pilgrim's Progress* (1678), the Slough of Despond is unusually large but not unrealistic. Labourers employed by the King's surveyors had sunk 'at least twenty thousand cart loads' of stone in its sagging maw:

> Here therefore they wallowed for a time, being grieviously bedaubed with the dirt; and Christian, because of the burden that was on his back, began to sink in the Mire.
>
> Then said Pliable, Ah, Neighbour Christian, where are you now?
>
> Truly, said Christian, I do not know.

People who lived and died in the same parish often had little idea where they were in relation to the shire or the kingdom, let alone the world. Their dialects had remained bafflingly distinct. North of the Trent, travellers from the south would sometimes employ interpreters as well as guides.

Trotting intrepidly through Derbyshire in the late 1600s, Celia Fiennes learned that 'the common people know not above 2 or 3 mile from their home'. She found the same scale of ignorance at Blyford in Suffolk, five miles from Southwold: 'they know scarce 3 mile from their home'. On his agricultural expeditions through England in the 1820s, William Cobbett was sometimes able to enlighten local people as to what lay over the next hill and how they might get there if they ever chose to leave their native plot.

This deep parochialism caused a startling proliferation of 'highest mountains in England'. In the late 1500s, the people of Lancashire and Yorkshire 'knew' from a rhyming couplet that 'Ingeleborrow, Pendle, and Penigent / Are the highest hills between Scotland and Trent'. Next door in Cumberland, it was equally certain that 'Skiddaw, Lauvellin and Casticand, / Are the highest hills in all England'.

When she was invited to admire 'the Reeke' (Wrekin) in Shropshire as 'the highest piece of ground in England' and a 'great mountaine' in Cornwall (probably Rough Tor or Brown Willy on Bodmin Moor) as the 'second highest', Celia Fiennes concluded that they must be considered such only by those who live 'in the heart of the Kingdom and about London': 'I thinke its better said the highest hill in each County.'

These localist myths of pre-eminence conjure up an island continent of tiny principalities, each with its own proud Everest and mighty Amazon. Even when Britons began to see their nation as the navel of an empire, and even in the mole-hill mediocrity of the East Midlands, there were glorious extremes. Hurtling through Leicestershire at over forty miles an hour in a vortex of soot and smoke, with no 'intervening village inns' at which 'honest information' could be obtained, passengers on the 'iron road' were alerted by *Mogg's Handbook for Railway Travellers* (1840) to the interesting fact that the neighbourhood of Packington 'is said to contain the highest ground in England' (Bardon Hill is 912 feet high, 2,231 feet lower than Scafell Pike). The 'fact' had been reported many times in 'official documents'. As speed shrank the landscape, the old local giants lived on.

*

THE BREED OF British human which attracted most anxious attention from Church and State in the fourteenth and fifteenth centuries was endemic in a type of habitat which covered one-third of Great

Britain. 'Waste' was a catch-all term for uncultivated land – moor, heath, wildwood and chase. It was a rare journey of more than a few hours that did not include several miles of 'waste' seemingly undisturbed by human hand. The steeples of a town might appear in the distance while the traveller was still passing through landscapes of an earlier age. In *The Monastery* (1820), Walter Scott accurately described the civilized Central Belt of Scotland as it was in the 1500s on the forty-mile highway from one great city to another:

> At length they arrived upon the side of an eminence, which commanded a distant prospect over a tract of savage and desolate moorland, marshy and waste – an alternate change of shingly hill and level morass, only varied by blue stagnant pools of water. A road scarcely marked winded like a serpent through the wilderness, and the pedlar, pointing to it, said, 'The road from Edinburgh to Glasgow.'

The 'county reports' produced at the end of the eighteenth century by the Board of Agriculture warned of the threats posed by the semi-nomadic denizens of the wastes. In the Lincolnshire Fens, 'so wild a country nurses up a race of people as wild as the fen'. In Brecknock, as in most other parts of mid-Wales, 'those who live in the neighbourhood of great wastes are still an idle and lawless set of people'. Even in Middlesex, no part of which was more than eighteen miles from the centre of London, the wastelanders, presumed to be beggars and thieves, were 'an absolute nuisance to the public'.

In the Middle Ages, people who lived in 'that barbarous state of society' were considered to be dangerously detached from the tethers of manor, parish and *vill.* The more wooded the land, the more likely it was to harbour vagrants and rebels and, later, heretics and witches. In parts of the Weald through which the peasant army passed unchallenged in 1381, in Sherwood and other forests where squires and parsons rarely ventured – Arden, Brewood, Cannock, Charnwood, Dean, Feckenham, New, Savernake and Wychwood – free men and women lived like pioneers colonizing a damp desert.

Some scratched a living from the stingy plots whose expressive names, from Lowland Scotland to the English West Country, are strikingly and inexplicably similar to the names of *lieux-dits* in northern and central France: Awkward Croft, Beggarall or Buggerall, Dangerous Furlong, Famish Croft, Goodfornothing Acres, Isle of Want, Judas Field, the Mistake, Rats Castle, Seldom Seen, etc. Some of these 'microtoponyms' are verbal phrases, which is a characteristic of Brittonic (British Celtic) languages: Hungerhimout, Labour in Vain, Makemrough, Peck and Hope, Scrapehard, etc. Most are attached to a field, a cottage or a croft.

Only two, like the heroes of rags-to-riches tales, have achieved the status of a village: Pityme near Padstow in Cornwall and Pity Me on the northern edge of Durham. We passed through the second Pity Me early one morning in 2023. At a pedestrian crossing, a woman asked where we were headed. 'North to the border.' 'Aah,' she sighed, 'that sounds like an adventure. *I*'m off to work, worse luck.'

*

THE VALUE OF 'waste' as a source of pasture, building material and fuel was often unrecognized by manorial authorities. Few suspected that economic and social change would come from the greenwood where a hardy breed of 'masterless men' specialized in various crafts and industries – coal-mining, charcoal- and lime-burning, carpentry, joinery, iron-working, tool-making and cloth-weaving. It was in villages on the forest edge that many of the new, occupational surnames sprang up: Bowyer, Collier, Cooper, Dyer, Fletcher, Mason, Tanner, Turner, Wainwright, Wheeler.

Every community, the subservient and the self-governing, the enclosed and the unenclosed, owed its security to its traditions and initiative. Across the Channel, villages and woodland settlements were frequently ravaged by rampaging armies. In Britain, the main threat to peace and order came from roving criminal gangs, none of which were of the philanthropic Robin Hood variety. The moated farms and manor houses, especially frequent in Suffolk and Essex, had been built to keep out bandits and, in some cases, the small 'armies' of feuding families and their servants, but increasingly they served an ornamental purpose. The ladies and gentlemen who scanned the countryside from stone battlements did not expect to be pierced by a sudden arrow.

This state of relative stability seems to contradict the later notion that a prosperous country requires a strong and frequently interfering central power. Medieval England was wealthier than almost any other European country, yet the hand of national government was felt in laws and taxes rather than in conscription and forced labour. In this state of affairs, the proposal of one of the leaders of the 1381 Peasants' Revolt that each county should have a king sounds more rational than revolutionary.

Pending his execution, Jack Straw explained his revolutionary idea: all lords and bishops would be culled and new laws would be passed and enforced regardless of birth and social status. In recognition of regional differences, 'we would then have created kings and appointed them – Walter Tyler in Kent and one in each of the other counties'. Faced with the uniquely large and undevolved administrative region called England, modern governments have contemplated similar reforms (without the culling of lords and bishops) but have been unable to bring themselves to institute them except in a piecemeal and lordly fashion.

Those sub-kingdoms already existed, each with its own unwritten constitution and local foreign policy. But their interconnections were feeble or non-existent. In self-regulating towns and villages, in hidden hamlets on the woodland's edge, in heathy dells and moorland denes, the ebb and flow of history was the rumour of a distant ocean. Within a single lifetime, change was almost imperceptible and, when it came, largely incomprehensible. Jack Straw's dream of overturning the old hierarchy would come true only in a partial, nightmarish form, and it would leave the common people more beholden to their superiors than ever before.

*

In bare chronologies, the second half of the fifteenth century is dominated by a conflict between the royal and would-be royal Houses of Lancaster and York. The Wars of the Roses – another name coined by Walter Scott – were spread over thirty-two years (1455–87) and the seven reigns of five kings: Henry VI and Edward IV twice each, then Edward V, Richard III and finally the first of the Tudors, Henry VII.

Actual campaigning took up only sixty-six weeks – an average of two weeks a year. Of the twenty-two significant engagements, thirteen were major battles – including the oddly unfamous Battle of Towton in Yorkshire (1461), which is thought to be the bloodiest battle ever fought on English soil. Most of the others were skirmishes with few or no casualties. They would have been hard to tell apart from the violent squabbles and rebellions of lords and their liveried retainers. As the names of the battlefields suggest, military commanders preferred open country: Blore Heath, Hedgeley Moor, Edgcote Moor or Danes Moor, Bosworth Field, Stoke Field and Losecote Field. The last name is associated with the shedding of tell-tale red insignia by fleeing Lancastrians, but its true origin is 'hlōse-cot' (pigsty cottage).

A few battles were fought in the Welsh and Scottish Marches, and one across the Irish Sea in County Kilkenny, but most took place along the old Roman corridor of the Great North Road. Terror spread over a wider area only when Henry VI's queen, Marguerite d'Anjou, gave the English a taste of war *à la française* by inviting her army to lay waste and plunder as it went.

The shocking novelty of these sporadic conflicts was the unusual arc of the reaping scythe. Never before had such a small proportion of the rank and file died in battle. Edward IV and the 'kingmaker', the Earl of Warwick (first Yorkist, then Lancastrian), ordered that the common soldiers on the losing side should be allowed to run away and that the nobles and gentry should not, as custom demanded, be held for ransom. Instead, the defeated aristocracy would be executed after the battle.

In this way, half the nobility of England, which 'hath long been mad, and scarred herself', perished. These were the words of Shakespeare in his *Tragedy of Richard the Third*, which was performed in the reign of Henry VII's granddaughter, Elizabeth I. Five months after his victory at Bosworth Field (1485), the Welsh and Lancastrian Henry VII '[united] the white rose and the red' by marrying Elizabeth of York.

The culling of nobles proposed by the peasant rebel Jack Straw had been carried out, not by commoners but by their lords and masters. Instead of a king for each county, there would be one king or queen, more powerful than their predecessors, for the whole self-scarred kingdom.

Two years after the Battle of Bosworth Field, on high open ground by the Fosse Way in the southern reaches of Sherwood Forest, Henry VII confirmed his supremacy by defeating the supporters of Lambert Simnel at Stoke Field. Simnel was the ten-year-old son of a carpenter impersonating the Plantagenet heir. He had been talent-spotted by a priest who took him to Oxford, that hive of scholars and pretenders, and taught him to speak and behave like a royal prince.

After the battle, the boy's life was spared. He was given a job more befitting his age and lowly station and became a turnspit in the royal kitchens. The function of turnspit was normally performed by a dog which, caged in a tread-wheel, turned the roasting spit and its dripping carcass and dreamt of what might have been and what might yet be.

17
The Good Fight

Jenny Geddes and the Dean of St Giles' Cathedral.

The lesson of history, in my mother's view, was broadly this: while most people wanted to love and be loved, or to tolerate and be tolerated, others – whom she considered a small minority because it was important to be optimistic when helping the helpless – spent their lives looking for reasons to hate or to be desperately offended. Why things had to be this way, she had no idea, but she found the unfathomability in some way consoling.

My father's view was that we were put on this earth to fight the good fight, not necessarily in the sure and certain knowledge of redemption (*that* lay in other hands), but because it was the right thing to do. If we ploughed a straight furrow with a glad heart we were less likely to make ourselves and other people miserable. Issuing strict instructions that he was not to be contacted, he left on the annual family holiday a few days after his new Assistant Chief Probation Officer had taken up his post. Naturally anxious, the new ACPO asked my father to leave him a list of priorities. On his first day in charge, he arrived at the office to find a single sheet of paper on which my father had written this and only this:

> Where there is no vision, the people perish; but blessed is he that keepeth the law.*

If my parents had been asked to come up with a consensus statement, they might have agreed that much of history – apart from war, oppression and major natural disasters – was 'a great big fuss about next to nothing'.

*

THOUGH HE WAS born in 1921, almost four centuries after Henry VIII appointed himself 'the only supreme head in earth of the Church of England', dissolved the monasteries and expropriated their lands and revenues, my father seemed to have lived through the last days of the British Reformation. He was the son of an Edinburgh policeman whom he remembered as a credulous, newspaper-believing bigot whose agricultural upbringing had made him heir to a lifetime's fund of self-righteousness: 'When I was your age, laddie, I was drivin' a pair o' horse!'

On the Sabbath, the two daughters and four sons were allowed to read only the Bible (the 1611 King James Version, unillustrated) and *Pilgrim's Progress* (1678, also unillustrated), which gave an extra zest to the thrilling flippancies of *The Dandy* and – his first encounter with what their author called 'social work' – the *Just William* stories in which knife-wielding boys turn the temperance Band of Hope meeting into a bloody pandemonium before returning to their separate homes, 'battered and bruised, but blissfully happy'.

The family had once spent their annual holiday in England, just across the border in Northumberland. The town in question lacked any decent place of worship (Presbyterian or Church of Scotland),

* Proverbs 29:18.

and they were forced to attend a Church of England service. Sergeant Robb bristled audibly at all the pagan frippery and furbelows of the nominally Protestant but, to him, flagrantly popish temple with its maniples and chasubles and monkish intonations.

Too young to know the difference, my father was delighted by the Anglican pantomime. After the first hymn, the man in fancy dress invited the congregation to join him in a game. At the words, 'let us pray', they were to kneel on the embroidered cushions at their feet. The obligation to kneel during Communion had been imposed by King James VI in 1618 but angrily rejected in 1638 by the Reformed Church of Scotland, along with the illustrated edition of the King James Bible. Before my father's knees had touched the hassock, he was raised up by a mighty hand and plonked back onto the pew like a juvenile miscreant: 'Bide where y'are, laddie!'

*

MY FATHER TOLD this tale as an example of his father's dogmatic inflexibility, yet he himself evoked with smiling approval the hurling of a 'creepie-stool' (a folding stool) by a market woman at the head of the Dean of St Giles' Cathedral in Edinburgh. This happened on Sunday 23 July 1637, the first day on which the revised Book of Common Prayer, authorized by King James's son, Charles I, was introduced in Scotland.

The new Book was supposed to be acceptable to the Scots: changes had been made to reassure them that they were not being treated as inferiors ('debts' for 'trespasses', 'presbyter' for 'priest', 'Yule' for 'Christmas'). Kneeling was retained – but this was not, the Book hastened to add, a sign of papist idolatry, for 'as concernynge the sacramentall bread and wyne, they remayne styll in theyr verye naturall substaunces'.

The stool-thrower, Jenny Geddes, is the first common woman to be identified as a significant figure in British history. The missile, miscommemorated by a three-legged 'cuttie-stool' on a plinth in St Giles' Cathedral, became a symbol of Scottish resistance to English impositions. It is often used as a historical aide-mémoire. Like the ape-flung leg bone in the opening scene of *2001: A Space Odyssey*, it seems to have triggered a coherent evolutionary sequence. The stool-throwing, which was probably an agreed signal, caused a riot in

Edinburgh and other cities. The riots led to the signing, principally by Lowland Protestants, of a Scottish National Covenant and the expulsion of all bishops from the Church of Scotland, which now became wholly Presbyterian.*

This in turn caused the two botched invasions of Scotland by Charles I, the counter-invasion and occupation of Newcastle and Northumbria by the Scottish 'Covenanters', the Catholic rebellion in Ireland, the English Civil Wars and thus the beheading of Charles I, the Puritan republic, the restoration of the monarchy and the notoriety of the second female commoner to play a major role in British history – Nell Gwyn, the comic actress and self-titled 'Protestant whore' of Charles II.

This retrocausal view of history leaves almost everything unexplained. The distant events which cast a pall over our Sunday mornings remained obdurately confusing. Why did we have to attend the depressingly modern Presbyterian church in Worcester and then, when the minister's mawkish sermons had my father reaching for a stool, the Methodist church, when there was a half-empty medieval cathedral a few yards up the road with royal tombs and mesmerizing stained-glass windows?

I understood impatience with pompous ritual, but Presbyterians and Methodists had rituals too. How much ritual was the right amount? Why did *we* get just a few cursory window units in primary colours? Why did I have to go to church anyway? My best friend and my best girlfriend were both Catholic, but *they* didn't have to attend a service every Sunday.

The differences between the protesting and the devout seemed to centre on confession, incense, graven images, length of sermon and rules of conduct – for example (I had this on good authority) not crossing your legs in front of a priest if you were wearing a skirt. Only to the elect, apparently, was it given to know the mysteries of the kingdom of heaven.

*

* Governed by elected elders or 'presbyters' instead of by bishops appointed by the monarch.

School history lessons offered a detailed but fundamentally simple explanation. All the big developments in the English Reformation had been driven by politics, economics and royal whim. In 1521, the thirty-year-old Henry VIII published a snarling attack on that 'infernal wolf', Martin Luther. He dedicated his book to the 'chief bishop', Pope Leo X, who awarded him the title 'Defender of the Faith'. Even after breaking with Rome in 1534 in order to divorce his sonless first wife, Henry retained this papal seal of approval. Like a war medal purchased second-hand, it has been sported by British monarchs ever since.

Henry had told the Pope, indiscreetly, that, since reaching the age of discretion, he had 'found that Religion bears the greatest sway in administration of publick affairs, and is likewise of no small importance in the Commonwealth'. This was the most significant article of faith in the next century and a half of theologically coloured policy-making. The Church was a tool to persuade the populace that obedience to the King and his government was a Christian duty and the path to salvation.

Henry died a Catholic, but his politicization of religion fostered a revival of iconoclasm compared to which the drinking songs of Goliard minstrels were schoolboy jokes. Tearing down priestly props and trappings became a popular sport. Icons were repurposed as dolls, altar stones as doorsteps and Communion bread as dog food. Recipe books found a common-sense use for holy water,

> which is also a very good medicine for an horse with a gall'd back: yea, if there be put an onyon thereunto, it is a good sauce for a gibbet of mutton.

The openly Protestant regency council of Henry's only surviving son, Edward VI (r. 1547–53), seemed to authorize this riotous behaviour. Thomas Cranmer, the first Protestant Archbishop of Canterbury, replaced the Latin service with an English liturgy. The blood and body of Christ were no longer considered to be literally present. The number of saints was reduced, altars and vestments were simplified, priests were allowed to marry.

The Catholic Restoration of Henry's elder daughter, Mary Tudor

(r. 1553–8), who was also Queen of Spain, served the long-term interests of militant Protestantism. Nearly three hundred Protestants were burned at the stake as heretics. They included Bishops Cranmer, Latimer and Ridley. The site of their incineration is marked by a cobbled cross set into the tarmac of Broad Street in Oxford, which makes an appropriately uncomfortable memorial for the thousands of cyclists who judder over it every day.

In this way, the new Protestant religion acquired its own catalogue of home-grown martyrs. At least fifty-five of the 'Marian martyrs' were women; twenty-four were clergymen. Most of the remaining three-quarters were skilled or semi-skilled tradesmen and artisans, urban rather than rural, representing forty-six different occupations – from barbers, brewers and bricklayers to upholsterers, weavers and wheelwrights.

The killing spree of 'Bloody Mary' sealed all Catholics in lasting infamy, at least until the Catholic emancipation laws of the nineteenth century. Any sign of Catholic counter-insurgency was amplified and commemorated – the plot to assassinate Mary's sister Elizabeth and to replace her with her cousin Mary Queen of Scots (1586), the scattering of the Spanish Armada (1588) by a patently Protestant Jehovah and, later, the cack-handed plot to blow up the Houses of Parliament (1605).

'Catholic' became a synonym of 'conspirator'. The 1593 act against 'popish recusants' (1593) asserted that those 'wicked and seditious persons . . . terming themselves Catholics' are in fact 'spies and intelligencers': they 'do secretly wander and shift from place to place within this realm, to corrupt and seduce her majesty's subjects'. Under the Act, all Catholics were to return to their homes and report themselves to the local minister and constable. If they strayed more than five miles from their registered place of abode, they would forfeit everything they owned. In 1605, after the discovery of the Gunpowder Plot, James VI and I added some extra 'disabilities': Catholics were obliged to take an oath of allegiance to the King and to renounce the Pope and were forbidden to practise law or medicine and to educate their children.

*

Seen in the costumes of their propaganda, the Protestant regimes of Edward VI, Elizabeth I and her cousin James VI and I were revolutionary governments in full sail with a strengthening tail-wind of patriotic indignation. Like all revolutionaries, to quote Balzac, 'they carried with them at all times an absolution for any crime they might happen to commit'.

British monarchs both Protestant and Catholic are conventionally described as 'devout'. The nature and quality of a person's faith is elusive and of little use in explaining political conduct. Prime Minister Theresa May made public professions of her Anglican faith and upbringing while pursuing, as Home Secretary, cruel, unchristian policies designed to make life unbearable for suspected undocumented migrants.

In Tudor times, the personal faith of monarchs was indistinguishable from political subterfuge. When Tudor governments equated Catholicism with conspiracy, they did so as conspiracies ratified by law. Their propaganda provided a simple rationale for their actions which, centuries later, retains its simplifying power – more to the benefit of politicians than historians. When Prime Minister Rishi Sunak rejected the 'unpatriotic' findings of British slavery scholarship in April 2023, he made an unusually forthright defence of this politically convenient view of history: 'Trying to unpick our history is not the right way forward.'

The segment of the national tapestry which depicts Elizabeth I as a true servant of the Protestant God has remained almost entirely unpicked. The glorious defeat of the storm-wrecked Spanish Armada is taught in schools and celebrated in general histories and television documentaries. The Elizabeth of the national syllabus addressed her troops at Tilbury, convinced that God was on England's side, as the commemorative medal affirmed: '*Flavit et Dissipati Sunt*' ('[God] blew and they were scattered').

The missing sequel is one of the obscurest disasters in British history. The following spring, a much larger 'Counter-Armada' of over twenty-seven thousand Englishmen sailed from Plymouth to finish off the battered Spanish fleet. The naval commander was Sir Francis Drake. Ignoring the Queen's orders and sensing mutinous intent in his crew of jailbirds and layabouts, Drake turned the expedition into another piratical treasure hunt. After stumbling on the wine cellars of Corunna, the soldiers drank themselves stupid and thirteen hundred English lives were lost besieging a town of four thousand people.

For every seven who sailed, one returned. The survivors spread disease through Plymouth, killing four hundred English subjects. A mendacious account of the disaster was widely disseminated at home and abroad to counteract the true reports. The monarchy was more impoverished than ever and nothing official was ever said on the subject, except in Spain, where one of the women who inspired the defence of Corunna by stabbing an English soldier with his own spear is a Galician national heroine.

As one of the few who knew the truth, Elizabeth may have concluded that God had changed his mind in 1589. In her speech at Tilbury, she had twice spoken of 'my God, my kingdom and my people'. 'My God' was not an acknowledgement of the personal nature of faith: it meant the omnipotent King of kings 'who has constituted me ruler of Your people'. 'God', 'people' and 'kingdom' – which included the Church of England – were inseparable. There was also a Spanish God and, as Elizabeth was nervously aware, countless other Christian gods were coming to life in the equally devout minds of her subjects.

18

'Perillous Dayes'

'The Pourtraicture of His Sacred Majestie in His Solitudes and Sufferings' (1649).

At the dawn of the seventeenth century, over a thousand Protestant works totalling more than four million copies were in circulation. The tracts, sermons, prophecies, visions and politico-religious manifestos printed by Baptists, Quakers, Puritans, Grindletonians, Muggletonians, Ranters, Seekers, Diggers, Levellers and lone visionaries make it impossible to conceive of Protestantism as a coherent system of belief. To the newly literate, the revelation that anyone could have their own thoughts about God was exciting or disturbing and sometimes infuriating. Yet a reigning spirit seemed to be at work. For the first time, the now-familiar irony of social media appeared in British history – the profusion of individual voices creating pervasive uniformities.

Despite the ritual condemnation of Catholic 'superstition', the Protestantism of the early printed tracts was not primarily rationalist: at times it was barely religious. Just as Jenny Geddes' stool had more to do with national, regional and class identities than with the nature of God, souls and salvation were often moral codes or simple allegories of social change. As a religion, it would be better named Anticatholicism. Its creeds consisted almost entirely of negative statements. The Scottish National Covenant of 1638, which many Scots were forced to sign, was written in a characteristically pugnacious, hate-filled idiom: 'detest and abhor', 'abhor and detest', 'detest and refuse', 'condemn', 'punish', 'search, apprehend and punish all contraveners'.

Enforcement of the stridently worded laws of Elizabeth, James and his son Charles I was inconsistent and often fell far short of the standards of cruelty implied by the legislation. Meanwhile, in the teeming world of print, hatred and malice were the marks of the devout Anticatholic, even in the cherished books which took pride of place on many a cottage shelf.

The tone had been set by John Foxe, an Oxford historian who diligently researched and recounted the persecution of Protestants and dissenters from the time of Christ (when Rome ruled the world) to the present (1563, when a Romish despot sat on Caesar's throne). Foxe's *Actes and Monuments of these Latter and Perillous Dayes* (1563) – commonly known as *Foxe's Book of Martyrs* – is still in print. Laudably, he wanted to 'cleanse' the historical record of 'monkish miracles', but he swallowed all the fictitious tales of early British martyrs, and as successive writers updated his compendium with the latest religious propaganda, the book became increasingly unhinged.

The original woodcut illustrations played a large part in its success. They showed martyrs in the process of being starved, stripped, plucked, racked, smashed, grilled, flayed and rubbed with salt or lime, hung upside-down or buried upright, pasted with pitch, tweaked and torn with pincers, detoothed, debrained, castrated and beheaded.

For the next three hundred years, in the eyes of Jerome K. Jerome, countless children were exposed to this sado-pietistic horror show while parents imperilled their immortal souls by masturbating to the illustrations. As a child in the 1860s, Jerome remembered spending Sundays poring over an illustrated Bible and Foxe's *Book of Martyrs*:

> Children were encouraged to wallow in its pictures of hideous tortures. Old Foxe may have meant well, but his book makes for cruelty and lasciviousness. Also, I worried myself a good deal about Hell.

Protestant polemicists found their natural audience in children. One of the most successful, in Britain and America, was Benjamin Harris's *The Protestant Tutor, instructing children to spel and read English* (1679; eighth edition, 1720). An easy-to-read summary of the New Testament was followed by verbal vignettes of 'popish tortures practised by those bloody idolaters upon poor Protestants': children had been forced to hang their own parents; martyrs had had their hands lopped off and their eyes put out and were left 'to pine away in misery'. Babes were torn from the womb and thrown in a ditch or reinserted into their eviscerated mothers 'and there strangled'.

While learning to read and spell, children could acquire the rudiments of modern history in the form of fake news: some ships of the Spanish Armada were found to have been carrying chains, whips and knives with which to 'enslave, torment and murther the poor English Protestants'; the Papist Church in Ireland had changed the names of all the English places into Irish Gaelic. The Great Fire of London had been started by a Catholic equipped with 'three fire-balls'.

The hectoring voice of this cheerless pedantry can be heard in almost every *bien-pensant* Protestant text – in Bunyan and in Milton and even in the words of gentle visionaries such as George Fox, one of the founders of the Religious Society of Friends (Quakers).

In the winter of 1651–2, George was walking south from Derby where he had been jailed under the Blasphemy Act of 1650 for claiming that God 'dwells not in temples' and that priests have no power to sanctify. One day, he saw on the horizon the three spires of Lichfield Cathedral and was assailed by a vague memory of the thousand early-Christian martyrs of Lichfield (all fictitious). Making a bee-line for the cathedral ('I went by my eye over hedge and ditch'), he left his shoes, as instructed by God, with some astonished shepherds and entered the city, where it was market day, crying as he went through the streets, 'Woe unto the bloody city of Lichfield!'

This prophetic text gives a rare glimpse of the unradicalized, well-intentioned majority who, after remaining invisible to history for centuries, would come to the fore in the English Civil Wars:

> And so at last some friends and friendly people came to me and said, 'Alack, George, where are thy shoes?'

*

THE SURGE OF Protestant vituperation was a symptom of intellectual panic. Some of the better-organized sects – Quakers in northern England, Baptists in Wales – established or reinforced networks of mutual assistance which had been weakened by social mobility, economic hardship and the decay of feudalism. Other groups, unnerved by the boundless sea of speculation, clung to the jagged rocks of sectarian dogma.

Anticatholicism morphed during the Civil Wars into a more intimately intrusive set of teachings promoted by an evangelical Parliament. The seasonal 'idleness' of peasants would be condemned. Many people would live under the unblinking eye of moral judgement as though trapped in a confession box with a religious or civil authority. The Puritan parody of Christianity would strike foreign visitors as a form of social tyranny. The word 'cant' was imported into French in the early eighteenth century to describe this English disease. When Anticatholicism became less virulent in the home nation, the disease would spread to the colonies.

Protestant pedagogy favoured the pre-Christian Old Testament. Reading the Bible to ward off the boredom of a church service, I found it a source of hilariously extremist statements. I sometimes tried them out on my father. 'It says here, "For he that curseth his father or his mother shall be surely put to death." Does that still apply?' My father, who appeared to have memorized the entire Bible, would produce some equally psychopathic pearl of wisdom: 'Aye, it does, and "his lamp shall be put out in obscure darkness", as it ought to be at your bedtime.'

*

THE MAN WHO inadvertently did more than anyone else to bring about a Puritan dictatorship was Charles I. The Book of Common

Prayer had been intended as a compromise. Even now, it seems to work quite well as a 'middle way'. Two of the three Anglican churches in Nicholforest parish still use the 'BCP' (1662 revision). The feathery pages refer to 'the late unhappy confusions', as though the English Civil Wars had ended only recently. On separate occasions in the last six years, two Catholic women – one English, one American – attended services in the parish and were amazed to find virtually no difference between the Protestant and Catholic liturgies.

The imposition of the revised Book of Common Prayer in Scotland by the Archbishop of Canterbury under Charles I ran counter to the Anglican spirit of diplomatic mediocrity. The King's belligerent response to the Jenny Geddes incident reignited anti-popery and militant Puritanism. In 1641, false rumours spread that the killing of three thousand Ulster Protestants in the Irish Catholic Rebellion had been authorized by Charles. The massacre would be brutally avenged by Oliver Cromwell in 1649–51.

When Charles tried to purge Parliament of its Puritan zealots Parliament asserted its 'privilege' or legal immunity and Charles fled west to Hampton Court, Windsor and then Oxford. The first Civil War (1642–6) began as a struggle between supporters of the King and radical Parliamentarians, most of whom wanted political concessions, not an end to the monarchy. The Royalists fought for control of London and the trade arteries of the Thames and the Severn – hence the strategic prominence of Oxford and Worcester and the main watershed lines of central and southern England.

*

IT WAS THEN, in the spring of 1642, when both sides were mustering men and seizing local arsenals, that a third force raised its fretful head and showed that war itself had found an enemy. Compared to the religious wars on the Continent, it seems a distinctly English variety of revolution, yet even historically minded politicians never mention this powerful third force.

In about thirty of England's thirty-nine shires, through much of Wales and the Welsh borders, and in boroughs from Newcastle upon Tyne to Sandwich in Kent, peasants first, then county justices and gentry forged pacts of neutrality or non-aggression. That 'oddly stable substratum' of Anglo-Saxon England came back into play: the ancient shire boundaries became the frontiers of demilitarized zones enforced by common agreement.

In some counties, particularly Lancashire, there was a clear divide between Papist and Puritan; almost everywhere else, neutralism was the norm. Towards the end of the first Civil War when the Royalists were decisively defeated at Naseby, civil defence associations of vigilante 'Clubmen' counted tens of thousands of peace-seeking irregulars. Some Clubmen acted as negotiators, others as a shire police force with authority to punish plundering soldiers of either side. Some were more pacifist than others. The 'Peaceable Army' of Glamorgan twice came close to taking Cardiff Castle, where it intended to declare the independence of South Wales.

The battles of Naseby (1645) and Stow on the Wold (1646) – both fought on the watershed line which divides East from West – ended the first English Civil War. The second, not-so-English Civil War (Royalist uprisings in England and Wales and a Scottish invasion of northern England) ended with the execution of Charles I (30 January 1649). Only a tiny minority of Parliamentarians voted for the King's death. Practically no one found it a cause for celebration. It made a martyr of the bungling monarch. As a victim, Charles Stuart acted impeccably. His co-written or ghosted *Pourtraicture of His Sacred Majestie in His Solitudes and Sufferings* was a posthumous bestseller.

After six years of skirmishing, disrupted trade and fear of foreign invasion, the tax-funded New Model Army commanded by Oliver Cromwell conducted a military coup. England and Wales became a republic or a 'Commonwealth and Free State' on 6 January 1649. The war-wracked land would be governed by an evangelical Puritan oligarchy. Charmed by the mirage of virtuous wealth evoked by Pilgrims returning from the Promised Land of Massachusetts, the home nation had effectively colonized itself.

Charles's son had taken refuge in the Dutch Republic. He was proclaimed King Charles II by the Scottish Parliament six days after his father's death, sixteen weeks before his nineteenth birthday. He was crowned at Scone Abbey near Perth on 1 January 1651, having agreed to accept the Covenant and to make the whole country Presbyterian once the Covenanters had defeated Cromwell. Much later, in another ironic reversal, he would promise to make England a Catholic monarchy (pp. 165–6).

*

THE SCOTTISH COVENANTER army under Charles II, having suffered several defeats on home soil, headed south – secretly, they thought – in a race to reach London before Cromwell. They entered Worcester on 22 August 1651. Soldiers were sent out to fortify and partially destroy the bridges over the Teme at Bransford and Powick. Then they rested for five days – long enough for the New Model Army to cross the Severn at Upton and advance on Worcester from the south.

Twice a year, at Christmas and at the end of the school year, we trooped up to the church of St Peter which stands outside Powick village on a knoll. The main object of childish interest was the vandalized tower: it had been pockmarked from top to bottom by the muskets of English 'Roundheads' who had been trying to prevent the 'Cavaliers' from enjoying the view of the Malvern Hills and Worcester Cathedral. The other vantage point, on the opposite side of the village, was Ham Hill, accessible by a lane called King's End Road.

The first skirmishes took place in and around Powick. If I had taken a keener interest in local history, I might have been able to present my father with the breaking news that my hedge-headquarters on Ham Hill was quite possibly the closest point that a Presbyterian Scottish army ever came to London.

19

'The Field Has Eyes, the Wood Has Ears'

Wyre Forest.

FROM TIME TO time, all children must wonder about the possibility and means of passing undetected from one place to another. For some children, the thought is ever-present. The hedge-den above Powick village, one mile from home, could, in theory, be reached without being seen. Much later, as a thought experiment, I wondered if it might ever have been possible to pass invisibly from one end of Great Britain to the other. (Map 1.)

The den was the headquarters of a group of boys and one girl which, as a result of our move from Stafford to Worcester, holidays in Scotland and a French pen-friend, had grown into an international organization with a command structure, rules, passwords, insignia and no clear purpose other than self-concealment. Its original name was RAPS (Rescue and Police Service), but because there was already a police force and no one needed rescuing unless we created the necessity, the letters DWAS had been added (Detective Work and Spying), which fitted what most of us did anyway.

A boy of Viking name and descent who begged to be sent on dangerous climbing missions and insisted on signing the gang register in his own blood had supplied us with an ingenious armoury of defensive weapons. It included the safety-pinned half table-tennis ball disguised as a RAPS badge which contained a quantity of pepper to be thrown, after yanking the badge off the pullover or jacket, in the face of an attacker.

Though a person who lies hidden is likely to have a restricted view, the half-moons and slivers of visibility acquire a periscopic intensity. The Nazi invasion planners noted in 1940 that the stone walls and hedgerows which straggle over much of lowland England 'provide good sources of cover, but not, however, against attack from the air'. In an age of non-reflective juvenile clothing, the hedge on Ham Hill made an exceptionally good observation post. Yet we never once noticed the inexplicably truncated line of telegraph poles which ended a few yards into the field on the other side of the lane.

It is probably a good thing that we didn't, because, in accordance with official RAPS procedure, we would certainly have investigated and tried to lever up the metal plate that was set into the ground. Thus we would have stumbled on a top-secret underground network. Established in 1962, it was still operational throughout the United Kingdom. While we sat in our den passing the time of day, three men, each known only by a number, were on duty at the bottom of a ventilation shaft in two concrete rooms equipped with shelves, chairs, metal bunk beds, monitoring equipment and a chemical toilet. One of those nameless monitors was responsible for the GZI (Ground Zero Indicator), a four-directional pinhole camera designed to capture the first blinding flash of a nuclear explosion.

*

AT POWICK BRIDGE and in the suburbs of Worcester, on the afternoon and night of 3 September 1651, an army was annihilated. In a matter of hours, Cromwell had neutralized the Royalist threat.

Doomed by the war-weariness of his supporters in Wales and the West Country, the King may have felt unlucky to be so completely overwhelmed. According to a historian of seventeenth-century espionage, 'Civil War battles were more often the result of armies meeting accidentally rather than [of] any intelligence coup.' On the other hand, the campaign in Scotland had proved the worth of 'scoutmasters' and 'intelligencers', and Parliament's improvements to postal services had made it easier to intercept secret messages. These were usually enciphered in a childishly simple system of numbers and letters compared to which the RAPS codebook was a masterpiece of obfuscation.

The fumbling but ruthless parliamentary intelligence network was about to be tested by a twenty-one-year-old rustic in tattered clothes, an assortment of ordinary British citizens and the resources of a half-wild, half-civilized English countryside with so many varied guises that even an unusually tall man with an unforgettable face could camouflage himself successfully in almost any setting.

Some time after midnight, the capture of the 'King of Scottes' was announced just as a group of riders was leaving Worcester by the town ditch. Cromwell's soldiers were ransacking the cathedral, the churches and the homes of wealthy citizens. Desperate Scots were being rounded up and civilians presumed to be Royalist executed. Near St Martin's Gate, a humungous hay wagon loaded with ammunition lay on its side, preventing immediate pursuit of the riders as they trotted north along Foregate Street past the grammar school and over the Barbourne bridge.

That morning from the tower of Worcester Cathedral, Charles Stuart had seen the gun smoke rising from outposts beyond the river Teme. He had marched out to Powick, then returned to Worcester to lead a cavalry charge at Red Hill in the east of the city during which several of his commanders were killed. Parliamentary soldiers had spotted him in the vanguard of his troops and so the reports that Charles had been wounded and taken prisoner were quite credible.

The plan was either to reach Scotland – which Charles himself thought suicidal – or, his strong preference (as he told Samuel Pepys in 1680), to cut his hair very short, dress himself 'in a country-fellow's habit' – grey breeches, leather doublet, green jerkin – and, after heading north, to turn again and walk all the way to London. By the warehouses of the Vintry in Thames Street, where Bordeaux wine merchants unloaded their crates, a passport would be waiting at the tavern of the Three Cranes for 'Will Jackson' . . . His ultimate goal was France, where his widowed mother, the aunt of Louis XIV, was living wretchedly in the palace of Saint-Germain-en-Laye.

Hundreds of fleeing Royalists were galloping north on the post road. It was conceivable that a small band which kept to tracks and open country would elude the search parties. Among the King's companions was a scoutmaster who knew something of the country beyond Worcester. After twenty miles they reached the limits of his geographical knowledge. Passing to the east of Kidderminster, they stopped at dawn on the heathlands beyond Kinver near the edge of the Wyre Forest. All around were the unsignposted byways of a country magnified by ignorance but mistakenly shrunk to a third of its true size by the only guidebook which purported to show accurate distances – Matthew Simons' *A Direction for the English Traviller by which he shall be inabled to coast about all England and Wales* (1643).

It would be another forty-seven years before Parliament ordered guide-posts to be placed at crossroads and more than a century before the order was enforced. Fortunately, the Earl of Derby, who had ridden down from Preston a few days before, knew of a hunting lodge north of Wolverhampton where a recusant family with experience of hiding Catholic priests would be willing to harbour the King. Six weeks later, the Earl and his servant were both caught and executed.

*

Approaching from the Black Country on canals and back streets through the subterraneous suburbs and centres of Birmingham and Wolverhampton and the long, unlit Coseley Tunnel which echoes with dripping stalactites, we reached the watershed of the rising land after Codsall on 13 September 2022. To the west, we saw the first wide-open view in two days of cycling. On a vast plain overlooked by the distant pyramid of the Wrekin, the surgically-supported trunk of the Royal Oak is the most noticeable and also the weirdest feature in the landscape for miles around. For that reason, it made an excellent hiding place.

For three days, Charles hid at Boscobel House and neighbouring properties near the Staffordshire–Shropshire border. One day was spent ensconced on the natural platform of the giant pollard oak with a picnic of bread, cheese and beer. From his leafy cage, he saw the soldiers 'going up and down' and 'peeping out of the wood' a few yards to the west. At one point, the search party came so close that he 'heard all the discourse how they would use the King himself if they would take him'.

On the night of Friday 5 September, he set off on foot with his host along sunken paths to reach the Severn at Madeley. The new plan was to vanish into the Welsh mountains, like Caratacus fleeing from the Romans, and 'get either to Swansey, or some other of the sea-towns that I knew had commerce with France'. But the crossing of the Severn at the future site of Ironbridge was guarded and the ferry boats had been impounded. The countryside was infested with soldiery: at one moment, he was forced to lie low in a wet hedge. Footsore and despairing, he returned to Boscobel. The only possible direction now was south, towards London and the coast.

Meanwhile, sixteen miles away at Bentley near Walsall, the twenty-five-year-old sister of a colonel in the Royalist army was preparing to visit her pregnant cousin at Bristol. When Jane Lane left Bentley on 9 September, she was accompanied by a tall servant with a West Midlands accent. He wore a sweat-stained steeple hat and mismatched stockings darned at the knees. The man was quite clearly an English patriot. At Bromsgrove, where his mare had to be reshod, he asked the smith for news of Charles Stuart. The traitor, he was told, was still at large, probably 'in some lurking-hole in England'. The smith would be 'not a little glad to catch him', 'because then the Parliament would pay me down a thousand pounds for my labour'.

> I told [the smith] that if that rogue were taken he deserved to be hanged, more than all the rest, for bringing in the Scots. Upon which he said that I spoke like an honest man.

So began a month-long, five-hundred-mile apprenticeship in the art of moving invisibly through enemy territory.

*

The lessons of Boscobel were these: first find a hiding place which looks too obvious to be worth searching, then, if possible, remain motionless. The micro-habitats of rural Britain can still provide effective cover. In January 2023, in a village to the north of Preston, a woman left a dog and a phone on the banks of the river Wyre. Drones, helicopters, high-powered sonar, forty police detectives and countless glassy-eyed social-media 'detectives' searched in vain. Nearly a month had passed when two dog-walkers found her body in riverbank reeds less than a mile from her last known location.

If the fugitive is unable to stay put, detailed knowledge of the country is essential. In 1464, after the Battle of Hexham during the Wars of the Roses, Henry VI managed to elude his pursuers for two months and two hundred miles by tracing an almost uninterruptedly lonely route through the Pennines, the Lake District and the Forest of Bowland. Charles was fleeing through busier, less rugged country, yet he managed to string together a sequence of at least forty-nine heaths – some, in the Birmingham and Bristol conurbations, now almost impossible to picture, others, in the Cotswolds and the West Country, practically unchanged.

Since heath-dwellers (literal 'heathens') were considered suspect, heathland was an ideal setting for a suspicious-looking man. However, if only one viable road or track exists, even a wide moor can be reduced to a thin corridor. Fleeing the pandemic and a political crisis in 2020, Prime Minister Johnson hurried off to the sparsely populated hundred-square-mile Applecross Peninsula in northern Scotland. He rented a shiny white cottage visible from a distance, failed to observe that the entire peninsula is served by only two narrow roads, and trespassed on neighbouring farmland. All this made accidental encounters practically inevitable. Even in Chaucer's day, it had been known for 'many yeres' that 'feeld hath eyen and the wode hath eres'. Photographs of an incredulous and disgruntled Prime Minister soon appeared in the national press.

Without preparation and cunning, the fugitive is helpless. Charles talked to common people and, as he put it, 'tuned' his voice accordingly. He rubbed his face with walnut leaves to smudge and tan his aristocratic pallor. He studied the 'lobbing' gait of peasants and servants and reduced his apparent height (6 ft 1 in.) by several inches. In a house near Bristol after the second day's ride with Jane Lane, 'a certain bragging fellow' boasted that he had fought at Worcester and seen the King twenty times:

> His Majesty asketh what manner of man the King was? Then looking earnestly upon the King, [the man] saith, 'He is taller than thou by four fingers.'

Sometimes, the ruse consisted simply of behaving as though everything was normal. Outside Stratford-upon-Avon, on the first day's ride, some Parliamentarian soldiers were grazing their horses by the roadside. 'I begged Mrs [*sic*] Lane softly in her ear that we might not turn back, but go on, if they should see us turn.' Later that day, they passed the same men in town, greeted them openly and were saluted in return.

*

The Roman Fosse Way, which sidles like a thief along the margins of the very few villages it passes, provided eighteen quiet miles between Stow and Cirencester. Once over the Cotswolds and the Mendips, Charles and Jane followed the equally peaceful trails of unenclosed country and the ancient tracks by which drovers bound for Salisbury or London avoided toll bridges.

At Bristol, England's second largest port, he learned that no ship would be ready to take him to France for another month. London was now out of the question. The homes of Royalists were being searched and the whole country seemed to know of the thousand-pound bounty on his head – a sum equivalent to the daily wage of thirty thousand soldiers in the New Model Army. Instead, he turned south, hoping to sail from an unwatched stretch of the Dorset coast. On the far side of the Avon Gorge he said farewell to Jane and presented her with his handsome silver and crystal pocket watch.

Leaving behind the dangerously overcrowded seventeenth century, he rode through landscapes of the Iron Age – Blackmore Vale, the Dorset Downs and Cranborne Chase – on the warpaths of long-forgotten kings, under the chalk ramparts and grassy folds of a dozen ancient hill-towns, from Cadbury Castle to Old Winchester Hill where, according to local people, he played a game of bowls. On 6 October he would ride to the edge of Salisbury Plain to see the 'great wonder' of Wiltshire, 'and there we staid looking upon the stones for some time'. He counted the monoliths and triliths of Stonehenge twice, happy to disprove the superstition that no one can count them more than once and arrive at the same total.

The threadbare servant had disappeared some time before. The tall travelling man in a travelling cloak was now the daring lover of the adventurous Miss Juliana Coningsby, a young relative of a Royalist officer he had met near Sherborne. There was nothing suspicious about an eloping couple behaving secretively . . . For the next five days, Juliana rode behind him on his horse. On 22 September, a mile and a half east of Lyme Regis, they reached the sea at Charmouth. The village was known to Jane Austen in 1803–4 as a genteel watering hole: 'its sweet, retired bay, backed by dark cliffs'. 'The fragments of low rock among the sands make it the happiest spot for watching the flow of the tide.'

That night, Charles stood on the edge of England with the wind of freedom on his face. The boat which had been hired at Lyme by Juliana's cousin failed to materialize. Proclamations had just been posted up in ports along the south coast requiring vessel-owners to obtain a special licence before taking passengers. The boat's captain was blameless: his wife had guessed the identity of the passenger and locked her husband in his bedchamber.

Next morning, Juliana and Charles rode on to Bridport. The town was swarming with soldiers about to embark for Jersey, where Royalists were holding out against Cromwell. The ostler at the George Inn thought he recognized the bridegroom's face but could not quite place it. Meanwhile, back at Charmouth, the blacksmith had been discoursing on the interesting subject of horseshoes. In his expert opinion, the couple's horse had last been shod somewhere to the north, perhaps in Worcestershire . . .

The authorities were alerted; homes of the local gentry were searched and a beautiful young lady was arrested because someone thought she might be a man in disguise. Troops were despatched to Bridport.

Later that day, Charles and Juliana trotted out of Bridport and turned up a lane on the outskirts of town just before cavalry from Charmouth went galloping past on the road to Dorchester and London. The site is marked by a stone bearing a quotation from *A Panegyrick to His Majesty on His Happy Return* (1660):

When midst your fiercest foes on every side
For your escape God did a lane provide.

*

THERE WERE SO many false sightings of Charles Stuart in those six weeks that Cromwell's officers were drowning in intelligence. Newsbooks reported him in Wales, in the North of England, in a castle four miles from Kendal, boarding a boat at Pevensey with the aid of a famous highwayman, crossing to Wandsworth on a Thames barge and in the capital itself, walking over London Bridge with a male companion.

No one seemed particularly surprised to see a man they believed to be the King. Coincidences – that bane of detective inspectors and delight of amateur sleuths – were even more common than they are today. While researching the King's journey, I found that I had personal knowledge of almost the entire escape route from Powick to the Boscobel oak. After Boscobel, Charles had passed within three streets of the house at Codsall where I lived as an infant. The oak was just up the road. My sister tells me (I was too young to remember) that we visited Boscobel House and tried to climb the oak tree.

As a teenager, I had walked with a friend at dead of night through the concrete heart of Birmingham from Spaghetti Junction to Bromsgrove, through this 'Heath' and that, expecting to be mugged. Amorously oblivious to the fourteen miles there and back, I had often walked to another 'Heath' on the north side of Worcester to hide in an attic room in my girlfriend's house before returning to Powick in the small hours – more conspicuously than in the daytime. On the way home, where Charles had crossed the Severn to inspect the outposts at Powick, I was regularly stopped by two bored policemen who ordered me to empty the contents of my pockets onto the bonnet of their patrol car.

As many hill-walkers know, in reputedly remote regions of Britain, a familiar face can pop out of the mist at any moment. A friend of my parents was walking alone through woods on the lower slopes of Lochnagar in the Grampians. (He told this tale as though recounting the sighting of a rare animal.) A tall figure emerged from the trees. There was a cheery hello and then a pleasant exchange with the man who was recently crowned King Charles III.

The prevalence of coincidence is not a trivial phenomenon. Unlike France, Britain is small enough to foster a comforting, even disappointing sense of uniformity and stability. In the seventeenth century and probably long before, nearly everyone knew at least one person from another part of the country and could quickly understand their patois. Familiarity breeds contentment. Even in a Puritan republic, stirring up factional hatred was hard work.

At Charmouth, according to one of the King's helpers, the man who called out the troops was the rigidly Puritan parson Bartholomew Westley (*sic*), great-grandfather of the Methodist leader John Wesley. He went to the inn and accused the landlady of shaming herself by cosying up to the traitor: 'Charles Stuart lay last night at your house, and kissed you at his departure.' She, however – quoted 'in her own language' – seems to have harboured ardently neutralist feelings:

> 'If I thought it was the king, as you say it was, I would think the better of my lips all the days of my life; and so, Mr Parson, get you out of my house, or else I'll get those [that] shall kick you out.'

*

WHATEVER HER POLITICAL inclination, the landlady had kissed the lips of a living legend. For the last month, printers and pamphleteers had been propagating what was meant to be a humiliating caricature of Charles Stuart as a 'plaine country fellowe' with 'haire cut in the country fashion' (a good guess), cowering with his companions 'in the Wood, where every noyse put them into a feare of being surprized', darting out to scavenge hips and haws. A monarch was just a man after all . . . The effect of this propagandist satire was to place 'the King of Scots' in the same thrilling category as Hereward the Wake, Robin Hood and philanthropic highwaymen.

The new, populist form of Royalism was not the nostalgic feudalism of the manor houses which piously gave shelter to the King. It was the spirit of the English Revolution turned against the government it had helped to create.

On 14 October 1651, he reached the tiny seaside village of Brighthelmstone (Brighton). A coal-brig called *Surprise* was chartered. It had been commandeered by the Royalist Navy in 1648, on which occasion its master had met the young Charles Stuart. Having been well treated on that occasion, he vowed to set him safely on French soil. The tipsy innkeeper, like the Charmouth landlady, was excited by the recent changes in the social edifice, but for a different reason. Finding the King alone at the fireside on the eve of his departure, he seized his hand and kissed it (as Charles told Samuel Pepys):

> 'I beseech God to preserve and keep you, [because] if I am not mistaken, I shall be an Earl and my wife a Countess.'

*

CHARLES STUART SAILED for France from Shoreham the following morning. He would not return until 1660, twenty months after the death of Oliver Cromwell. There was much to look forward to. He would commission an atlas of the principal roads of Britain with all distances accurately measured 'by wheel'. He would pursue his interest in prehistoric stone circles and order an excavation of the henge at Avebury. He would shower his supporters with ridiculously expensive gifts – including another watch for Jane Lane, gold and bejewelled, to be passed down through the female line.

There would be no more skulking in priest-holes and hedges. In the Great Fire of London (1666), he went out to help the fire crews by passing buckets of water. After the Fire, he ordered a survey to be made that would turn London into a city of brick and stone, with wide avenues on which he would parade his mistresses. No British monarch had ever lived so much in the public eye. None was so practised in the art of hiding in plain sight.

He felt the *frisson* of concealment in politics and diplomacy. By 1670, the Crown was on the brink of bankruptcy. A treaty with France was signed that year at Dover. There was also a Secret Treaty of Dover to which only two ministers were privy. It remained secret for more than a century. In exchange for a personal annual pension of two hundred and thirty thousand pounds (nearly equivalent to the army's annual budget), Charles promised to assist Louis XIV in his conquest of the Dutch Republic. He also promised to declare himself, at a time of his choosing, the Catholic head of a Catholic state. Six thousand French troops would be made available to extinguish any Protestant rebellion.

In 1685, after suffering a stroke, he honoured the Secret Treaty and converted to Roman Catholicism. A few days later, he made his final escape, leaving his Catholic younger brother James to battle with a Protestant Parliament. It was largely because of Charles's money-grubbing ruses and the revenue reforms of George Downing – formerly Cromwell's scoutmaster-general in Scotland – that Parliament would gain control of the public purse. Monarchs would thenceforth be servants of the body politic, and with a burgeoning fiscal bureaucracy, it would become practically impossible even for the obscurest citizen to remain invisible to the State.

20
Megalopolis

'The Burning of London in the Year 1666'.

When James II ascended to the wobbly throne in 1685, the new world which had come into being in the far south-east of Great Britain had acquired sufficient mass to exert the force which Thomas De Quincey described more than a century later. Pondering the 'vast droves of cattle . . . upon the great north roads, all with their heads directed to London', he was gripped by the sensation of a remote but irresistible 'attracting body':

> A suction so powerful, felt along radii so vast . . . operating, night and day, summer and winter, and hurrying for ever into one centre the infinite means needed for her infinite purposes . . . crowds the imagination with a pomp to which there is nothing corresponding upon this planet.

Two fields east of the Great North Road in Lincolnshire, a young Isaac Newton was lazing under apple trees on the family sheep farm at Woolsthorpe. As he often told friends and interviewers, it was there that he conceived the notion of a force called gravity. It would take twenty years of agonizing calculations to produce that heaviest fruit on the modern Tree of Knowledge: *Philosophiæ Naturalis Principia Mathematica* ('Mathematical Principles of Natural Philosophy'). The book was published in London in 1687. On its title page, 'Is. Newton' was slightly less prominent than the imprimatur of 'S. Pepys', recently elected President of the Royal Society and an expert in his own way on the forces which governed Europe's biggest city.

As new realities foster fresh perceptions, science in turn provides timely metaphors. 'Possessed of a centripetal force exceeding our terrestrial gravitation a thousand times and more', Newton observed, the Sun should now be considered to occupy 'the lowermost region of the universe' (towards which all objects fall) and thus, counter-intuitively, 'the centre of the system'.

*

THE DISPROPORTIONATE CONCENTRATION of wealth, power and people at the bottom of the island of Great Britain made London a country in its own right. 'The Nation of London' was the title of De Quincey's essay. Before the fall of the royal House of Stuart in 1688, it had sucked in more than half a million people. Londoners outnumbered Edinburghians by thirteen to one. A century later, the population would exceed one million. Three times as many people lived in London as in the ten next largest English towns together. The second largest was the former capital of Anglo-Saxon East Anglia, Norwich, where twenty-five thousand people occupied an area of less than one square mile. London's five hundred and fifty thousand were crammed into four square miles (omitting half a square mile of river Thames).

The funnelling effect experienced by De Quincey as he sat in a 'lock' (traffic jam) ten miles from the centre of London was intensified by a lack of bridges. Work did not begin on a second bridge – Westminster – until 1739. With its high-rise houses in which one-thousandth of the population lived in the 'hellish and dismal cloud of sea-coal', London Bridge looked like a grand urban street migrating to the other side of the river. It was an embodiment of economic growth simultaneously stimulated and stifled by private interests – those of the Company of Watermen and Lightermen and the West Country Bargemen, the toll-rich burghers of Southwark, the Mayor of London and the Archbishop of Canterbury, and Charles II, flagrantly wealthy but with crippling cash-flow problems, who scuppered the plan for a second bridge in exchange for a 'loan' (non-refundable) of one hundred thousand pounds from the City of London Corporation.

Westminster and Southwark were no longer distinguished from the whole mass of London. The mesmerizingly detailed map published in 1682 by the King's Cosmographer, John Ogilby, and his successor, William Morgan, was titled *London &c. Actually Survey'd.* It was illustrated with engravings of the principal buildings – religious, civic, financial and commercial. The Royal Exchange, which most Londoners knew as a luxury shopping centre, was depicted next to St Paul's Cathedral and the equestrian statue of Charles II trampling on an irate Cromwell whose spiked head and weathered face were still exhibited on a pole attached to the roof of Westminster Hall.

Upstream of London Bridge, from Three Cranes Stairs to Horse Ferry, the *London &c.* map shows the river milling with passage boats, tide-boats (propelled by the tides) and tilt-boats (equipped with awnings). Downstream, a barge is approaching Wapping with a flock of sheep on board. The three-masted merchantmen attended by lighters are especially dense in front of the eleventh-century Tower of London and the seventeenth-century Custom House designed by Christopher Wren after the Great Fire of 1666.

The biggest sea-going vessels were partially unloaded sixteen miles downriver at Erith before proceeding to the Custom House. The thirty-three-year-old Samuel Pepys, who was then a chief administrator of the Navy Office, rode to Erith docks on 16 November 1665 – sending 'my money and boy down by water' for safety – to visit the most recently captured ship of the Dutch East India fleet. Some of its riches, originating in Japan, China, Siam and Bengal, had leaked out in the usual way – silver and jewels had gone to important men and their wives; spices for medicine as well as cookery were being sold secretly in an obscure tavern at Gravesend near the mouth of the Thames by sailors who had risked their lives to steal them but were pitifully ignorant of their current market price. The treasure-congested bowels of the ship still contained enough to give a palpable measure of the cargo's value in the capital of klepto-commerce:

> My Lord Bruncker . . . and Sir Edmund Pooly carried me down into the hold of the India shipp, and there did show me the greatest wealth lie in confusion that a man can see in the world – pepper scattered through every chink, you trod upon it; and in cloves and nutmegs, I walked above the knees – whole rooms full – and silk in bales, and boxes of copperplate, one of which I saw opened. . . . as noble a sight as ever I saw in my life.

*

On 13 May 1665, from his office in Seething Lane, Pepys took a Hackney carriage along Fenchurch Street and Cornhill to the Royal Exchange. There, he collected a handsome new watch, probably from the watchmaker who had supplied Charles II with the timepiece he had given to Jane Lane in Bristol.

In the multiplicity of urban pleasures, it was unclear to Pepys how much mechanical inventions might contribute to happiness. Those nominally useful, eye-pleasing playthings were not sturdy tools to be passed down through the generations, tended and smoothed by fatherly hands. Less than two months later, his new watch stopped working. The speedy decline and obsolescence of intricate devices was good for business but not for the individual consumer. It led, however, to Pepys's discovery – because the watchmaker lent him one while his watch was being mended – of the 'larum wach', which helped him 'to be up betimes'. This intelligent machine proved particularly useful after the Great Fire when nearly three-quarters of churches in the City were destroyed along with their bells.

Leaving the Royal Exchange, he took a carriage for Woolwich Dockyard in a peculiar state of mind that was neither pleasure nor its opposite. The condition he described, probably before any other writer, would one day be known as technology addiction:

> But Lord, to see how much of my old folly and childishnesse hangs upon me still, that I cannot forbear carrying my watch in my hand in the coach all this afternoon, and seeing what a-clock it is 100 times. And am apt to think with myself: how could I be so long without one – though I remember since, I had one and found it a trouble, and resolved to carry one no more about me while I lived.

Though the weather was hot, he was still wearing his winter clothes, in addition to which his tummy was grumbling 'from my fasting so long and want of exercise'. Something about the city made it hard to ignore trivial ailments of the sort that country people barely noticed.

'Watch' was the modern word for a clock held in the hand. It still carried suggestions of vigilance. Its diligent ticking seemed to make demands on its owner. It blurred the distinction between need and desire. A few months later, it would induce Pepys to record the amount of exercise he took, thereby improving his health and making his body a subject of scientific investigation. By the end of that summer, he was using a watch with a minute hand to time his walks from Woolwich to Greenwich and Deptford Dockyard and found that he came 'within two minutes constantly to the same place at the end of each quarter of an hour'. A calorie counter and heart-rate monitor would have made parts of his diary unreadably tedious.

*

According to Newton's *Principia*, 'absolute' time is unobservable. Human beings are restricted to relative or 'common' time, which is measurable 'solely with reference to the objects of sense perception'. London time had its own megalopolitan characteristics. Whereas a peasant taking an animal or some produce to market rarely included duration in the calculation of profit, time in London was practically a commodity in its own right. A street song first written down in 1744 significantly associated the quarter-hour-chiming bells of London with the tinkling of money and the reverberations of economic activity: 'You owe me five farthings, / Say the bells of St. Martin's. / When will you pay me? / Say the bells at Old Bailey, / When I grow rich, / Say the bells at Shoreditch.'

The acceleration of time in London had a converse effect on the hinterland. For every square mile that was added to the mass, the outlying regions appeared to age by several decades. In the fields beyond St Pancras and in the satellite hamlets of Bethnal Green, Hackney, Mile End and Bow, Londoners wanting to unwind would take the healthsome air, eat at ivy-clad taverns, enjoy the clean rain and the undistracting monotony of the soon-to-be-urbanized countryside. Nostalgia created a market for the bucolic meditations of Izaak Walton's deliberately anachronistic bestseller, *The Compleat Angler* (1653). Walton's philosophical fishing manual begins on the upper reaches of the river Lea, which forms the border of Middlesex and Essex. From its confluence with the Thames opposite Greenwich, the river could be followed, first on streets, then on lanes and paths, past Stratford-by-Bow and Tottenham Hill to quiet places where people and houses still decayed slowly at their leisure. In London, whole streets might be demolished in a day and carted off to a rubbish heap.

Getting lost had never been so easy. A French physician, Samuel de Sorbière, lived in Covent Garden in 1663–4 and reckoned that a year was not enough to grasp London's 'vast extent'. His confused account of London geography proves his point: what he took to be its greatest width – more than forty-five minutes from Southwark by the bridge to Moorfields – was actually its narrowest. A Swiss writer, César de Saussure, who trusted Sorbière's account, memorized his walking routes as though laying a thread through a labyrinth. One evening in 1725, after idling in St James's Park to watch the crowds, he found that the Horse Guards gate in Whitehall through which he had passed was closed. A frantic night of aimless wandering ensued:

> I could not make a driver understand me . . . The only thing I could do was to walk from street to street, in the hopes of recognising some landmark or other; but after hoping this for about an hour I found myself in an entirely unknown part. It was now past midnight . . . I did not know what to do. I sat down on a seat in front of a shop and longed for day.

*

ALONE IN LONDON for the first time at the age of seventeen, I lost my way in the illogical environs of Covent Garden and Leicester Square, formerly Leicester Fields and, before that, a nameless patch of ground near St Martin's on which women spread clothes out to dry. I asked a pair of policemen for directions: they continued their conversation as though I existed in a different time zone. Later, I discovered that the most useful navigational aid in a city – more useful than in almost any natural setting, and certainly more useful than a Metropolitan Police officer – is a compass. Later still, I noticed a reliable correlation between the likelihood of getting lost and the number of coincident periods in a given district.

In much of central London, the ghost trails of Roman and Saxon streets have survived the centuries of uncontrolled private enterprise so that several eras coexist in the present. This topographical synchrony was already a fact of urban life in the late sixteenth century. John Stow, who 'attempted the discovery of London, my native soyle and countrey', published his majestic *Survay of London* in 1598. Even then, large portions of the city he had known as a child had vanished.

Between the Tower and Aldgate, there had been a farm where horses and a herd of thirty or forty cattle grazed: 'I myself in my youth have fetched many a halfpenny worth of milk.' The farm and the Minories abbey had been replaced by military warehouses and workshops. 'Carpenters' yards, bowling allies and divers houses' had been built over the old open ditch outside the city walls. The ditch had been so wide and deep that several people, 'watering horses where they thought it shallowest, were drowned, both horse and man.'

Some features of London had become untraceable in history. On the main road east, an incongruous hill topped by trees and trampled by cattle and treasure-hunters loomed over Whitechapel. After 1757, it even overshadowed the monumental London Hospital. Whitechapel Mount had been used as a fort during the Civil Wars and, in fact or only in legend, subsequently fattened by bodies from the Great Plague and rubble from the Great Fire. It may originally have been a Saxon earthwork or the accumulated waste of countless centuries or even a geological remnant of pre-human London. It survives only in three street names and a slight incline on Mount

Terrace which runs past the evocative incinerator chimney of the Royal London Hospital.

*

THE NEW BREED of human spawned by the city required new forms of expression. Shakespeare's weighty histories and wordy fairylands were falling out of fashion. An avid theatre-goer, Pepys judged *A Midsummer Night's Dream* at Drury Lane 'the most insipid ridiculous play that ever I saw in my life': it was redeemed only by 'some good dancing and some handsome women'.

Between the stage and the daily drama of the streets, the gulf was too wide. 'City comedies', satires, guidebooks and diaries were better able to express the turbulence of the urbanized mind. Like Baudelaire, who devised a well-sprung poetic prose that could cope with the shocks and 'innumerable interconnections' of 'enormous cities', John Stow, the discoverer of London, took a fifteenth-century song, 'London Lickpenny' ('money-sucking London'), stripped it of its tidy rhymes and metre and used a rapid, jolting style to convey the excited discombobulation of a Kentish consumer consumed and ejected by the city:

> In Westcheape he was called on to buy fine lawn, Paris thread, cotton umble and other linen clothes . . . in Cornhill, to buy old apparel and household stuff, where he was forced to buy his own hood which he had lost in Westminster hall: in Candlewright street drapers proffered him cheap cloth, in Eastcheape the cooks cried hot ribs of beef roasted, pies well baked and other victuals: there was clattering of pewter-pots, harp, pipe, and sawtry, yea by cock, nay by cock, for greater oaths were spared . . . but he wanted money to abide by it and therefore gat him into Gravesend barge and home into Kent.*

Pepys's daily diary gives a similar sense of the great flighty swarm of tempting goods, the constant nagging novelty and the invigorating

* Lawn: linen. Cotton umble: unknown; perhaps tufted cotton. Sawtry (or psaltery): a type of zither. 'By cock': euphemistically, 'by God'. 'To abide by it': 'to keep it up'.

insults of the city. While ladies and gentlemen in rural retreats mused on morality and the meaning of life, he felt the urgent need to adopt, for peace of mind, a *philosophie de circonstance*:

> So home, and there find my wife come home and seeming to cry; for bringing home in a coach her new Ferradin waistcoat,* in Cheapside a man asked her whether that was the way to the tower, and while she was answering him, another on the other side snatched away her bundle out of her lap, and could not be recovered – but ran away with it – which vexes me cruelly, but it cannot be helped. (28 January 1663)

A few hundred yards from the scene of the robbery, I sat in a pub with a friend from university who, after working as a firefighter, had taken a senior position at Lloyd's, the descendant of the maritime insurance market which evolved in a London coffee house in the 1680s. Just below the ground-floor window where we sat, the front wheel of his locked bicycle was being quietly removed. He was telling me that after living in London for many years, he had trained himself to think of theft as an inescapable local tax, payable at surprisingly frequent intervals. On that occasion, it led him to the rapid invention of a simple but cunning harness which allows a one-wheeled bicycle to be transported by a pedestrian with minimum effort. Cities can be as conducive to innovation as apple orchards.

*

LONDONERS' BEHAVIOUR BECAME a common subject of provincial speculation, as it still is. In small towns and villages, a 'stranger' was usually someone whose business was obvious to everyone – a pedlar, a beggar, a drover, an itinerant preacher. In London, almost everyone was an alien. The city made strangers out of its own inhabitants. They formed colonies and nests in the coiled mass: Welsh in Lambeth, Irish in St Giles, Scots by the Strand and Charing Cross. Flemish weavers and merchants had been living in Holborn, Bishopsgate, the Vintry

* Ferradin: probably a woollen fabric from northern Italy. (Women's waistcoats were worn to be seen.)

and Southwark since before the Peasants' Revolt of 1381 when many of them were killed by the rioters. After some tentative or implicit relaxation of legal anti-Semitism under Cromwell, Sephardic and Ashkenazi Jews arrived in Whitechapel. Huguenots fleeing the pogroms of Louis XIV settled in Spitalfields. By 1700, French Protestants accounted for about one-fifth of London's population.

The home territory of most Londoners was smaller than that of a wood mouse. All but the very wealthiest lived in conditions of intense intimacy. They could hear and smell their neighbours and talk to them across the rooftops. The labyrinth of blind alleys and courtyards with no obvious entrance or exit presented the enforcers of lockdown during the Great Plague with an impossible task, as Daniel Defoe learned from his uncle:

> For example, in Coleman Street [by Moorgate] there are abundance of alleys, as appears still. A house was shut up in that they call White's Alley; and this house had a back-window, not a door, into a court which had a passage into Bell Alley [now Great Bell Alley]. A watchman was set by the constable at the door of this house, and there he stood, or his comrade, night and day, while the family went all away in the evening out at that window into the court, and left the poor fellows warding and watching for near a fortnight.

New varieties of sociability came to life in the maze. The catalysts were coincidence and eye contact. Anonymity was an aphrodisiac. Alleyways were accomplices. Pepys is often mincingly described as 'libidinous', though there is precious little evidence beyond his diary to give a sense of what was normal. Abuse of power for sexual pleasure is hardly unknown today. Surveys of London commuters over the last eighty years suggest a large overlap between people who disapprove of extra-marital sex and those who go in for it.

Another insoluble puzzle of the streets:

> Going to Whitehall I had pleasant *rancontre* of a lady in mourning, that by the little light I had seemed handsome; I passing by her, I did observe she looked back again and again upon me, I suffering her to go before, and it being now duske. I observed she went into

> the little passage towards the privy water-gate, and I fallowed but missed her; but coming back again, I observed she returned and went to go out of the Court. I fallowed her, and took occasion in the new passage now built, where the walke is to be, to take her by the hand to lead her through; which she willingly accepted, and I led her to the great gate and there left her, she telling me of her own accord that she was going as far as Charing cross; but my boy [Pepys's servant] was at the gate, and so yo [I] durst not go out con [with] her – which vexed me; and my mind (God forgive me) did run après her todo [all] the night, though I have reason to thank God, and so I do now, that I was not tempted to go further. (17 February 1669)

Pepys (pronounced 'peeps') turns his readers into private detectives. Why was this lady heading for the privy water-gate when she claimed to be on her way to Charing Cross? For whom was she wearing that most respectable and fetching form of dress? And who was she? The water-gate was reserved for royalty and people with Court connections . . .

As a commodity, sex was one of the mainstays of the London economy. For the consumer, it was a source of dubious pleasure, for the supplier, a cause of wretchedness and disease. In *The Testament of Laurence Lucifer* (1604), attributed to Satan and probably written by the playwright Thomas Middleton, the retail outlets of service-industry sex were commended as a miraculously profitable form of real estate.

'Lucifer' owned tenements in Westminster, Clerkenwell, Farringdon and Shoreditch. If those properties were correctly maintained and the assets frequently furrowed and fertilized, they would yield a rich harvest and the bulk of the cost would be borne by the providers:

> Let no young wriggle-eyed damosel, if her years have struck twelve once, be left unassaulted . . . For one acre of such wenches will bring in more at year's end than an hundred acres of the best-harrowed land between Deptford and Dover.

*

Six days after his encounter with the woman in mourning, on his thirty-sixth birthday, Pepys took his wife and two young cousins Barbara and Betty to see the tombs at Westminster Abbey. He described their visit in one of his most cheerful diary entries. It was Shrove Tuesday, the last feast day before Lent, and several other people had had the same idea, but 'by perticular favour', he and his party were given a private viewing. They saw the desiccated and well-preserved body of the famously beautiful Catherine de Valois, queen of Henry V and grandmother of the first Tudor king.

> [I] had her upper part of her body in my hands. And I did kiss her mouth, reflecting upon it that I did kiss a Queen, and that this was my birthday, 36 years old, that I did first kiss a Queen.

If Pepys had been suspected of Catholic sympathies, kissing a relic would have been a dangerous display of idolatry, but the kissing of the corpse was a happy celebration of his birthday and the thrilling liberties of London. A cat might look at a king and a commoner might kiss a queen, albeit a dead one. Democracy of a sort was trickling down through the uppermost levels of the social hierarchy.

21
From the Neck Down

A sheepfold in the Luttrell Psalter.

UNTIL THE SECOND World War, British historians had little or nothing to say about the countryside. Land was usually mentioned as a source of private wealth or as the setting of intellectual and mechanical improvements. Before the end of the nineteenth century, most historians were landowners or recipients of produce and income from a family seat. Many were clergymen who had the benefit of a glebe. Echoes of this rural rootedness could still be heard in the 1980s among the ageing fellowship of Exeter College, Oxford. The one subject guaranteed to galvanize a long meeting of the governing body was the planting of a new tree in the Fellows' Garden. In the Senior Common Room, the latest *Country Life* was in greater demand than the daily newspapers.

Few historians of repute dwelt on the essential activities which filled the lives of half the population – herding and milking; ditching and hedging; dung-spreading, sod-turning, harrowing and ploughing; planting and sowing; reaping and mowing; binding, shocking and carting. The indoor activities of women were mentioned even less – cleaning and mending, spinning and weaving, preparing and cooking food, rearing livestock and children.

My French tutor, Dr Hiddleston, told me of a Fellow, then retired or deceased, who, on being asked, 'What is your field?', witheringly retorted, 'I do *not* work in a "field".' This was the period in which the ground-breaking landscape historian W. G. Hoskins unwisely (by his own account) accepted a university professorship at Oxford. He was never appointed to a college fellowship but was left to his 'field' and only occasionally invited to sit at someone's High Table.

By then, most of the intelligentsia, along with most of the middle class, had been thoroughly urbanized. The countryside was a mere backdrop. The reality itself might be boring, mysterious or intimidating, depending on experience and taste. I know from certain visitors to our mud-defended enclave on the Border that Evelyn Waugh's incurably metropolitan Mr Salter in *Scoop* (1938) is scarcely parodic.

> [Mr Salter held] the obstinate though admittedly irrational belief that agriculture was something alien and highly dangerous. . . . There was something unEnglish and not quite right about 'the country', with its solitude and self-sufficiency, its bloody recreations, its darkness and silence and sudden, inexplicable noises; the kind of place where you never know from one minute to the next that you might not be tossed by a bull or pitch-forked by a yokel or rolled over and broken up by a pack of hounds.

*

As London grew, so did its supply zone. The city's needs primed the pumps of agriculture and industry. By 1750, slightly less than half the population still worked on the land, but the land was twice as productive as in 1600 and there was more of it to farm. Fens and levels had been drained, commons enclosed and smallholdings subsumed into larger farms. New crops changed the colours of the countryside.

The titchy English turnip, eaten as a horticultural treat, was shouldered out by its hulking Flemish relative. The sheep-fattening root was used in the new Flemish rotation system of wheat, turnips, barley and clover or ryegrass. This was known from the 1730s as the Norfolk four-course system and credited to the English statesman and brother-in-law of Robert Walpole, Charles 'Turnip' Townshend. Fields left fallow became the mark of the stick-in-the-mud traditionalist.

'Agrarian Revolution' was the promising heading we inscribed in our History exercise books at school. But instead of riots and bloodshed, we were presented with the seed drill, the horse-drawn hoe, the cast-iron plough and the selective breeding of livestock. The human tilth in which Britain's agricultural eminence germinated was represented only by a handful of geniuses who interested themselves in soil, tools, vegetables and manure.

Leaving behind the horror-strewn Middle Ages, we discovered a more familiar landscape of turnpike roads and tidy fields in which each dawn brought a new 'improvement'. In 1700, a twenty-seven-year-old Berkshire farmer applied methods he had observed in French vineyards to English wheat fields. In what seemed to us a retrospectively obvious innovation, Jethro Tull's mechanical seed drill planted the corn evenly in neat rows at the ideal depth.

The stagecoach of progress had set off for the future, leaving most of its prospective passengers still sitting in the familiar fug of the old coaching inn. Tull was attacked for impugning the wisdom of Virgil's *Georgics*, published in 29 BC. His own labourers bridled at the insult to their seed-scattering expertise. Fifty years after his great discovery, almost no one was using the revolutionary seed drill, as the editors of Tull's *Horse-hoeing Husbandry* lamented:

> These people are so much attached to their old customs, that they are not only averse to alter them themselves, but are moreover industrious to prevent others from succeeding.

The Huntingdonshire fields through which William Cobbett rode in 1830 were a scene from the Middle Ages – 'few Swedish turnips, and those not good', the wheat not 'drilled' but 'broad-cast' 'in a most careless manner', as though flung from a shovel. 'Other parts contained only here and there a blade' or were 'so thinly supplied as to make it almost doubtful whether they had not been wholly missed.' The Agrarian Revolution had come and gone like a typical British weather front of scattered showers, giving one field a good soaking and leaving its neighbour bone dry.

*

THE SCHOOLBOOK TALE of brilliant inventors blazing a trail to national wealth and imperial power had the unintended effect of making our ancestors look stupid. Why had it taken them so long to realize that evenly planted seeds would produce a richer crop? Had no one ever thought to apply the simple verities of the kitchen garden to the open field or observed grain dropping punctually between the loose planks of a moving hay wain? No doubt someone *had* noticed – just as many farmers had been cultivating the Flemish turnip eighty years before Turnip Townshend launched his campaign.

Tull himself was a Janus-faced prophet. So smitten was he with the prolific vineyards of Montpellier where vines naturally thrived in poor soil that he conducted an anti-manuring campaign, insisting that unfertilized land yields a better wheat crop than a field fed with dung. Evidence-defying notions were passed down like worthless heirlooms from parent to child. A character in Tobias Smollett's *Humphry Clinker* (1771) is struck by a 'strange phenomenon' at Alloa on the north bank of the Forth. The peasants left their fields encumbered with rocks and boulders. 'A gentleman well acquainted with the theory as well as practice of farming' assures him that when he had cleared a field of stones, the crop was poor, but when the stones were put back, the crop was as good as ever. The same improbable experiment had been 'tried in different parts of Scotland with the same success'.

It is an obvious fact that the more rigidly exclusive the hierarchy, the shallower the reservoir of talent, just as a government whose ministers are picked from a pool of cronies is likely to be not only unrepresentative but also incompetent and prone to corruption. When most of the previously all-male Oxford colleges admitted female students and the proportion of state-school pupils increased, the intellectual standard improved, as did the social maturity of the student body.

Much of Britain's intellectual capital lay fallow. Even ignoring what the former Parliamentarian soldier Walter Blith in his bestselling *The English Improver Improved* (1652) called the 'prejudices against improvement' of 'a confused heady people', there were no established means by which the insights of an agricultural labourer could filter upwards into the executive realm or sideways into a neighbouring shire. Workers who were paid only 'from the neck down' had little or no incentive to share their knowledge and no training other than tradition. Nepotism was the norm at all levels of society. A man with no special aptitude for his father's occupation might spend a lifetime as a wheelwright or a blacksmith before bequeathing his worn tools and muddled notions to his son.

The Statute of Apprentices (1563; repealed in 1814) had regulated the wages and employment of agricultural as well as urban workers, but it did little to disseminate advances in the art of agriculture. Agrarian legislation reflected local private interests and, in a unique case, concern for animal welfare: under Charles I, the Parliament of Ireland made it illegal to attach a plough to the tail of a horse and to pluck the wool off living sheep.

With the dissolution of the monasteries under Henry VIII, whole areas of expertise acquired by centuries of toil and experiment had slipped away, just as the mysteries of land and field drainage were lost in the trenches of the First World War. Drainage engineers today are often gleefully aghast at the hydraulic ignorance of farmers who ruin their machinery in soggy fields. The situation at Evelyn Waugh's Boot Magna Hall was not untypical:

> The lake was moved by strange tides. Sometimes . . . it sank to a single, opaque pool in a wilderness of mud and rushes; sometimes it rose and inundated five acres of pasture. There had once been an old man in one of the lodges who understood the workings of the water system . . . but he had been in his grave fifteen years and the secret had died with him.

*

For Walter Blith, the 'greatest hindrance' to the draining of fens was the workforce. With onomatopoeic synonyms of 'slovenly', he evoked the ditch-diggers' 'slothful and sleathy slubbering' and their 'abominable lusts': gambling, fornication and drunkenness. Beer and wine were weaker than today, but inebriation was normal at all levels of society. Even Samuel Pepys in his lofty position at the Admiralty would sometimes exceed his customary 'morning draught' (one or two pints of wine) and become unfit for business.

The printed advice available to farmers suggests a peasantry which found the most elementary tasks and truths of earthly existence insuperably challenging or unfathomably mysterious. The most widely read manual was Thomas Tusser's *Five Hundreth Pointes of Good Husbandrie*, written mostly in rhyme. It was first published with only 'a hundreth pointes' in 1557 and remained in print for nearly three hundred years. Tusser's tips were on many a lip. Only a snob would have sneered at their simple accuracy:

If sunne be at westward, it setteth anon,
If sunne be at setting, the day is soone gon.

As bud by appearing betokneth the spring,
and leafe by her falling the contrarie thing.

Take heede how thou laiest the bane for the rats,
for poisoning seruant, thy selfe and thy brats.

I often heard similar nuggets dispensed by a North Cumbrian cattle farmer. For those who had ears, he liked to rehearse the plain verities of a farmer's life. Rain follows rain and has nowhere to go but the already sodden ground. In autumn, the leaves fall from the trees and clog up the drainage channels.

Describing what seems obvious is the beginning of practical wisdom. A mind blurred by the multiplicity of farming jobs, numbed by the dangerously hypnotic momentum of strenuous tasks, needs to hear the constant babble of basic truths. 'Let the saw do the work'; 'Swing the hips, not the knees'; 'Better safe than sorry'.

By 1700, rural England was productive enough to become a net exporter of grain, yet the clanking of horse-drawn machinery was a rare sound in British fields until the late nineteenth century. To most farmers, change meant risk. It was reassuring to see an innovator come to grief. Enjoyment of other people's stupidity is a powerful force in agrarian history. The two estate workers who taught me the expression 'paid from the neck (or shoulders) down' were never happier than when performing a task under the ignorant instruction of a wealthy landowner. Instead of replacing a rotting fence cheaply in half a day, they would be told by the would-be cost-cutting owner to repair the fence one sagging section at a time, which entailed the enormous extra expense of tea breaks, chinwags and travelling to and from the worksite.

In the 1670s, the biographer and natural philosopher John Aubrey thought that 'grosse stupidity' had greatly diminished since the Civil Wars. Before then, ''twas held a strange presumption . . . even to attempt an improvement in husbandry'. Scrutinizing 'the ways of nature' was considered a sin and it was not 'good manners' to be 'more knowing than [one's] neighbours'. Meanwhile, ignorance forged its own wavering path. The prejudice against experts would spread to the urban intelligentsia where it produced the 'wise countryman' type, the fount of unwritten ancient lore. In *Mr Harrison's Confessions* (1851), Elizabeth Gaskell sneeringly depicted an agronomist who believes (correctly) that hedges should be trimmed and that manure should be scientifically studied. This know-it-all is contrasted with the local farmer:

> [It] struck me that, if Mr Bullock had the fine names and the theories on his side, the farmer had all the practical knowledge and the experience, and I know which I would have trusted.

At that time, Mrs Gaskell was starting a garden at her house in Manchester and could clearly have done with some scientifically studied manure: 'Clay soil it will be, and there is no help for it.'

*

Active ignorance survived the increasing availability of sound information. The two may be inversely related: the more powerful the flow of information, the more dogged the resistance. 'To take no notice at all of what is dayly offered before our eyes' was one of John Aubrey's definitions of stupidity. Patently incorrect notions can survive for centuries. It was not until I read Oliver Rackham's *Woodlands* (2006) that my brain recorded what my eyes already knew – that alders dislike standing in water and thrive only in *flushed* ground, and that the roots of tall trees are shallow not deep, as conventionally depicted.

No one presumably still believes that earthworms eat corn, that hedgehogs suck milk from cows' udders, that the badger 'hath the legs on one side shorter than of the other', and that the nightjar lives up to its popular name of 'goatsucker'. But one of the commonest British mammals, by spending most of its life a few inches underground, has remained a creature of myth. Almost all information commonly dispensed regarding the mole is demonstrably wrong.

Just as all ages tend to patronize the past, the future will find us short of practical sense. Eternally biodegradable plastic tree guards have been littering woodland and strangling trees for decades. Diesel-producing biomass destroys habitats with monoculture and diesel-powered machinery. The coveted photogenic 'bluebell wood' is often an overgrazed, depleted copse in which only the sheep-spurned bluebell survives.

It was once common knowledge that woods must be thinned and coppiced to ensure their survival. In the twenty-first century, woodland left 'wild' quickly degenerates into worthless scrub and shrubbery of little use to humans, animals and native plants. Oxford University's Wytham Woods is probably the most knowledgeably managed and studied woodland in the world. When a sector of the woods is being thinned or coppiced, word spreads that trees are being felled in Wytham Woods and protestors drive there to denounce the desecration. A professor or a student is then sent out to explain how trees grow and flourish and how they have evolved.

Agronomists who travelled the country in the eighteenth and nineteenth centuries looking for signs of improvement might have been impressed by the creation of public bodies with responsibility for the environment. But Government and Nature are not always well acquainted. An officer of Natural England was asked to come and assess the condition of the part of our woodland which is designated 'ancient'. We stood together in a grove, surrounded by native trees in full distinctive foliage. The officer noted the dampness of the ground and then, looking about, said, musingly, 'I'd expect to find alders here . . .' All around us, the crinkly leaves of sixty alders whispered vainly in the breeze.

22
A New Earth

Brown hare near Laxton.

More than any vegetable or invention, it was the quarter of a million miles of barriers erected during the longest conflict in British history that stimulated agricultural and then industrial growth. Ever since the first deliberate sowing of seed, the enclosure of land by hedge, fence, wall or dyke had been one of the basic elements of husbandry. Animals must be kept from the crops – the cow from the young corn, the rabbit from the lettuce, the goat from almost anything ingestible.

By 1600, enclosed pasture and arable accounted for about half the land surface of England. In Kent and Essex, Devon and Cornwall, most of Wales, the Welsh borders and Cheshire, farmable land had been divided into small fields, much of it in pre-Roman times. Unenclosed farmland was still dominant in a diagonal swathe from Somerset to the West Riding of Yorkshire and in the Scottish Lowlands. These were the regions in which enclosure sparked protests and riots from the thirteenth to the mid-nineteenth centuries.

The unenclosed or 'open-field' system was probably a late Anglo-Saxon innovation. When the first villages were taking shape, the hinterland was divided into large fields, then subdivided into strips or 'selions' (from the Old French for 'furrow'). The selions were shared out so that each family had the same proportion of good, bad and middling earth. Typically, the land was farmed with a three-course annual rotation – a year of wheat, a year of peas, barley or oats, then a year in which the land lay fallow. Crops were protected by movable hurdles, ridges of ploughed earth or natural hedges which grew wherever wind and terrain decided. Sometimes there was a pinfold in which stray animals were impounded and – one of the happier examples of child labour – 'bird boys' armed with stones and wooden clappers or, failing boys, a dead crow on a stick or a straw-stuffed cloth 'werel' holding a bent bow.

Like the similar Scottish 'runrig' system, open-field farming was founded on mutual assistance. It was commercially inefficient but socially beneficial. The whole able-bodied population spread out over the fields following the trampled ways or *gaits* which led to each strip. In the partially drained peatlands of the Isle of Axholme in northern Lincolnshire, the agriculturist Arthur Young discovered a farming society tending its tiny plots 'with all [the] minutiae of care and anxiety', 'very poor respecting money, but very happy respecting their mode of existence'.

Many tasks and customs such as manure-spreading, bonfire-building and stone-gathering were performed and observed in common. A jury appointed by a manorial court or 'court leet' inspected the fields in autumn and levied fines on offenders. According to the only known native account of the open-field way of life, 'inclosure came and destroyed [the stone-gathering custom] with hundreds of others – leaving in its place nothing but a love for doing neighbours a mischief'.

*

It took over five hundred years for the old open-field system to disappear. When it did, almost nothing of it survived in writing, painting and physical reality. An entire chapter of British history went missing. The most intensive periods of enclosure were the late 1400s to the early 1500s, and c. 1750 to 1850, when enclosure was imposed, often by Acts of Parliament, on about one-fifth of England and Wales. Hundreds of minor battles were fought against landowners who fenced, hedged and ditched the land into a state of enhanced profitability and prevented villagers from exercising their grazing and other rights on 'common' land.*

A few enclosure riots involved thousands of people – Kett's Rebellion in Norfolk in 1549 and the Midland Revolt of 1607 which spread through Leicestershire, Northamptonshire and Warwickshire. Most were small but no less bitter. Some of the medieval uprisings were provoked by wool magnates converting farmland into enclosed pasture. As Thomas More complained in 1516, they turned much of England into sheep feed: 'fields, houses, towns, everything goes down their throats'. Other miseries were caused by landscaping fanatics like the wealthy parasite of Goldsmith's 'Deserted Village' (perhaps echoing the emparkment and relocation of Nuneham Courtenay near Oxford):

> . . . The man of wealth and pride
> Takes up a space that many poor supplied;†
> Space for his lake, his park's extended bounds,
> Space for his horses, equipage, and hounds:
> The robe that wraps his limbs in silken sloth,
> Has robbed the neighbouring fields of half their growth.

By far the most brutal example of offensive enclosure was the partitioning of the Debatable Land by Scotland and England in the sixteenth century. To stymy the horse-riding natives, paddocks and

* Apart from small portions of waste amounting to four per cent of all English land, no land was 'common' in the modern, open-access sense by 1600.

† I.e., land which provided many poor people with a living.

cornfields were created with double quickset hedges and ditches as deep as a horse is tall. These were to serve as the bastions of a baffling fortress. Access paths would be 'narrow and somewhat crooked' so that 'the enemy or thief' could easily be ambushed and killed by a bowman. This agro-military zone comprised the entire border region from Newcastle to Carlisle. Freeholders were ordered to pay for 'little closes or crofts' to be built around their towns and villages and to reinforce the sea-to-sea obstacle course by planting a 'quantity of hips and haws, and shoots of ash trees'.

These and other flagrant, usually legal acts of land-grabbing have been used to present the seven-hundred-year-long conflict as a poignant tale of 'little people' standing up for their rights. The curled lip of the evil landowner and the sad cringe of the dispossessed peasant are deeply rooted in Romantic tradition. This well-meant but condescending simplification became entrenched in the British mind when Victorian and Edwardian city-dwellers asserted their right to fresh air and recreation on what they took to be common land.

As ever, History fails to confirm the fiction. Many of the early Tudor enclosure riots were organized by lords or gentry objecting to the fences and fox coverts of a neighbouring lord or gentleman. The rebellions which posed a serious threat to order were urban rather than rural. Resistance normally took the form of petitioning, court appeals, vandalism and grumbling. A great deal of enclosing was initiated by villagers and carried out with the agreement of the whole community. Not everyone was wedded to subsistence farming. The daily trudge to distant strips too narrow and finicky to allow the use of modern machinery was not to everyone's liking.

*

THE ONLY LIVING remnant of the system which covered a third or more of England is in the parish of Laxton on the edge of Sherwood Forest. Approaching from the south in May 2023, we saw several black-eared hares race towards the bicycles one at a time along the tarmac road as though fleeing from the village. They inspected the half-human interlopers, sprang into the long grass of the verge and reappeared a few moments later a hundred yards into a vast and weedy field.

Laxton has the impossible task of representing more than half a millennium of social, physical and visual experience. The colourful Laxton map in the Bodleian Library (1635) depicts more than three thousand swerving selions, each parcel of strips on a slightly different alignment. The scene of ant-like complexity was muddied by the introduction of farm machinery to Laxton in the early twentieth century. Now only three of the original open fields survive. This nine-hundred-acre island-in-time has the same butterfly-free, floral paucity of the modern farms that surround it.

The court leet still has jurisdiction and sits in the Dovecote Inn but the jury members will eventually be replaced by actors or information panels. Ten years ago, there were eighteen farmers in Laxton; now there are twelve. There is no shop or bus service. Between the West Field and the Mill Field, a mile west of the village on the site of an old farmhouse, the National Holocaust Centre and Museum stands like a chapel in this roofless temple to remembrance.

The historical reality is as elusive as the brown hare. About fifteen years ago, an archaeologist visited Laxton and was appalled by what he took to be the sight that must have filled the eyes of Midland peasants every day for centuries: 'the openness . . . has to be seen to be appreciated; in wintertime these are very bleak places indeed'.

The self-taught poet John Clare would have been shocked to see the old open-field system described as 'bleak'. The son of an agricultural labourer and a shepherd's daughter, born in Helpston, Cambridgeshire in 1793, he watched in horror as the pasture, meadows, arable, commons and wastes of Helpston and neighbouring parishes were devastated by 'the axe of the spoiler and self interest'. This went on from 1809 to 1820.

> O samely naked leas, so bleak, so strange! . . .
> To see the ploughshare bury all the plain,
> And not a cowslip on its lap remain;
> The rush-tuft gone that hid the skylark's nest . . .

To Clare's loving eye, bleakness was not an attribute of open-field farming (a term he never used): it was the result of enclosure. The old landscape had held more secrets than a city – its shady woods and

'Gipsey' camps; 'a cow-pasture with its thousand paths'; the puddly lovers' lanes; the twittering hedges from which winter fuel was cut. Clare's Cambridgeshire poems describe a land lost twice over – first in reality, then in recorded memory.

Clare is the only writer to have described the appearance of a newly enclosed landscape, before the hedges had grown up to cover its nakedness and the birds had come back to nest. He saw it in all the ugliness of its infancy. The result of this devastation would be the beloved patchwork countryside of lowland Britain which picture agencies file under headings such as 'typical English landscape': it belongs with thatched cottages, dry-stone walls and heathery hills, chalk downs and contented livestock browsing under skies of white cumulus. To Clare, those stitched-up fields and meadows were the mark of bloodsuckers and bullies.

In most cases, the results were similar. As land came to be farmed more efficiently with fewer hands, food production increased and the numbers of villagers dwindled, providing modern industry with a willing or reluctant mobile workforce.

*

IN 1689, THE Catholic king James II was replaced by his Protestant nephew and niece in the so-called Glorious Revolution. A cabal of Protestant lords had invited William and Mary of Orange to invade England with Dutch ships, troops and money. At that time, British industry was still in its pre-'satanic' stage. Lucifer had left his sooty smear only in a few out-of-the-way places where the tropical swamps of the Carboniferous Period had turned into coal beds and rushing hill streams provided power for pumps and mills.

Industrial landscapes brightened many a tour through tedious country. Almost all pre-1700 industry was located in what are now considered holiday destinations for the moderately energetic: the lead mines of South Lanarkshire and Alston Moor in Cumberland, the copper mines of Coniston in the Lake District, coastal salt works from Tayside to Sussex, the wood-fuelled ironworks of the Kentish Weald and the Forest of Dean, the coal-rich valleys of Ebbw Vale and Blaenavon above Cardiff and Newport. Most of these sites had been worked since prehistory. Several are included in the Iron Age atlas of the British Isles.

Riding to Land's End in 1698, Celia Fiennes was astonished to find the area between St Austell and Redruth thickly sprinkled with copper and tin mines. The Cornish furnaces were fuelled by coal from Bristol. Since the few trees in that land of slate and granite had been used for pit props, there was only turf to heat the houses: 'It makes one smell as if smoaked like bacon.'

This was the cranky face of modern industry in the late seventeenth century. Its remoteness and makeshift machinery belied its international importance. In the 1720s, heading for Halifax up and down the unforgiving moors to the east of Blackstone Edge, Daniel Defoe stumbled on a sight he believed to be unique in the world: the hills were covered on every side by the cottages of an invisible indoor population of hard-working, healthy cloth-makers.

The upper Calder Valley was like a factory town with no streets. 'Hardly a house [stood] out of a speaking distance from another.' Gutters and pipes divided the torrents so that 'none of those houses were without a river . . . running into and through their work-houses'. The sun came out and light blazed from the white cloth stretched out on stone-supported frames or 'tenters' before each house: 'I thought it was the most agreeable sight that I ever saw.'

For several decades, the Calder Valley had been exporting most of its cloth to Germany and the Low Countries via agents from Leeds and Wakefield and the port of Hull. Deep in the roadless Pennines, the effects of wars and plagues and fluctuations in foreign money markets were felt as keenly as in the London Exchange.

The feeble scratchings and smeltings of early British industry had exasperated 'The English Improver', Walter Blith. What was needed, he wrote in 1649, two centuries before the first geological survey of the British Isles, was 'a thorough searching of the Bowels of the Earth, a business more fit to be undertaken by . . . the whole Commonwealth, than by any particular man'. Machinery would transform every industry and find new uses for human muscle and endurance. One day, and for thousands of days to come, those 'bowels' would be a hell on earth.

*

THE STAGE ON which the Industrial Revolution was about to erupt was neatly sketched by a thirty-two-year-old French playwright and *philosophe* in *Letters Concerning the English Nation*, published in London in 1733. After being beaten up on the orders of an aristocrat, imprisoned without trial and banished from Paris, Voltaire spent two and a half sociable years in Wandsworth and London (1726–8) discrediting his home nation. Compared to the French autocracy, the English government, with its happy 'harmony between King, Lords and Commons', was practically a philanthropic institution.

Greedy monarchs could no longer rummage in the pockets of the poor. On arriving from the Netherlands, William and Mary had been dismayed to find that the public purse was not their private treasure chest. Monarchy was now as much an ancient tradition as an active principle of government. By 1721, under the reign of George I of the House of Hanover, the most powerful men in the kingdom were a commoner, Robert Walpole, leader of the Commons, and his brother-in-law, Viscount 'Turnip' Townshend, leader of the Lords. Both men came from Norfolk and both had been educated at Eton College and King's College, Cambridge.

In Voltaire's rosy analysis, the 'English' state already had a machine-like momentum:

> Posterity may be surprised to learn that a small island whose natural resources consist of modest quantities of lead, tin, fullers' earth [used in the processing of woollen cloth] and coarse wool has gained such power through commerce that [in 1726] she was able to send three fleets at once to three ends of the Earth.*

Trade had 'made the English masters of the sea'. Naval supremacy 'enriched English citizens, contributed to their freedom and thereby increased trade'. While France was a medieval mosaic of internal customs barriers with provincial populations of mutually incomprehensible serfs, the liberated 'peasants' of England (Voltaire was probably referring to yeoman farmers of the south-east) provided

* Gibraltar at the mouth of the Mediterranean, Porto Bello (Portobelo, Panama) and the Baltic, to blockade the Russian fleet.

manufacturers with a sophisticated market: the 'peasants' ate white bread, wore shoes instead of clogs and roofed their houses with tile instead of thatch.

Luxury and staple goods flowed through Europe's biggest customs-free zone, which included Scotland after the Acts of Union of 1706–7. The value of land increased, largely because of enclosure, but land tax did not. The latter was very nearly that rarest of birds, a popular tax – consensual, locally administered, keyed to wealth and leaving the business and merchant sector relatively unaffected. Income tax had proved unworkable. The latest poll tax had been scrapped in 1698 and no government would be foolhardy or callous enough to introduce another one until 1989.

For Voltaire, the main driving force of the British machine was freedom of conscience. Non-Anglicans were excluded from the English universities and most professions, but the effect was to create a class of independent-minded dissenters who believed that rational thought was compatible with faith and whose gods rewarded temperance and hard work.

*

WITH HIS LONDON-CENTRIC view, Voltaire was unaware of the dramatic fluctuation in Britain's socio-economic magnetic field. The old North–South imbalance had become interestingly unstable. I compiled a list of the thirty most influential pioneers in the British Industrial Revolution up to the end of the eighteenth century. The list includes inventors, engineers, factory developers and entrepreneurs. Many were Nonconformists (Presbyterians, Quakers, Unitarians). All but one came from regions with a strong tradition of dissent: eight from Lancashire, six from Scotland, six from the Midlands and the remainder from Wales, Cornwall, Devon, Lincolnshire, Cumberland and Yorkshire. Nearly all were born and worked north of the Trent and west of the Exe. A map of their origins could be mistaken for a map of the poorest counties.

More than four days by coach from London, a new nation was coming into being. Some villages were now towns; towns had turned into cities. The growth spurt had come so quickly that some of the old urban centres no longer deserved their official designations.

The 'cities' of Bath, Rochester, Peterborough, Carlisle and York, Defoe observed in 1725, were poor, shrivelled places compared to the 'towns' of Birmingham, Liverpool, Manchester, Sheffield, Leeds and Hull. Twelve days north of London, cloth manufacturing and foreign trade had made Glasgow 'the cleanest and beautifullest and best built city in Britain' after London. Constrained by its hills, 'Auld Reekie' (Edinburgh) was the smelliest, most overcrowded city in the land with the longest and loveliest central avenue: Princes Street.

The onslaught of non-metropolitan enterprise and ingenuity would leave few parts of the British Isles untouched. Anything might now happen within a single lifetime, even in John Clare's rural Cambridgeshire. Like the Hampshire parson Gilbert White whose *Natural History of Selborne* (1788) he hoped to emulate and which revealed some previously undescribed animal species, Clare had written about his infant world as though creation was still fresh and only now being classified and named.

Enclosure of the countryside had cast his bucolic childhood far into the past. His was the first generation to experience sudden change as a regular occurrence. The God of Genesis had made the world in six days. Now, new worlds could be created by the gods of profit and efficiency in almost the same period of time. The heaven and earth of Revelation had passed away and it was no longer certain that God had retained his ancient rights over the land, nor that the latest change would be the last.

Five years after the completion of enclosure in the Helpston area, in the patch of ancient woodland near Clare's cottage, the world was about to be recreated once again:

> Saw three fellows at the end of Royce wood who I found were laying out the plan for an 'Iron rail way' from Manchester to London – it is to cross over Round Oak Spring by Royce Wood Corner . . . I little thought that fresh intrusions would interrupt and spoil my solitudes after the Inclosure.

23
The Home Empire

First World War memorial in Derry / Londonderry.

IT TOOK THE best part of a century for the British Industrial Revolution to build up a full head of steam. Thomas Newcomen's five-horsepower engine (1712) was used to pump water out of a coal mine near Dudley. Its 'snifting valve' made the sound of a sick man with the sniffles. James Watt's less hissy, more fuel-efficient steam engine (1776) performed the same obscure function in a nearby colliery between Tipton and Coseley. His catch-all patent ensured that the Newcomen would remain the mine owners' choice until the end of the century. Shortly after the patent expired, Richard Trevithick's high-pressure 'Puffing Devil' carriage, which Watt considered an accident waiting to happen, chuffed and swaggered up a hill in Camborne – running backwards for technical reasons, which explains the Cornish miners' commemorative song:

The horses stood still, the wheels went around;
Goin' up Camborne Hill comin' down.

Later versions of the song placed the puffing pride of Cornwall in a context of greater social importance: 'White stockings, white stockings she wore'; 'He heaved in the coal, the steam hit the beam'; 'I 'ad er, I did, it cost me a quid'. Farce before tragedy was the rule in early industrial history.

Britain's natural as well as self-inflicted handicaps proved to be strokes of luck. The chronic shortage of timber and the need to find alternative sources of energy stimulated innovation. At the same time, the population grew in almost biblical proportions. It nearly tripled in size between 1750 and 1850. This was due to lower infant mortality rather than heightened adult vigour.

Britons were now eating all the wheat they produced and could no longer be fed without imports. Food riots were common even in the wealthiest parts, east of the Exe and south of the Trent, where the staple was expensive white bread rather than barley or oats. Fortunately for industrialists, the multitude of wage-dependent men, women and children concentrated in ever smaller areas created a convenient and seemingly inexhaustible labour force. Crucially, this included the 'Celtic' nations – Wales, Scotland and Ireland – which had become a largely quiescent domestic empire.

*

THE 'CELTIC FRINGE', as an American historian pointed out in 1982, was 'not so much a fringe as a hemisphere'. In 1801, the population of England was 8,502,000; the population of the 'fringe' was 7,400,000. Approximately the same number of people lived in Ireland (5,216,000) as in all English counties south of the Wash and the Dee (5,576,000). Ireland itself is two-fifths the size of Great Britain. To most Irish people – and not just Irish people – the British habit of referring to Great Britain as 'the mainland' is a case of exaggerated self-importance.

The 'peripheral' nations had long been treated as an unruly nursery of tribes, clans, Catholics, dissenters, Royalists and other enemies of English governments. They were the restive and poorly coordinated rear end of the pantomime horse (an image recently applied by an English historian to post-Union Scotland).

Wales had once, briefly, had its own parliament (1404–5) when Owen Glyndŵr's dream of an expanded Welsh kingdom led him to within sight of the Malvern Hills. After his submission to England in 1414, Glyndŵr and his dream had vanished into legend.

In 1536, Wales was officially absorbed by a constitutional diktat. The insulting Act of Union affirmed that Wales 'ever hath been' (since Edward I) 'annexed . . . and subject to' English rule. All the 'singular and sinister usages and customs' of the 'dominion' would be utterly 'extirped' along with the Welsh language, which was 'nothing like nor consonant to the natural Mother Tongue used within this Realm'. Monolingual Welsh-speakers would be excluded from all official positions.

At the dawn of the Industrial Revolution, Scotland was completing its own internal colonization. The ravaging of the Debatable Land (1552–1608), the colonization by Lowlanders of the Highlands and Islands (1595–1630s), the Massacre of Glencoe (1692) and the extinction of Jacobite rebellions (1715 and 1745) were all carried out by Scottish as well as English troops.

The 'Young Pretender' Bonnie Prince Charlie, grandson of James II, took the city of Carlisle, which was no great military feat, and reached the river Trent five miles south of Derby. Cold-shouldered by English Jacobites, he headed back to Scotland and was defeated at Culloden near Inverness by an army which included four Scottish and Highland units. Even before Union with England, 'sending Scots to fight Scots' had presented no serious difficulties. After 1750, many of the evictions lumped together under the heading of 'the Highland Clearances' were the work of clan chiefs.

The nations of the 'Celtic fringe' had become an asset rather than a military or economic nuisance. In 1707, many people in England opposed union with Scotland as an expensive rescue package for a bankrupt economy. Now, as industrialization accelerated, Scotland and Wales were more likely to be seen as important, if inferior contributors to England's wealth. When the electoral Reform Acts of 1832 reorganized the old constituencies, favouring the new industrial towns – and, for the first time, explicitly *ex*cluding women – Scotland

and Ireland, with different degrees of property ownership, remained under-represented compared to England: 4.8% of the whole population had the vote in England and Wales, 2.7% in Scotland and 1.2% in Ireland.

Ireland was still living through the long agony of colonization which had begun with the Anglo-Norman invasion of the late twelfth century. All the brutal bolsterings of Protestant supremacy were fresh in inherited memory – the confiscation of Irish lands and their conversion into English 'plantations'; their use as a dumping ground for deported rebels; the atrocities of Cromwell's reconquest of Ireland which ended with the siege of the plague-racked city of Galway in 1652; the 'Bloodless Revolution' during which William of Orange massacred the Jacobites at the Boyne in County Louth and Aughrim in County Galway.

In 1798, a five-month revolutionary war of independence ineptly assisted by the French Republic had been crushed. Two years later, when the Acts of Union dissolved the separate Irish Parliament and created the United Kingdom of Great Britain and Ireland, this seemed to many Irish people, as it still does, yet another act of repression.

*

In the summer of 1965, thanks to my mother's campaign to get my father to take the family on a foreign holiday – preferably to France or Switzerland – I discovered the Republic of Ireland. It would have taken less time and trouble to cross the English Channel, but Ireland was subjectively closer to home and potentially less complicated. This was during the Scientific Revolution of the 1960s, touted by the Yorkshire-born Labour Prime Minister Harold Wilson as the economy-boosting successor to the Industrial Revolution.

Holidays with a 'primitive' component (rented cottage, caravan, canal barge or tent) were acquiring a vicarious nostalgic appeal. My father had seen advertisements in the Sunday papers by a company in Galway which offered self-guided tours in three- or four-berth 'gypsy caravans' (gas stove, tinned food and horse included). My mother had swiftly organized the passports, since when my father's increasingly unironic renditions of 'Galway Bay' had etched that wistful dirge for ever in our brains.

This being the Scientific Revolution, we were to fly to Dublin from Manchester Airport while my father took the Ford Anglia by ferry from Liverpool, once famous for Irish immigrants and Chinese sailors and now for Beatles. Mr B—, the father of a friend at primary school, had offered to drive us the forty-five miles from Stafford to Manchester on the recently opened M6 motorway which was already sending thousands of day-trippers to join the twelve-mile tailbacks that were clogging up the Lake District.

Mr B— was a man of his time, which, in the mid-1960s, meant ahead of his time. He prospected sites for the towering electricity pylons. To the poet Stephen Spender, pylons embodied the shameless intrusion of modernity: he thought they looked like naked giantesses. This placed Mr B— high on the playground scale of Dad prestige, as did the fact that he drove an S-type Jaguar sports saloon. The car could do 118 mph, more than twice the top speed of the eponymous feline. Despite the rising death toll, there was still no national speed limit. On the virtual runway of the M6, we raced north through the Midlands and saw the pylons fall away to the east.

Soon after Stafford, we bypassed Stoke-on-Trent, the conglomeration of six industrial towns where Josiah Wedgwood, pioneer of factory discipline and the division of labour, had mass-produced his luxurious but affordable stoneware. The first consumers of Wedgwood pottery discovered that mild state of pleasant alienation which was now a part of everyone's mental furniture. No human trace of the Jaguar's manufacture remained. It was as pristine as the scene of an impeccable crime. Owner and factory worker were cleanly separated by the proud fact of ownership.

The car's message was that things were better than they had been and were getting better all the time. Its charm was its delusive self-sufficiency: it demanded constant attention and petting. The driver and the front-seat passenger had independent arm-rest and ventilation options. All five occupants had access to a flip-top ashtray, of which Mr B— and my mother unstintingly availed themselves. Mr B— had a pull-out map tray; my mother had the use of an elasticated magazine pocket. The tobacco-stain-coloured veneer and the stubby black gear-lever with its scrotal bag suggested a child's den refitted for serious adult pleasures.

Compared to the ethereal form of public transport, the car was already out of date. Once safely airborne, I pressed my face to the porthole and marvelled at the accuracy of the map: Anglesey and the north coast of Wales looked exactly as they were supposed to, with similar colour-coding for fields, mountains and sea, and the added three-dimensional decoration of clouds.

Far below on the western edge of Britain, English travellers had made their weary way to Holyhead to board the packet to Dublin. On atrocious Welsh roads, carriages had been taken to pieces and carried to the Menai Strait by native porters. Thomas Telford's wondrous suspension bridge across the Menai Strait (1826) and then the railway from Chester (1850) shortened the journey, but until the twentieth century, Ireland was as far in time from London as New Zealand is today.

*

VISIBLE TO 'THE mainland' only from a few remote Scottish headlands, the country that was 'steeped in legend' according to the guidebooks was also pickled in English prejudice. In 1775, the parson of Selborne, Gilbert White, had written of Hibernia as a Dark Continent awaiting discovery:

> Some future faunist . . . will, I hope, extend his visits to the kingdom of Ireland; a new field, and a country little known to the naturalist. . . . The manners of the wild natives, their superstitions, their prejudices, their sordid way of life, will extort from him many useful reflections.

Though he lived in Manchester with the daughter of an Irish mill worker, Friedrich Engels, the son of a factory owner and friend of Karl Marx, was categorically racist about the 'uncivilised', thick-skinned Irish who forced down the wages of 'the Saxon native'. In *The Condition of the Working Class in England* (1845), the 'wild Milesian' (Gaelic Irish) was said to be sly, drunken and filthy. He lived in damp cellars with a pig and went barefoot like a savage.

> With the Irish, feelings and above all passion reign supreme; reason must bow before them. Their sensuous, excitable nature

retards the development of reflection and quiet persistence. Such a people is utterly unfit for industry in its current form.

Anti-Irish prejudice was still rampant in the 1960s. If something was 'Irish', that meant that it was amusingly skewed, ungrammatical or didn't work properly. The tatterdemalion brawling Irishman and the friendly, fatalistic believer in leprechauns – both permanently sozzled – were stock comic characters in a world outside History.

*

WE MET MY father at Dublin Airport and drove west in the Ford Anglia on the prehistoric trans-Hibernian route of the Esker Riada, the series of gravel mounds and ridges which divides Ireland into north and south. We saw peat-coloured people cutting peat in the endless boglands and heard again (and again) the descending semi-tones of the sun going down on Galway Bay.

In Galway, we waited outside an office and a stable for the caravan owner to return from the pub. Women in the street were speaking a language which I felt sure I would understand if I eavesdropped long enough. The man bowled up. Unlike the Irish types on television, he was not pretending to be drunk. To my father's delight, he slowly crushed two feathery gas-mantles between thumb and forefinger while showing us how to work the lamp. The four-berth caravan had sunk in a bog on the back roads of Connemara but we were not to worry: the three-berth caravan would be nearly as good and a bit cheaper too.

An exhausted grey mare was led out on a rope, snuffling in a nosebag. My mother asked for its name. Its name was 'the Horse'. We ambled through the suburbs of Galway and inched out onto the open road. The nameless mare was the gentlest large four-legged creature I ever met. Her top speed was four miles an hour, less with the caravan attached and no miles an hour if my father bent double and joined us on board. He quite happily resigned himself to a walking holiday with a horse on a rope: he talked to her in Aberdonian Scots and fed her oats from his palm. My mother was assessing her two contrasting roles – a skivvy in a claustrophobic galley on wheels and a lady of leisure pretending to be a Romany – when we saw clip-clopping smartly towards us a caravan of the same covered-wagon type but beautifully painted and driven by real Romanies. The children stared; the adults looked at the road ahead; my mother shrank back into her galley.

She consoled herself with the thought that our excruciating neo-colonial excursion might be an education for her children. We dutifully collected sociological data: Alison counted the nuns, I did the monks, and we were into the hundreds by the second day. We thought they might be missionaries sent to care for the rural population which seemed to lack basic comforts. Barefoot boys on country lanes played the shin-shattering sport of hurling with sticks ripped from a tree and a stone for the ball. Many of the fields had been left to the weeds. In some, a donkey or a mule was standing still or lying down, crippled by unclipped hooves.

Seventeen years after Ireland was declared a republic, agriculture was still 'the dominant occupation and way of life in Ireland', yet because of mass emigration, a great deal of land was unfarmed. Most farmers were smallholders. Few in the west of Ireland had any education beyond primary school. In 1965, four out of five primary schools were run by the local parish priest. Free secondary education would not be introduced until 1967.

*

MY FATHER DECIDED to give the mare and my mother a holiday and, leaving the former at a horse-friendly 'motor hotel', we drove to the Dingle Peninsula. On the deserted three-mile-long beach at Inch, we played in the Atlantic Ocean under a cloudless sky. Having developed an interest in astronomy, I wondered if it might in reality be possible, using powerful lenses, to 'light a penny candle from a star'. This intriguing experiment in cosmic combustion was mentioned in 'Galway Bay' as an example of something impossible, like the attempts of 'the English' to stop the Irish 'being what we are'.

I assumed until recently that 'Galway Bay' had been written by an Englishman on holiday or a middle-class Dubliner on the verge of retirement who liked to tickle fish in 'the trout stream' and found the rural Irish endearingly stuck in their ways. In fact, it was written, probably in the 1930s, by a doctor from a Catholic family in Enniskillen who graduated from University College, Galway and spent most of his professional life as a neurological specialist in Leicester.

Arthur Colahan's song was schmaltzy but realistic. We had seen 'the barefoot gossoons [young lads] at their play' and 'the women in the meadows making hay' (or cutting peat). We had smelled 'the turf fire in the cabin' and heard people 'speak a language that the English do not know'. Since potato production in the 1960s was small-scale and local, we might also have seen 'women in the uplands digging praties'. For all but the most ignorant, the vision of women forking up potatoes summoned up the ghosts of the Irish Famine.

My father sang the older version, not Bing Crosby's 1947 worldwide hit, in which 'the English' was replaced with 'the strangers'. Even euphemistically, the political sting was palpable. The 'strangers' still 'scorned us just for being what we are'. Most of the English-speaking and especially Irish-American audience, knew exactly how the English had come 'and tried to teach us their ways'.

Colahan himself had direct experience of British imperialism. In the First World War, he had been a captain in the Royal Army Medical Corps and served in India. According to the biography of the Colahan family in the *Journal of the Galway Archaeological and Historical Society*, Arthur 'was exposed to mustard gas which badly affected his health for the rest of his life, and, probably, contributed to the breakdown of his unhappy marriage: they had no children'. The Rawalpindi experiments in which more than five hundred Indian soldiers were exposed to mustard gas by British army scientists and doctors did not begin until the 1930s, but mustard gas was already being recommended for use in 1919 against the people Winston Churchill called 'recalcitrant natives'.

'Galway Bay' was heavy with history. Shaking their heads at the stubborn Irish stuck in the past, the colonizing powers had departed, leaving the post-colonial population to live through the long epilogue.

*

THE UNEXPECTED ADVANTAGE of the fake gypsy caravan was that only it was fake; everything else was real. As a vehicle of discovery, 'the Horse' outstripped the Jaguar by an Irish mile. Statistics create a similar illusion of streamlined simplicity. Exports can be useful indicators of a country's wealth, but not in this case. Despite the creeping pace of agricultural reform and the unmotivated tenantry of its plantations, Ireland supplied the industrial powerhouse of Great Britain with a cornucopia of foodstuffs.

The trade figures make for sinister reading. Throughout the Irish Famine of 1740–41, food exports continued as before while close to one-eighth of the population died. During the Great Hunger of 1845–52, the same proportion perished (about one million people) and more than a million fled abroad. In some of those years of misery, exports of livestock (including rabbits), vegetables (including potatoes), fish and dairy products actually increased. Huge quantities of grain, some of it processed into Guinness and whiskey, flowed through the ports of London, Bristol, Liverpool and Greenock (for Glasgow). Unless grain prices rose or the pubs ran out of whiskey, it was easy for most Britons to ignore their suffering neighbour. After the partition of Ireland in 1921, the United Kingdom showed no inclination to offer the Irish Free State a favourable trade deal.

On 12 August 1969, four years after our tour of western Ireland, violent battles between Catholics and Protestants broke out in the streets of Derry / Londonderry. To the combatants and their victims, this was history in the raw. The matted roots of the struggle lay in the Ulster Plantation and the aggressive settlement under James I which brought Protestants from Lowland Scotland and northern England.

Prime Minister Harold Wilson and my father's new boss, the Home Secretary Jim Callaghan, hurried back to Westminster from their summer holidays. There were echoes of the 1798 rebellion in unconfirmed reports of French students helping the Catholic militants with weaponry and advice on guerrilla tactics. A British army regiment was placed on standby.

The leading article in *The Times* on 14 August, titled 'The Madness', was written by the editor, William Rees-Mogg. Like Friedrich Engels, he resorted to the histrionic language of colonial superiority. In Rees-Mogg's opinion, this was no longer a purely political matter; it was 'something much more primitive and volcanic, tribal fears and hatreds'. Now it was 'the turn of Westminster to renew its acquaintance with the Irish question – a prospect that any sensible politician must pray he may yet be spared.'

The ensuing Troubles dealt repeated blows to Ireland's vital tourist industry. Attempts to attract motorists were unsuccessful: they came and went, spending very little money. Instead, just as 'Galway Bay' was said to have done more for western Ireland than the Irish Tourist Board, it was the 'primitive' aspects of the country that appealed to foreigners. Cruising on sunlit waters and gazing at 'the ripple of the trout stream' proved surprisingly lucrative. It was sadly appropriate that one of the most dynamic performers in the vanguard of resurgent Irish tourism was the horse-drawn gypsy caravan.

24
Speed

From Turner's Rain, Steam, and Speed.

As we sailed ahead the river contracted. The day came, and soon, passing two lofty land-marks on the Lancashire shore, we rapidly drew near the town, and at last, came to anchor in the stream.

Looking shoreward, I beheld lofty ranges of dingy warehouses, which seemed very deficient in the elements of the marvelous; and bore a most unexpected resemblance to the ware-houses along South-street in New York.

Twenty-seven days after boarding a merchantman in New York, the nineteen-year-old Herman Melville sprang ashore on 4 July 1839 at Prince's Dock in Liverpool and for the first time 'felt dusty particles of the renowned British soil penetrating into my eyes and lungs'. He described his adventure ten years later in the largely autobiographical novel *Redburn: His First Voyage*. During the crossing, he had memorized every detail in the guidebook his father had used when visiting Liverpool as a merchant-importer. Now, as he began his exploration of the new Old World, he found that *Picture of Liverpool, or Stranger's Guide* (1805) 'bore not the slightest resemblance' to present reality.

Chrono-displacement disorder was a fact of daily life in Liverpool. In 1565, the port of Litherpole, which meant 'muddy creek', had one hundred and thirty-eight householders and seven ships. In 1700, the year a slave ship from Liverpool was first recorded (at Barbados), the population reached 5,714. Over the next century and a half, as the North-West became the pounding heart of industrial England, its busiest port grew by a factor of sixty-six. By 1851, there were 375,955 Liverpudlians, of whom a quarter were born in Ireland and one-tenth in Scotland or Wales. No British city apart from London had more domestic immigrants.

Liverpool had weathered 'the struggle between sordid interest and humanity'. Melville knew about the 'unhappiness' from his abolitionist father. For a hundred years, slaves had been imported from Africa, sold in Liverpool, then exported to the New World. The slave trade, but not slave ownership, had been abolished in 1807, but by then, marketing one and a half million human beings had established Liverpool as 'the second city of the British empire'. The town on the muddy Mersey boasted the world's first commercial floating harbour or 'wet dock', which allowed deep-sea ships to be loaded and unloaded without waiting for the tide. The port was fed by the world's first integrated canal system, which had been spreading since the 1760s like the blood vessels of a healthy human embryo.

Melville found no trace of what had 'once constituted the principal commerce of Liverpool': 'Not a negro was to be seen', not even in the naked chained figures at the base of the monument commemorating Nelson's victories. It still stands on the square called Exchange Flags behind the Town Hall. All four cowering captives have European features. This was clearly a nation that was prepared to extend the privilege of servitude to all peoples . . .

Slave-picked American cotton had replaced African slaves. The bales had no memory of the suffering that produced them. The black people Melville saw were sailors from the ships, though there were also several

Africans and people of African descent in Liverpool – former slaves who had sided with the British in the War of Independence and the children of African chiefs who had been sent there for an English education. In Liverpool, 'the negro steps with a prouder pace, and lifts his head like a man'. The black steward from his own ship promenaded in the streets of Liverpool arm in arm with 'a good-looking white woman':

> In New York, such a couple would have been mobbed in three minutes; and the steward would have been lucky to escape with whole limbs.

*

FROM THE OPPOSITE bank of the Mersey at the northern end of the Wirral Peninsula, the Liverpool skyline looks like a dreamscape of New York. I saw it for the first time as an adult in 2022 after cycling up from Chester on the Shropshire Union Canal. The rubbly strand of the river between Port Sunlight and Birkenhead was deserted apart from a dog-walker and a beachcombing gull. The ebb tide had unveiled the unrecyclable detritus of a port city – wires and tubes attached to remnants of machinery and enough heavy red bricks to build a small workshop. An installation artist could turn this industrial graveyard into a submersible monument to four centuries of development and decay. Liverpool is one of the birthplaces of modern science fiction. On his maiden voyage to England, Jules Verne took the steam ferry across the Mersey to Birkenhead where he marvelled at Laird's immense shipyards. Ten years later, in *Twenty Thousand Leagues Under the Sea*, he made Birkenhead the place where the hull of Captain Nemo's submarine *Nautilus* is manufactured.

I had always thought of Liverpool as the great city at the end of a branch line. Waiting for trains at Manchester or Crewe, I had sometimes gone to stand on the platform for Lime Street Station to listen to the melodious accents known as Scouse or Merseyside English. Historical linguisticians revel in the unique features of Scouse and ponder its indefinable origins. 'Fur' and 'fair' are homophones. In 'Birkenhead' or 'Brookside', the 'k' is reminiscent of the Welsh or Scottish 'ch'. 'Tea' or 'Beatles' are pronounced with a soft slurred 'ts', which may come from Ireland.

The sense of local identity is unusually strong in Liverpool. Melville had the physical sensation of it one Sunday when he left the flagstoned city and followed the London Road ('smooth as an entry floor') until a 'wide sweep of view' opened up, probably in the vicinity of Everton and Mount Vernon. Slums and factories had yet to hide the meadows and woodlands of the Cheshire Plain. 'And then, indeed I saw England, and snuffed its immortal loam – not till then.'

It would soon be quite ordinary to live in a city without ever coming into contact with the natural terrain. When we entered twenty-first-century Liverpool with the grit of towpaths and Mersey glaur on our shoes, the magical history tour had an authentically anachronistic flavour.

*

Collieries, dye works and the nascent chemical industry coloured the rivers and canals of Merseyside brown, purple, green and black. The overspill of people and their sewage spread the effluence far afield. Smokestacks grew taller and the rain brought the airborne smuts back down to earth. Streets which had yet to be paved were tarred with a slippery mixture of coal dust, soot and cinders.

Industrialization would come to be associated with drab uniformity in buildings and people. Faceless workers moved en masse towards faceless factories. The greater connectedness of towns and cities overwhelmed the intervening villages with urban creep but without the insidious sameness that would come with later forms of industry.

There was also an opposite effect. In the industrial Midlands, small workshops with masters and apprentices on comfortable wages were more common than factories with a hire-and-fire workforce. Burgeoning export markets exaggerated local differences. In this period, Britain was beginning to look like the 'Counties of England and Wales' jigsaw puzzle, organized like a nationwide department store and hardware emporium: gloves came from Worcester, hats from Bedford, shoes from Northampton, leather goods from Leicester, pots and pans from Stafford, and lace and hosiery from Nottingham – which may be the origin of the lively belief that Nottingham girls are the prettiest in England. Each county in turn could be subdivided into specialities. In 1830, William Cobbett found the entire village of Mosborough south of Sheffield 'employed in the making of sickles and scythes'.

After a fortnight riding through Yorkshire, it occurred to Cobbett that he had only twice seen a stack of wheat. 'But this is all very proper: these coal-diggers, and iron-melters, and knife-makers, compel us to send the food to them, which, indeed, we do very cheerfully.' In 1832, in the Tyne valley where the Carlisle–Newcastle railway was being laid, he noticed the signs of prosperity and the remarkable scarcity of orchards and gardens. One day soon, instead of being haggled for at a market or dug out of a field, daily essentials would arrive on the train and be bought in a shop.

The biggest change in the social texture of Britain was not uniformity but the creation of powerful new urban identities. Historical phonetics records the change as crisply as a phonograph. Scouse was indistinguishable from common Lancastrian until the mid-to-late nineteenth century. Geordie, the English of Tyneside, had only recently evolved from broad Northumbrian, and Brummie, the speech of Brummagem or Birmingham (pronounced 'Baernegum'), sounded like standard West Midland until the end of the eighteenth century. These cherished 'traditional' forms of speech are no more than two centuries old.

*

At the time of Melville's Liverpool adventure, much of Britain's geography was being tailored to fit the needs of trade and industry. Its uncooperative hills were disciplined by cuttings, tunnels and aqueducts. The Mersey was in continual communication with the Humber, the Trent, the Severn and the Thames. Since the opening of the Rochdale Canal in 1804, it had been possible to cross the Pennines without noticeably going uphill and to be towed on waveless waters from Merseyside to Birmingham, Bristol or London and to any of a hundred canal ports and settlements. Many still exist in seeming isolation (except on sunny weekends), with their lock keepers' cottages, watermen's inns and red-brick terraced houses roofed with barge-transported Welsh slate.

In the early 1970s, all I knew of the two-and-a-half-thousand-mile-long canal network was a two-mile stretch of urban squalor and decay. The Worcester and Birmingham Canal, built between 1791 and 1815, was a stagnant conduit for household rubbish, dead animals and typhoid along the treacherous towpath of which we were made to go on 'a cross-country run' on Monday mornings to be sneered at by fag-smoking truants from the nearby secondary modern school. This alleged masterpiece of engineering followed the ugliest and slowest possible route through crumbling brick canyons, past the blank back-sides of factories and warehouses from the Severn at Worcester to 'Brummie Land'. School history and cross-country experience suggested that the canal revolution, like the Monday-morning run, had ultimately been a massive waste of time and effort, especially since railways were about to be invented.

Perceptions of speed are hard to recapture. A former colonial army clerk, George Head, who set out to explore the canal system of northern England in the summer of 1835, was delighted by 'the ease and rapidity with which passengers are conveyed by the quick passage boats'. These canoe-shaped vessels had names such as 'Water Witch', 'Swiftsure' or 'The Express', unlike modern longboats which typically celebrate idleness – 'Drifter', 'Patience', 'Lazy Days', 'Moonshadow', etc. 'Northern Powerhouse', which I saw painted on a houseboat slumbering on the Bridgewater Canal near Manchester, was a sarcastic variation on the theme, as was 'May Contain Nuts' at Gloucester Docks.

In Preston, George Head boarded the seventy-foot 'Water Witch', which plied the Lancaster Canal. No sooner had his luggage hit the deck than a whistle blew and two horses broke into a canter. They were trained to respond to the sound of a whistle (speed up) and a horn (stop).

> So quick were our movements, that frequently, on whisking round a corner, a traveller was seen waiting for a passage; and within the space of twenty seconds from the moment the boat stopped till she proceeded on her way – from the blast of the horn to the sound of the whistle – the packages and our new companion . . . were all together gliding away on our voyage.

This happy (but not for horses) form of transport buoyed up industry and commerce for more than half a century. One of the most popular passenger routes was the Forth and Clyde Canal: its 'swift-boats' covered the fifty-six miles between Glasgow and Edinburgh in seven hours. The 'fly-boats' on the Grand Junction Canal between London and the Midlands carried fifteen-ton cargoes at four miles an hour. This might sound slow, but unless the canal froze solid, the recipient of the goods could expect them to arrive in one piece rather than shattered by a potholed turnpike road or delayed by a river which overflowed in winter, dried up in summer and travelled in only one direction.

*

MERSEYSIDE NOT ONLY had the first entirely new canal – the coal-carrying Bridgewater Canal, opened in 1761, which ran in a great lockless loop from Runcorn to Manchester – it also had the world's first fully functioning, all-steam, inter-city railway.

The Liverpool and Manchester, built by the Northumbrian locomotive pioneer George Stephenson, had a double track for two-way traffic, steam locomotives only (no horses), a signalling system consisting of arm-waving company policemen, and a full timetable. The L&MR ran a daily service of four first-class and two second-class trains, the latter costing four shillings, which was equivalent to the weekly rent of a working-class family in Manchester. The train was twice as fast as the coach. A Manchester cotton broker could wake up at a civilized hour, conduct his business in Liverpool and be home in time for tea.

At the grand opening (15 September 1830), the train carrying the Duke of Wellington stopped halfway to Manchester at Parkside Station. Ignoring the official advice, William Huskisson, Member of Parliament for Liverpool, left his carriage to have a word with the Duke. The oncoming locomotive was the famous *Rocket*, designed by George Stephenson's son Robert. The *Rocket* had recently attained a speed of thirty miles an hour. As he clutched the out-swinging door of the Duke's carriage, Huskisson was fatally maimed and thus, according to the trackside memorial, 'brought home to every bosom the forgotten truth that "*IN THE MIDST OF LIFE WE ARE IN DEATH*"'.

The fatal train steamed on to Manchester. The general opinion was that Huskisson had provided everyone with a timely lesson. All the early railway guides told tales of gaucherie and gore but insisted that train travel was perfectly safe if a few simple rules were observed: sit near the centre of the train to minimize the effects of a collision; sit with your back to the engine to shield yourself from cinders; when occupying a roof seat, remain seated, especially on the approach to tunnels and bridges. A frequently reprinted *Treatise on the New Art of Transport* (1850) used examples from all over the British Isles to illustrate the rules:

> Beware of yielding to the sudden impulse to spring from the carriage to recover your hat which has blown off, or a parcel dropped.
>
> If you travel with your private carriage, do not sit in it on the railway.

This was a reference to the misadventure of the Countess of Zetland on the Great Central Railway in 1847. Showered by coals from the engine's chimney but invisible to the guard at the rear of the train, her London-bound carriage caught fire near Lutterworth in Leicestershire. The Countess and her maid waved their handkerchiefs and called to 'several policemen on the road, none of whom took any notice of us'. At Rugby Station a few minutes later, shaken but unsinged, the Countess informed the stationmaster that her terrified maid had leapt out onto the track. An engine was sent back up the line at walking speed and eventually spotted the maid lying on the rail, motionless but alive. Unfortunately, braking systems had not kept up with locomotive technology and the engine was unable to stop in time.

As in the world of early and present-day motoring, occasional carnage was felt to be a price worth paying for the miracle of high-speed travel. The disquieting advertisements in *Bradshaw's Monthly Railway and Steam Navigation Guide* (from 1839) seem to have had no deterrent effect. They recommended powders for nervous complaints, trusses and remedies for hernias and ruptures, ointments for skin infestations, ten different life insurance companies and, 'for the attention of railway directors', a new kind of brake which 'has no tendency to fly off when left to itself'.

*

Over the next forty years, stoked to bursting point by private enterprise and feverish share-buying, the railway network grew by an annual average of three hundred miles. Whole districts of London were gutted; both living and dead were evicted from the villages of Stepney and St Pancras. In the countryside, anciently intricate patterns of path and field were cut across by the rails which refused to go uphill or down or to turn sharp corners. To Charles Kingsley in 1848, those silent iron lines vanishing into infinity had 'an awful waiting look about them'. At unfrequented embankments and bridges on a branch of the Great Western Railway near Powick, my friend Simon and I would go a-trespassing in summer to enjoy the sense of peace and imminent doom.

The stagecoach, that sociable mode of transport which was such a boon to novelists, had introduced whole sections of the population to one another. A coach could carry no more than sixteen people whereas a train could absorb a crowd of one hundred and eighty. After Gladstone's Railway Act of 1844, all companies were obliged to run at least one third-class train a day, Sundays included. These cut-price trains, popularly known as 'parliamentaries', had seats and roofs and cost no more than a penny a mile. Osborne's railway guide recommended train travel to 'the student in human character': it would be hard to find 'more heterogeneous groups'.

Rail passengers were better behaved than stagecoach travellers who refreshed themselves at every tavern. Strict rules governed the handling of luggage. A station clock began to tick in the head of every citizen. Travellers were now the bumbling servants of a super-efficient service. They were expected to acquaint themselves with complex information-sharing processes: Bradshaw's railway timetables were a bamboozling innovation. The only Victorian character fluent in the runes of Bradshaw is Dr Watson. Charles Dickens never mastered the computations of connections and exceptions. In 'A Narrative of Extraordinary Suffering', he described the floundering of 'Mr Lost' in the topsy-turvy world of Bradshaw: 'It was his horrible fate to depart from Cirencester exactly an hour before he arrived there, and to leave Gloucester ten minutes before he got to it!'

By 1871, extreme competition had placed almost the entire population of mainland Britain less than ten miles from a railway station.

More than seven and a half thousand stations, halts and depots were owned by one hundred and thirteen separate railway companies. That year, within fourteen miles of central Oxford, where Charles Dodgson ('Lewis Carroll') was writing *Through the Looking-Glass*, there were twenty-two stations. To his first readers, Alice's disorientation was understandable and realistic:

> 'Now then! Show your ticket, child!' the Guard went on, looking angrily at Alice. And a great many voices all said together . . . 'Don't keep him waiting, child! Why, his time is worth a thousand pounds a minute!'
>
> 'I'm afraid I haven't got one,' Alice said in a frightened tone: 'there wasn't a ticket-office where I came from.' . . .
>
> 'So young a child', said the gentleman sitting opposite to her (he was dressed in white paper), 'ought to know which way she's going, even if she doesn't know her own name!'
>
> . . . And after that other voices went on . . . , 'She must go by post, as she's got a head on her [like a postage stamp]—' 'She must be sent as a message by the telegraph—' . . . and so on.

In railway Wonderland, reality was always ahead of the passengers. Beyond a certain limit, speed itself acquired strange, mind-defying properties. The *Treatise on the New Art of Transport* explained in 1850 that so many people stepped off speeding trains and were killed because of the preternatural smoothness of motion: 'A railway train moving at the rate of a fast stage-coach seems to go scarcely as fast as a person might walk.'

The first railway users invariably likened locomotives to birds because nothing else in common experience moved at such a speed. It was 'as if some huge steam night-bird had flung you on its back, and was sweeping through unknown space with you, most probably towards London'. To a person standing at the trackside, the sound was 'like the flapping of mighty wings'. Inside the covered carriage, there was the 'continuous burring noise' of metal on metal, the creak of carriages in front and behind, and 'the sudden startling clatter' when the train crossed a bridge or entered a tunnel. As top speeds increased – forty-five miles an hour in 1839, seventy in 1871 – the whooshing became the furious ticking of an overwound mechanism. The nonsense poet Edward Lear told an inquisitive Albanian prince in 1848 that while the sail-less ship went 'squish-squash, squish-squash, squish-squash, thump-bump', the horseless coach said 'tik-tok, tik-tok, tik-tok, tokka, tokka, tokka, tokka, tokka – tok'.

*

AT THE VANISHING point of the rails a black speck appeared. The Bristol-bound train from Paddington, pulled by a Fire Fly-class locomotive with its tall black chimney, shot across the new viaduct at Maidenhead on Brunel's Great Western Railway through a vortex of steam and rain. In a boat on the Thames two people looked on; on the track ahead a brown hare ran for its life.

This speed-distorted scene was painted by J. M. W. Turner in 1844 from an imaginary viewpoint. It is sometimes mistakenly described as 'nearly abstract'. According to Lady Simon (Jane O'Meara), who shared a carriage with Turner on the same line in 1843, *Rain, Steam and Speed* was 'perfectly and wonderfully true'. Though a rainstorm was beating down over the West Country, the artist had stuck his aged head out of the window somewhere near Bristol to register the 'chaos of elemental and artificial lights and noises'.

It took a rare kind of genius to portray reality in its accelerated state. In 'the eternal coal smoke' of London, where trains and barges went underground or passed high over busy streets, the teenage Arthur Rimbaud trained himself to describe these counter-intuitive landscapes with perfect objectivity. His prose poem, 'Métropolitain', was named after London's under- and over-ground railway – 'from the asphalt desert fleeing with the sheets of mist arrayed in fearsome ranks in the writhing, recoiling, descending sky . . .' This was the extreme edge of the avant-garde in 1872. It was also the natural idiom of an observant artist-journalist, Fred Jane, travelling on the Metropolitan Railway twenty years later:

> Off again [from Blackfriars to Mansion House], a fierce light now trailing out behind us from the open furnace door . . . revealing overhead a low creamy roof with black lines upon it that seemed to chase and follow us. . . . Then again we would seem to stop,

> and to fall down, down, down, with always the wild shrieking surge and ceaseless clatter of the iron wheels.

*

For the travelling public, a new age of accidental discovery had dawned. While reduced journey times contracted space, the geography of Britain unfolded its treasures. Because of intractable terrain, stubborn landowners or jealous turnpike and canal companies, railway surveyors often projected their lines through roadless swathes of lonely countryside, sometimes unwittingly retracing the route of a long-abandoned Roman or Iron Age road. Half an hour and a four-shilling ticket from city centres, unfamiliar domains opened up. As the trains of the Liverpool and Manchester Railway reached the five-mile section of floating track bed between Glazebury and Eccles, the passengers peered out at the quaking black-peat desolation of Chat Moss. They saw plough horses plodding over a spongy expanse with wooden pattens fastened to their hooves and a solitary crofter staring back at the cavalcade of city-dwellers from his crooked plank cabin.

Thousands of miles of quiet countryside traversed by railway lines were a stimulus for the criminal economy. In 1854, a parliamentary committee was warned that the mail train which served the Potteries from Whitmore was unguarded despite the fact that the North Staffordshire Moors were known to be 'very insecure'. Not far from several centres of industry, the heathy solitude of Cannock Chase, which travellers found 'an attractive sight', was the scene of 'mysterious robberies'. The crew of an overnight goods train

> systematically stopped opposite to the wildest part of the chase, rifled the most promising truck, and hid the spoils in a regular smuggler's cave that they had constructed.

On New Year's Day 1849, two masked men equipped with wool-stapler's hooks inched along the narrow ledge of a Great Western mail train as it raced through the Somerset Levels between Bridgwater and Bristol. Money letters amounting to two hundred thousand pounds were taken from the mail coach. This, the committee learned, was 'the greatest robbery that the Post-office has ever sustained'.

Another unsuspected wilderness, more remote in reality than it appeared on the map, was the Vale of Aylesbury between Leighton Buzzard and the Chiltern ridge. Sixteen miles from the centre of London, it is still possible to cycle on disused railway lines below the Chilterns and to meet more wild animals than human beings. Osborne's railway guide predicted in 1840 that the verdant vale would inspire passengers with 'feelings of delight and admiration'. Close to the point at which the guide expected those feelings to be 'crushed by the sight of one of those modern prisonlike workhouses', the Royal Mail train from Glasgow was stopped by an improvised red signal. This was on the night of Thursday 8 August 1963. The driver and his secondman were handcuffed, then the engine and front two coaches were detached and shunted half a mile down the track to Bridego Bridge, now better known as the bridge of the Great Train Robbers.

Fleeting scenes of desolation framed by carriage windows were not confined to rural parts. They could be viewed in districts which swarmed with humanity and from which every trace of nature had been wiped. In the bowels of industrial Manchester, the Manchester and Leeds railway cut through a zone of hideous squalor. Manchester had been designed, according to Friedrich Engels, so that a member of the 'money aristocracy' could commute to its centre every day from pleasant suburbs without ever glimpsing – unless he peered down a side street – 'the grime and misery that lie to right and left'.

One day, near Victoria Station, where the fetid stream of the river Irk vanished into brick caverns, Engels noticed that the new extension of the Leeds railway had obliterated a section of slums. As a result, some previously hidden courts and alleys had been exposed:

> Directly under the railway bridge stands a court which far surpasses all others in filth and horror. So secluded and inaccessible was this court that simply working out how to get there was an arduous task. I had thought I knew the whole area quite well, but I should never have discovered it myself without the holes punched through it by the railway viaduct.

25

Muddling Through

Chartist Meeting on Kennington Common.

In derelict oak woods near my house, in a sunless gorge known only to birds and animals light enough to skip over its floor of fathomless mud, a burn (or a beck) crashes through the ravine, snapping off branches and tumbling rocks over the cataracts. One day when the water was unusually low, I peered down through the leafy gloom and was shocked to see traces of human activity. In that place where no one ever lived, the bed of the stream resembled a section of paved street. Grasping bendy stems of hazel, I slithered down to investigate.

Flat stones of similar size had been arranged in neat rows. Undislodged by the torrent, they were held in place by iron girders which, in more populous parts of Cumbria, would have been prised up and carted off long ago by metal thieves. This incongruous cobbling continued for some distance around a double bend until, in the deepest shade where the burn passes under a field and a lane, I saw twenty feet above me the parapet of a colossal dark arch.

Etiolated branches had tried to penetrate the fortress but not a single brick was out of place. Weep holes on the abutments (for drainage and ventilation) looked like arrow slits in a castle wall. This monumental arch was the entrance to an elegant tunnel through which I was able to walk upright to the other end. Where a modern engineer would be content with a simple concrete drainage pipe, this trifling tributary of the Liddel, like thousands of other culverted watercourses all over the British Isles, had been honoured with two arches built to last for centuries and an unnecessarily long and extravagant avenue of nicely laid stones. Few people, and certainly none of the passengers travelling on the old Border Union Railway, ever saw this work of art.

Half a mile downstream of the culvert, the 1863 Ordnance Survey map shows a rectangular structure three hundred feet from our front door. No trace of it remains above or below ground. This was the temporary home of a Yorkshire railway superintendent, his Irish wife and a sixteen-year-old Scottish railway labourer listed in the 1861 census. The culvert and its cobbled approaches were built in 1860–61 by 'navvies' (originally the builders of 'navigation canals') working on 'the hardest of all the routes in the kingdom along which any train runs at express speed'. Houses were few and far between, as they still are today, and so most of the thousand or so navvies would have lived in accommodation too transient to be recorded by the census – a dry-stone room with a brushwood roof and a stone floor, a plank shack or a kind of turf igloo. According to an early historian of *The English Railway: Its Social Relations and Revelations*, there were also 'many women but few wives'.

This was the domestic British empire in the full flush of mature ambition, engaged in the self-destructive but mutually profitable enterprise of creating a national infrastructure. From the hills of northern England, then 'pouring in masses from every county in the empire' (wrote the historian), with nothing but basic tools and 'great animal strength', a horde of Huns and Vandals on good wages had come to serve 'the workshop of the world'.* These 'savages in the

* The expression 'workshop of the world' is credited to Benjamin Disraeli (warning the House of Commons in 1838 of 'social misery and

midst of civilisation' emptied the streets of respectable towns on pay day, desecrated beauty spots, 'vitiated' sons and 'dishonoured' daughters. 'Stones were thrown at passers-by; women were personally abused; and men were irritated.' Thousands of navvies died in rock falls and explosions, of disease and alcohol poisoning, and in pitched battles between English, Scots and Irish.

One of the men who worked here when the culvert was built was kicked to death in a fight at the local inn. This was just a few weeks after the national census was taken. The census listed only people with an address and so the murdered Scot called John Donnelly appears only in police and newspaper reports. While passenger deaths were deplored and publicized, the deaths of navvies were not separately recorded and collected. A plausible estimate is three fatal accidents for every mile of railway in the United Kingdom. In 1861, the cumulative number of deaths would have exceeded thirty thousand. Practically every tunnel, cutting, bridge and culvert in the British railway network is a memorial to the dead.

*

THE DUKE OF Wellington had come face to face with some of these rugged enablers of national prosperity at the opening of the Liverpool and Manchester Railway in 1830. At Manchester, he came under sustained bombardment from vegetables and verbal insults hurled by crowds of labourers and unemployed. Several thousand of the protestors sported the insignia of French revolutionaries.

The hero of Waterloo was reviled for his opposition to electoral reform. Not far from the station, at St Peter's Field, tens of thousands of men and women had demonstrated peacefully on 16 August 1819

---

political disaster' if agriculture were sacrificed to the needs of a few industrialized counties). However, it was probably first used in 1816, in an equally critical context, by Thomas Evans in *Christian Policy the Salvation of the Empire*, referring to the hogging of land by a plutocratic elite. In 1841, thirty-six per cent of the workforce was engaged in manufacturing industry, twenty-two per cent in agriculture (the lowest proportion in Europe) and thirty-three per cent in services (domestic, professional, public, military, etc.).

against the farcically antiquated system of representation which gave two parliamentary seats to the vacant ruins of a thirteenth-century town on an Iron Age hillfort (Old Sarum) but none at all to the ballooning populations of Manchester, Sheffield, Leeds and Birmingham, which had a combined population of nearly half a million.

Manchester magistrates had foolishly ordered the cavalry to charge the unarmed mass. Eleven or perhaps eighteen people (reports vary) had been killed at St Peter's Field and hundreds wounded, including a disproportionate number of women. 'Peterloo' was the name given to the massacre in pointed allusion to Wellington's fluky defeat of Napoleon at Waterloo in 1815 with the aid of the Prussian army and a European force of Scottish, Welsh, Irish, English, German and Dutch-Belgian soldiers.

In the days following the Peterloo Massacre, as more reliable information came in from the North, *The Times* candidly changed its initial opinion of the protests as the work of dangerous agitators. This was an example of that polite and pliable British 'fairness' and 'versatility' which surprised and sometimes exasperated foreign revolutionaries and promoters of class war:

> All such suspicions sink to nothing before the dreadful fact, that nearly a hundred of the King's unarmed subjects have been sabred by a body of cavalry in the streets of a town of which most of them were inhabitants, and in the presence of those Magistrates whose sworn duty it is to protect and preserve the life of the meanest Englishman.

French citizens have often congratulated me on belonging to a country which sailed with 'Anglo-Saxon' sangfroid and aplomb through the age of revolutions as smoothly as a butler delivering a tea tray. 'You decapitated your king', they would say, 'a century and a half before we got rid of ours.' While France was afflicted by government death squads, ideological maniac dandies and self-crowned emperor-adventurers, England got on with the respectable business of making money. I could have mentioned the fanatical anti-Catholic Gordon Riots in London (2–9 June 1780) in which soldiers shot dead nearly three hundred rioters who refused to disperse, but I knew that this was small beer compared to the long series of bloody coups d'état and the traditional mowing down of protestors by heavily armed police.

*

AFTER PETERLOO, THE next shining milestone on the long march of 'the masses' – a term which came into use in the 1830s – was the imprisonment and transportation to Australia in 1834 of six farm labourers from the Dorset village of Tolpuddle. They had asked in a civil fashion to be paid a living wage and were sacrificed to the Government's fear of 'combinations' (trade unions).

All British newspapers, whether Whig or Tory, expressed outrage at this heartless punishment. Thirty-five thousand protestors marched through London in orderly ranks by an agreed route from King's Cross to Whitehall. *The Times* reported that 'the utmost decorum prevailed': the workers were a 'striking' example of 'military array, discipline and good order'. The six Tolpuddle Martyrs eventually received a conditional pardon in 1836. Five of them later emigrated to Canada, disgusted by the hatred that continued to dog them as 'strife-makers' and 'criminals'. But that hatred was mostly local and petty and, in the case of the Church of England, provoked by the eloquence of the leading martyr, George Loveless, who was a Methodist lay preacher.

When there was violence, as in the machine-breaking riots in the south of England in 1830–31 and the 1839 Chartist uprising at Newport in South Wales, the rioters were met with violence and, usually, transported to Australia. Peaceful mass protest was generally tolerated. By the mysteriously efficient process which came to be known as 'muddling through', successive governments continued to equip the workshop of the world with safety valves and emergency brakes. Revolution's 'jour de gloire' would never dawn on the north side of the English Channel. To this very day, while French schoolchildren call for the furrows of the fatherland to be watered with the blood of tyrants and traitorous kings, the British ask God to allow the monarch to 'defend our laws' and 'reign over us' for as long as possible.

*

Two YEARS AFTER his full-steam retreat from Manchester, Wellington was defeated in the House of Commons by his own Tory party. The Great Reform Act of 1832 was exceedingly modest but it proved that the ship of state could change course – very slightly – without losing its rudder. The new Whig administration then set about reforming all those bungling local fiefdoms of which the Manchester magistracy was a glaring example. The Commission on Municipal Corporations did not mince its words. Out of two hundred and eighty-five town councils from Berwick-upon-Tweed to the Isle of Wight, only nine were deemed satisfactory. The rest were found to be self-electing petty oligarchies run by politically partisan, ignorant, senile or totally inert mayors, magistrates and other officials.

This was the fusty world in which the self-congratulating cranks, pedants, sadists and lazybones of the novels of Charles Dickens lived their pernicious lives. Many of his characters were black shadows of corrupt individuals mentioned in government and newspaper reports. They lived in the minds of readers who loved justice almost as much as laughter and who particularly enjoyed the humiliation of public officials.

The main working-class reform movement, Chartism,* ended in what seemed an amusing muddle before mutating into something vast and ungraspable, politically impotent but socially dynamic. As a political force, it fizzled out spectacularly at Kennington Common in London on 10 April 1848. The organizers told the public to expect a crowd of two million and a petition of five million signatures weighing a ton. The defence of the metropolis was directed by Wellington. The Foreign Office barricaded its ground-floor windows with bound volumes of *The Times*. Queen Victoria and her family were evacuated to the Isle of Wight.

Only twenty thousand Chartists turned up. A daguerreotype shows empty space between the platform and the oil of vitriol (sulphuric acid) factory. The crowd is almost exclusively male. Top hats are

* The People's Charter of 1839 made six demands: the vote for all men over twenty-one; annual parliamentary elections; secret ballots; no property qualifications for candidates; salaries for all MPs; constituencies roughly equal in population.

surprisingly prevalent. Few of the figures are blurred by movement. This is a crowd which has faith in the power of institutions to change.

Two hundred miles away, barricades were still being cleared from the streets of Paris after a victorious workers' revolution. In two weeks' time, a French Constituent Assembly would be elected by universal male suffrage. Two months after that, thousands of striking workers would be killed or transported to Algeria by the new revolutionary government.

Three 'crazy cabs' – the smallest and cheapest kind – were all it took to deliver the famous petition to Parliament. The governmental Committee on Public Petitions determined its weight to be less than one-third of a ton. It had been signed by nearly two million people, but the sheets had lain about in workshops, taverns, clubs, chapels and other places accessible to schoolboys and jokers. Consequently, like most big petitions of the time, it registered many different shades of opinion and mood.

A Chartist who had read the Committee's report was more accurate than he knew when he told a meeting in Merthyr that the petition was 'the voice of the sovereign people'. 'Victoria Rex [*sic*]' had signed it, as had the Duke of Wellington, Mr Punch and Cheeks the Marine (from Captain Marryat's sea stories). There were also many lesser-known individuals such as Pugnose, Flatnose, Wooden-legs and, inexplicably, No Cheese, as well as 'other signatures obviously belonging to no human being'.

After analysing a random sample, the member for Cirencester, Joseph Cripps, alerted the House to what he felt was the final proof of inadmissibility: 'that in every 100,000 names there were 8,200 women' who, as women, should not be counted. One of the most popular and militant leaders of the London Chartists was the son of a black slave from St Kitts. None of William Cuffay's fellow Chartists questioned his right to a vote. The movement included many female activists, orators and intellectuals – and, as a male supporter of truly universal suffrage observed in 1846, a great many stupid men – yet the enfranchisement of women had been omitted from the Charter in case it caused the less radical demands to be rejected. Feargus O'Connor, the Chartist member for Nottingham, believed that such a measure 'would lead to family dissensions'. More than that, it would have been a revolution to astonish the world.

26
Black Country

'China-Making at Stoke-on-Trent'.

All the people in the Kennington Common daguerreotype – the top-hatted, the flat-capped, the bonneted and the uniformed, all the 'classes', as they were now called – lived in a world that had only recently come into being. No other country had been so swiftly and comprehensively industrialized. None had ever so copiously soiled and disbeautified itself.

> Loud scream the Daughters of Albion beneath the
> Tongs & Hammer,
> Dolorous are their lamentations in the burning Forge.

As the work of a visionary in a world gone mad, William Blake's *Jerusalem: The Emanation of the Giant Albion* (1804–27) has undeniable objective weight. Literary scholarship tends to diagnose insanity when dealing with accurate descriptions of social and institutional derangement. James Thomson's long poem, *The City of Dreadful Night* (1870–73), is habitually analysed as the work of an alcoholic depressive though it deftly describes a common condition which recent studies of past and present societies have identified as Industrial Revolution post-traumatic stress.

> The street-lamps burn amid the baleful glooms . . .
> The air so thick it clotted in my throat;
> And thus for hours; then some enormous things
> Swooped past with savage cries and clanking wings . . .

These and other 'visions' are strikingly similar to plain prose observations of industrialized Britain. Millions of people saw widening fans of coal smoke stretch for twenty and thirty miles from the centres of cities. They were still there, with added chemicals, in the 1950s and 60s. Writing for the *About Britain* series of books published to celebrate the Festival of Britain exhibition in 1951, W. G. Hoskins recommended 'a whole day's exploration' in the Abberley Hills on the edge of the Midland Plain:

> From the heights of Abberley Common one would see . . . the dark cloud over Birmingham, extending for miles to the left over the towns of the Black Country, as if it were on another planet inhabited by prisoners or madmen.

After 1846, the whole area between Birmingham and Wolverhampton became known as the Black Country. At first, the name referred with grim humour to the benighted mill workers and miners, 'more barbarous' than the peoples of the *terrae nigrae* (Abyssinia and Sudan). Soon, 'Black Country' was generally taken to describe the great Midland bulge of slaggy waste through which the railways ran – the starless dark deepened by the red flares of pot banks and blast furnaces, the perpetual daytime twilight, the landscapes of 'cinder hills' with sparse slopes of sooty grass cropped by despondent ponies.

Surveyed from Dudley Castle, the Black Country 'unrolled before you like a smouldering carpet', according to J. B. Priestley in 1934. 'Black Country' was one of those rare regional names which exactly matched the appearance of the place. When the Robb family lived there in the early sixties, it was a giant scrapyard of offensively useless junk left behind by the previous occupants. Cooling towers, gasometers and chimneys, shop windows and advertisements for beer, cigarettes and cleaning products, children squatting on pavements and frolicking on demolition sites – everything was grimy. Looking out from the false security of the Ford Anglia, aged five, I found it frankly frightening.

The Black Country was where my father went to tame juvenile delinquents. They lived in places with names which seemed to have no sense beyond their ugliness – Bilston, Smethwick, Sedgley, Walsall, Gornal, Dudley. Perhaps it was the way my father pronounced them: 'Coseley' and 'Cradeley' sounded like a mockery of nursery comforts. It was in such places that children in books and comics were kidnapped or abandoned. As we drove into the black heart of Bilston under railway bridges weeping with rain, my father would suggest it was time to shake the glass jar in which I had concocted an apotropaic potion with mysterious liquids and powders taken from the larder. The key ingredient was cake colouring. Eventually I overfed the mixture and it turned into an impenetrable swirling fog with no magic power.

Middle-class train passengers and newspaper readers of the nineteenth century were fascinated by the thought that human beings lived in that vomitus of coal mines and factories. Everyone knew that the filth of the Earth's bowels was the source of Britain's wealth and there was a general feeling that something ought to be done to allay the suffering of the ant-like multitude and to prevent it from destroying its masters.

*

ONE SUMMER, I worked in a die-casting factory two bus rides from home on an industrial estate in north Worcester. It involved standing at a work bench from nine to five with an hour for lunch, holding in my ungloved hand a file with which I screechingly scraped the burrs off the tiny holes in aluminium pub tables fresh from the furnace. The job was unmechanized. No eye protection was provided. Each pub table had approximately seven hundred holes. At home, I ate, slept in front of the TV and went to bed. In the hours between shifts my brain filed tables. I lasted six weeks. Conditions were relatively good. My fellow filers, Dolly and Blossom, had worked in the factory for years and were quite sanguine about losing all sensation in their fingertips. It meant that they could no longer knit or sew. As a temporary worker, I was spared the initiation ritual which involved denudement and industrial grease. Though I worked at less than half the speed of Dolly and Blossom, I was never fined, thrashed or threatened with the sack, and I was never in serious danger of mutilation. This would once have been considered a cushy job.

'Getting used to it' was the key to a lifetime of drudgery. Upper- and middle-class people with their 'slaveys' (junior housemaids) had the daily spectacle of domestic servitude before their eyes. They now discovered, mostly by reading about it, that the labouring classes could 'get used to' the most appalling hardships. In the textile mills of Lancashire, Ulster and the Scottish Lowlands, the machines required auxiliary parts made of human muscle. Labour-saving devices greatly increased the amount of unrewarding, repetitive manual labour. Once conditioned to work regular hours, the more or less able-bodied population of an industrial town could be activated and synchronized by a factory 'buzzer' (a steam whistle) or a knocker-up tapping at windows with his long pole. The crescendo of clattering clogs would commence and then, for the next twelve or fourteen hours, the town would throb with the beating of hammers or the clank and rattle of looms.

While suffering wear and tear and irreparable damage, the human machines showed an amazing capacity for mental and physical adaptation. Thirty years ago, my sister lived in the small mill town of Hadfield near the border of Derbyshire and Greater Manchester. She saw women who had worked in the cloth mills 'talking' to each other in the near-silent 'mee-mawing' speech of mime and mouthing which had evolved when the deafening looms had made the mill-workers 'cloth-eared'.

As in the cotton industries of Uzbekistan and parts of Southern India today, children were found to be eminently enslavable. Some of their duties became quite famous. 'Mule scavengers' crawled under the spinning mules to rescue cotton fluff from the snickering spindles. 'Trappers' as young as five crouched in the endless night of mines for ten hours or more a day opening and closing ventilation doors for the slightly older 'hurriers' or 'thrusters' who pushed and pulled the coal up from the coal face.

Industrial horror stories of infants performing numbing tasks in cramped workshops were read as eagerly as the sensationalist 'penny dreadfuls' or 'penny bloods' which became popular in the 1830s. The account of an orphan boy 'farmed out' from the St Pancras workhouse to a cotton mill near Nottingham in 1799 was a bestseller. It was published in Manchester and then London in 1832, five years before the serialization of *Oliver Twist* and a year before the Royal Commission on Employment of Children in Factories. Robert Blincoe's lingering evocation of a pretty ten-year-old girl caught by the apron in a drawing frame appealed to a variety of tastes:

> He heard the bones of her arms, legs, thighs, &c. successively snap asunder . . . as the machinery whirled her round, and drew tighter and tighter her body within the works, her blood was scattered over the frame and streamed upon the floor . . . When she was extricated, every bone was found broken! . . . her clothes and mangled flesh were apparently inextricably mixed together . . . I shouted out aloud for them to stop the wheels! When I saw her blood thrown about like water from a twirled mop, I fainted.

The girl survived but 'was for ever rendered a cripple'.

Digests of parliamentary reports in the *Manchester Guardian* and most other newspapers revealed a ghettoized sub-society on the verge of moral collapse. Infanticide was common, bastardy the norm. Menstruation was irregular or delayed; at fifteen, boys still had squeaky voices. Babies were left with day nurses who offered discounts if the baby had been dosed with an opiate 'quietening mixture': Godfrey's Cordial, Mrs Winslow's Soothing Syrup and Atkinson's Royal Infant's Preservative were standard items in working-class as well as middle-class households. Doctors frequently recorded 'failure to thrive' as a cause of death.

The family itself was falling apart. Teenagers who earned more than their parents were becoming rude and selfish. Women, who were usually paid less than men, made up a majority of the manufacturing workforce: they had the skills and habits of endurance required by housework. Friedrich Engels saw the world turned upside down: a man from Leeds had found his old friend unemployed and living in a damp cellar in St Helens. He was darning his wife's socks! 'Is it possible to imagine anything further removed from sanity and common sense?'

*

THE MILL OWNERS who were questioned by the Royal Commission on Employment of Children in Factories in 1833 were wrestling with unfamiliar complexities. They were not in the business of making people suffer. Some shop-floor tyrants and practically all parents used the strap and other humiliations to maintain discipline; manufacturers preferred fines and dismissal. Many saw the employment of young children as a 'working system' of 'cruelty and degradation'. From the benevolent regimentation practised at New Lanark by the Welsh reformer Robert Owen, they knew that humane treatment could foster efficiency and that children who had been drilled in the rudiments of education made better factory workers.

Parliament debated the mill owners' equations of profit and morality. If manufacturers were made criminally responsible for accidents – which 'generally arise through carelessness' – the workers would be out of work. If hours were reduced – the new Factory Act (1834) set a limit of nine hours for children up to the age of thirteen – foreign companies would benefit and then Parliament would have to 'legislate for the whole world'. Moreover, as almost every mill owner discovered, the workforce had a mind of its own: 'Parents are so anxious for money that they push their children into the mill as soon as possible.'

The time lag between exposure of abuses and framing of legislation was often short by recent standards. The first laws were sketchily enforced, if at all, and applied only to certain industries. Factory inspectors owed their positions to parliamentary patrons, some of whom had factory-owning friends. Yet the laws were passed by Whig and Tory administrations, and senior civil servants became ever more inclined to appoint sub-inspectors who were competent rather than well connected.

The 1842 report on the employment of women and children in mines was a professionally conducted uncovering of 'barbarous and cruel slavery'. A condensed version was produced for general readers. It contained poignant testimonies from children as young as six, translated into standard English, and – for the first time in a government report – a gallery of unforgettable etchings showing misshapen creatures squirming through tunnels as tight as coffins. A bill was drafted and became law three months later.

The spirit of industrial legislation was more philanthropic than punitive, and although the causes of poverty remained obscure, it was not normally assumed that paupers were scroungers and cheats or simply too stupid to manage a budget. The Beerhouse Act of 1830 abolished duty on beer, ending the licensing monopoly of local magistrates and spawning twenty-four thousand beer shops in the first six months. The equally well-intentioned Truck Act of 1831 banned the practice of paying workers in overvalued goods and forcing them to buy expensive food at the company shop.

The Poor Law Amendment Act of 1834 was clumsy but not unkind. It obliged the poor, unless disabled by age or injury, to enter the parish workhouse in order to qualify for relief. The workhouse, invariably a grim and graceless structure, was to be 'a place of comparative comfort' but not so comfortable that it dissuaded the idle from seeking other employment. It was not supposed to be worse than the worst possible job, and although the separation of married couples could be a cruel imposition, for some women and children it was a godsend. A useful occupation, a regime of 'regularity and discipline' and a ban on spirits and tobacco were intended to provide a safe asylum and an alternative in many cases infinitely preferable to what would later be termed 'care in the community'.

The guiding principle was the centralization of power in national government. In France, after the crushing of popular revolts and the coup d'état of Louis-Napoléon Bonaparte in 1851, state control would be synonymous with surveillance and repression. In Britain, political exiles found a disorientingly polite and even pietistic faith in national institutions. Victor Hugo and his fellow exiled representatives 'wasted no time', as the French Vice-Consul was told by his spies, 'in taking advantage of the licence that English law affords the spoken and written word'. In the land of laissez-faire, where, as Hugo noted, even dogs were allowed to go about unmuzzled, tyranny took more humble and pervasive forms. In the Channel Islands, he felt the clammy pressure of a self-policing society:

> To the English, I am 'shoking', 'excentric' and 'improper'. I fail to wear my tie in the correct fashion. I have my hair cut by the local barber . . . which makes me look like a 'workman'. . . . To cap it all, I am a poet and, therefore, not very popular.

*

1851 WAS THE year in which the railway historian published his account of the rampaging horde of navvies (p. 223). A French reader would have found his remarks a peculiar melange of conservatism and socialism. The author, John Francis, contended that the volatile nomadic workforce should be brought into the bosom of society, educated and 'treated like men, not left to themselves, like beasts'. They should be provided with decent accommodation and encouraged to contribute to a health-insurance scheme. Capital should be used not just to create more capital but to remedy the ills it had caused.

The man who wrote this was not a radical reformer; he was an officer of the Bank of England and its official historian. His views are more typically Victorian than the 'Victorian values' of modern political discourse. Instead of calling for the 'savages' to feel 'the full force of the law', he insisted on the Government's moral and pragmatic duty to care for the physical and mental welfare of its citizens and servants.

It is easy in any age to find examples of cruelty dressed up as rectitude and common sense. Some later laws were framed in such a way that they served as tools of punishment. One government minister ordered that female prisoners should be shackled to iron bedsteads while they were in labour or giving birth. People who were housebound because of physical or mental incapacity were ordered by another minister to find work they could do at home or lose their entitlement to poor relief. Another policy was promoted by a Home Secretary in early winter when the weather was turning cold: homeless vagrants sleeping in the streets would be fined and have their shelters torn up and taken away. Anyone providing such shelter would also be subject to a fine. Yet another minister, a cherub-faced man who might have been auditioning for a role in a Dickens drama, learned that cheerful murals depicting funny faces had been painted on the walls of hostels which took in lone refugee children. The youngest refugees were nine years old. The minister ordered these murals to be painted over, which they very soon were, at a cost of £1,550.

The first of these acts of uncharity dates back to 1996, the others to 2023.

27

Classrooms

The school-room in The Old Curiosity Shop.

In the great muddled proliferation of educational establishments, schools founded by factory owners were among the best organized and the least effective since children who had worked a seven-hour shift were prone to fall asleep at their desks. Workhouse children fared somewhat better: the 1834 Act stipulated at least three hours of schooling a day. As a result, child paupers were often more literate than their peers.

Unlike France, Prussia and the United States, Britain had nothing that could realistically be called an education system. Schools were not lacking. On nineteenth-century maps, the word 'school' is attached to many thousands of small buildings: it crops up even in the most thinly populated regions. Here in Liddesdale, most schools were sited on high ground, convenient for farms and hamlets on either side of a watershed. One was endowed by the Church, another by the parish. The others were probably 'dame schools' run by a widow or a spinster who charged less than a shilling a week per pupil for day care and basic instruction.

A typical dame-school curriculum consisted of reading (parroting set phrases) and writing (copying out, always with the right hand). Instead of writing, girls practised knitting. Textbooks, where available, made the basics bafflingly exotic, especially for children who spoke only a local dialect or another British language. William Mavor's *The English Spelling-Book* was one of the most popular. It recreated English as a dead language, first with words of two letters – 'It is to be on. He is on my ox. Is it so or no?' – and then with three: 'Let the cat be put in a bag. I can eat an egg. The dog bit my toe.' The advanced texts in Mavor's manual were cautionary tales of greedy, mendacious, ungrateful, cowardly, lazy or ignorant children, and descriptions of common beasts of farm and field, plus the bear, the lion and the elephant.

> A horse knows his own stable, he dis-tin-guish-es his com-pa-ni-ons, and . . . is less useful when dead than some other animals are.

Hundreds of charity schools had been founded in the eighteenth century by the Anglican Society for Promoting Christian Knowledge and its Church of Scotland counterpart. After 1844, nearly all large towns also had a 'ragged school' for infant pariahs rejected by other institutions as uncontrollable or likely to spread disease. There were Sunday schools for all denominations and an astounding number of unpaid, untrained teachers. The 1851 census shows more than three hundred thousand of them in England and Wales. This was three per cent of the adult population. This enormous army of uninspected amateur teachers, which cost the government nothing, has been blamed for '[keeping] the teaching profession in its chronically depressed state throughout the nineteenth century'.

*

THE BEST-KNOWN TYPES of educational establishment are those that generated the intense romantic intimacies which served the needs of novelists and dramatists. No more than fifty thousand children were taught in their own homes by governesses and tutors and about the same number in 'public schools' (boarding) and endowed grammar schools (non-boarding). Together, these over-represented institutions account for less than five per cent of children in schooling.

For girls of 'good families', there were 'academies' or 'seminaries' which claimed to provide the kind of moral and intellectual dressage that would make a young lady ready for the marriage market. The seminary run by the 'excellent but rather venomous' Mrs Wackles and her three daughters in Dickens' *The Old Curiosity Shop* (1841) gives a fair idea of the female curriculum:

> English grammar, composition, geography, and the use of the dumb-bells [for physical education], by Miss Melissa Wackles; writing, arithmetic, dancing, music, and general fascination [making oneself interesting and attractive], by Miss Sophia Wackles; the art of needle-work, marking, and samplery, by Miss Jane Wackles; corporal punishment, fasting, and other tortures and terrors, by Mrs Wackles.

Along with these moderately serious and profoundly frivolous 'accomplishments', a superior establishment would also offer conversational French, taught, ideally, by a French-speaking governess advertising herself as Parisian and Protestant.

It is fortunate that relatively few boys were educated at the prestigious public schools.* Even after Dr Thomas Arnold of Rugby and other reforming headmasters, the public schools were notorious for rotting the moral fibre of the sons of the privileged and powerful. The teachers examined and punished but left instruction to older boys who were sent into the classrooms like corrupt sub-consular officials assigned to an underdeveloped province.

* In 1861, the nine establishments officially named 'public schools' (originally free grammar schools) were, in order of foundation, Winchester, Eton, St Paul's, Shrewsbury, Westminster, Merchant Taylors', Rugby, Harrow and Charterhouse. 'The Seven Great Public Schools' of 1868 (p. 246) were these, minus Merchant Taylors' and St Paul's.

This 'monitorial' system produced generations of prigs, bullies, sycophants, cowards, liars, cheats and rapists. Academic intelligence was not an asset. Some painfully timid 'gentlemen' emerged quivering from their years of scholastic misery saddled or, as some saw it, equipped with all the adult vices. Many looked back on 'the best years of their life' with undying hatred. As a day boy at Harrow, Anthony Trollope was constantly flogged. Having so often bared himself to the headmaster, he suspected that Dr Butler 'did not recognise me by my face'.

*

ALL TEACHERS, PARENTS and, after escaping into the outside world, most pupils agreed that regular corporal punishment was one of the fundaments of pedagogy. Samuel Johnson was not unusual in professing humble gratitude to the tireless flagellator who taught him Latin at Lichfield Grammar School: 'My master whipt me very well. Without that, Sir, I should have done nothing.' His biographer Boswell added that 'while Hunter was flogging his boys unmercifully, he used to say, "And this I do to save you from the gallows."' (He was alluding to a loophole in English law – closed in 1827 – which allowed a convicted man to escape execution by proving that he could read Latin, thus pleading 'the benefit of clergy'.)

Attitudes to children which now seem uncaring or cruel were governed by social and economic realities. While staying with African friends in Nairobi in 1986, we were shocked to see small children with tidy satchels on their way to school being roughly hauled off public buses, with general approval, to make room for adults on their way to work. This all seemed to be a matter of course, as it would have been in Victorian Britain. The lachrymosity of Victorian fiction with its winsome waifs and tortured angels struck J. B. Priestley as a paradox until it occurred to him that perhaps

> the Victorians liked to weep over their novels and plays, not because they were more sensitive and softer than we are but because they were much tougher and further removed from emotion, so that they needed good strong doses of pathos to move them at all.

Parliament's reluctance to intervene in education conformed to the general opinion that people should be left to make their own arrangements and spend their income as they saw fit. The first baby-step towards state education was the granting of twenty thousand pounds for school buildings in August 1833. Twenty thousand pounds was 0.04% of that year's government expenditure. In the same month, to win support for the Abolition Act, a sum of twenty million pounds was pledged to slave-owners as compensation for the loss of 'services'.

Even after it was decided that all children should receive an elementary education and that control should be exercised over the quality of teaching, the child was secondary to the system. The Revised Code of 1862 made grants of public money dependent on attendance figures and examination results: this was the 'payment by results' scheme, recently revived with all its original disadvantages. Its most significant short-term effect was the creation of an aggressive bureaucracy.

The Code was couched in punitive terms with finger-jabbing italics and sub-clausal hierarchies redolent of regimented office buildings. For each 'failure to satisfy the inspector' in one of the three Rs, the school would forfeit one-third of the grant paid for each pupil. An inspector in north-west England and north Wales reported a common 'inconvenience' of the Code: on the day of inspection, he would arrive in the classroom 'to hear paroxysms of whooping cough [and] observe the pustules of small-pox'. Sick children had been dragged out of bed and brought to school to prevent forfeiture of the grant.

The entire grant could be withheld if, for example, girls were not being taught 'plain needlework', or 'reduced by no less than one tenth' for 'untidiness in the children' or 'badly kept registers'. The registers 'must be stoutly bound and contain not less [*sic*] than 500 ruled pages'. In a later refinement, teachers were instructed that if the school caught fire, their first duty was to save the register. Only when the register was safe would the children be led into the playground by the approved exit.

To men and women who worked 'at the chalk face', this cheerless orgy of regulation looked ridiculous. School inspectors – notably Matthew Arnold, the poet and son of the Rugby headmaster – travelled thousands of miles like missionaries through a heathen land.

They saw village schools whose pupils were 'cowed and sullen, or wild, fierce and obstinate' and who had to be taught to 'sit without crouching like a sheepdog'. Inner-city schools contained 'sharp-witted, restless little creatures' who had seen more of life than anyone cared to know. A man in a Scottish Victorian spa town once informed me that 'teachers know nothing about the real world'. In some places, half a day of classroom teaching can still supply enough reality to last a lifetime. School was an education for everyone, including the parents.

*

In the edifice of British state education, we are still just a few doors down from the office which produced the 1870 Education Act. Ten years after the Act, elementary education from ages five to ten was made compulsory. Eleven years after that, fees in state schools were abolished. The 1902 Education Act allowed the new Local Education Authorities to provide training for teachers. When my parents started school in the late 1920s, the leaving age was fourteen. In 1969, when I entered the Worcester Royal Grammar School (WRGS), the statutory obligation to spend most of childhood and adolescence at a desk or on a playing field seemed to have existed for ever, like cars, cigarettes and football, yet it was only twenty-five years since secondary education had been made compulsory and free to all British children.

With its tripartite post-primary system of secondary modern, grammar and public schools, British education continued to mirror and magnify the class system. Success at the eleven-plus examination, which was known to disadvantage working-class children, separated my sister and me from three-quarters of the girls and boys we had played with at primary school. Some of the village children who passed the exam went to a secondary modern anyway because a sister or a brother was already there or because grammar schools 'aren't for the likes of us' and in either case because 'free' education at a grammar school was more expensive. A third of the WRGS *School Rules* (June 1967) was devoted to clothing: 'games' alone called for five different outfits. It was conceded, however, that some pupils might have to subsidize their own schooling:

> If a boy is to do justice to his School work and find time for reading and hobbies there is not really opportunity for him to undertake casual or part time employment. *The School asks parents to agree that their son will not be so employed during term time unless financial circumstances make it imperative. Boys engaged in any such employment must not wear school uniform.*

Ideally, the full-time pupil would live in a large house in which a room would be 'put at the boy's disposal where absolute quiet is enforced'.

Apart from the total absence of girls (only one-third of grammar schools were coeducational), my sub-section of the junior population was more socially representative than its pre-war equivalents. Of my three best friends at school, numbers 1 and 2 did not regularly go on summer holidays, 2 and 3 came from single-parent families, 1 was the child of immigrants, 1 and 3 were Catholic, 3 presented himself fallaciously but convincingly as a member of the distressed aristocracy. One of the fathers worked on a factory production line, one of the mothers ran a small corner shop. When the school 'went private' shortly after we left, we thought it a sad development. We would probably never have met, and most of our middle-class contemporaries who took up middle-class professions would have had an even narrower view of the society in which we all lived.

Two of our teachers appeared to 'have it in for' working-class children. A boy in my sixth-form class whose domestic duties included childcare and who was forced to 'undertake casual or part time employment' told me one day that he had been ordered to get his hair cut. Our comparative measurements showed his well-tended working-class locks to be a good inch-and-a-half shorter than my straggly middle-class mane. Those teachers might have espoused the views of the minister in Lord Palmerston's government who championed the 'payment by results' scheme in 1867, though they would have chosen slightly different words:

> The lower classes ought to be educated to discharge the duties cast upon them. They should also be educated that they may appreciate and defer to a higher cultivation when they meet it;

> and the higher classes ought to be educated in a very different manner, in order that they may exhibit to the lower classes that higher education to which, if it were shown to them, they would bow down and defer.

No plots were hatched in the WRGS staffroom to shackle the 'lower classes' with an inferior education, but there was a perceptible current of class-consciousness. The Sixth Form debating society rejected by a large majority the scandalous motion proposed by the German master, Mr Orton, that 'dustmen should be paid the same as civil servants'.

The eleven-plus examination had already set us apart from three-quarters of our contemporaries; the grammar school introduced a further discrimination of the intake by dividing us into four 'streams' based on presumed academic ability. After the second year, forms C and D would continue to practise woodwork, while forms A and B, having completed their teapot stands and bird houses, would pursue their studies in Latin. In this way, no pupil in C or D would be able apply to Oxford or Cambridge Universities, which, we were told, required O-levels in Latin and Mathematics for all degree courses. The assumption was that these pupils would leave school at the earliest opportunity.

*

As in Victorian times, most of the senior teachers at the grammar school held degrees from Oxford or Cambridge. They wore their graduation gowns in the classroom. With its time-worn furniture and decorous buildings, the school exuded a pungent air of tradition. Our hefty oak desks were engraved with ancient football results and the nicknames of forgotten teachers. These gnarled palimpsests were sometimes revarnished but never scoured: my own rutted desk-lid preserved a pallid pea from some prehistoric school dinner. Some of the older teachers were still known by their original nicknames. The German master was 'Spiv' because he had arrived at the school after the war in a demob suit. Why the Latin master was called 'Dinky', we had no idea. He looked old enough to have spoken Latin as his native tongue. The brittle brown pages of the *Basic Latin Vocabulary*, to which Mr Protheroe had contributed, testified to his antiquity.

The rituals of British grammar- and public-school education can strike Americans and Europeans as a strangely musty form of snobbish eccentricity. To us, grammar-school life had the convivial irony of humorous boarding-school tales. Even minor corporal punishment – a board rubber flung at the head of a chattering boy – was softened by tradition. It was all part of a self-conscious performance which foreign friends later identified for me as 'the famous British irony'. One of our most popular and effective teachers once spent an entire lesson ironically slippering every boy in the room. It had a pronounced cohesive effect on the class. The rule book itself had passages of dry levity. If a boy developed an infectious disease, the Headmaster was to be informed without delay, '*preferably by telephone*'. Parents were asked to 'co-operate by seeing that . . . their boy does not go out late in the evening, *particularly when he has no definite object in leaving the house*'.

Political and religious ideology had little to do with it. Since the Act of 1870, religion had been treated in an optimistic spirit of compromise. Where an Anglican, Nonconformist, Catholic or Jewish school already existed, it was allowed to continue with state funding, provided that the religious instruction was non-denominational. The calculated wishy-washiness of Anglican doctrine lent itself well to this 'dual system'. Only a handful of boys at the Royal Grammar School – two Muslims, one Hindu and one Jew – availed themselves of the right to miss morning assembly with its hymns and homilies. Most boys in the chaplain's RE class claimed to be non-believers, but they were obliged to attend assembly because the school did not believe in atheists.

The philosophical backbone of British education was almost invulnerably soft-centred and supple. The guiding principle was not the constituted form of government as it was in France and the United States but the seemingly self-evident truths of civility and social hierarchy. The pinnacle of the system had been established by the Public Schools Act of 1868, which placed the seven 'Great Public Schools' beyond the jurisdiction of elected bodies. These autonomous institutions became the models which lesser institutions would strive to imitate.

*

It was fitting that our self-fictionalizing world owed many of its distinctive features to a work of fiction. Thomas Hughes, a former pupil of Rugby, idolized its headmaster. In *Tom Brown's School Days* (1857), Dr Arnold's 'manly piety' was said to have turned the school into a nursery of God-fearing, academically able and occasionally blubberingly sentimental leaders of men and apostolic builders of empire.

In a spirit of competitive emulation, we were encouraged to believe that we were 'just as good as' or better than any public school, especially Eton, as though it cared. The *Short History* that was handed out to every boy began with this quotation: 'The Royal Grammar School of Worcester has an antiquity that makes pale the antiquity of Eton.' As the fifth oldest school in Europe, we beat Eton College by a good century and a half, or, admitting secondary evidence from the Hwiccan period, by seven hundred and fifty-five years. Institutionally, however, we were younger siblings of Eton, Harrow, Winchester and Rugby.

To them, we owed the division of the pupil body into opposing 'houses' and the weekly dressing up as Army, Navy and Air Force 'cadets'. Pacifists were called 'pioneers' and allowed to go and dig old people's gardens instead. It was also because of the Victorian public schools that we studied Latin. This was one of the accomplishments which the government minister of the 1860s thought would cause the lower orders to bow down and defer to us. It would be inaccurate to call this 'anachronistic'. Very recently, it was a view widely held in the general public and among his parliamentary colleagues and opponents that the Etonian prime minister's ability to spout Latin quotations was a mark of Mr Johnson's intelligence.

The most palpable public school import was the game invented at Rugby School in 1845. The scholarly Dr Arnold was not keen on sport. Rugby football involved not only fractures but also the brazen bullying which Arnold endeavoured to stamp out. According to Thomas Hughes, the only time the Doctor used physical violence was when a boy misconstrued 'triste lupus' in Virgil's third *Eclogue* as 'the sorrowful wolf'. As any boy should have known, 'triste lupus stabulis' means 'a sad thing for stables is the wolf'.

The necessity of contact sports in the moral development of the child was an obsession of the Doctor's adoring pupil. The author of *Tom Brown's School Days* was a sports enthusiast. He regretted the disappearance of the brutish game once played by Berkshire yokels under the shadow of White Horse Hill in his native village of Uffington. The winner was the one who first drew blood from an adversary's head by bashing him with an ash stick attached to a basket handle. The game was called 'back-sword'. During the Napoleonic Wars, it had been recommended as a plebeian form of fencing practice, 'though the fire of artillery now generally rules the battle'.

It was because of Hughes that we had to play rugby instead of association football (soccer), which was incorrectly presumed to be working class. My friends and I were passionate about football. We arrived early at school to play it in non-accordance with rule G.6: 'No ball games are to be played anywhere on the School premises.' At lunchtime, we played football at Worcester racecourse, sometimes against an improvised team of stable lads and apprentice jockeys.

Hughes's book was written in the immediate aftermath of the Crimean War (1853–6). He believed that the manliness and resolve of English youth required stiffening by frequent exposure to injury. *We* were playing in the age of thermonuclear weapons, when that sort of thing was a matter of personal choice. The country was not depending on us to win renown for 'the fleets and armies of England'.

It so happened that the 'Beak', A. G. K. Brown, who was a gentle and undemonstrative headmaster, had won silver and gold medals in the 400 and 4x400 metres at the Berlin Olympics in 1936. One of the boarders was Imran Khan, the cricketer and future prime minister of Pakistan. He was unhappy in the chilly boarding house but extremely popular for his astronomical cricket scores. Both Brown and Khan were champions; none of us were. Tradition had cast us in the role of bookish subversives. Our unauthorized alternative school magazine was gratifyingly banned. As 'Oxford material', we were supposed to bring honour to the school only after we left.

According to public-school tradition, all boys in the final year were sub-prefects with limited powers of punishment (copying out pages of the *School Rules*), whereas the athletically but not always intellectually proficient were full prefects with their own 'office'. Thomas Hughes might have approved of this adjustment of the hierarchy which favoured muscle over mind, though he would have shuddered at the pin-ups and ashtrays in the prefects' den and their back-slapping assertions of heterosexuality in the showers after rugby.

This historical adherence to upper-class traditions of 'manliness' entailed the banishment of all femininity from the school, apart from the school secretary and the boarding-house matron. The unscalable wall separating us from the independent girls' school next door was like an ethnic frontier. We only once saw its girls enter our hallowed halls: we fought them in a fencing contest and, by their skill and our bashfulness, they soundly thrashed us in foil, épée and sabre.

28
Playing Fields

The Crystal Palace destroyed by fire.

IT WAS ALL very well for Thomas Hughes to urge the 'stalwart sons' of England to ride onto the 'battlefield' of life with that 'silent endurance so dear to every Englishman' – preferably gibbering with cold on the roof of a stagecoach rather than cosseted 'in those fuzzy, dusty, padded first-class [railway] carriages'. This type of pseudo-stoicism was called 'muscular Christianity'. It ignored the obvious fact that even in schools like Rugby with pupils of 'good stock', the British breed displayed wide variations in size and mettle.

Army recruiting surgeons had discovered in 1845 that over a third of young male Britons were pigeon-chested, knock-kneed, flat-footed and unfit to fight. In January 2024, when the head of the shrinking British army warned that it would be necessary to reintroduce civilian conscription if the country went to war with Russia, the population had see-sawed to the opposite extreme. Two-thirds of adult Britons were now overweight. One newspaper headline paraphrased the chair of the National Obesity Forum: 'Obese Britain will be crushed by Mad Vlad's army in WW3.'

The creator of Tom Brown was captivated by the boundless gift the nation had given itself. In the endless wet dream of empire, he saw the swell of distant oceans and the never-setting sun. He imagined scenes of reminiscence over tea or a glass of port in the headmaster's study. His fellow Rugbeians would be thinking fondly of their alma mater 'in country curacies, London chambers, under the Indian sun, and in Australian towns and clearings'. Hughes recited to himself the classroom litany of English victories over foreign but not domestic foes – Crécy and Agincourt, battles fought 'with hand-grenade and sabre, and musket and bayonet, under Rodney and St. Vincent, Wolfe and Moore, Nelson and Wellington'.

Conscription was not introduced until January 1916, and so the weapon most public-school pupils would wield in adult life was the steel pen, just as ours would be the biro and eventually the mouse. Most would see action only on a playing field, locked in a heaving scrum or fleeing across the field, their thighs suddenly clamped by muscly arms, buttocks serving the adversary as shock-absorbers as they fell flat on their face in the mud.

*

How Britain came to acquire its miscellaneous empire of dominions, colonies, protectorates, former trading posts and other 'possessions' and 'dependencies' was never very clear. The Cambridge historian Sir John Seeley put it this way in his lastingly popular lectures on *The Expansion of England* (1883): 'We seem, as it were, to have conquered and peopled half the world in a fit of absence of mind.'

Several French observers attributed Britain's global dominance to the 'virile' education of the sporting upper classes. It was Count Montalembert, a liberal peer with a Scottish mother, who first claimed that the Duke of Wellington, on a nostalgic visit to Eton, had pointed to boys at cricket practice and said, 'Twas here that the battle of Waterloo was won.' It was an odd moment at which to praise the English upper classes, thirteen months after the catastrophic charge of the Light Brigade (1854) in the Crimean War where veterans of Waterloo tirelessly demonstrated the arrogant ineptitude of the British top brass.

Wellington's words are almost certainly apocryphal: he had no fond memories of Eton. By his own account, he was shy, idle and unpopular. His mother had removed him from Eton and sent him to the Royal Cavalry Academy at Angers in 1786 shortly after the young Corsican Napoleone Buonaparte, born the same year as Wellington, graduated from the military academy at Brienne.

To Matthew Arnold and many other intellectuals, the 'playing fields of Eton' remark was typical of upper-class self-delusion:

> Disasters have been prepared in those playing-fields as well as victories; disasters due to inadequate mental training – to want of application, knowledge, intelligence, lucidity.

Waterloo had been won by the rank and file, the sons of yeomen and peasants who played 'very clumsy cricket' on the village green (G. K. Chesterton), not by the 'ignorant, pretentious and blundering' private schools (H. G. Wells). In the 1920s, the Old Etonian Eric Blair (George Orwell) found that his education in 'snobbery' helped him in the Imperial Police Force in Burma. He remembered the faces of 'subordinates I had bullied and aged peasants I had snubbed, of servants and coolies I had hit with my fist in moments of rage'. It also helped him with his later qualms of conscience: 'Nearly everyone does these things in the East, at any rate occasionally: Orientals can be very provoking.'

Just as the British Empire was not a monolithic whole, British attitudes were various and fluctuating. They were rarely what came to be known as jingoistic until the end of the nineteenth century. To many Victorians, the Empire was an epic tale of stirring failures and embarrassing victories. There were widespread doubts about the ability of Britons to manage such a monster. The American colonies had been lost, in Seeley's words, through 'languid incompetence'. Eighty years after the Declaration of Independence, the savagely repressed Indian Mutiny (1857–9), which induced the Government to take control of the East India Company gravy train, brought home the notion that the sub-continent inhabited by millions of people of 'alien race and religion' had never really been 'conquered' by the island kingdom which lay five thousand miles and six months to the west. 'Natural superiority' was a tasteless fantasy. Only one-fifth of the two hundred and eighty thousand troops in India were British.

The modern political notion of the Empire as a source of nationalist pride can be dated from 24 June 1872. In the Crystal Palace which had housed the Great Exhibition of 1851 (it was moved from Hyde Park to Sydenham in 1854), Benjamin Disraeli, leader of the Conservative Opposition, made a speech in which he sought to weaponize what he took to be the imperialist fervour of the common voter. The nation could either continue to fritter away its colonial possessions and be 'a comfortable England' closely tied to its European neighbours, or it could be

> a great country – an imperial country – a country where your sons, when they rise, rise to paramount positions, and obtain not merely the esteem of their countrymen, but command the respect of the world.

Disraeli saw Queen Victoria as the fairy on his imperial cake. In 1876, he had her officially titled 'Empress of India'. The Liberals under Gladstone considered this title un-English and despotic: it smacked of French and German imperialism. Victoria herself did not have to be persuaded. In her mind, she already was the Empress of India. Three days before Disraeli's speech, she noted in her journal:

> Then [I] saw the Duke of Argyll, who said there was a hitch about the Burmese Envoys, who did not want to prostrate themselves in their customary fashion when appearing before sovereigns. As Empress of India I must insist on this, otherwise I could not receive them.

*

THE COMMON VOTER Disraeli hoped to woo with flag-waving imperialism was elusive. Some, like Charles Dickens, saw the Empire as a training or dumping ground for unpromising progeny who might otherwise have been consigned to an office, a vicarage or a shop. Taxpayers worried about the drain on public finances and the seemingly fruitless responsibilities and perils. Some were simply indifferent or unable to grasp the enormities of distance and ambition.

Readers who followed the great adventure in newspapers were confronted with horrors, committed or suffered, which offended a Christian sense of decency: the seizure of Hong Kong (1842) and the cynical promotion of opium addiction to pay for Chinese tea imports; the defeat of the British army by Zulus at Isandlwana (January 1879), the massacre of the British mission in Kabul by Afghan troops (September 1879), the occupation of Egypt and the humiliating slaughter of the garrison at Khartoum by the Islamic Mahdist 'dervishes' (1885). The rhymes of Tennyson's 'The Charge of the Light Brigade' still hammered away in British heads – 'thundered', 'wondered', 'sundered', 'blundered'. There was also that dainty sense of inadequacy, the feeling that there could never be enough Britons to bestride the globe. 'The smallness of our numbers' had been one of the concerns of the 1870 Education Act:

> If we are to hold our position among men of our own race or among the nations of the world we must make up the smallness of our numbers by increasing the intellectual force of the individual.

After the electoral reforms of 1867 and 1884, about three-fifths of the male population were eligible to vote, but members of Parliament were still unpaid and thus, almost to a man, wealthy and upper or upper-middle class. Governments seemed to steer the ship of state through storms and dangerous waters, heedless of the passengers' desire for cosy comforts. 'And therefore', wrote Seeley, assessing the mental state of the nation in 1883,

> . . . public opinion does not know what to make of [our Indian Empire], but looks with blank indignation and despair upon a Government which seems utterly un-English, which is bureaucratic and in the hands of a ruling race, which rests mainly on military force, which raises its revenue, not in the European

> fashion, but by monopolies of salt and opium, and by taking the place of a universal landlord, and in a hundred other ways departs from the traditions of England.

*

EIGHTY YEARS AFTER the fall of Khartoum, my knowledge of the British Empire came from my stamp collection, some household mementos of great-aunts and uncles – Canadian ashtrays and an Indian table and ivory elephant – and the 'pink bits' on the globe (p. 32). The wooden Scout hut in a Worcester suburb was decorated with Ashanti masks, Zulu shields and stuffed animal heads. Our Boy Scout games referred to Zulu warriors, Red Indians, Robin Hood and the British bulldog. I earned my 'Housekeeping' badge by making up a bed with hospital corners, brewing a pot of PG Tips tea and preparing a plate of kedgeree – the fish, egg and rice dish adapted to British palates by the East India Company.

Given the fact that he had at his disposal the Foreign Office, the diplomatic service and a private secretary, I feel that, on balance, I was no more ignorant of the British Empire than Prime Minister Tony Blair when he attended the ceremony at which Hong Kong was handed back to China in 1997:

> Jiang Zemin [the President of China] explained to me that this was a new start in UK/China relations and from now on, the past could be put behind us. I had, at that time, only a fairly dim and sketchy understanding of what that past was. I thought it was all just politeness in any case. But actually, he meant it.

The Boy Scout movement was a happy result of the Great Boer War (1899–1902), fought against the South African republics of Dutch colonists and their descendants. The movement's founder, Lieutenant-General Baden-Powell, briskly recounted the war in his *Scouting for Boys* (1908): 'In South Africa we had to drive out the Dutch and then fight the natives for our foothold . . . and though it has cost us thousands of lives and millions of money we have got it now.'

The ambition of this child-friendly war hero was the regeneration of the now majority-urban population of street-corner hooligans and 'hysterical' football crowds, those cigarette-smoking cowards and 'wasters'. This was the nation once known for its 'stolid, pipe-sucking manhood, unmoved by panic or excitement, and reliable in the tightest of places'. A citizen worth his salt should know how to lay a fire, tie a knot in the dark, find his way through a strange town, memorize the contents of a shop window in a minute, seek out and rescue drowning women, recognize criminals by their boots and hunt down animals ('a better game than stamp collecting'). 'Scoutcraft' was not just honest fun but a matter of national self-preservation. The average man of the modern metropolis 'is no more good when war breaks out than an old woman, and merely gets killed like a squealing rabbit'.

Baden-Powell was not a warmongering chauvinist. He wanted all nations and races to learn discipline and practical skills from the American Indians, the people of the Himalayas, the Samurai, the Ashanti, Sherlock Holmes and even the French and Germans. He hoped that Britain would help to abolish 'the existing brutal anachronism of war' and the spectacle of 'extreme poverty and misery shivering alongside of superabundant wealth'. He urged girls to take as their models Florence Nightingale, Lady Lugard (who coined the name 'Nigeria'), the explorer Mary Kingsley 'and many devoted lady missionaries and nurses'. Several girls unexpectedly attended the first Scout rally at the Crystal Palace in 1909, which led to overheated correspondence in *The Spectator*. Girl Scouts were reported to be roaming the country carrying long poles and returning home 'in a state of very undesirable excitement'.

*

THE BRITISH PUBLIC first heard of Baden-Powell as the officer who held out against the Boers from October 1899 to May 1900 in the besieged town of Mafeking on the borders of the Transvaal. Surrounded by open veldt, Mafeking contained a thousand white men, six hundred white women and children and – a detail missing from many accounts – seven thousand of the Barolong people. In the Boer bombardments, the British lost two hundred and twelve, the Barolong four hundred.

Newspapers seized on this uncomplicated tale of heroic endurance as an antidote to readers' confusion and 'war fatigue'. The heroes of Mafeking represented the 'British' values and virtues of fairness and unflappability which only the British human race was thought to possess. With his dummy minefield, his illusory barbed wire and various vital pieces of equipment made out of biscuit tins, Baden-Powell was the hero of a boy's adventure tale complete with a stiff upper lip and a wealth of cricketing metaphors: '200 not out', he reported on 29 April, 'and they have tried every bowler but don't seem to get us out'. *The Times* adjusted its prose accordingly: 'No man in our day has done so much with such slender means. None has shown a more unquenchable cheerfulness in the presence of crushing dangers.'

This was the style of the New Journalism, brilliantly exploited by the recently launched *Daily Mail*. Here in 1900 is one of the first clear sightings of the text-driven age in which we live. Rapidly gathered information was delivered to the public in the form of vivid prose, photogravures, advertisements and merchandise. From now on, important events would arrive with their dramatic potential extracted and displayed. Rationalists like Professor Seeley, who was familiar with the muddle of real events, would look unpatriotic by comparison.

The *Daily Mail* seemed to have a crystal ball wired up to the electric telegraph and the undersea cable. Before the siege had been lifted by Canadian troops, the paper was already setting out the chairs and tables for 'Mafeking Night'. Headlines such as 'Waiting for News' and 'Still in Suspense' kept readers on tenterhooks while telling them exactly 'How the Relief of Mafeking Will Be Celebrated'.

> In every town and village a mass meeting of inhabitants ought to be held simultaneously at seven o'clock in the evening for the purpose of singing the National Anthem.

There would be – 'make no mistake' – spontaneous 'shaking of hands, and laughing shouts of "Good old Baden-Powell", and fireworks'. At Stone in Buckinghamshire, Baden-Powell's faithful dog, Bob, would make an appearance in a torchlight procession. The correct type of firework should be obtained from Messrs Pain and Sons of Walworth, as advertised within:

RELIEF OF MAFEKING.
PATRIOTIC REJOICINGS.
PAIN'S FIREWORKS SUITABLE FOR THE OCCASION.
Empire Rockets. Red, white, and blue. Empire Instantaneous Illumination Fires. Red, white, and blue. . . . Port Fires for Lighting, complete in case, £5 5s., carriage paid. Specially manufactured for Patriotic Rejoicings; order early; there is a great demand.

The celebrations of 18–19 May 1900 were a tremendous victory for the halfpenny press. Circulation figures were stupendous. This media-inspired event is still used in its original wrapping to illustrate 'public feeling'. Scepticism, indifference, sympathy for the Boers – all shades of opinion were momentarily blown to kingdom come by the bells, bands, mass singing, factory buzzers and fireworks. It was, inevitably, 'a very temporary spasm of jingoism'. The briefest inspection of the Mafeking toy box shows how the wonders worked. There are hundreds of pictures but no unretouched photographs of the night itself. The euphoria lasted just long enough to ensure a Conservative victory in the 'khaki election' that September. Then the fireworks fizzled out and jubilation gave way to equally traditional British queasiness at the horrors of war.

Reuter's news agency telegraphed details of the 'scorched earth' policy used against the Boers. The British army was no longer the 'gallant little garrison' of underdogs but the efficient military machine run by the imperialist Goliath, General Kitchener. The farms which generations of Boers had scratched out of the veldt and taken from the natives were burned down. Wells were poisoned and animals destroyed. In the stinking, understaffed British concentration camps, nearly twenty-eight thousand died of starvation and disease. Four thousand were women, twenty-two thousand were children, black as well as white.

A Cornish peace activist, Emily Hobhouse, compiled an illustrated report on the British 'war against women and children'. Her findings were confirmed in 1901 by an all-woman Commission appointed by the British Colonial Office. The *Daily Mail* discarded its mask of jubilation. Both Emily Hobhouse and 'the pro-Boer press' were ignorant and biased; they were helping the enemy to spread its propaganda.

It quoted General Sherman, the annihilator of Atlanta: 'War is war and not popularity seeking'; 'to the civil population of Atlanta . . . he replied that they "might as well appeal against the thunderstorm".' The vilification of Hobhouse inspired some 'patriots' to issue death threats to journalists of the *Manchester Guardian*.

*

THE GLOVED FIST and accusatory index finger of General Kitchener pointing at 'YOU' appeared on posters pasted up on every street corner as soon as war was declared on Tuesday 4 August 1914. By January 1915, more than one million had volunteered to serve. Press photographers set up tripods and ladders outside army recruiting offices and took razor-sharp shots of men massing in the street, hemmed in by police horses. These new 'instantaneous' photographs would stiffen resolve and shame the shirkers. High-speed shutters could immobilize a split second and enable an editor to walk among the frozen figures and imbue them with meanings which time would have washed away.

The photographs most often reproduced today show cheerful men in the uniform of their social class – in order of prevalence: flat caps, boaters, bowler hats and trilbies. None of the heads are bare; smokers are holding fire. They look like public opinion made flesh. In the eyes of the future, all these men are innocent, as they are in Philip Larkin's photograph-inspired poem, 'MCMXIV': 'Never such innocence again . . .' Having seen the later photographs and the footage of the Somme offensive, we can easily picture those grinning jaws on fleshless heads.

With so many volunteers setting their affairs in order before sailing for France, the photographers had plenty of recent wedding practice. They had sure-fire jokes at the ready, guaranteed to raise a smile. Facial-recognition software could probably identify each joke from the gestures and expressions: 'Does the missus know you're off to France? . . .' In one guffawing throng outside Walworth Town Hall in South London, a lone woman on the edge of the crowd seems to find the pleasantry only mildly amusing.

The best-known scenes of cheering men outside recruiting offices are not typical. Almost every British citizen supported the cause, but unanimity was based on individual decisions rather than mass emotions. Most of the photographs show the flickering moods of people living in that most elusive time zone of historiography, the present moment. They look distracted or disgruntled, bullish or doubtful, resolute or giggly, happy to be out of the office or shop, wary of the man standing just behind them. About one in ten seems to be enjoying the bank holiday. Some look sly or rakish: perhaps the girlfriend they are leaving behind has got herself 'in the family way' . . . Many have been stirred by news of the torture and murder of Belgian civilians or shamed by a procession of girls holding banners marked 'My Dad's at the front. Where is yours?'

Poignant delusion is what we are now invited to see in the smiling faces. 'It will be over by Christmas' is supposed to have been the thought in every mind. There is no contemporary evidence for this. Even when prompted by later interviewers, veterans would fail to recall a mood of optimism. Dread and defiance were the dominant emotions. The face of Kitchener on the ubiquitous posters was a reminder of the back-and-forth years of the Boer War. Everyone knew that the war in Europe was likely to be bloody and protracted. *The Times* had confidently announced the beginning of 'the great catastrophe' on 3 August: 'The losses in human life and in the accumulated wealth of generations . . . are frightful to think on.' Within a few weeks of the first battles (Mons and the Marne), local newspapers were publishing soldiers' letters home from 'Hell on Earth': 'It is nothing but killing your fellow man.' Compared to this, the Boer War was 'a picnic'.

From one end of Britain to the other there was an 'absence of gaiety' (noted by the *Cornish Guardian*). On Sauchiehall Street in Glasgow, 'people of all ages were walking rather aimlessly about and talking without reserve to those who would talk to them'. Women wept and prayed. In London, the *Hampstead Record* reported not 'the slightest sign of "Mafficking"'.

Baden-Powell the hero of Mafeking issued 'an appeal to village lads' in his capacity as Chief Scout. It was printed in newspapers all over Britain and the Empire:

> Boys of Britain! Don't go about waving flags because there is war. Any ass can do that. . . . Come and do something for your country. She needs your help.

A fleet of fifty bicycles stood ready outside 116 Victoria Street in Westminster. The corridors and offices of Boy Scout headquarters were swarming with Scouts waiting to be despatched with urgent messages. A thousand Scouts proficient in semaphore headed for Suffolk and the east coast to watch for strange ships and signals. By 12 August, three thousand boys were guarding railway junctions and defending telegraph and telephone wires from foreign saboteurs. Letters poured in from Scout troops requesting permission to sail to Calais or Dieppe to help with the French harvest.

When naval bombardments of eastern sea ports began in November 1914 – soon to be followed by airship raids on Norfolk and Humberside – Boy Scouts volunteered as stretcher-bearers. Some went to Red Cross depots and acted as wounded soldiers to provide nurses with battlefield practice. Knowledge of first aid and the art of keeping calm in a crisis were still Boy Scout priorities fifty-seven years later. On a Scout weekend at the youth hostel in Malvern, I was covered with frighteningly realistic plastic wounds and told to lie still at the foot of a stone staircase. One quick-witted boy known as 'Squirrel' ran off at once to find a telephone. Ten minutes later, an ambulance arrived. A sensitive young Scout had to be comforted. No one can tell how a particular individual will behave in an emergency. A bar-room bully turns out to be a quivering jelly; a milksop has nerves of steel.

Some Scouts were old enough to enlist before the end of the war. The lower age limit in 1916 was eighteen but a determined boy could usually find a way. One sixteen-year-old ex-Scout behaved heroically at the Battle of Jutland; many others died in indistinguishable carnage. The Chief Scout's advice was to 'be a man' and 'play the game':

> Your forefathers worked hard, fought hard, and died hard, to make this Empire for you. Don't let them look down from heaven, and see you loafing about with hands in your pockets, doing nothing to keep it up.

Baden-Powell was thinking of Henry Newbolt's imperialist poem of 1892 in which a hard-fought game on the school cricket field becomes a valiant last stand in the Sudanese desert.

A bumping pitch and a blinding light,
An hour to play and the last man in.
. . .
The Gatling's jammed and the Colonel dead,
And the regiment blind with dust and smoke.
. . .
Play up! play up! and play the game!

When the first official film of trench warfare brought the spectacle of mass slaughter at the Battle of the Somme to more than twenty million cinema-goers in 1916, the Victorian Age had retreated into a foggy past. The Queen herself had died in 1901. The silent *Battle of the Somme* – seventy-four minutes, with captions – showed Welsh, Scottish, English and Canadian soldiers scrambling over trench parapets and stumbling into the mud. The camera lingered over the gigantic shells and howitzers, the busy stretcher-bearers, the 'nerve-shattered German prisoners', 'Tommies offering cigarettes' to the enemy, the craters and the corpses, heaps of dead men and horses, 'the Manchesters' pet dog' who 'fell with his master'.

Henry Newbolt watched the film and, as a contributor to the War Propaganda Bureau, wrote a poem for the leader page of *The Times*. His old-fashioned verse with its Victorian dying falls spoke with the voice of a well-dressed corpse in a deep grave. His poem was somewhat challenging and self-contradictory. It plodded like a shell-shocked casualty who seemed not to know what he was saying.

O living pictures of the dead,
  O songs without a sound,
O fellowship whose phantom tread
  Hallows a phantom ground—
How in a gleam have these revealed
  The faith we had not found.

29

Semi-Detached

Violet Carson as Ena Sharples in Coronation Street.

IN LETTERS HOME from the war, and especially in novels and poems, the middle- and upper-class England which hovered over the trenches like an unconvincing hallucination smelling of ether, cordite and new-mown hay tended to evoke the wold or fen country within easy cycling distance of Oxford or Cambridge where flower meadows swayed and slow chalk streams whispered of long afternoons and beloved paintings – the Lark, Stour and Cam, the Cherwell, Evenlode and Windrush.

Approaching the Roman Fosse Way and the more ancient border of Gloucestershire and Worcestershire in late summer, we ran into pockets of heavily armed resistance. The traffic had become impatient of vulnerable road users. In the miniature tourist Mecca of Stow on the Wold, tank-sized vehicles were circling and reversing. 'The capital of the Cotswolds' was occupied by an army of steel-panelled conveyances so numerous and enormous that only the upper storeys of the honey-coloured houses could be photographed.

Three miles on the other side of Stow, we dismounted on the grassy pavement of a narrow bridge over the Evenlode and the railway line to look down on a station which no longer exists. Wing mirrors whizzed past an inch from our ears. A metal plaque fixed to the parapet indicated the likelihood of collision, in which event, 'please phone the Rail Authority as quickly as possible: the safety of trains may be affected'.

Down a curving lane in the nearby hamlet we found that rarest of travellers' conveniences: a clean bench sheltered by an open shed. I was sorry not to have discovered it long before. The hamlet lies just beyond the outer limit of our Sunday morning bike rides out of Oxford. We used to pedal off in darkness or early light so as to be home before the opening of DIY stores and the churchgoers' rush hour. The back wall of the shed was covered with an incongruously large-lettered sign in the brown-and-cream livery of the Great Western Railway. It was removed from the platform when the station was closed in 1966 and is now its only vestige.

ADLESTROP

Yes. I remember Adlestrop –
The name, because one afternoon
Of heat the express-train drew up there
Unwontedly. It was late June.

The steam hissed. Someone cleared his throat.
No one left and no one came
On the bare platform. What I saw
Was Adlestrop – only the name

And willows, willow-herb, and grass,
And meadowsweet, and haycocks dry,
No whit less still and lonely fair
Than the high cloudlets in the sky.

And for that minute a blackbird sang
Close by, and round him, mistier,
Farther and farther, all the birds
Of Oxfordshire and Gloucestershire.

Edward Thomas, who had only recently started to write poetry, had left London that morning on the 10.20 from Paddington. The poem suggests a lone passenger but he was travelling with his wife. They were to arrive at Great Malvern at 2.45. This was on 24 June 1914 – 'a glorious day', he noted in his journal: 'tiers above tiers of white cloud with dirtiest grey bars above the sea of slate and dull brick by Battersea Park'. In that morning's *Times*, the weather forecast warned of 'rain later, thunder locally'. On page seven, there was an account of the Anglo-German naval review at Kiel where the Germans had unveiled their new Dreadnought battleships, and Kaiser Wilhelm, as a grandson of Queen Victoria, had boarded a British warship in a British admiral's uniform. Both sides officially looked forward to a return match the following year. Four days later, before the review had ended, Archduke Franz Ferdinand was assassinated at Sarajevo.

*

THE 'EXPRESS-TRAIN' FROM Paddington was actually a stopping train: the 'unwonted' halt at Adlestrop is shown on the timetable. In the scheduled minute, the engine hissed and the blackbird sang. Adlestrop was the eighth station after Oxford. Three stations up the line, in fields outside Campden near the edge of the Cotswold escarpment, Thomas saw the willowherb and meadowsweet and heard someone clear his throat. War was declared six weeks later. The poem was written five months after the declaration, in January 1915. On Easter Monday 1917, at the close of the Battle of Arras, Second Lieutenant Edward Thomas, aged thirty-nine, stood up and was about to light his pipe when a shell exploded.

The pre-war pastoral 'Adlestrop' became a 'war poem' because it contained its own future. The memories of a train journey, tidied up and brought into line, fitted into sixty seconds (which is also the time it takes to recite the poem) and attached to a waiting steam engine, created an illusion of short-lived timelessness. Poetry, said Baudelaire, is 'that which is entirely true only in another world'. The name itself is an accidental creation. 'Tatlestrop' or 'Tatel's farmstead (a Mercian name) had morphed into the more mellifluous 'Attlesthorpe' in the early 1300s. Five centuries later, when Jane Austen visited her uncle and cousins in the manor house, the name had become 'Adlestrop'.

The place in which Edward Thomas never set foot embodied that solid but ever-changing England which, in small and relatively undisturbed areas, can comfortably accommodate all the upheavals of its history – the rebuildings of the early Norman church, the enclosure of the fields, the laying out of the manorial park and then the Great War. In the graveyard a modest monument was erected by a stonemason and his wife to commemorate their two 'dear boys', both killed in 1917.

As we sat on the bench, I recorded the sounds that rose above the slur of traffic on the A-road: the hoo-hooing of a wood pigeon, the chatter of a blackbird and the clip-clop of a horse which seemed to draw near but never appeared. Our way to Oxford lay between the manor and the graveyard, through a hidden gate and beside a nameless tributary of the Evenlode which forms the boundary of a cricket field. Within sight of the Oxfordshire border, I recorded the sounds again. Here, the resident blackbird's song was slightly different. The 'mistiness' of that choir of all the birds of two shires covered a land of many thousands of separate territories, each about the size of a suburban house and garden.

*

'TEMPORARY GENTLEMEN' WAS the term applied to the lower-middle-class men who were brought in to supplement the 'officers and gentlemen' of the regular army. Army manuals explained to the new soldiers how a gentleman officer should behave: 'When in officer's uniform you must travel 1st class.' 'Never address a Captain by his military rank alone – it is only tradesmen who do that.' Those 'ghastly little men', hen-pecked and unheroic, who lived contentedly in their horrid little houses, had been sneered at for several decades by 'toffs' and newspapers aimed at middle- and upper-middle-class readers. With a war to fight, the temporary gentlemen fitted in quite smoothly, were proud of their humble origins and were generally treated as equals.

The official hope was that after the war these 'TGs' would return to their former occupations, refuse to join a trade union and continue to defer to their upper-class managers. In 1918, the degentrified officers found the old country in a muddle. Clerical and mechanical jobs, especially in munitions, had been 'devalued'. More than a million women had been performing the same tasks at least as efficiently and not always on lower pay. There was a perception in Government that men in certain skilled occupations had always exaggerated their indispensability. A senior official in the Labour Department wrote in July 1918:

> It is conclusively proved that the vaunted skill of the mechanic can be much more easily acquired than the mechanic had given the world to believe.

The working classes had benefited from higher wages and more assertive trade unions. Middle-brow newspapers of the 'it's all right for *some* but what about *me*?' persuasion painted a picture of working-class men awash with money, splashing out on 'pianos, furniture, good quality boots and shoes for their children and even gramophones'. Working-class women and girls had entered the world of work like an army of internal migrants. The wages of shorthand typists almost doubled. Women were seen in mid-price London restaurants dining alone or with a friend. They wore make-up and short skirts and smoked cigarettes in public. Some even wore trousers like the Land Girls who had driven tractors and felled trees. Women in factory teams had been playing high-quality league football in front of thousands of spectators.

The social revolution which the government hoped to moderate or reverse by sending women back to their own or someone else's kitchen had taken place with astonishingly little fuss. No one had suffered a heart attack because the railway guard, bus conductor, firefighter or bank clerk was a woman. In 1918, four years after the last force-feeding of a hunger-striking suffragette, propertied women over thirty were given the vote. The Sex Disqualification (Removal) Act of 1919 entitled women, unless the Crown decided otherwise, to hold a range of civil and judicial posts – barrister, solicitor, magistrate, civil servant – and to serve as jurors, though in many cases, even long after the Second World War, they would be expected to resign their post once they had assumed their 'natural' role as wives and child-bearers. 'How will you look after your children?' was a question I heard posed to a female applicant for an Oxford college fellowship in the late 1980s.

Class was a different matter. The term 'working classes' was used in housing legislation, but there was no legal definition of 'class'. George Orwell imagined that while every Briton in 1910 could be instantly 'placed' by clothing, manner and accent, after the war, an entirely new subspecies emerged: 'people of indeterminate social class' (indeterminable to Orwell himself). The German invasion handbook of 1940 more correctly observed that 'the extensive [employed] middle class [has] its own elaborate internal hierarchy'. It adapted to changes in society, not by abolishing itself, but by evolving ever-greater degrees of division.

This was not just a taxonomic puzzle for social historians, who tended to disagree with their subjects' self-classification. It was vital to know to which class everyone belonged: oneself, one's superiors and inferiors, one's neighbours, friends and even members of one's own family. It became increasingly common for children to be embarrassed by their parents and vice versa. In *Tess of the d'Urbervilles* (1891), set in 1870s Dorset, Thomas Hardy described the irreversible social alienation, despite their mutual affection, of an eldest daughter (Tess) and her mother:

> Between the mother, with her fast-perishing lumber of superstitions, folk-lore, dialect, and orally transmitted ballads, and the daughter, with her trained National teachings and Standard knowledge under an infinitely Revised Code, there was a gap of two hundred years as ordinarily understood.

However complicated the situation became as a result of war, marriage, relocation or economic circumstances, it was advisable to identify the limits of reasonable aspiration or subterfuge. The defence of a social territory required the right kind of voice, plumage and nesting habits. In lower-middle-class Bromley, nine miles from central London, the mother of H. G. Wells stoutly placed herself in 'that upper-servant tenant class' to which, as a lady's maid, 'her imagination had been moulded'. She did all the household drudgery herself but simulated 'respectability' by giving the impression that she employed a servant.

Social manoeuvring could occupy almost every spare minute of a lifetime without having the slightest effect on one's standing. There was only so much a hat, hairstyle and cosmetics could achieve if the mouth still spouted malapropisms and the body betrayed its occupant with a weathered face, calloused hands, missing teeth or a gait imparted by a certain form of manual labour, and all the other indelible clues which enabled Sherlock Holmes to pierce the most cunning disguise.

*

MATERIAL OBJECTS HAD begun to acquire a magic-carpet life of their own. As Mrs Wells's son Herbert George noted, 'furniture shops that catered for democracy had still to appear', but it had been recognized for some time that second-hand ornaments and fittings which gave off faint whiffs of gentility could lift a careful owner into a slightly higher social sphere.

The first great revelation of purchasable respectability had been the Crystal Palace Exhibition or 'World's Fair' of 1851. The products of the wider world had been politely admired and even caused some anxiety at the progress of rival nations, but they were outnumbered and outshone by the Aladdin's Cave of British-made fabrics, furniture, ironmongery, machinery, scale models, trinkets and curios, some undoubtedly useful such as horse-trimmers and whisker-scissors from Sheffield, others, such as the Lord's Prayer etched on a slip of gold the size of a pin-head, having no purpose other than to please the discerning eye and prove the owner's good taste. Special 'shilling days' had been introduced so that the working classes could attend. These lesser visitors became objects of interest in their own right: '[Will] they come sober? will they destroy the things? will they want to cut their initials, or scratch their names on the panes of the glass lighthouses?' In the event, they 'surpassed in decorum the hopes of their well-wishers'.

One of the most visited exhibits was a sort of castellated cottage comprising four 'model dwellings'. At the insistence of the organizers, this insight into a future without slums was erected beyond the perimeter of the Exhibition grounds, despite the keen patronage of Prince Albert, who was President of the Society for Improving the Condition of the Labouring Classes. Each model dwelling had its own private staircase and the latest kinds of grate, ventilator and damp-proof, sound-proof brickwork.

Those futuristic walls would receive the enormous clutter of late-Victorian and Edwardian households with their rugs and tinted photographs in fancy frames. 'Wherever you can rest', the influential John Ruskin had decreed, 'there decorate'. The stained-glass fanlight above the front door and the yellow gleam of gaslight would illuminate all the immovables and breakables of the hallway, the décor of which, according to Mrs Panton's *Homes of Taste* (1890), 'could make or break a friendship' and 'denote that [the owners] are worthy of cultivating'.

At the dawn of the twentieth century, all but the poorest homes were a permanent exhibition. Daisy Ashford, a nine-year-old from Surrey, wrote a novel in 1890 which was published with the original spelling in 1919 and became a bestseller. The hero of *The Young Visiters*, Mr Salteena, wishes to be 'more like a gentleman' and seeks the expensive advice of the 'earls' (as opposed to 'mere people') who live in 'compartments' in the Crystal Palace. He and his young girl-friend Ethel visit Bernard who lives in a mansion with many servants.

> The toilit set [in Ethel's room] was white and mouve and there were some violets in a costly varse. Oh I say cried Ethel in supprise. I am glad you like it said Bernard . . . My own room is next the bath room said Bernard it is decerated dark red as I have somber tastes. The bath room has got a tip up bason and a hose thing for washing your head. . . . It also had a step for climbing up the bath and other good dodges of a rich nature.

Mass advertising explained the social meaning of each possession. The soap manufactured by Lever Brothers at Port Sunlight was promoted with coupons, free gifts and frameable cards. One advertisement showed emblazoned crates of the soap in a Flanders trench at the feet of a marksman, a soldier with a head wound and another vigorously washing his face . . . The image was published eleven days after the first phosgene gas attack on British lines: 'The <u>CLEANEST</u> fighter in the World – the British Tommy.'

Slogans and ditties trotted through the mind of every citizen. Even in the drabbest room, there would always be some corner redolent of a happier place.

> Oh Hurrah shouted Ethel I shall soon be ready as I had my bath last night so wont wash very much now.
>
> No dont said Bernard and added in a rarther fervent tone through the chink of the door you are fresher than the rose my dear no soap could make you fairer.

Human beings became part-time servants of their fittings and appliances. The lower-middle-class 'Mr Pooter' of *Punch* magazine in his rented end-of-terrace house by a railway line in a North London suburb is forever nailing fans up on the wall, tacking down carpets, straightening Venetian blinds and trying to find an honest tradesman to mend the boot-scraper or the cistern.

People spent ever more time doing things they were not good at. It would be another century before most of the population became typists and worked with a tool that would 'welcome' its owner and then absent itself for half an hour while it treated itself to an 'update'. But the battle with paint pots and appliances was already under way. As leisure time increased, so did the means of filling it. The 'safety bicycle' of 1885 was a thrilling liberation for women as well as men, but it could take a heavy toll on patience.

> Three times he said: 'Thank Heaven, that's right at last!'
> And twice he said: 'No, I'm damned if it is after all!'
>
> . . .
>
> Then he lost his temper and tried bullying the thing. The bicycle, I was glad to see, showed spirit; and the subsequent proceedings degenerated into little else than a rough-and-tumble

> fight between him and the machine. One moment the bicycle would be on the gravel path, and he on top of it; the next, the position would be reversed – he on the gravel path, the bicycle on him. Now he would be standing flushed with victory, the bicycle firmly fixed between his legs. But his triumph would be short-lived. By a sudden, quick movement it would free itself, and, turning upon him, hit him sharply over the head with one of its handles.

*

IT WAS NOT until after the First World War that the 'model dwellings' promised by the Great Exhibition began to snake through the suburbs, on and behind arterial roads and out into the peri-urban countryside. Two weeks after the armistice in November 1918, the Liberal Prime Minister Lloyd George gave his 'Homes for Heroes' speech at the Grand Theatre in Wolverhampton. He promised the traumatized and unemployed survivors of the war new houses, jobs and welfare. Naturally, his chief worry was political turmoil, as he told his Cabinet:

> Great Britain [will] hold out against the alarming spread of Bolshevism only if the people . . . [are] made to believe things [are] being done for them. We [have] promised them reforms, time and time again, but little has been done. We must give them now the conviction that this time we mean it.

One-third of all the houses now standing in Britain were built between 1918 and 1939. It was then that large parts of England and Wales acquired the semi-detached physiognomy which strikes some European visitors as a peculiarly British expression of arrested gregariousness. The typical post-war examples had three bedrooms, one or two living rooms, a scullery, a larder, a coal store, a bathroom and a separate toilet. In Scotland, where almost half the population had lived in one or two rooms before the First World War, the climate seemed to demand pebbledash render the colour of a leaden sky.

One-third of English villages in 1942 still drew their water from a well, a quarter of farms had no electricity and a third of all houses in

1951 had no bath, yet much of the population now enjoyed comforts and maintenance problems unknown to previous generations.

Today, more than three-fifths of Britons live in a 'semi'. At Cowley in East Oxford, Margaret and I lived for thirteen years in a startlingly thin and tall 1917 detached 'semi', the other half having never been built. The rear of the house was hideous but the front had an air of frumpy but cautiously playful distinction. It had a gabled facade, two white stucco ornaments resembling funerary urns and a stone lintel above the front door engraved with the word 'HOME'. The previous owners had treated the front parlour in the time-honoured way by 'keeping it good'. With its dust-softened décor of paper flowers and picture frames, it looked like the scene of a wake before the arrival of the coffin. These parlours may originally have been intended as spare bedrooms for returning servicemen who were unable to manage the stairs.

In the aneurysmal conurbation of London, many of the inter-war houses for the lower middle class were furnished by the warehouses of Benjamin Drage (né Cohen), who sold low-price furniture on the hire-purchase credit scheme. He later gave homes, including his own Surrey mansion, to thousands of Jewish refugees and orphans. In the class-conscious suburbs, buying on credit carried a stigma and so the advertisements reassured 'ladies' who paid 'the Drage way' that their furniture would be delivered in 'plain motor lorries'.

A golden age of snobbery had begun. Some who could afford better homes saw the various types of semi-detached house as upstart architectural immigrants who disguised their poor taste and penury with supposedly 'upper-class' bay windows and tiled porches, mock-Tudor half-timbering and 'period' touches of the kind used in model villages like Port Sunlight. Despisers of lower-middle-class mediocrity drove out to 'Metro-land' to patronize and sneer at the tea rooms, petrol stations and picnic sites where 'little people' dropped their aitches and their litter. One of the best-known mockers of mock-Tudor was John Betjeman (né Betjemann), the son of a successful manufacturer of high-end dressing-tables and accessories. He wrote 'The Outer Suburbs' in 1931 at the age of twenty-five after snooping about the semi-detached North London suburbs where he taught at a prep school:

And bright within each kitchenette
The things for morning tea are set.
A stained-glass window, red and green,
Shines, hiding what should not be seen,
While wifie knits through hubbie's gloom
Safe in the Drage-way drawing-room.

I was born in a 1930s semi-detached house backing onto a railway cutting and I began to grow up in another of the same period on an arterial road near Wolverhampton. I loved the intangible jewels that the fanlight scattered over the hallway carpet, and every night I fell asleep under the fairy beams of headlamps passing over the ceiling of the bay-windowed bedroom I shared with my sister.

As the estates and roadside developments decayed or were refurbished, they came to accommodate broader cross-sections of society. Victorian rows of narrow houses had uglified parts of London, notably the Euston Road area, with their strips of sunless garden and dingy basements peeping onto the pavement. These were now divided up into flats and bedsits where a class identity was hard to maintain in the hotchpotch of diets, dialects and etiquettes. The houses on our Wolverhampton road had been targeted at skilled manual workers and white-collar workers on modest salaries. The neighbourhood had since become more varied. Thirty years after the houses were built, within the range of my Rudge tricycle, I could interact with or try to avoid three working-class Scottish children, an older girl with a bigger tricycle who operated a pavement checkpoint and a boy with a bedroom full of expensive toys which I investigated when the front door had been left open. Next door to us, a retired local tradesman and his wife were dismayed to find themselves sharing a wall with a young 'black' family from India.

*

While the suburbs showed signs of permeability, in the country as a whole, the class structure seemed to be rooting itself more firmly than ever in Britain's economic geography. The old industries of coal, iron, shipbuilding and textiles had stagnated and failed. The areas of growth were now technology, chemicals, consumer goods – especially electrical appliances – and motor vehicles manufactured in the Midlands and the South. Bleak reports on the state of the nation appeared throughout the 1930s. A series in *The Times* on 'Places Without a Future' (County Durham and South Wales) where 'industry is not depressed but dead' confirmed the truth of the hellscapes in J. B. Priestley's *English Journey* (1934): 'long sad roads; a few stinking little shops; pubs with their red blinds down'; 'workless lads in a workless world'; 'a suspicious policeman or two'; 'docks and slums, docks and slums'. What Britain urgently required was 'a national scheme'.

After years of dawdling, the Government commissioned four 'provincial' universities in 1934 to survey a smattering of ill-defined 'Special Areas' which suffered from high unemployment: a sliver of West Cumberland and two sub-Pennine towns (Alston and Haltwhistle), a selection of coal towns in the North-East, two mining areas of South Wales, and Scotland (about thirty places dotted about the Central Lowlands). Northern Ireland was not included. Along with Merseyside, the 'Special Areas' – also labelled 'deprived', 'depressed', 'distressed', 'derelict', 'desolate' and, tellingly, 'peripheral' – would receive grants of varying size, but there was to be no 'national plan' and no post-Depression New Deal.

The Chancellor of the Exchequer, Neville Chamberlain, whose Birmingham constituency was doing well out of the car industry, instructed the surveyors to reach certain conclusions. They were to find that the Special Areas were basket cases and that their 'surplus labour' (the unemployed) should 'out-migrate' (leave home and go south). Furthermore, the surveyors were to note the 'failures of local government'.

These surveys reinforced the London-centric mental geography of Britain and popularized the tribalist use of the terms 'the North' and 'the South'. Limbs would be allowed to rot and drop off the national body for the sake of the healthy parts. A helpful diagram was published by *The Listener* magazine in 1935. At the top, crowds of unemployed workers waited to migrate from the four 'Northern Areas' to the 'Southern Areas' at the bottom. Though Cardiff is on the same latitude as London, the Northern Areas included Wales.

Defying their strict instructions, two of the surveyors flagged up the likely consequences of Chamberlain's mass-removal scheme. The author of the Durham and Tyneside report noted that large-scale movements of people entailed 'an immense waste of social capital' (extra housing, schools, hospitals, etc.) and created a 'residue of persons who cannot be transplanted and must therefore become a charge on public funds'.

When we moved to our first semi-detached house in the late 1980s, we found living evidence of a Special Areas transplantation. The houses of Florence Park in East Oxford had been cheaply built in the 1930s for unemployed Welsh miners. The ex-miners had come to work at the Morris Motors car plant and, being of Communist persuasion, were furious to discover that they had been brought to Oxford as strike-breakers. One of the transplanted Welshmen lived across the road from us and was still respectfully referred to as 'a Bolshie'.

Many of the migrant Welsh were involved in the campaign to bring down the infamous Cutteslowe Walls in North Oxford. In 1934, a speculative builder had turned two streets on the Cutteslowe Estate into cul-de-sacs by erecting seven-foot-high walls topped with iron spikes. His middle-class semi-detached homes were on one side and the council's working-class houses on the other. This forced all but the most athletic council tenants to walk an extra mile to reach the centre of Oxford.

War with Germany, which delayed the demise of 'the North' by reviving the munitions industry, also caused the destruction of one of the Cutteslowe Walls. During military exercises in 1943 in anticipation of the Normandy invasion, a tank crew mistook the literal class barrier for a practice obstacle and flattened it. The wall was rebuilt by courtesy of the War Office and survived until the reunification of the Cutteslowe Estate in 1959.

30
The Eastern Front

The Battle of the River Forth.

On Sunday, 3 September 1939, in Newton Mearns on the edge of Glasgow – and everywhere else in Britain and the Empire – for five minutes the only voice was that of the wireless. It spoke in the cavernous but fluty upper-class tones of patriotic English films and the British Broadcasting Corporation. Prime Minister Chamberlain was inviting the world to 'imagine what a bitter blow it is to me that all my long struggle to win peace has failed'.

My mother, Joyce Gall, was fourteen years and three hundred and sixty-four days old. When she described the scene to us, she tut-tutted at her younger self: the first casualty of war would be her birthday. This, as a responsible older sister, she could bravely accept. But as her father interpreted the wireless oracle, it dawned on her that her dream of seeing France was dashed, perhaps for ever. In the morning, she felt even angrier with herself when she found out why her mother was in tears: her oldest brother – my mother's beloved Uncle Ackie – had sailed from Glasgow on 1 September on the *Athenia*, bound for Quebec and Montreal.

Alexander Wotherspoon was Chief Purser on the Glasgow-built passenger liner. She had called at Belfast and Liverpool before heading out into the Atlantic. Most of the eleven hundred and three passengers were British and North American; there was also a large contingent of European refugees, most of whom were women, children and babies. With reports of U-boat activity in the North Atlantic, the *Athenia* was steering a judicious zigzag course, avoiding the sea areas where the trade routes converged. Wotherspoon and Chief Officer Copeland had been summoned urgently to the Captain's quarters shortly after eleven o'clock on 3 September. They were ordered to draw up a notice informing passengers and crew that war had been declared: 'The important thing, of course, is not to alarm the passengers.'

As a senior reporter on the *Glasgow Herald*, my grandfather would have received the news before it hit the newsstands on my mother's birthday. The *Athenia* was about two hundred and fifty miles off the north-west tip of Ireland when the Tourist deck was spattered with lumps of coal, iron, wood, luggage and human flesh. An explosion sent black clouds of diesel smoke billowing from the engine-room bulkhead. The ship reared up and tilted. Distress signals were sent out: '*Athenia* torpedoed 56.42 north, 14.05 west.'

Some passengers spotted a U-boat surfacing off the port beam: it remained visible for a minute and a half, fired two shells at the wireless rig, then vanished. The *Athenia* was amply equipped with lifeboats, but as she began to sink stern first, the listing and lurching made it impossible to launch the boats safely. One slipped from its davits and crashed into the sea; another capsized. At midnight, when the first rescue ship, a Norwegian oil tanker, reached the darkened *Athenia*, its propellers shredded another lifeboat full of people. In all, one hundred and twelve would die.

When the remaining lifeboats could take no more passengers, twenty-two crew members assembled on the Officers' deck. The head barman had been able to rescue a bottle of whisky and there was more than enough pipe tobacco to go around. The officers shook hands and said goodbye.

My Great-Uncle Ackie was at that time 'a silver-haired veteran of nearly four decades at sea'. He still had his full helmet of soft silver hair when I met him in his bungalow at Bearsden outside Glasgow. I was nine or ten years old. He took me out to his garden shed, which creaked under the weight of forty years' worth of *National Geographics*, and told me that I could take as many as my father would agree to stow in the car. We located the issue which reported the discovery of Pluto. I would have liked to take at least another dozen, but the car already had a full load of holiday luggage. Over afternoon tea, Uncle Ackie told my mother that he expected to die before the year was out. She urged him not to give up hope though he seemed perfectly calm and cheerful about the prospect. I could picture him on the bridge of the *Athenia* at the moment when the Norwegian tanker, having boarded all the passengers it could hold, unexpectedly returned to take the officers off to Galway on the west coast of Ireland.

*

THE SINKING OF the *Athenia* was the first act of aggression in Western Europe after the declaration of war. The first wounded to be welcomed back to Britain were its passengers and crew. The United States ambassador in London, Joseph Kennedy, sent his twenty-two-year-old son John F. to interview and reassure the American survivors in various Glasgow hotels. German High Command feared the effect on public opinion in the States.

Scotland was then attacked on two fronts: the Atlantic and the North Sea (commonly called the German Ocean until 1914). A man who was standing outside his stone cottage near the naval base of Scapa Flow in the Orkneys was the first British civilian killed in a bombing raid (16 March 1940). During the Blitz, on the nights of 13 and 14 March 1941, shipyards, factories and working-class districts in the Glasgow conurbation were pounded by bomber fleets more than two hundred strong. All but one-fifth of the town of Clydebank was annihilated. In front of Glasgow Girls' High School, Joyce Gall and her best friend practised their choir singing by mimicking in two-part harmony the baleful glissandos of the 'Take Cover' siren.

One night in May 1941, shortly after bedtime, the Gall family heard a twin-engine plane flying over their house at Newton Mearns. At six minutes past eleven, in a field on the edge of their housing estate, a farmer helped a well-spoken German gentleman disentangle himself from his parachute. Rudolf Hess, Hitler's deputy since 1933, had fled from Berlin in his Messerschmitt 110 in the hope of negotiating a peace deal with the British Government. Shortly afterwards, he became the last in a long line of state prisoners to be held in the Tower of London.

At the age of eighteen, after doing well in her French and German higher exams, Joyce Gall signed up for nursing duty in a VAD (Voluntary Aid Detachment). She would have preferred the Wrens (Women's Royal Naval Service), whose smart uniform would have complemented her Deanna Durbin hairstyle, but she had the consolation of being posted to one of the most inspiring film locations in Britain – the great granite fortress which looks down over the Firth of Forth. French prisoners had languished in its vaults during the Napoleonic Wars. Edinburgh Castle now contained a military hospital with sixty-eight beds, an operating theatre and a 'mental ward'. Its first prisoner-patients had been a German aircrew shot down in the war's first air battle (16 October 1939), watched by the passengers of a train crossing the Forth Rail Bridge. A local fisherman had rescued three airmen. On a Gaumont newsreel, the fisherman showed off the gold ring he had been given by the pilot as 'a souvenir for saving his life'.

On Joyce's first day on the ward, the Sister shouted, 'Nurse Gall! Number Fifteen needs his bag changed . . .' Having never seen such a thing, she was fascinated by the surgeon's ingenuity. The changing of the colostomy bag was her first close encounter with the enemy. 'Fraternizing' was forbidden, but it was impossible in such intimate circumstances not to show kindness by practising her German. She liked to hear the grateful wounded call out 'Schwester!' and they liked to hear her recite the silly verses which had stuck in her mind since school:

Es ging die Riesentochter zu haben einen Spaß
Herab vom hohen Schlosse, wo Vater Riese saß.*

It must have been the training they had received: the prison hospital seemed to exaggerate national characteristics. Germans: always up early, clean shaven, clothes folded; Italians: still in bed. As the war went on, the POWs came from farther away. Wounds became dangerously infected on the long train journey up through Britain.

Italy surrendered on the fourth anniversary of the declaration of war. Then came D-Day (6 June 1944) and the Normandy landings. The German prisoners arriving at the Castle were increasingly young, some not even the age of her little brother. 'Brainwashing' was a word not used until 1950, but the practice was well known. The Germans seemed to have been told that the British subjected their captives to terrible tortures. After dark, nightmares stalked the wards. An amputee who refused to be helped by the nurse repeatedly screamed, 'Heil Hitler!'

Once it was obvious that the Allies would prevail, the atmosphere changed. The ban on fraternizing was no longer strictly enforced. For years, my mother kept her kirby grips in a German Red Cross tin marked 'Schokolade'. It was emblazoned with a black eagle sporting a swastika. A young prisoner from a village in the Rhineland had given it to her at Christmas 1944 along with its bitter black chocolate and a sad slice of black bread. He showed her a photograph of his fiancée, Gertrude – a pudgy peasant face stared out from under a hideous cloche hat. When the war was over, Nurse Gall must come and visit them at their home in the Rhineland, where giants sat in lofty castles. She knew that the RAF had been carpet-bombing the whole area since October 1942. He would be lucky to find his home still there and his Gertrude still alive.

*

THREE YEARS AFTER the end of the war, Joyce Gall, having passed her nursing exams, took a one-year social-work course at Glasgow

* 'Down from the lofty castle where Daddy Giant sat, / The giant's daughter went off to have some fun.'

University. In the class on child development, she noticed a tall, well-built man with dark eyes and a truthful face. Everyone said that Gordon Robb was 'very good with children'. The children he was especially good with were boys from the slums of Edinburgh and Dundee who had run wild during the war and who, as a matter of routine self-defence, sewed double-edged razor blades into their lapels. Faced with adult small talk, he was practically mute. In a book written by the minister of his church in Edinburgh, he had underlined a quotation from St Augustine: 'Our need is not much speaking but much prayer.'

Joyce never spoke to him at the time, but she remembered thinking, 'I bet *he* did something brave in the War.' By chance, she saw him again a year or two later on a rainy Sunday in Manchester when, because the cinemas were closed, she attended a service at the Presbyterian church. After the service, he asked her out to the theatre. Either because he was nervous or because he wanted to see what she was made of, he had also invited a lively contingent of Manchester slum boys. For a later date, he took her climbing in the Lake District along Striding Edge in a heavy fog which concealed the precipices on either side.

My father only once broached the subject himself, and some of what I know comes from documents in filing cabinets, but he made no secret of his wartime activities. If you asked him a question, he would give you an adult answer. As a young child, I once asked him what happens when you die. He said that he had often been with people as they lay dying, some in such an appalling state of mutilation that it was a wonder they still had breath to speak, and yet, just before they slipped away, they suddenly became lucid and asked him to say a prayer or left him with a message for a loved one.

*

GORDON WAS EIGHTEEN years old when war was declared. At that time, he was helping to run a youth club in Edinburgh's grimy Old Town. He had been inspired by George MacLeod, the First World War hero and Church of Scotland minister who gave up his comfortable parish in the West End of Edinburgh and went to work in the depressed shipyard area of Govan. My father had discovered in the teachings of Christ a complete instruction manual for helping the so-called 'enemies of society'. Like millions of Britons in the 1930s, he believed in the rightness and efficacy of militant pacifism.

In September 1939, a new National Service Act was rushed through Parliament: all males aged between eighteen and forty-one were to register for service. He saw a clear path open up before him and registered as a conscientious objector. To his disgust, all the other young men in the peace group at his local church ditched their principles and signed up to fight. His own father disowned him; his older sister never forgave him. The next time she spoke to him was to give him news on the telephone in 1958: 'Your mother's dead, and *you* killed her!'

Local tribunals were sentencing 'conchies' to imprisonment pending appeal. Some, like the poet Norman MacCaig, had been locked up in Edinburgh Castle. The Appellate Tribunal in Parliament House dismissed most of the appeals. Its chairman was the 16th Lord Elphinstone, brother-in-law of the Queen and holder of the record for the biggest moose shot in Alaska. In 1943, Elphinstone's misinterpretation of the new Service Act was denounced in the House of Lords by the Duke of Bedford as unreasonable and abusive: Elphinstone had repeatedly insisted, in contradiction of the law, 'We are the final judges and we say that there can be no unconditional exemption.'

The Duke of Bedford's view was shared by most of Parliament: conscientious objectors performed valuable work. It was important, he said, 'to prevent the unfortunate spectacle of a Government professedly fighting for freedom and democracy inflicting fines and sentences of imprisonment upon people whose consciences do not allow them to obey the orders of the State'. He mentioned one rogue magistrate, a brigadier-general, who had told a follower of Christ, 'Don't talk twaddle.' A Mrs Bailey of Sheffield sentenced every C. O. who came before her to a year in jail and thought it a pity that they couldn't all be sent to Germany. The Duke went on,

> It seems to me to be a pity that Mrs Bailey does not consider joining the Russian Air Force. . . . Surely a Valkyrie like Mrs Bailey would make a much better bomber pilot than member of a tribunal. A lady of such ferocity employed on the Eastern Front would very likely be more than the equivalent of a Second Front.

The eighteen-year-old objector impressed Lord Elphinstone with his fighting spirit. Gordon Robb was allowed to volunteer for Air Raid Precautions rescue work. He asked to be sent to London or Coventry. After the fall of France and the evacuation from Dunkirk, these devastated cities were on the front line of British resistance. Instead, he was sent to a place which, to the annoyance of its proudly suffering citizens, newspapers were allowed to identify only as 'a northern coastal town'. Of Kingston upon Hull, he knew almost nothing, except that it lay on the same Eastern Front as his home city of Edinburgh.

His principal function was to rescue the wounded and retrieve the dead from bombed-out buildings. Relative to its size and population, Hull was the most heavily bombed urban area in Britain in the Second World War: more than ninety per cent of it was damaged or destroyed. Its docks, factories and silos were primary targets of the Luftwaffe; it was also bombed by German aircrews returning from Liverpool and Manchester to jettison their remaining ordnance before heading home across the North Sea. From the air, the gigantic pointing finger of the Humber Estuary made Hull easy to spot.

Night after night, the sky glowed orange. After the high-explosive bombs and the oil and magnesium incendiaries came the new parachute mines, a single one of which could wreck hundreds of houses and cause damage a mile from the point of impact. On average, from 1940 to 1945, there was one air raid every twenty days. The rubble had to be searched by hand. Miscellaneous body parts were collected and recorded before being placed in a mass grave: 'In Cleveland Street: a female scalp, forehead and right eyebrow' (10 March 1941).

He took a room in the house of a married couple. In his spare time, he worked at a boys' club which had moved to West Dock Avenue when its premises were required for a bandage factory. He got on well with his landlord and landlady until, one day, the husband told him he would have to find lodgings somewhere else: his wife's colleagues were making life difficult for her because she had taken in a conchie. He had made a few friends at the first-aid station. One of them went mad and was placed in a lunatic asylum; another was tormented by his wife because of his pacifism and committed suicide. 'I learned to plough a lone furrow,' my father told the minister of his church half a century later.

My sister and I used to tease him about his epic infrastructure projects which involved lugging gigantic stones about the garden, demolishing sheds with a sledgehammer and bleeding on my mother's clean kitchen floor. Unmechanized heavy construction was his favourite weekend activity. After the War, he had worked as a stonemason's labourer on the Isle of Iona and helped to rebuild the ancient abbey. The Holy Spirit and his unwitting servant Adolf Hitler had provided him with the necessary experience. It was a view of ordainment and causality that neither I nor my mother were able to fathom, though we could see the good that might come of it.

*

After storing these various family experiences in a mental scrapbook – the sinking of the *Athenia*, the visit of Hitler's henchman to my mother's neighbourhood, the prison hospital in Edinburgh Castle and the blitzing of Hull – I felt I had a rough idea of what had happened in the Second World War. The British army had fled in little boats across the Channel, raised the drawbridge and melted down all the iron railings in the kingdom. Spitfires had – quite easily, it turned out – stymied the German invasion, which meant that it had not after all been necessary to remove all the old signposts from country lanes. Eventually, Hitler had committed suicide and, as my mother put it when she was tired of the television 'harping on about the War', it was now 'just a bad dream'.

I realized, however, that each family member had a different story and that each required a different explanation. What, for instance, had my mother's little brother Billy been doing when he was photographed in khaki shorts in what appeared to be a tropical setting? (This was in 1945, near the end of the Burma campaign against Imperial Japan.) Why had my father's youngest brother John sailed to Murmansk in the Arctic Circle and then to Japan with the United States Navy? Uncle John had photographs of a plain of ruins and trees stripped bare, taken when a shore party from his minesweeper went for a walk in Nagasaki.

These were events which seemed to belong to a different time. Many veterans of campaigns beyond Europe felt – and were – forgotten. Their contributions were not celebrated in the comics which some boys gloated over at school in which screaming, square-jawed Germans were blasted into kaleidoscopes of carnage. The Nazi concentration camps were never mentioned.

My mother and father were older than the parents of most children my age.* Most other parents were too young to have served. I knew from my mother that not everything that was said about the war was true. Though she had loved dancing and popular music, she had no recollection of hearing 'The Forces' Sweetheart' Vera Lynn sing the mawkish 'White Cliffs of Dover'. (This was not a title to tug at Scottish heartstrings.) Who wanted to listen to that stiff-upper-lip and trembling-tear stuff anyway when there were American singers with perfect hair and teeth and dance routines to cheer people up?

No one who had experienced the War in a bombed city believed that the entire nation had pulled together and formed orderly lines at bus stops. Queuing in 1939 was an irksome novelty enforced by bus conductresses: Jerome K. Jerome believed that 'the queue system' 'came from Paris'. In Glasgow, my mother had seen a ferocious 'clippie' refuse to allow a fur-coated lady and her lap dog to board the bus: 'Workin' dugs only!' Not everyone had shared my grandmother's admiration of Winston Churchill: many people had hated him as a self-serving warmonger and, unlike Churchill himself, were not surprised when he and his party were comprehensively defeated in the 1945 general election.

Wartime censorship had suppressed demoralizing news. In the 1960s and 70s, unheard stories filtered out to the general public. Resting from his labours on Sunday afternoons, my father would summarize the latest long-delayed bulletins published in *The Observer* and *The Sunday Times*. My grandmother had to be dissuaded from watching a television documentary in which Churchill was said to have known that the *Athenia* would be torpedoed but did nothing to prevent the disaster because it might force the United States to enter the War. The story had been invented by Joseph Goebbels and published in the Nazi Party newspaper in 1939. The submarine

* In 1958, the mean ages of parents at the birth of a child in England and Wales were 27.6 (mothers) and 30.6 (fathers). My parents were both seven years older.

commander admitted his guilt at the Nuremberg trials. On the other hand, it was undeniable that the firebombing of civilian targets in Germany, cheerfully directed by Arthur 'Bomber' Harris, was an atrocity with few parallels in European history.

My father died in 2000, my mother in 2016, by which time the Second World War had become controversial. Opinions of the war were influenced more than ever by party politics. In Parliament, it frequently cropped up in debates on immigration. The tone and substance of speeches were sometimes suspiciously reminiscent of Pathé newsreels and the boys' comics of my generation and even of the jingoistic adventure tales of the early twentieth century. The alleged unanimity of 'the people of this country' was contrasted, contradictorily, with the unpatriotic scepticism of an equally fictitious minority. Chamberlain, who was hailed as a heroic preserver of peace before September 1939, was reviled for his policy of appeasement. The very word 'appeaser', used in unrelated contexts, has become a term of abuse. Yet there are risks in seeking to gain political capital from Britain's victory. With so many researchers delving into newly released records, the war and its aftermath can still turn up some nasty surprises like an unexploded bomb in a suburban garden or a sea mine washing up on a beach.

31

This Happy Breed

Tarsem Singh Sandhu at the Chiswick bus depot.

THE WAR HAD made Britain more insular than ever, impatient with rationing but never seriously short of tea, and, at war's end, more inclined to believe that isolation from Europe had been the key to victory. It was only half a joke to say that one of the best things about being British was that everyone else was foreign.

The lighthouse nation which – unlike its dependencies, the Channel Islands – had escaped the horrors of occupation had drawn heavily on the resources of allies and the Commonwealth. The army and the RAF, but not the navy, had relaxed their colour bar. Men and women had come from East and West Africa, South Africa (black as well as white), India, Australia, New Zealand and Canada – indigenous peoples as well as those of European descent – and from the Caribbean. Thousands of French and North Africans, Poles, Czechs and Slovaks had fought under British commanders. The Americans had been fairly useful too . . .

Britain was officially grateful to her allies and expected her gratitude to be reciprocated. Eight decades after VE Day, one of the commonest platitudes of political oratory is the boast that Britain has a long and proud tradition of welcoming foreigners. The special adviser of a Home Secretary recently told a researcher:

> One of those phrases we always put into every speech is the one about having a long and proud tradition of protecting refugees. So then when you announce the [immigration] policy everyone is happy; we're protecting the system from abuse and protecting those in need.

The best evidence of official post-war benevolence is the Polish Resettlement Act of 1947 which gave more than two hundred thousand Poles the right to remain in the United Kingdom in recognition of their wartime service. Yet this Act had to be pushed through Parliament in defiance of the press, the trade unions, public opinion and political opposition, both Conservative and Communist. Jews had been discouraged from coming to Britain before the War: in 1938, the Home Secretary had told Parliament with devilish logic that an influx of Jews must be prevented because it would foster anti-Semitism. When the Kindertransport scheme brought Jewish refugee children to Britain, they were not allowed to bring their parents.

Under the Labour Government of Clement Attlee which drew up the Polish Resettlement Bill, a secret Home Office meeting was called in October 1945. 'Undesirable Chinese seamen' were to be 'rounded up' and compulsorily 'repatriated'. The plan was not to be discussed in Parliament or anywhere else. If questioned, ministers and officials were to deny all knowledge. This was important because the proposed deportation was illegal.

Some thirty-six thousand merchant seamen had died in the Atlantic convoys that kept wartime Britain supplied with arms and food. A large proportion of the merchant navy came from Liverpool's four-generations-old Chinese community. Many seamen of Chinese origin had married local girls and started families. Late in 1945, just as life was returning to normal, husbands began to disappear. Identity papers were seized and altered by squads of Special Branch officers. Houses were raided at night. False criminal records were created. Some children were informed that their fathers had abandoned them. Many decades later, a woman born in 1946 found her respectable and law-abiding mother listed in an official document as a 'prostitute'.

No one knew what had happened: Daddy had gone out to the corner shop and was never seen again. A small number of the two or three hundred deportees made it back to Liverpool from Shanghai in the early 1950s. At least one was re-deported. The surviving documentation was unhelpful: names had been misspelt or had never been recorded. One ship's manifest named only the two first-class passengers, who were French and Danish. The rest were treated as anonymous livestock: '100 Chinese seamen shipped by the Home Office.' The Labour MP for Liverpool Exchange, Bessie Braddock, tried to penetrate the wall of silence in 1946 but was told by the Home Office that if they stopped deporting seamen now 'it might embarrass the immigration officer . . . the police and the shipping companies concerned'.

*

THE FUG OF chip fat and pipe smoke leached out while Mrs Rudd stood at her front door complaining to my mother about the cooking smells from the 'coloured' family next door. (The word was still widely used.) Their 'colour' was like the light-brown in my box of crayons. Ours was the pinkish one labelled 'flesh' which wasn't really a colour at all.

For a long time, my only conscious experience of 'racial' prejudice was 'that silly woman' next door to us in the outskirts of Wolverhampton. In my four-year-old world, bus drivers and bus conductors were brown. When my mother accidentally left me on the bus one day, a conductor looked after me and made the driver wait at the next stop until my mother came running along the pavement. The only other 'coloured' person I interacted with was the grumpy man who delivered the coal.

In July 1967, a twenty-three-year-old Sikh bus driver in Wolverhampton returned from sick leave wearing a beard and a turban. In India, he had been a teacher. When the superintendent sent him home to shave, he refused to comply and was sacked. He found his union, the TGWU, 'evasive and non-committal'. However, its members voted to support him by a majority of 346 to 204. The story became an international news item, but the Wolverhampton Corporation Transport Committee sat firm:

> If we had said 'yes' to this one request, we would have to give way on other things. This sort of thing ferments.

A year later, Tarsem Singh Sandhu, still bearded and turbaned, was hired as a bus driver at the Southall garage in West London. On his first day at work, drivers at the garage two stops away in Hanwell showed their disgust with this flouting of the dress code by turning up for work in sombreros and Muslim topis.

Twelve weeks before the sacking of Mr Sandhu, the Conservative MP whose constituency included Wolverhampton city centre and my primary school had given a speech in Birmingham. Enoch Powell had once condemned the barbarity of the British repression of the Mau Mau uprising in Kenya. He had championed the recruiting of Indian and Pakistani doctors and Caribbean nurses for the National Health Service. But on 20 April 1968, in a state of simmering exuberance, as his friend on the Wolverhampton newspaper noted with alarm, he launched his new political identity with 'a rocket' of a speech.

The new Race Relations Bill would enable immigrants to 'organise . . . and campaign against their fellow citizens'. Their descendants, being 'born in England', would be almost impossible to root out. Alluding to the myth of the founding of Rome by descendants of Aeneas and the Trojans as described by Virgil, he foresaw, like the frenzied Sybil of *Aeneid*: Book VI, 'rivers of blood'. (As a former Professor of Greek at the University of Sydney, Powell had a habit of seasoning his speeches with snippets of Classical literature, however inapt.) He also quoted one of his white constituents: 'In fifteen or twenty years' time the black man will have the whip hand over the white man.'

Most of Powell's colleagues found his call to arms vile and egocentric. He was sacked by the Conservative Opposition leader, Edward

Heath. The shadow Fuel and Power spokesman (*sic*) Margaret Thatcher thought this unwise. Polls suggested that three-quarters of the population sympathized with the views of 'Enoch'. In the fortnight following his speech, he received one hundred thousand letters of support. Many of them accused the 'elitist' BBC of painting a rosy picture of 'coloured people' and promoting 'the permissive society'.

Watching television had become the most popular leisure activity in Britain. Commercial television was even more alarming than the BBC. In 1968, Thames Television had hired a young woman from Jamaica as an interviewer of celebrities and members of the public. Accompanied by a camera crew, she enjoyed being able to walk down a street without being spat at. Almost every day, letters arrived from viewers demanding that 'the n . . .' be taken off their screens. Barbara Blake-Hannah was dismissed without apology and went to work for ATV in Birmingham, to which she had to commute from London because no Birmingham hotel would take her. Shortly after his 'rivers of blood' speech, Enoch Powell agreed to give an interview to ATV but only on condition that 'the black girl' was not in the studio. She was sent out to conduct open-air interviews on what she remembered as an exceptionally chilly day.

*

After the speech, physical attacks on immigrants increased. In South London, the fourteen-year-old British-born Hanif Kureishi was threatened by passers-by with imminent deportation. 'Knock, knock, it's Enoch,' they would say. The new Race Relations Bill, voted into law in October 1968, might have placated some of the moderates. The 1965 Act had criminalized 'incitement to racial hatred' and certain forms of discrimination. Most of the new Act was a reiteration: it was an offence to refuse housing, employment or services 'on the ground of colour, race or ethnic or national origins'. The wranglings of committees were plain to see in the exemptions: owners of 'small premises' could refuse to house 'persons of different colour' if they lived there themselves. Also exempted were places of work in which 'a reasonable balance' of ethnicities might be upset. This was accompanied by a 'good luck with this one' clause which attempted a definition of 'reasonable'.

Enochs came and went but immigration never acquired the explosive power it had in France or the United States. For letter-writing television viewers, immigration was just one of many signs that the country was going to the dogs. Long hair, mini-skirts, drugs, students protesting (more considerately than the students of Paris with their home-made napalm), white English pop stars singing like black Americans, Beatles pretending to be Indian and marrying foreign women. Abortions and divorces were legalized; sodomy was decriminalized. The hangman had been out of work since 1965. Nothing was sacred, not even the Church. By 1980, less than one-eighth of the population attended a weekly religious service.

There were television programmes so weird that only children could understand them. For some parents, the BBC's enchanting historical animation, *Noggin the Nog*, was eerie and disturbing. Utterly mysterious foreign animations were dubbed into dubious English. It was the twelve-to-fifteen age group which first had a taste of Pythonesque humour in *Do Not Adjust Your Set*, featuring the indefinably obscene Bonzo Dog Doo-Dah Band with its excessively well-spoken lead singer.

Television seemed to be gleefully sabotaging itself. By 1968, the once-terrifying *Doctor Who* science-fiction series was appreciated mainly for its distinctly British make-do-and-mend monsters and special effects based on washing-up suds and thinly disguised household objects. By comparison, the *Thunderbirds* puppet series made in Slough was disconcertingly sophisticated. The characters' American accents were a cause for concern. *The Times* deemed the upper-class English 'dummy called Lady Penelope' with her 'pseudo-Roedean aroma' (a reference to the public school) somewhat offensive, but the reviewer approved of the foreign-sounding villain – 'a sinister oriental gentleman called the Hood, whose eyes light up, and who lives in a temple thick with incense and statues with eighteen arms'.

*

Racial prejudice took so many forms and assumed so many disguises that there was always something new to discover. The categories into which adults divided the human race were of obvious interest to a child, but my *New Golden Encyclopedia* (1964) had nothing to offer but common sense. (The encyclopedia was written by the American anthropologist, Dorothy A. Bennett.)

> Mankind: All the people on earth are very much the same . . . Combinations of [their] physical characteristics are used to define race. But races and the groups within races have mingled so much that it is hard to know what they were like originally . . . Furthermore, the variations within racial groups are almost as great as the differences between them.

'Cunning yellow bastards' was a phrase I heard from a visiting ex-army officer who had volunteered for the Probation Service. He was inviting my father to admire his new Japanese camera. Apparently, the man had been a prisoner of war of the Japanese in Burma. I learned about the Italian community in Worcester in my first year at grammar school when my best friend was briefly bullied as an 'Eyetie'. I found out about the inherited prejudices of two of my classmates only when our French master, Mr Fawbert, appalled by what he had read, quoted excerpts from their homework essays on 'Immigration'. They may not have changed their minds but they were properly ashamed.

At Oxford, our group of friends included a Black British undergraduate: I believe he was the only West Indian in his year. Thanks to R., we were familiar with the 'some of my best friends' kind of racism. He knew that it was not just because of his pleasant personality and intelligence that he was invited to so many parties. If the topic arose, it was usually muffled by conversational silence.

Here in Cumbria, where the population is 97.6% white and 0.2% black, some relatively uncommon sub-types of ignorance can be found. A Pakistani postmaster and shopkeeper who served his small-town clientele with unfailing courtesy despite occasional racial insults kept a display of racist dolls in his shop window next to the toy tractors. He had acquired the stock from the previous, white owner of the shop and was keen not to offend local people by getting rid of the 'golliwogs'. Recently, at Carlisle Magistrates Court, a mother and daughter were found guilty of racially aggravated harassment because they were in the habit of shouting 'Paki!' at a white Polish man every morning on his way to work. I live with a foreign immigrant who holds a British passport but, of course, 'that's different'.

I first witnessed racism in the raw while working as an immigrant labourer in Paris in 1976. One day, I saw my landlord refuse lodging to a white woman because he had spotted her husband waiting outside on the boulevard. 'Can you believe it?' he said in a loud voice as she left in disgust, 'A beautiful woman like that married to a black man!'

In Britain, racial hatred was more often self-deceiving or deniable. The new arrivals from Trinidad in Sam Selvon's novel *The Lonely Londoners* (1956) find life in foggy London as confusing as the bus and Underground network. Having arrived ten years before at Tilbury Docks and on the boat train to Waterloo, Moses tries to prepare the eager innocents for life in the imperial capital:

> '. . . the old Brit'n too diplomatic to clamp down on the boys or to do anything drastic like stop them from coming to the Mother Country. But big headlines in the papers every day, and whatever the newspaper and the radio say in this country, that is the people Bible.'
>
> 'In America you see a sign telling you to keep off, but over here you don't see any, but when you go in the hotel or the restaurant they will politely tell you to haul – or else give you the cold treatment.'

British racism sported the tattoos of its long history. Even after the Holocaust, the Fascist pseudo-science of eugenics still had adherents. More common was the old stockbreeding analogy. The earliest recorded example of 'race' in the sense of 'ethnic group' dates from 1572, when it referred to the intermarriage of English colonists with Irish natives in the Ards Peninsula: 'The Englishe race, overrunne and daily spoiled, . . . degenerated.'

Underlying the rhetoric was the disquietude of people like our retired neighbours in Wolverhampton who had begun to feel like strangers in their own patch of the West Midlands. Before the Scottish Robbs moved in next door, there had been the Van-someones from the Netherlands or perhaps South Africa. The Robbs would be gone within three years, and then who would be next? Sooner or later, Horace Rudd would look like an immigrant unless he swapped his flat cap for a turban . . . It was all very unsettling for him.

Every politician knew the potential of that hornets' nest. For the sinister Classics professor with the upper-class moustache, it was a simple matter to channel those uncoordinated energies into a ray gun that would stagger his opponents and produce the bloodshed he predicted. As a member of the 'elite', he offered respectability to the 'decent' majority who revelled in 'the sense of being a persecuted minority'.

Powell knew exactly what sort of 'troubles' he was inciting. Everyone had heard about the Notting Hill 'race riots' of 1958. The Home Secretary had been told that they were caused by black hooligans fighting white hooligans, though constables who were there had reported mobs of 'n . . .-hunting', 'Keep Britain White' Teddy Boys. Terrified West Indians had fled or tried to defend themselves and their families. Eyewitness accounts of policemen at the scene were retained in secret files and not made public until 2002.

Seven months after the battle of Notting Hill, Basil Dearden's crime mystery, *Sapphire*, won the Best British Film award of 1959. Two police detectives investigate the murder of a light-skinned Caribbean woman on Hampstead Heath. Turning his forensic eye on his junior colleague, Chief Inspector Hazard shows himself to be a policeman ahead of his time:

> 'You'd really like [the culprit] to be this coloured boy, wouldn't you?' . . .
>
> '. . . These spades are a load of trouble. I reckon we should send them back where they came from. We wouldn't have half the bother if they weren't here.'
>
> 'Well, I suppose you're right . . . Just the same as you wouldn't have old ladies being covered [with guns in a hold-up] if it weren't for the old ladies. . . . Given the right atmosphere, you can organise rioting against anyone – Jews, Catholics, Negroes, Irish . . . even policemen with big feet.'

*

In 1979, because my girlfriend Fiona was working in Harrods Food Hall and I couldn't bear the thought of male customers pretending to feast their eyes on the quails' eggs and taramasalata, and secondarily because she had a room with a view in South Norwood, I found a summer job in London. It happened to be in Brixton, where many Caribbean British citizens had been living since 1948.

Though it suffered from unemployment, poverty and crime, Brixton was a collection of neighbourly neighbourhoods. Despite newspaper reports of 'no-go areas', there was no 'colour bar', neither in the pubs where some of the best reggae bands in the world played for next to nothing in an atmosphere thick with ganja smoke, nor at the shabby bazaar of Brixton Market, where expats and adventurous cooks could load up with yams, sweet potatoes, plantains, okra, cassava, breadfruit, mangoes and pawpaws. Herbs and leaves were sold in shopping-bag-sized bunches instead of tiny sachets.

After work each day, I waited for the South Norwood bus outside Woolworths' on Brixton High Street. Invariably, a pair or trio of police officers would stop black youths – always black, some still in school uniform – and order them to empty out their pockets in full view of the bus queue. The justification was 'the sus law' (the Vagrancy Act of 1824), which stated that anyone who looked suspicious to a policeman could be searched and even arrested. This humiliating procedure, which was already known to be a waste of police time, caused bitterness throughout the community.

These were the days of the Anti-Nazi League and Rock Against Racism, when there was often little to distinguish an anti-racism demonstration from a free open-air rock concert and poetry performance. The 'Nazis' were National Front supporters, more active than the average bar-stool racist. Some were just as happy putting the boot into white supporters of a rival football team or gay men of any colour.

On 4 May 1979, Margaret Thatcher became prime minister. Outside 10 Downing Street, bulwarked by three senior police officers, she recited the apocryphal Prayer of St Francis: 'Where there is discord, may we bring harmony; where there is error, may we bring peace . . .' Ten days before, a white schoolteacher from New Zealand had been killed with a blow to the head by an officer of the Metropolitan Police Special Patrol Group. This was at Southall – home of the first turban-wearing bus driver – during a demonstration inspired by the racist murder of a Sikh teenager. The demonstration and ensuing violence are still described as 'a race riot'. This was to be a common theme.

In the depressed St Pauls district of Bristol – a city with a three-hundred-year-old tradition of paupers' rebellions – a riot took place in April 1980. This, too, was called a race riot, as were the riots in Brixton in April 1981 and Toxteth (Liverpool) three months later. 'Race riot' suggested the extreme social disorder of American urban ghettos, yet photographs of all these English rebellions show black and white protestors in the same crowd confronted by riot police.

That summer, frustration with the police burst out in carnivals of destruction. Returning from France in July 1981, Alison and I saw mile upon mile of burnt-out cars and smashed windows on the South Circular Road. Two months later, I started training as a teacher at Goldsmiths' College of the University of London. Four hundred yards up the road, in a fire-gutted house in New Cross, thirteen young black people had died in January at a birthday party. The police knew of other racist arson attacks in the borough, but neither they nor the Government showed much interest. In February, forty-eight people died in a fire at a nightclub in Dublin. The Queen and Margaret Thatcher sent their condolences. No such messages had been sent to the bereaved British families of New Cross. A protest march was organized. 'Thirteen dead, nothing said' was the slogan. Skirmishes with police were reported in the *Daily Star* as a 'terror riot'. The *Sun*'s headline was 'Day the Blacks Ran Riot in London'.

Since contemporary social history was being written by the forces of order, it was vital to inform the public by other means. Large open-air audiences heard the poet Linton Kwesi Johnson celebrate 'di great insohreckshan' of Brixton as the 'event af di year'. His reggae-backed poetry was the sound of English shrugging off its stuffiness and making the Mother Country proud of her imperial heritage:

an I wish I ad been dere
wen wi run riat all owevah Brixtan
wen wi mash up plent police van
wen wi mash up di wicked wan plan*
. . .
evry rebel jusa revel in dem story
dem a taak bout di powah an di glory
dem a taak bout di burnin an di lootin
dem a taak bout di smashin an di grabin
. . .
dem seh babylan dem went too far
soh wha?

*

IN THIS FURROWED field of British history, a historian has to walk with one foot in the present and the other several decades in the past. In 1993, a black teenager waiting for a bus in South-East London was stabbed to death by white racists. The case could have been cleared up quickly but was allowed to grow cold by the Metropolitan Police. In 1999, an independent report found the service to be 'institutionally racist'. In 2012, two of the murderers were convicted. In 2023, a journalist discovered that the police had known of another perpetrator but had ignored their own evidence. The police apologized to the teenager's mother, now Baroness Lawrence of Clarendon, and promised to explain their failure to act. When I wrote this in 2024, she was still waiting for an explanation.

British West Indians who had lived and paid tax in this country for forty years or more were hounded by the Home Office. Some lost their jobs, others were detained and even deported. In 2013, reviving an initiative of the Labour Government, Home Secretary Theresa May introduced policies intended to create 'a really hostile environment' for people who might or might not turn out to be undocumented immigrants. 'We can deport first and hear appeals later,' she explained to the House of Commons. Ordered to provide evidence that they had arrived before the 1971 Immigration Act, some of the victims

* The 'Swamp 81' stop-and-search operation.

discovered that the landing cards which might have proved their entitlement had been destroyed by the Home Office, despite protests by their own staff.

Many had arrived in 1948 on the *Empire Windrush*, a reconditioned Nazi cruise ship named after the river Windrush ('white fen'). As citizens of the Commonwealth, they were British subjects with the right to live in the United Kingdom. Contrary to the heart-warming *Windrush* legend, the Government had not invited them to come to Britain: it hoped to see them driven back across the Atlantic by uncongenial conditions. 'They won't last one winter in England,' said the Colonial Secretary in June 1948. In 2024, a Government compensation scheme set up in 2019 was still working through the claims. Fifty-three of the claimants had since died.

As for the Liverpudlian Chinese seamen, until July 2021, the Home Office, despite the written evidence, denied that the deportations had taken place. In the House of Commons, Kim Johnson, the first Black MP for Liverpool Riverside, made several attempts to obtain an official apology:

> I have asked the Prime Minister [Boris Johnson] directly for an acknowledgement and an apology during Prime Minister's questions, but my request was met with bluster and a clear lack of understanding.

32

'Exceptional Hardship'

The first day of the National Health Service.

DESPITE THE SLOGAN adopted by the Conservative Party in the general election campaign of 1979 – 'Labour Isn't Working' – unemployment grew in the first two months of Thatcher's premiership from 4.2 to 5.3 million and continued to rise until it hit the all-time high of 11.9 million in May 1984. At the suggestion of my girlfriend's brother, I spent several hours in a phone box near Harrods with a pocket full of 10p coins, leafing through the directory and calling every department store I could think of. Not a single one was hiring. Fiona had introduced me to her uncle, a doorman at Fortnum & Mason's, who bewailed the fact that chauffeurs were no longer permitted to pick up their parcel-laden aristocrats at the rear entrance. Some old stores had already closed down.

At the local labour exchange, the only temporary job on offer was

'Monster'. This would have involved standing outside Hamleys toy shop in Regent Street wearing a goofy head and a full-body suit of synthetic fur while being goaded by children and probably teenagers. I went back to the phone box and called every London borough council that came to mind.

In this way, I stumbled on a curiously buoyant sector of the labour market. In less than thirty minutes, I had two offers. Wandsworth wanted a lifeguard for the municipal swimming pool: apparently, my inability to swim 'probably wouldn't matter'. The other job required nothing but the ability to sit at a desk and hold a pen. Next day, I hopped on the bus and presented myself for an interview at the new Lambeth Town Hall extension on Brixton Hill, where a man in a grey suit told me that I'd be better off on the dole (receiving unemployment benefit), the job was that boring. I turned up for work the following Monday.

The glaringly expensive new office building (completed in 1977, demolished in 2020) was viewed by the struggling – and later to be poll-taxed – rate-payers of Brixton as a glass-fronted insult. The top floor was notable for its subsidized restaurant, not open to the general public, and a roof garden of exotic plants and penthouse views over West London. Twice a day, a food trolley which would not have disgraced Fortnum & Mason's *salon de thé* sashayed out of the lift and glided through the open-plan offices. This was the signal to put away the crossword puzzles and the transistor radios tuned to the horse-racing.

My job was in the Work Study Department. The only time the place looked busy was when a trade union boss passed through on his way to a meeting, harrumphing at the obvious signs of capitalist sloth. I see now that the *Oxford English Dictionary* defines 'work study' as the 'analysis of methods of working in a business or industry, in order to maximize output and efficiency'. In the Lambeth Town Hall version, there was almost no output to maximize.

'That's what I like to see – someone stupid!' said the cheery head of my sub-section as he passed my desk on my second day: 'Working! . . .' He had just returned from the customary two-hour lunch break at the White Horse to find that I had finished the task of writing out in alphabetical order on sheets of yellow foolscap the names of all the streets in Lambeth, of which there are more than a thousand. I was desperate to keep boredom at bay, but there were only so many pencils that needed sharpening.

At the end of my second week, having run out of tasks, I was given a promotion: my new job was to analyse the work cards which all labourers employed by the borough were obliged to fill in. Plasterers were the largest category, with carpenters and gravediggers not far behind. The results of my 'analysis' would determine what would be considered a reasonable amount of time for each task and thus the appropriate remuneration. Normally, this would have required qualifications and experience. Perhaps, if I stayed there long enough, I would end up running the whole department . . .

'Self-reporting' was the only kind of time-and-motion study the unions would accept. The nature of the scribbled work cards was a problem. Some had clearly been copied word for word from others. I compiled a sheaf of suspiciously identical work cards and asked my supervisor for guidance.

go to site – no tools – return to depot	1 hr 20 m
go to site	30 m
remove bicycle from chimney	45 m
paint skirting boards	3 hrs
return to depot	50 m

Bicycles had been removed from chimneys at several different addresses. Was this a peculiarity of Lambeth borough? Was it in some way connected with Santa Claus or a recognized method of concealing stolen property? My supervisor glanced at the cards. 'Ours not to reason why, Graham . . . If that's what it says, just put it down as a job.'

This kind of publicly funded skivers' paradise was quite common at the time. Before he moved to Brixton, the punk poet John Cooper Clarke had worked as a fire-watcher at the Naval Dockyard in Plymouth: 'If anybody asked how many people worked there, the answer was always the same: about ten per cent.'

The leader of Lambeth Council was a *bête noire* of the Conservatives. The Trotskyist Ted Knight ('Red Ted' to the tabloid newspapers) refused to implement the Government's cuts to public services. A future architect of New Labour arrived at the council just after I left. Peter Mandelson lasted less than three years, frustrated by the class-based politics and the treatment of trade unions as equal partners in policy-making. If Thatcherite infiltrators had been sent to vindicate the Prime Minister's anti-Keynesian economic advisers – high public spending meant high taxes and served only to subsidize inefficiency – they might have created something very much like the Lambeth Work Study Department.

When I left in late August, the departmental head dumped on my desk a heap of folders, binders and pieces of office equipment – stapler, hole-punch, rulers and protractors – none of which I needed. 'You'll need this at university,' he said. 'Go on. If *you* don't take it, someone else will.' Everyone in the office knew that the institution was rotten beyond repair. A slightly shamefaced hilarity was the prevailing attitude. I decided to write an article about my experience for a national newspaper. My father sought advice from a colleague who had written for *The Guardian*. He said that I would have to name names . . . All the people I had 'worked' with had been welcoming and kind and I couldn't bring myself to write the article.

In such seemingly innocuous ways, institutions safeguard their interests at the expense of the wider community, while the institution's 'esprit de corps', as William Hazlitt wrote in 1821, offers its servants 'every kind of comfort and consolation'.

*

Like all twentieth-century British citizens, I had grown up in a world of institutions. Until the rise of industry induced the State to concern itself with the lives of individuals and local organizations, the only national institutions were Throne, Altar and Navy. They had since proliferated to such an extent that society was unimaginable without systems of finance, law, education and welfare.

As early as 1815, Jeremy Bentham described institutions as 'instruments of delusion employed for reconciling the people to the dominion of the one and the few'. Instead of 'more or less obnoxious individuals' (king, bishop, judge, landowner), 'abstract fictitious entities' were created which seemed to deserve respect and even veneration (Monarchy, Church, Law and Property). Hazlitt observed that these 'corporate bodies' exerted a powerful influence over their servants. The abstract body, feeling 'neither shame, remorse, gratitude, nor goodwill', 'extinguished' individual consciences: 'the most refractory novice in such matters becomes weaned from his obligations to the larger society'.

Democratic institutions became a source of patriotic pride – preeminently the National Health Service, which was largely responsible for the shocking ejection of Churchill in the 1945 general election. Never before had so much been done to make people happy and useful to the State. With free hospital care, child and disability allowances, a minimum wage and old-age pension, the citizen would be supported 'from cradle to grave'. When Minister of Health Aneurin Bevan introduced 'the new health service measures' to the Institute of Almoners in 1948, he presented them, not as charity but as an empowerment of the People:

> Echoes would reverberate throughout Whitehall every time a maid kicked over a bucket in a hospital ward.* For a while it may appear that everything is going wrong. As a matter of fact, everything will be going right, because people will be able to complain. They complain now, but no one hears about it. What will happen after July 5 is that a public megaphone will be put in the mouth of every complainant.

This great democratic experiment, said Bevan, 'would be watched by almost every nation in the world'. It would be an indirect consolation for losing the Empire. When Britain had its knuckles rapped by the United States for the ill-judged Franco-British-Israeli invasion of Egypt during the Suez Crisis of 1956, it was undeniable that Britain was the juvenile partner in what only the British knew as 'the special relationship', but at least *we* had a national health service.

*

* Traditionally quoted as 'The sound of a bedpan falling on a hospital floor in Tredegar [Bevan's South Wales constituency] should reverberate around the Palace of Westminster.'

The NHS was given pride of place in the opening ceremony of the 2012 London Olympics, along with Glastonbury Tor, the Industrial Revolution, the Queen, James Bond, J. K. Rowling and the bungling 'Mr Bean' character. Naturally, there would always be resentment of those who received their State 'hand-outs' while enjoying 'luxuries' such as televisions and mobile phones (required for claiming benefits). Populist politicians knew that a society could tolerate only so much fairness . . . 'Fairness,' said Prime Minister Liz Truss in 2022, two weeks into her seven-week premiership, 'is an argument of the Left.'

The institution which saw the greatest expansion was the legal system, especially in its regulation of road traffic. Motorists are the largest class of offender in the United Kingdom. Only in 'traffic court' do magistrates see a broad social and economic cross-section of the population. Only there are middle-class defendants a frequent sight. In 1988, a new, undefined legal concept called 'exceptional hardship' was introduced. A mother who steals food from a supermarket to feed her hungry children cannot plead exceptional hardship. The plea is reserved exclusively for motorists, who, if successful, will be allowed to continue driving despite having been found guilty of offences which might have endangered the lives or livelihoods of other people.

In the ten years to 2022, the 'exceptional hardship' of more than eighty-three thousand offenders was recognized, often for questionable reasons. One example cited in Parliament was the need to take a dog for a walk. Other popular excuses include children being forced to walk a short distance to school or reluctance to use public transport. Several of the eighty-three thousand 'hardship' sufferers went on to kill or injure other road users.

Except in solicitors' firms which specialize in exploiting the loophole, there is little overt support for this vague provision. The workings of institutions are sometimes so obscure or gradual that it can be hard to trace the origins of a particular legal provision. The unique category of 'exceptional hardship' is one of those gifts that institutions give to their servants. The servants in this case are motorists (who include several magistrates), 'weaned', as Hazlitt put it, from their 'obligations to the larger society' and tolerant of anti-social behaviour to which they coyly or mirthfully confess in private conversation.

*

Public institutions in the twenty-first century have a great power of benevolence which can coexist with low-level corruption like a body with its parasites. Like the Victorian workhouses and orphanages, they can acquire negative connotations simply because of their *raisons d'être* – sickness, poverty, delinquency, ignorance or abandonment. Even the most beneficial can be condemned as a drain on the public purse or blamed for the ills they seek to remedy.

In 1982, as part of my Post Graduate Certificate in Education, I taught for one term at a large, underfunded comprehensive school in a graceless part of East London. Several of the classrooms were prefabricated sheds with unbreakable window panes which trembled when the pupils stomped in. I was told by the head of languages that 'if all the children who were in the classroom at the start of the lesson are still there at the end, you'll have done your job'. One teacher, on his first day, locked the classroom door only to see the entire class exit by the windows.

Many of the pupils were visibly malnourished; a few had serious mental and social problems. One severely agitated girl had to be allowed to wander about the classroom. Her classmates hated her because she begged for food in the playground and the lunch queue. An eleven-year-old asked me to be extra-nice to his friend because 'he comes from a broken home'. It was later explained to me that his father's body had been dumped by gangsters a mile and a half from the school on Wanstead Flats.

Violence was normal in the neighbourhood. A small boy came to me at the end of the day and asked to be escorted part of the way home 'because they're going to beat me up'. After a lunchtime knife fight at West Ham market, uniformed police officers turned up at my classroom with a list of names and took the suspects off to be interviewed. A well-respected, long-serving teacher warned me in front of a first-year class (now called Year Seven) that their behaviour would degenerate as the term progressed. A week or so later, her glasses were smashed while she was wearing them. I was told by some weary teachers that my predecessor had left the school after being knocked unconscious and hospitalized. The aggressor was the East London junior boxing champion, which must have been a partial consolation.

For some pupils, sport offered a kind of salvation. Lister was the school of the Paralympic medallist Ade Adepitan and the England footballer Sol Campbell, who lived nearby in a tiny house with eleven brothers and sisters. West Ham United football ground was five streets away. This proved pedagogically useful. The slightest allusion to 'the Hammers' guaranteed a flicker of interest: 'Qu'est-ce que Trevor Brooking va acheter à la boulangerie?' 'What d'you just say, sir? . . . What'd 'e say?' I often wished I was teaching anything but French. In a class of twenty-five, there might be forty different languages. Some children recently arrived from Bangladesh might have struggled to buy a loaf of bread in a Plaistow bakery but they would be able to ask for *une baguette et deux croissants* if they ever went to France.

As a student teacher, I had a relatively light teaching load. Even so, I had never experienced such mental exhaustion. Most of the staff rooms I had visited in other London schools looked like smoke-filled dens for tranquillizer addicts. Two teachers at Lister School let off steam on Friday evenings by shouting obscenities at rowdy fifth-year pupils through the windows of a speeding car on their way to an epic drinking session at the pub. When the Welsh headmaster came to the staff room to warn us that some pupils had been throwing missiles at the janitor's dog, which was kept at the bottom of a concrete shaft, the response was 'Throw them in!' – which, as the headmaster observed, was 'not very helpful', though it was psychologically beneficial.

I was amazed at the dedication of the teaching staff and the fortitude of the pupils. In different circumstances, some of them would have been an intellectual match for students I later taught at Oxford. Along with all the disadvantages of urban poverty, they were coping with a double-pronged attack on the education system. On the one hand, 'child-centred' ideology as well as lack of funding had imposed mixed-ability classes as an antidote to the effects of inequality. Goldsmiths' College had sent us to observe two dazzlingly gifted teachers working in tandem in a lavishly funded school with a small class of intelligent, well-socialized children. This was supposed to prove the benefits of mixed-ability teaching. In normal reality, the system hampered everyone's progress. As the footballer Sol Campbell remembered, teachers at Lister School could either 'simply ignore the troublemakers and concentrate on those who want to learn something', or they could do the opposite. Either way, no one was happy.

While left-wing ideology strove to make its dream come true, schools came under fire from the political Right. As Education Secretary, Margaret Thatcher had given one of the first warning signs of a Devil-take-the-hindmost approach to public services. Her Education (Milk) Act of 1971 abolished the provision of free milk to primary-school pupils aged seven and above. The rationale appeared to be budgetary, but this short-sighted measure proved to be part of a moral–ideological reform of the entire education system. Under Prime Minister Thatcher, schools would be expected to pay their own way. These school-businesses would be subject to market forces. Those that failed would be starved of funding; the successful would be rewarded.

Many of the parents whose children attended Lister School were in no position to exercise their freedom of choice as 'consumers'. The local school was their only option. Generations of the same family had gone there. Some, like Imran Khan the lawyer who represented the family of the murdered black teenager Stephen Lawrence, suffered racist abuse from pupils as well as teachers. Some were proud of their survival skills and stoically amused by the mayhem. Despite all that, the institution, like the community it reflected, had a certain stubborn stability.

I couldn't wait to leave and I felt guilty when I told my pupils that I would be flying off to study at an American university. I still imagined that I would return to school teaching. There had been a faint but undeniable sense of common enterprise. Instead of being treated as a faceless trainee, I had been honoured with a nickname: 'Baz', short for 'Basil', due to a fancied physical rather than temperamental resemblance to the John Cleese character in *Fawlty Towers*. As my fellow trainees had discovered at other schools, many of the children had a keen understanding of the institution's purposes, means and special idiom. A second-year pupil declared to me after class one day, 'The reason I'm not doing well at French, Sir, is teacher expectations.' After that, I expected a great deal of him. I wouldn't be surprised if he became a teacher himself.

33

Secrets

Engraving by Simon J. Phillips.

I LEFT FOR THE United States in August 1982 after liquidating everything apart from a suitcase of clothes and a box of books. For four years, I was to study for a doctorate at the Baudelaire Studies Center of Vanderbilt University under the Sorbonne Professor of French. From then on, everything I wrote would be in French; almost everyone I taught would be American. It was like a double emigration. I missed my friends but hardly ever reminisced. Memories were vivid enough: preserved in photographs or revisited too often, they would become brittle and corrupt.

When I returned to Britain five years later, I was one half of a happy marriage. We had spent the previous year in East Africa and then in borrowed flats and houses in France. Winter in Provence was very long. Besieged by the Mistral, we recounted our respective histories until nothing would ever need repeating – childhood and adolescence, friends and lovers, schools, jobs, journeys and universities. We both enjoyed a spartan, future-oriented domestic and mental habitat. In Britain, we cycled from our home in Oxford in all directions but never visited any of the other places I had known in earlier life. I taught, then wrote books. Years passed before I allowed the first-person singular to talk for more than a sentence or two, and then only if it was going somewhere on a bicycle.

After conceiving this book and embarking on a series of sea-to-sea and end-to-end expeditions, I was struck by a lingering inquisitiveness attached to certain buildings and institutions. My Powick friend Simon Phillips and I had spent a great deal of time looking for and, when we failed to find any, inventing 'secrets'. They usually involved introverted adults behaving strangely, uninhabited cottages or holes dug in woods by animal or human. There was no shortage of such things in rural Worcestershire.

Simon had a secret which he kept from himself. It explained occasional intermissions in our friendship. For several weeks, he would refuse to answer when I knocked at his door in Hospital Lane; then, one day, he would turn up at my back door and we would go on as before. I last saw him in London in 1982, where he was creating intensely detailed miniature stage sets. In the early autumn of 1983, when I had been in the United States for a year, Alison telephoned from England to say that Simon had died in St Thomas' Hospital in London. The Institut Pasteur in Paris had only recently isolated the HIV virus. By 31 July, only fourteen cases of acquired immune deficiency syndrome had been reported in Britain. Simon was the thirteenth.

All I have of him is the engraving at the head of this chapter. He gave it to me when he was eighteen, along with a book of William Blake's poetry. On its blank pages he had copied out in delicate capital letters some verses of Donne, Milton, Michelangelo and Baudelaire, and this quotation from Jacob Bronowski:

> Of course, it cannot be literally true that what the sculptor imagines and carves out is already there, hidden in the block. And yet the metaphor tells the truth about the relation of man to nature that exists in discovery.

Almost every 'mystery' has been easy to explain and most of the discoveries made in the course of research for this book are of only anecdotal interest. I found out, for example, that Oscar Wilde's lover Lord Alfred Douglas was born in the red-brick house on Ham Hill between my hedge headquarters and Powick village. I wished I could have told Simon.

An Oxford philosopher I knew thirty-five years ago would have dismissed this sort of free-floating detail as 'brute fact'. A few discoveries, however, turned out to merit adult investigation. One was an odd sort of school I had visited as a junior footballer, the other was the Victorian hospital which loomed over Powick until it was converted into an unmysterious complex of 'luxury' flats. Both led back by unexpectedly short routes to the present, which is why I mention them here.

*

THE OFFICIAL SECRETS Act of 1911 captured the spirit of the pre-First World War espionage thrillers in which the doughty but naive island-nation swarmed with formidably cunning, gimlet-eyed German spies. The Act was tightened up in 1920 to cover every possible peep-hole:

> If any person for any purpose prejudicial to the safety or interests of the State approaches, inspects, passes over or is in the neighbourhood of, or enters any prohibited place within the meaning of this Act; or . . . obtains, collects, records, or publishes, or communicates to any other person any secret official code word, or pass word, or any sketch, plan, model, article, or note, or other document or information which is calculated to be or might be or is intended to be directly or indirectly useful to an enemy; he shall be guilty of felony.

In its revised form, the Secrets Act appeared to override some basic principles of English law. The term 'enemy' was to be understood to include 'potential' enemies. The standard of proof was lowered to the point of extinction. After the revision, it was no longer necessary to prove a suspect guilty of an act or an intention prejudicial to the State in order to find him or her guilty of such an act. 'Conduct' or 'known character' would suffice.

This legislation was tirelessly abused by Governments keen to elude public scrutiny until – and also after – the first British Freedom of Information Act (2000) came into effect in 2005. I witnessed it in action during my final year at Oxford.

Crossing Magdalen Bridge, I ran into the friend of a friend who had graduated the previous year. Norbert (not his real name) was on his way to hear a punk band at the Oranges and Lemons. Their name just happened to be 'The Russians'. I decided to join him. Someone had told me that 'Norbert' had been recruited by GCHQ – the Government's intelligence and security agency – and so I asked him, 'What sort of work are you doing?'

He lowered his eyes and smiled. 'Er, I'm not actually allowed to say . . .'

'No, of course. Silly of me to ask . . . But you're enjoying the work, I hope?'

With the same rueful smile, he said: 'I'm afraid I can't even tell you that.'

The punk band was deafening. We would have had to communicate in sign language or on scraps of paper. 'Norbert' had never been verbose: his taciturnity must have served him well in his GCHQ interview. It was kind and perhaps even reckless of him to divulge as much as he did. Even alluding to the Official Secrets Act could be an offence. Years later, I learned from our mutual friend Henry (his real name) that 'Norbert' had left GCHQ ages ago. I have no reason to doubt the truth of this, though of course there *are* reasons.

The effectiveness of this shroud of official secrecy can be judged by 'the Cambridge Five' ('five' is a low estimate) who lounged at the heart of the British establishment and passed thousands of documents to Soviet intelligence from the 1930s to the 1950s, causing the Americans to treat British intelligence as a putrid Swiss cheese of supercilious traitors and blinkered buffoons. None were prosecuted. Anthony Blunt, Surveyor of the Queen's Pictures, was unmasked in 1964. The Queen may have been told privately of his disgrace; Prime Minister Douglas-Home was left entirely in the dark.

*

All institutions have secrets. Some are known to exist, such as the cost of security for members of the Royal Family, others are not. The latter might be called unofficial official secrets.

Documents from the Home Office marked in a huge, attention-grabbing typeface 'TOP SECRET' occasionally arrived at our family home in reinforced packets containing envelopes within envelopes. As I was able to ascertain when my father left some of the enclosed papers spread out on the dining-room table, they were to all intents and purposes enciphered by unreadably boring prose.

When I was sixteen, knowing that I wouldn't blab – which I didn't, until now – he told me a secret so sensitive that it hadn't even been recorded in writing. The new maximum-security prison of Long Lartin had been built in the Vale of Evesham near the Three Shires Elm in what might once have been an inter-tribal buffer zone. My father had found a kindred spirit in the prison's reforming governor, Bill Perrie. He often went there to talk with inmates and to explain to local protestors why they should be happy to accept the building of a hostel for prisoners' families, most of whom were not well off and could barely afford the trip across the Irish Sea.

At that time (1974), several IRA prisoners were serving long sentences at Long Lartin. As far as the British public was concerned, the Government never talked to terrorists and would never under any circumstances grant concessions. Meanwhile, the IRA prisoners at Long Lartin were communicating freely with their commanders back in Ireland. These two-way communications were known to the Home Office. Nothing was done to prevent them, either because there would be rioting in Ulster and outrage in the British press or because secret attempts were already under way to agree a truce with the Irish Republican Army.

I believe my father told me this to show that not all important news was in the newspapers and that politics is not a simple science, especially when one party considers itself to be at war. It seemed that, as in the novels of Balzac, nothing could occur without some kind of criminal activity. Thanks to my father, who thought it might be 'useful experience', I spent several evenings in a hostel for institutionalized ex-convicts who were still finding their feet in the outside world. They shuffled about as slowly as the hands of a clock. They drank tea and watched television. They all behaved impeccably, with the possible exception of the man who gave me inside information on the horses at Leicester racecourse, thanks to which my friend Gerald and I won 75p at a betting shop.

A month after I left, the two junior probation officers who ran the hostel were found to have been selling off some of the pharmaceuticals on the black market. I now wonder: was I placed there as a mole? If so, it was a waste of time – I hadn't noticed anything suspicious.

*

The visiting psychotherapist at Long Lartin Prison was a Welshman, Arthur Spencer, who lived in a Victorian villa half a mile from our home at Powick. The villa and all five hundred and fifty acres of Powick Mental Hospital and its grounds were sectioned off by high brick walls until the 1950s when Dr Spencer, a former Baptist lay preacher and world expert on the therapeutic use of LSD, had them knocked down and taken away.

Simon and I were regular visitors to Powick Hospital. His parents and sister were nurses there and his brother-in-law was a doctor. The Powick asylum had always been more progressive than the average psychiatric institution. From 1879 to 1884, the young Edward Elgar lived nearby at Lower Broadheath by an ancient track which forms the quietest route into Worcester from the west. Edward was in charge of the hospital staff orchestra. It performed the jaunty polkas and quadrilles which he composed for the inmates' sanative entertainment.

In 1852, the first medical superintendent had brightened the airing courts with flowering shrubs, the wards with bird cages and fish tanks and the well-tended grounds with dovecotes and rabbit hutches. He hoped to prove that a pleasant environment made padded cells superfluous, even for patients who had been delivered to the asylum manacled and trussed like chickens.

Rabbits still multiplied at the back of the hospital under a concrete shelf. Prisoners of instinct, their noses jammed up against the wire, they were fed at irregular intervals by an absent-minded patient. The squirming leporine mass faced the Malvern Hills. In the foreground were two tennis courts, one grass, one hard, both usable but potholed.

It looked like a scene of decayed post-Revolution gentility from *Dr Zhivago*. While we knocked our tennis ball to and fro, a few patients would emerge from the hospital and fall asleep on the sloping lawn. A lobotomized man stood like a monolith while another studiously masturbated. There was no need to reserve the courts because no one else ever used them.

Simon would take me through the wards and introduce me to some of his favourite patients. The quieter wards were like waiting rooms for a form of transport that no longer existed. There were women who had arrived at the asylum fifty or sixty years before. Some had been admitted because they had borne a child out of wedlock or because they were suffering from post-natal depression. No one had come to retrieve them.

'These two ladies have been here for *ages*, haven't you?'

'*Ages*, yes!' they chanted in unison. 'We've been here for *ages*!'

'There's nothing wrong with them. They've just been here so long they can't leave. There's nothing wrong with you, is there? You could leave whenever you wanted, couldn't you?'

'Ooh no! We'd never leave now.'

Something interesting had always just happened. A man had woken up after surgery; a nurse had run screaming to the doctor: the man had picked out his stitches and was playing with several inches of intestine. Simon teased out an imaginary segment, tested it with his teeth and flung it over his shoulder like a feather boa. (He was later invited to Marcel Marceau's mime school in Paris.) 'The doctor told the nurse not to worry: it's good for the gut!'

Now and then, our visit took us to the Annex and Ward F.13 ('F' for 'female'). It had eighty beds and no partitions. Under the high Victorian ceilings the noise was astounding. I remembered it as an incessant hubbub of shouting, mumbling, wailing and wittering monologues, like a series of recordings made in various public spaces and played back simultaneously. Until recently, I assumed that shock had amplified the effect, but then I heard the same hullabaloo again in a 'World in Action' documentary broadcast by Granada Television in May 1968.

The film shows a typical day on Ward F.13 of Powick Hospital. 'Some people may find this distressing,' the presenter warns. Women are being dressed and undressed; one stands in a puddle of her own urine; another sits in full view on a toilet. Their hair is filthy; most are emaciated. Later in the film, in a more peaceful setting, a dishevelled woman called Helen is interviewed. She has been there for 'forty-four years nearly'. She is quite sure of this. She has no friends because no one can understand her. The fact has long been settled in her mind: the place is 'Hell'.

'Most comparable institutions would prefer to stay hidden,' says the unseen presenter. 'Powick didn't evade our enquiries, and the decision was surprising, for the hospital is ashamed of the Annex.' Dr Arthur Spencer is interviewed at length. His exposition has the eerie quality of a live hostage video. This is his chance to alert the outside world. Some people, he knows, will become 'incensed' at the appalling conditions; others will 'shut it out of their minds and reject the whole problem'. Colleagues will vilify him. (A flicker of mischief passes over his face.) Secrets whispered in inner rooms will be shouted from the housetops. Funding, of course, was a problem as was public indifference, but the evil was in the very walls of the Victorian asylum – one of hundreds still in operation. It had to be destroyed. Otherwise, 'we shall just go on, and on, as we are at present'. After more than a hundred years of misdiagnosis, incarceration, electric shocks and 'mind-loosening' drugs, the hospital itself was insane.

This rare example of self-denunciation by the head of an institution gone mad contains a lesson which transcends the walls of the asylum: it can sometimes be hard to control the historic bodies which govern the lives of all citizens.

*

At about the time that Simon and I began our hospital visits, a man who had played in the reserve team of Tottenham Hotspur Football Club moved into one of the new houses built at Collett's Green. Mr Baker was a public-spirited man who believed that, with its burgeoning population of boys, Collett's Green should have its own football team. (Despite copious evidence to the contrary, girls were presumed incapable of playing decent football.)

A meeting was held for parents and sons. A blue-and-white kit was selected from the Umbro catalogue. Having accidentally memorized the strip of all ninety-two teams in the Football League, I pointed out that the same combination of colours, cuffs and collars was already taken by Bristol Rovers. Mr Baker took my point but suggested that this was unlikely to cause confusion for the time being. Forms were signed, subscriptions paid and Collett's Green Football Club was born. A few weeks later, while village children scoffed from the touch-line, Mr Baker instructed us in the esoteric arts: passing the ball into empty space, maintaining a 4-3-3 formation, and so on. Twelve boys had turned up for the practice session, which meant that we were all picked for the team.

Because the local fixture list was already crowded, our first match was at Rhydd Court Special School, five miles south of Powick on the banks of the Severn. We were warned that the Rhydd Court boys were 'problem children' with 'learning difficulties'. We were to show due consideration and not treat them too roughly. As we clip-clopped out of the changing room, they were already on the field, performing vigorous stretching exercises. Whatever the 'problem', it clearly wasn't physical. The rules of football permitted the shoulder barge but not the head barge, the two-armed shove, the body sandwich and the leg scythe. None of these brutal tactics produced the slightest peep from the referee's whistle. They must have been so low on the scale of 'problem' violence that they failed to register in his brain.

The oddest thing was the absence of malice. When our smallest player was flattened and his brand-new kit besmirched, the Rhydd Court boys seemed genuinely upset, as though they were afraid that we might not play with them again. They eased off slightly and the final score was only nine–nil. It helped that the referee ended the game ten minutes early.

Next up on the fixture list was another 'problem' school, six miles away on the other side of the M5 motorway. Croome Court was the name of a Palladian mansion built by Capability Brown in 1760 for the 6th Earl of Coventry, the man whose feudal descendant received an annual cheque from my father. Seeing its landscaped playing fields and monumental trees on a Saturday afternoon in 1970, I felt the allure of those well-equipped boarding schools of juvenile fiction with their long-suffering masters. We found the boarders of Croome Court instantly appealing: we sensed that we might actually beat them. They were younger and flimsier than the Rhydd Court boys. Some of them could have played the part of Fotherington-Tomas in the *Skool* series of books:

> [Fotherington-Tomas] is goalie . . . and spend his time skipping about he sa Hullo clouds hullo sky hullo sun etc when huge centre forward bearing down on him and SHOT whistles past his nose.

The Croome Court boys were not obviously 'mental': we decided that they were just unusually shy and had to be protected from the rough and tumble of a 'normal' school. The only sign of aberration was the deranged marking of the pitch. It seemed to have been designed for a non-existent sport. The centre circle was a square and the penalty area a thin rectangle no wider than the goal-line. We guessed that this idiotic lay-out was the work of Croome Court's oddly stilted 'manager'. Perhaps he was new to football, or perhaps the school had a line-marking robot which could only draw straight lines.

We trotted out onto the pitch under the gaze of the Palladian mansion. A few parents had driven down from Collett's Green to cheer or criticize. The sparse home 'crowd' was notable for a group of hefty nuns who seemed to have taken a vow of silence.

The game quickly settled into an unfamiliar pattern. The Croome Court boys flitted about valiantly but were hampered by an aversion to physical contact. Their defenders fled before our advancing wingers. The Collett's Green forwards were able to establish themselves in the last quarter of the field, where they passed the ball between themselves for the sake of appearances before poking it into the net.

Twenty minutes in, with four goals to our credit and none against, we began to feel confident of victory. By the end of the first half, disarmed by Croome Court's earnest efforts, we felt like bullies. During the interval, we agreed that, without actually kicking the ball into our own net, we would help them to a consolation goal. This proved impossible. The final score was seventeen–nil. The 'manager' came to our changing room and thanked us for coming. Sadly, there was to be no post-match tea in the Palladian mansion. We played at

Croome Court on one other occasion but never had the pleasure of a return match in Powick.

*

We reached Croome Court from Pershore on a rainy afternoon in May 2022. It was included in our hastily planned cycle route simply because it happened to lie between two overnight stops. The mansion and its parkland now belong to the National Trust, which offers relaxing and instructive days out in a child- and dog-friendly environment. St Joseph's Roman Catholic Special School had closed in 1979. It had been run by the Sisters of Mercy of the Archdiocese of Birmingham and catered to boys aged seven to eleven who had suffered neglect or whose progress had been hampered by long illness. Most had been labelled 'retarded'.

The National Trust commemorates the school with a small exhibition. In 2018, it asked former pupils to contribute mementos of a heart-warming nature. They included a model aircraft, an Enid Blyton adventure story, a pre-decimalization penny, a jar of Brylcreem and, surprisingly, a football medal. The brochure evoked a jolly life of schoolboy escapades under the watchful eyes of the nuns. One amusing adventure took place in 1962.

Four boys grabbed some bicycles and pedalled off towards the motorway. They crossed the fields behind a straggly hedge and, after passing through the hamlet of High Green, came to that wonder of modern Britain, the recently opened M5. At the motorway bridge, it would still be possible, though dangerous and illegal, to re-enact the jaunt by slithering down the steep embankment and over the metal barriers.

On the smooth asphalt of the south-bound carriageway of the M5, the four boys would have made good progress towards Strensham five miles to the south where the motorway ended. Traffic was already quite heavy. Small boys pedalling furiously along the hard shoulder would not have escaped attention . . . That afternoon, a police van scrunched up the driveway of Croome Court and delivered the fugitives into the hands of the Reverend Mother.

*

For the National Trust, the motorway gang belongs to the fairy-tale worlds of Enid Blyton's *Famous Five*, Arthur Ransome's *Swallows and Amazons*, and J. R. R. Tolkien's *The Hobbit, or There and Back Again*. None of those books had been available at Croome Court. The former pupil who lent his Enid Blyton for the exhibition explained that he loved the books when he was little:

> My mum used to send them to me when I was in care before I came to Croome but when I got to St Joseph's I wasn't allowed to read books like this, and I missed my books.

Some had fond memories but most had felt like orphans with living parents. At the age of sixty-two, the man who contributed an old penny to the display could still not understand why his mother had never visited him: 'I got this penny so she could come on the bus and I wrote down how she could come but she never came.' The objects on display had other tales to tell. Brylcreem made the hair slick and slippery so that 'when the nuns tried to grab me by the hair their hands would slide off'. Football shin pads would have been a useful defence against 'the Karate Nun' who kicked out at boys when they complained about the food. Routine punishments included the strap – administered in private or in front of the whole school – and confinement in a room for several days, along with the cancellation of visits home, especially if bruising and lacerations were visible.

One boy I would not have seen, though he may have been watching from a window, was the former captain of the football team. He attended Croome Court in the 1960s and 70s. The PE teacher called him his 'star man' and fondled him in the minibus on the way to matches. One day, he raped him in his dormitory for five minutes. On another day, he was knocked out in the changing room and woke up in the dormitory with a sore anus. If he told anyone what had happened, he would 'never play for the football team again'. He decided to tell the Mother Superior. 'She suddenly became incredibly angry and I saw real hatred in her eyes.' He would certainly 'rot in purgatory'. Pending that, he was beaten every day and the football team lost its captain.

*

In 2015, an Independent Inquiry into Child Sexual Abuse was launched by the Home Secretary, Theresa May. Survivors were contacted and encouraged to testify in full. Their statements would be published online for everyone to read.

Croome Court was found to have been one of the organs of a loose but tightenable system of mutual protection. The principal perpetrators were priests of the Archdiocese of Birmingham. Below them were the savage Sisters of Mercy. Theirs was the common response of lower-tier management to the prevailing practices of a corrupt institution: while some shut their ears to the trumpet of Truth, others stamped it into silence.

Several sectors had contributed to the effort of concealment: obstructive diocesan secretaries, anonymous destroyers of records, the routinely unresponsive police and the fourth biggest landowner in Britain, the National Trust, which was lambasted by the Inquiry for deliberately painting a rosy picture in order to avoid 'reputational damage'.

Rhydd Court, too, had been a hunting ground. In this case (the object of a separate inquiry), the facilitating agencies were the county council and its insurance companies, which advised against admitting liability and caused vital information to be redacted from council reports, leaving the victims exposed to accusations of deceit or self-delusion.

These confederated institutions had enabled the frocked Gollums of the archdiocese to enjoy untroubled retirements and blessed after-lives. At the heart of it all, presiding over this Mordor of the former Hwiccan kingdom, was one of the wealthiest priests in the diocese. He was said to have exercised a mysterious 'power' over the Archbishop. Between the 1950s and 70s, the priest with 'jam-jar glasses' ('so you didn't actually know where he was looking') held 'special reading lessons' at his home and practised 'pseudo-religious' masturbation on children. This never-to-be-convicted priest, whose dementia saved him and the Church from judicial disgrace, was the storyteller's eldest son, Father J. F. R. Tolkien.

Advised that the Church would lose if the cases came to court, Archbishop Vincent Nichols authorized insultingly small payments to two victims ('without admission of liability') and refused to disclose an incriminating document. Cardinal Nichols, as he became in 2014, expressed 'regret' and told the Inquiry, snakily applying historical relativity to Christian morality, 'It's very difficult to judge actions in 1968 by today's standards, but by any standards today, what happened then was not right.'

Reminiscence is the enemy of truth unless it can be made to function like a Freedom of Information request. After this impromptu visit to the shady lanes of childhood, I knew that all along they had been humming with real secrets. *We* were the Fotherington-Tomases, skipping about under the sun-blessed clouds of the shire, unaware that – according to the Inquiry's estimate – one-tenth of the British population under the age of sixteen had been sexually abused by one and a half per cent of the adult population.

34
Accidental Journey

Old Sarum near Salisbury.

We arrived at the Royal Maritime Club in Portsmouth on the evening before our ship was due to sail. This was Day Zero of a meticulously planned five-hundred-mile bicycle tour of northern France. For sixteen months, Covid had cut us off from the Continent and, latterly, Scotland, the country on our doorstep. Facts had been hard to come by. Government ministers were still bragging about England's 'world-beating' vaccine roll-out: it was slower than those of forty-three other countries, including Wales. Contracts for protective equipment and IT systems had been handed out to friends and cronies using a 'VIP lane' known only to Conservative MPs and peers. The roll-out was said to have been made possible by 'Brexit freedoms' though all European countries had been free to follow their own procedures.

None of this now seemed to matter. Our doctor had given us the QR codes which proved that we were fully vaccinated and free to leave the country. 'Fair stood the wind for France' was playing on a loop in my frontal cortex. This is the first line of an Elizabethan ballad celebrating the Battle of Agincourt. It is also the title of H. E. Bates's Second World War thriller in which a wounded British airman escapes with his French lover from occupied France by boat, train and bicycle. In Portsmouth, the breeze was blowing from the south-east, but that didn't matter either: we were taking the ferry to Normandy and nothing could stop us.

We rode to the port early next morning, past the iron-hulled pride of the world-beating Victorian navy (HMS *Warrior*) and the Historic Dockyard which showcases the wreck of Henry VIII's flagship the *Mary Rose* and Nelson's *Victory* – the ship which flew the signal 'England expects that every man will do his duty' at the Battle of Trafalgar.

To be absolutely certain, I had studied the latest agreement between France and the United Kingdom and the users' guide for international airlines and ferry operators:

> Your travel customer will show their NHS COVID Pass. This will be on a smartphone, tablet or printed off as a paper PDF or paper version of the NHS COVID Pass letter.

The usual packing trials had shown that a smartphone weighs as much as a GPS unit, a spare inner tube and a pair of socks, and so the paper version was the obvious choice. At the ferry terminal departure desk the conversation involved several officials but amounted to this: they could not allow us to board the ferry because Brittany Ferries did not have 'the right kind of scanner'. We could either cycle quickly to Southampton ferry port and back (thirty-eight miles) or track down an authorized pharmacy (location unknown) in a Portsmouth suburb. The latter option launched us on a complex procedure which I can't bear to describe.

A fruitless five miles later, we pedalled back to the port and, keeping out of sight of the terminal departure desk, joined the queue of cars. Perhaps the official at the barrier would have the right kind of scanner . . . He didn't. The ferry sailed for France; we returned to the town centre and sat in Victoria Park staring at peacocks and cockatiels in an aviary, trying to blot out all the weeks of planning, while, in the ebb and flow of tearfulness and rage, a feeling akin to the excitement of playing truant came slowly to the surface.

*

We had often toyed with the idea of allowing the wind to determine the direction of travel. Here was our chance. For wherever the wind 'stood fair', there would we go until, after a fortnight of wind-assisted wandering, we would arrive at a place of the wind gods' choosing. This book was already well under way and so almost anywhere would be useful. In the event, atmospheric pressure and topography would place our northernmost point at Leamington Spa and our terminus, after five hundred and twenty-three miles and nine shires, at Basingstoke, which it had never occurred to me to visit.

With a hastily acquired Ordnance Survey map torn into pocket-sized segments, we skipped the outer suburbs of Portsmouth on a local train, then cycled west out of Winchester on the Roman road which leads to the Iron Age hill fort and former 'rotten borough' of Old Sarum (p. 225). Late that afternoon, looking south from the circumvallations, we saw at a distance of two miles the spire of a great medieval cathedral. It rose so high above the trees that the city at its foot was completely invisible.

After a night in Salisbury, an easterly wind ushered us over Cranborne Chase into Dorset. Most parts of Britain are so thick with history that the Aeolian tour guides had an easy job. The itinerary was a spontaneous masterpiece of time warp and coincidence. Rattling down a steep descent, I recognized the eighteenth-century model village of Milton Abbas. Then came 'Tolpuddle Martyrs' engraved on a stone arch by a chapel on the edge of Puddletown Forest where a signpost pointed to the cottage where Thomas Hardy was born, four hundred yards from the Roman road which took us into Dorchester.

The same wind prevailed for three days. On the third day, from the escarpment of the Wessex Ridgeway, we caught sight of the English Channel and I began to worry about the drawbacks of wind-driven travel on a narrow island: if the wind remains constant, the traveller soon runs out of land. Seven hundred yards from the Dorset–Devon border, we ate lunch in a graveyard in the hamlet of Marshwood. Below us in the middle distance we saw Lyme Bay and the sail-less sea. Charles II had passed through Marshwood in 1651 on his flight to the coast. A little girl from the neighbouring primary school marched into the church with her heavy viola and began to play a merry tune. When we returned to the bikes, the wind had changed.

A fresh south-westerly now sent us north over the undulating levels under Glastonbury Tor to the sand-blasted promenade of Weston-super-Mare and the vast beach with its own horizon created by the world's second highest tidal range. (The highest is in Nova Scotia.) On the other side of the Severn Sea, we could make out the coastal installations of another nation's capital city. By then, we had decided to ditch the French tour indefinitely and so we added Cardiff to the list of future destinations.

*

Six research expeditions followed, with or against the wind. The idea was to 'ground-proof' historical texts used in this book. Originally, I had planned the expeditions as shorter itineraries stitched together with train journeys. Traffic had become so dense and aggressive in the growing commuter zone of London that we had long ago given up cycling long distances in the south. Now, as a ripple of relief passed over the agued land, something green and pleasant seemed to have happened to England.

Cars had been growing fatter at a rate of one centimetre every two years. In Dorset, we watched in amazement as a living-room-sized car with one occupant brushed the hedges on both sides of a lane at the same time. Drivers, however, had become less murderously impatient. Some of them smiled and waved like actors in a car advertisement. About seven million Britons had taken up cycling during the pandemic. This greatly increased the likelihood that the cyclist on the road ahead would be personally known to the driver.

In monied areas with gated entrances and mown lawns, there were signs of greater social cohesion. Schools, church halls and village halls and large houses sported Ukrainian flags and banners welcoming refugees in English and Ukrainian. In food deserts which had become dependent on distant supermarkets, community-run village shops had made a comeback. This helped to reduce edible weight in the panniers and created more opportunities to interview natives. In talking with strangers, I noticed an unusual presumption of political unanimity. In a pub in Kent, a woman walked in from the street to announce the death of 'the wicked witch' (Home Secretary Priti Patel had just resigned), and the whole place cheered.

Two years before the Labour Party's victory in the 2024 general election, it had become almost as acceptable as it usually is in France to abuse the sitting government. At 10 Downing Street, Prime Minister Johnson had held drinks parties in contravention of his own Covid rules a few hours before the Queen sat alone, observing the rules, mourning her husband in St George's Chapel at Windsor. 'Boris' had lied to Parliament, apologized, then lied again and brought most of the nation together in a spirit of revulsion.

*

Post-lockdown conviviality was a contrast to the years of Brexit bitterness when the politically engaged section was reported to have split into two warring factions: 'ordinary people' (Leavers), condemned as racist and deluded, and 'elites' (Remainers), condemned as stuck up and unpatriotic. Adherents of both camps could be seen demonstrating every day on Parliament Square. Most of the demonstrators were quite willing to verbalize or even discuss the matter peaceably with passers-by. In France, there would have been burning tyres and battles with riot police.

Studies conducted shortly after the Brexit Referendum found that the groups most likely to have voted to leave the European Union were the poor, the unskilled and the unqualified who had been 'left behind' by economic growth and industrial change. The 'leave' group was often associated with 'the North'. (See map 7.) This reflected geographical prejudice rather than the minutely mottled maps of variations in income and well-being. The 2019 English Index of Multiple Deprivation identified concentrations of 'deprived neighbourhoods' in the London and Birmingham conurbations, on the Welsh and Scottish borders, along the Mersey–Humber corridor and within twenty miles of the coast, especially in the South-West

Peninsula and around the Wash. As a general rule, in England, if your neighbourhood is rarely troubled by scavenging seagulls, you are more likely to be affluent than needy.

Mounting poverty and regional inequalities had been exacerbated by the Covid pandemic. In one scarcely caricatural view, 'there was never any lockdown: there was just middle-class people hiding while working-class people brought them things'. The underpaid workforce of the ailing National Health Service was applauded – sometimes literally, in synchronized mass clapping events – as the nation's friends-in-need, while the Government was regarded as a chortling cabal of self-serving hypocrites and bunglers.

I was wary of this wholesale vilification of Westminster's six hundred and fifty freely elected representatives. At school, I had held the satisfyingly simple view that all politicians were more or less corrupt. I was surprised when my father insisted that all the MPs and even Home Secretaries he had worked with had entered politics with good intentions. Fifty years later, teenage cynicism seemed to be the default adult view. MPs were spattered with violent online and face-to-face abuse. In July 2024, the 'welcome packs' handed out to the three hundred and thirty-five new MPs contained panic alarms with GPS trackers. Two MPs have been murdered – Jo Cox (Labour) in 2016 and Sir David Amess (Conservative) in 2021. After the initial outrage, these definitive attacks on democracy had remarkably little resonance.

*

It was after our unexpected travel ban at Portsmouth that I began to take a historical interest in 'sleaze'. Either on the road or in the planning, long cycle journeys can generate random samples for various kinds of study. Between 2022 and 2024, we happened to pass through the constituencies of so many delinquent MPs that I had the idea of comparing the map of constituencies with the map of our expeditions. In this way I discovered that, with only a few intervals of innocence, it would be possible to ride from the far south-east of England to the borders of Cumbria, through town and city, o'er field and fell, like a latter-day Piers Plowman observing 'the mooste mischief . . . mountynge up faste' throughout the kingdom, without leaving the territory of a duplicitous politician.

The expenses scandal of 2009, which ended political careers in almost every party, accounted for the largest number. Five MPs and two lords were sent to jail. The leaked details lingeringly published in instalments by the *Telegraph* were damagingly memorable. A former Minister of Agriculture had charged the taxpayer for the cleaning of his moat. The MP for Gosport submitted thirty thousand pounds' worth of 'gardening expenses', including a floating duck island (£1,645) which the ducks of Portsmouth Harbour hadn't even used.

Since then, the list of violations had grown in number and variety. In 2023, the long-sitting Chair of the House of Commons Standards Committee, Chris Bryant MP, published a rogues gallery of offenders and a list of misdemeanours which included bullying of staff, racial abuse, sexual harassment and watching porn in front of female colleagues during a Commons sitting. Dim corridors in the labyrinthine Palace of Westminster were haunted by drunken gropers whose names were made known to new MPs and their staff. Bribes were offered and accepted in the form of party donations, tickets to concerts and sporting events, holiday homes, official honours and seats in the House of Lords. MPs took part-time jobs and sold their inside knowledge and influence to private companies.

Nepotism and 'venality' had plagued British politics until at least the end of the eighteenth century. Contracts were handed out to friends without competitive tendering, as they were during the Covid pandemic. On the other hand, corruption had been recognized as a blight forty years before the first Reform Act. One MP, Christopher Atkinson, was expelled from the House in 1783 for defrauding the Victualling Board: he was made to stand in the pillory outside the Corn Exchange. Two hundred and forty years later, abuse of privilege had reached historic depths. There is no comparable period in which two former prime ministers of opposing parties (John Major and Gordon Brown in 2022) denounced the Government of the United Kingdom as 'corrupt'.

Under the premierships of Johnson (1,140 days), Truss (49 days) and Sunak (619 days), the House of Commons was a Through-the-Looking-Glass chamber in which anything a prime minister said was likely to be misleading or untrue. In ministerial speeches, statistics changed place so that 'now' would look better than 'before'. Some figures were plucked out of thin air, and when they were shown to be fictitious, the official transcript was not corrected. In 2021, NHS trusts were instructed in a 'playbook' leaked by a whistleblower that any major refurbishment or unit tacked on to an existing hospital 'must always be referred to as a new hospital'. Thus the promised 'Brexit dividend' of forty or forty-eight new hospitals would become real without having to exist. In Carlisle, after the visit of Health Secretary Javid to open a treatment centre on the site of an unused hospital building, we still have one hospital but we also officially have two. A similarly Orwellian 'doublespeak' bill was passed in 2024 declaring Rwanda to be a safe country for deported migrants.

Mendacity on this scale was something new in post-Reform British politics. Each lie was a loutish chipping away at the pillars of democracy. Sometimes, the foundations were undermined in daylight. An unknown number of laws (three or four thousand) deriving from four decades in the European Union were to be instantly repealed in a 'bonfire of red tape'. Scrutiny of this 'Brexit freedom' was to be stifled by a five-week prorogation of Parliament. When this autocratic suspension was declared unlawful by the Supreme Court in September 2019, the Prime Minister's allies subjected the independent judiciary and some of their own colleagues to a mob-pleasing media campaign of intimidation. A cross-party House of Commons report found that these 'attacks on the legitimacy of Parliament itself' 'had significant personal impact on individual Members and raised significant security concerns': this was a polite way of saying that they had endangered the lives of their colleagues.

The blitz of mini-coups d'état reached its climax in September 2022 with the solo flight of Prime Minister Truss whose undebated, unapproved and ideologically simple-minded 'mini-budget' was an instant economic disaster.

*

By this time, Margaret was no longer always able to say, 'It's worse in the United States.' Histrionic populism with an American flavour is highly unusual in post-Reform British political history. Under Prime Ministers May, Johnson, Truss and Sunak (2016–24), the 'Brexit freedoms' most aggressively promoted were those most likely to cause chronic inconvenience or misery to certain groups. Journalists who reported whistleblowers' revelations would be subject to imprisonment. Unhitched from human rights legislation, the Royal Navy would be ordered to attack refugees crossing the Channel in dinghies with powerful sonic weapons which induced vomiting. In the first gust of mutiny since the Invergordon pay dispute of 1931, sailors serving in the navy let it be known that they would disobey such a command.

Children were a frequent target – the refugees in the 'little boats' used by people-smugglers, the thirty per cent of British children who lived in poverty and who lost their right to the free school meals they had received during the pandemic, the grown-up children who sought recognition of the abuse they had suffered. While the Independent Inquiry into Child Sexual Abuse was probing dark dungeons, Prime Minister Johnson used a masturbatory metaphor to lambast such inquiries as a waste of money: 'sixty million pounds I saw was being spaffed up the wall'.

When the personalities have slipped from public memory, it will be hard to explain why some beneficial measures were scarcely publicized while others were so venomous that they were unlikely to win votes from anyone. Many backbench Tory MPs found this exasperating. It was as though the Government had overestimated the mean-spiritedness of the electorate.*

The post-Brexit repeal of what Prime Minister Cameron had called 'the green crap' (environmental legislation) allowed privatized water companies to pump raw sewage into rivers and the sea. The fines for exceeding discharge limits were so lenient that it was cheaper

* Majorities in the 'first past the post' system can be powerfully deceptive. In the 2019 general election, 21% of registered voters voted Labour; 29% voted Conservative. This gave 202 seats to Labour and 365 to the Conservatives. In 2024, the same figures were 20% Labour and 14% Conservative, which gave Labour 411 seats but the Conservatives only 121. In this 'Labour landslide', almost 360,000 fewer people voted Labour than in 2019. With only another 2.4% of the popular vote, Labour won more than twice as many seats. When ministers claim to know 'what the people of this country want', they are referring, not to the ballot box, but to correspondence and unrecorded conversations on 'the doorstep'.

for water companies to carry on polluting. No one thought this a good thing. In September 2022, when French ministers were warning of an attack on the seafood industry by an armada of English turds bound for the Normandy beaches, a waitress in a seafront restaurant in Hastings told us as she set our table that she could no longer go swimming in the tidal toilet of Covehurst Bay.

*

As WE CYCLED through constituencies of the disgraceful and the disgraced, I pondered the mystery: all the hate-mongers and opportunists had been freely elected by a majority of local voters. Many were said to be 'good constituency MPs' respected by constituents and colleagues alike. Some, perhaps with an eye to their 'legacy', devoted themselves to philanthropic causes after leaving Parliament.

I thought of the cursed establishments we had visited in 2022. The neo-Gothic Palace of Westminster had all the hallmarks of institutional corruption: the perpetrators and facilitators, the guardians of reputations and turners of blind eyes, the ever-smaller inner circles spawning sub-institutions called 'cultures' which feed on the parent organism and threaten to destroy it.

The only element missing from the 'corrupt institution' model was the identity of the victims. This inevitably led to the concept of 'population abuse', which could prove useful in a non-partisan anthropological study of parliamentary behaviour. A separate study would have to account for the accidental evolutionary events which select certain individuals for the roles of instigator and leader.

At Oxford in early 1990s, I became friends with the peripatetic mathematician-philosopher Georg Kreisel, a pet pupil of Ludwig Wittgenstein at Cambridge in the 1940s. In the Exeter College Fellows' lunch room, he would sometimes drop a suggestive proposition on my plate. One of his favourite quotations, which he applied to himself, came from a conversation reported in Boswell's *Life of Samuel Johnson*:

> 'You are a philosopher, Dr Johnson. I have tried too in my time to be a philosopher; but, I don't know how, cheerfulness was always breaking in.'

One day, after we had been considering the eccentricities of a senior college official, Kreisel told me how the riddle of the stickleback was solved. This small fish of the Gasterosteidae family swims in shoals. Instinct tells it to follow the leading fish. But what tells the leading fish where to go? After dissection of a great number of sticklebacks, it was discovered that the leader is the individual whose brain is damaged or genetically defective. Its movements are random and unpredictable but vital for the functioning of the shoal.

It would be rash but not irrational to apply this finding to the whole of human history. In the tree of life, the common ancestor of hominids and sticklebacks existed more than four hundred million years ago, yet certain forms of behaviour recur on a basic level in all sentient creatures. Evolution relies on accident and chaos, including mass extinctions, of which there have been at least five. Unless the planet itself becomes terminally unhinged, we are not the last word.

*

THE RIVER ON the banks of which I have written this book is the home of another aquatic creature noted for its (to us) peculiar behaviour. Victor Hugo, who was for eighteen years the United Kingdom's most politically embarrassing asylum-seeker, was thinking of Napoleon III's regressive dictatorship when he wrote: 'There are such things as crayfish souls forever scuttling backwards into the shadows.'

In September 2023, in a Great Leap Backward, Prime Minister Sunak cancelled the Birmingham-to-Manchester leg of HS2. This is the projected high-speed railway which was intended to bring London and 'the North' closer together and, as in the Industrial Revolution, fire up the non-metropolitan economy. Passengers on the West Coast Mainline would no longer be stranded for hours in open country with nothing but light snacks and announcements. In Sunak's alternative vision, the money would be used instead to fill potholes and build more roads. He announced this at a party conference in, of all places, Manchester, to which he travelled by car instead of his usual helicopter.

To prevent a future administration from reviving the project, the land acquired for the construction was swiftly offered for sale in what was described as a spiteful act of vandalism. New platforms would still be built at Birmingham because, contractually, this was cheaper than not building them: they would be a memorial to something which never existed. Other legs of HS2 had already been cut off. The city of Bradford, where more people live than in Bordeaux, Strasbourg or Toulouse, and which forms one-half of the third largest urban agglomeration in the United Kingdom, would continue to be a dead-end.

History shaped by human beings has a poor sense of direction. Parliament had regressed to pre-Reform levels of corruption; the unelected House of Lords had become even less representative, swollen, when they chose to attend, with acolytes, donors and relatives.

Regression is as common in history as in a human life. The Magna Carta or 'Articles of the Barons' to which King John grudgingly affixed his seal in 1215 is embedded in legend as the keystone of ordinary people's rights. The 'ordinary people' in this case were twenty-five uppity Anglo-Norman plutocrats with their own armies. A few scraps of Magna Carta verbiage survive in English law and are occasionally quoted in English courts by self-named 'freemen' who have seen something historical on the Internet. The charter itself was declared 'null and void of all validity for ever' by Pope Innocent III seventy-five days after it was sealed.

Another crayfish manoeuvre announced at Manchester was the scaling back or strangling of policies intended to cut carbon emissions. The chaotic climate generated political energy: the Prime Minister used it to abolish measures likely to reduce traffic, pollution, injury and death. He warned of a plot hatched by a Sorbonne professor to force all citizens to surrender their cars and remain within urban sectors measuring fifteen square minutes. He courted and paid public homage to the world's leading purveyor of mis- and dis-information, Elon Musk, the loose-lipped conduit of bots, trolls and autocrats.

*

Every age lives under the shadow of its recurring nightmare. Once, it was the Day of Judgement and the inextinguishable fires of Hell. Some people now look back fondly on the dawn of the Campaign for Nuclear Disarmament and the Aldermaston Marches when we counted down the hours and minutes to the moment of Mutually Assured Destruction. The mother of a classmate at my Worcestershire primary school knew all about the blinding light at the end of Time from her husband who worked at the Royal Radar Establishment in Malvern. She felt that one hostage was enough: her son would remain an only child. The doctor prescribed anti-depressants which she was depressed and horrified to learn were the 'purple hearts' used by 'juvenile delinquents'.

Along with the lava lamp, the smokeless ashtray, the Pop-o-Matic dice shaker and other icons of the Space Age, the mushroom cloud was swept into mental deep storage by the prospect of planet-wide extinction. Not even the seasons would survive: the Home Counties would look like a scorched desert, as they did in the summer of 2022; in Cumbria, it would never stop raining. The jet stream was stuck for weeks on end, making it simpler to pack for long trips. Compared to this slow-motion Apocalypse, the enclosure of open-field countryside was a minor horticultural enhancement.

It would be surprising if no one ever denied the terrifying reality of human-induced climate chaos. The shadow activated powerful mechanisms of self-defence. Fear became the sign of a rational, well-informed mind. Cars queueing impatiently at recycling centres were a common sight. In 2022, according to the official Opinions and Lifestyle Survey, twenty-five per cent of British people aged sixteen and over were either not worried about climate change or 'neither worried nor unworried'.

Plant and animal populations including humans adapted to global warming by moving north. News outlets reported foreign insects crossing the English Channel in unprecedented numbers.

*

While I was writing these paragraphs in August 2024, I went out for a late-morning ride. The verges were heaving and swaying with meadowsweet, willowherb, bird's-foot trefoil, purple vetch, yellow loosestrife, wild rose and honeysuckle and thirty-two other native species. (The cycling brain tends to latch on to numerable data.) Nineteen miles of sun-bathed botanical beauty were being tossed about by the conspiring winds of the Cheviots, the North Pennines and the Border fells. Butterflies darted and dangled over the feast. I counted the species: the list began and ended with cabbage whites. Other types of winged pollinator were hovering but they were so few in number that I could probably have counted them too.

In 1866, the astronomer and inventor John Herschel wrote to the economist William Stanley Jevons:

> We are using up our resources and expending our national life at an enormous and increasing rate and thus a very ugly day of reckoning is impending sooner or later. . . . The enormous and outrageously wasteful consumption of every . . . article that the Earth produces . . . in two centuries . . . would even make the Earth a desert.

One hundred years later, the gigantic tree-swallowing slag heaps of carboniferous South Wales sagged up to the foot of gardens and infected valley communities with bitter nostalgia for a past that was well within the memory of the youngest child. In 1966, one of those spoil tips engulfed a school. Our Welsh headmaster at Powick took us in a coach all the way to Aberfan to see where one hundred and sixteen children had died under the black mountain created by their fathers. We were not asked to write about what we saw. We were being presented with a fact.

Climate chaos is not conducive to reminiscence. On this morning's ride, I thought only fleetingly of the butterfly-cloaked apple trees of a Worcestershire childhood. What I saw from the saddle were the memories of someone else's future.

Despair has never been so obviously futile. The good news is that most of these changes are not happening by accident and, in the present political system, the next election is never more than five years away.

MAP CAPTIONS

1. Beacons and triangulation points, mutually visible, south to north and west to east (triangles). South to north: Start Point, Pilsdon Pen, Oakhill (Beacon Hill), Worcestershire Beacon, Wrekin, Axe Edge, Ward's Stone, Cross Fell, Hart Fell, Ben Lomond, Ben Nevis, Sgùrr na Lapaich, Ben Klibreck, Sgribhis-bheinn (Cape Wrath). West to east: Carn Llidi, Foel Cwmcerwyn (Precelley), Pen y Gadair Fawr ('Cradle'), Worcestershire Beacon, Arbury Hill, Dunstable Downs, Therfield Heights, Lovecotes Hill, Great Wood Hill, Fersfield Common, Ant Hill (Ilketshall), St Margaret's (Lowestoft). The other symbols trace various attempts by fugitives to cover long distances undetected. Three of the five successfully reached the sea and sailed for France. From top to bottom: Charles Stuart ('Bonnie Prince Charlie') after the Battle of Culloden (1746); Thomas Percy, Earl of Northumberland, after the Catholic Rising of the North (1569–70); Henry VI after the Battle of Hexham (1464) in the Wars of the Roses; Thomas Becket fleeing Henry II in 1164; Charles II after the Battle of Worcester (1651).

2. The historic shires of Scotland, England, Wales and Ireland. The English shires are ancient, the others mostly medieval. The dotted lines labelled 'RR' in central and southern England represent the only significant coincidences of shire boundary and Roman road. (p. 78)

3. Navigable rivers in the late Middle Ages. These are the recorded stretches of river accessible to cargo-bearing vessels. The cross in the middle of England marks Coton in the Elms, the farthest point from the sea in the British Isles.

4. British and Irish towns mapped by Iron Age Britons in five separate maps (p. 42), shown here on a modern projection, from the data preserved but muddled by Ptolemy in c. AD 150. The probable dates (AD) at which the information was collected are indicated in the seas, along with the graticules (grids) and orientations of the original maps. The dotted line meandering through southern Scotland and northern England shows the route of the Great Caledonian Invasion (c. AD 180) led by a British general called Arthur.

5. British kingdoms, c. 780. The line which cuts through the shire boundaries on the Anglo-Welsh border represents the dyke of the Mercian king Offa (r. 757–96). The shires of Mercia are distinguished by their aortic central rivers. These boundaries appear to predate the kingdom of Mercia by several centuries. (p. 75)

6. Danish place names in Great Britain and the Isle of Man. Some years after King Alfred defeated the Danish king Guthrum at the battle of Ethandun (Edington in Wiltshire) in 878, a treaty set the border between Wessex and the Danelaw. While the demarcation line ignored the shire network, Danish settlers continued to observe the ancient boundaries. (p. 79)

7. Perceptions of a North–South divide. On the ambiguity of Latin 'superior' and 'inferior': p. 37. The river Trent has often been treated, since at least the Middle Ages, as a cultural or political border. The 'tea' (N) – 'dinner' (S) line traces the current prevalence of words for the evening meal. 'Grass' is more often pronounced with a short 'a' in the North and a long 'a' in the South. The Morrisons–Waitrose line is based on a playful but scientific analysis of the frequency of lower-priced (N) and more expensive (S) supermarkets. The same team of social scientists has drawn a similar distinction between the northern-oriented Greggs (associated with sausage rolls) and southern-oriented Pret A Manger (avocado wraps). The 'Dorling line' is based on education, unemployment, poverty, house prices and

life expectancy statistics: Danny Dorling, in N. M. Coe and A. Jones, eds, *The Economic Geography of the UK* (London: Sage, 2010), ch. 2. The south-west–north-east trend happens to mirror the Jurassic Limestone Belt.

8. The twelve administrative subdivisions of the United Kingdom created in 2003 by the European Union's NUTS initiative (Nomenclature of Territorial Units for Statistics). The NUTS regions were replaced post-Brexit with the nearly identical ITLs (International Territorial Levels). 'North West' lumped together the Liverpool–Manchester mega-conurbation and the sparsely inhabited uplands of Cumbria more than a hundred miles to the north. Statistics produced for these artificial entities are almost worthless on a local level and yet have been adopted by various organizations, commentators and even weather forecasters so that the people of the Cheshire Plain in the lee of the Welsh mountains and the people of the Anglo-Scottish borderlands are regularly presented with a false socio-economic identity and someone else's weather. The population of each region is shown in thousands. 'London' (Greater London) and 'South East' account for 28 per cent of the United Kingdom's population.

9. Coastlines of Britain in 2020, 2120 (probably) and in a future without glaciers and ice caps when seas may be sixty-six metres above present levels. In the diminished British Isles, it would still be possible to cycle from Land's End to within about fourteen miles of John o' Groats. The largest unsubmerged city would be Birmingham, advantageously situated thirteen miles from each coast: the Irish Sea near Kidderminster and the North Sea near Tamworth, former capital of the kingdom of Mercia.

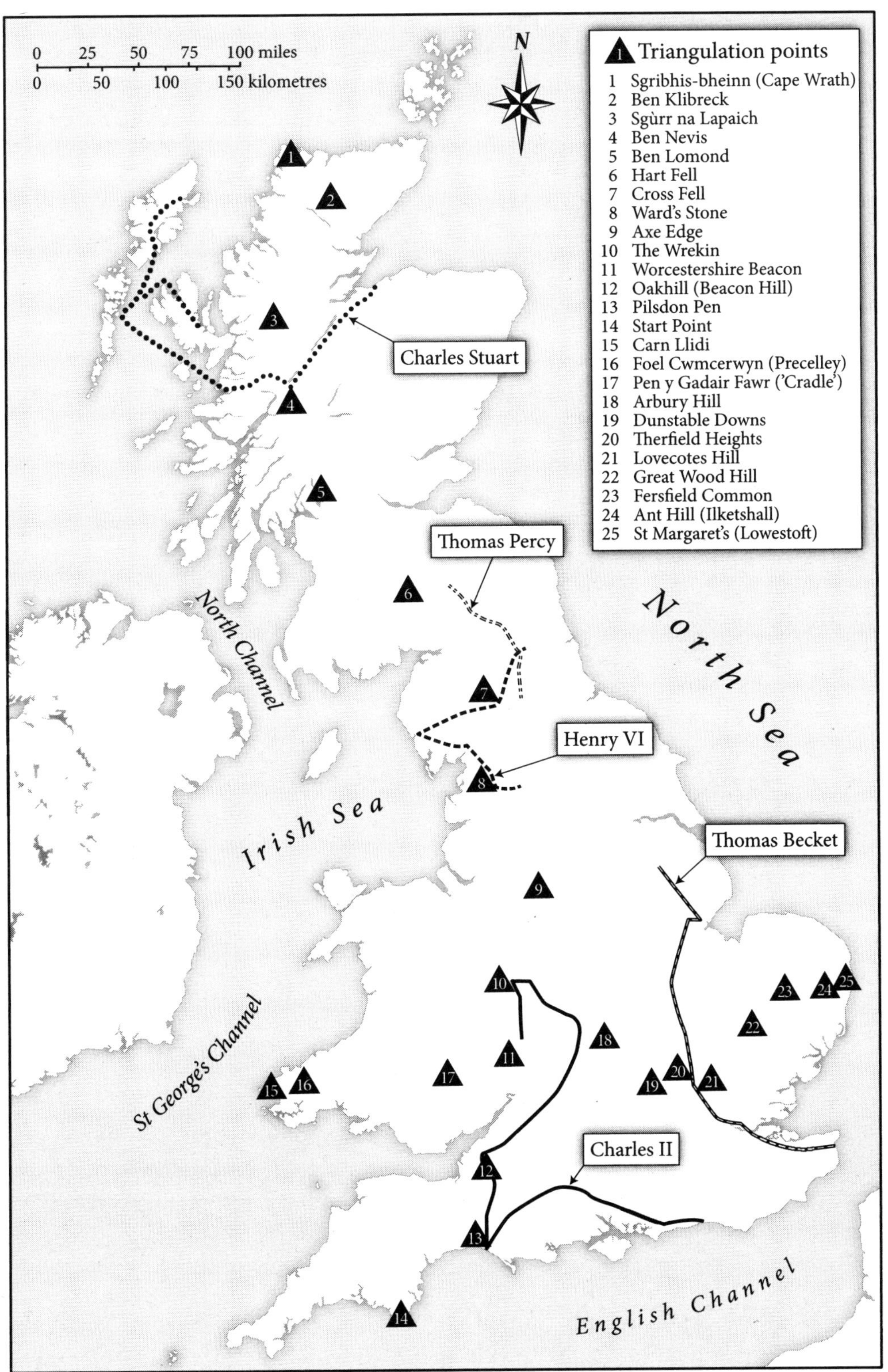

Map 1. Beacons and triangulation points.

Map 2A. The historic shires of Scotland, England, Wales and Ireland.

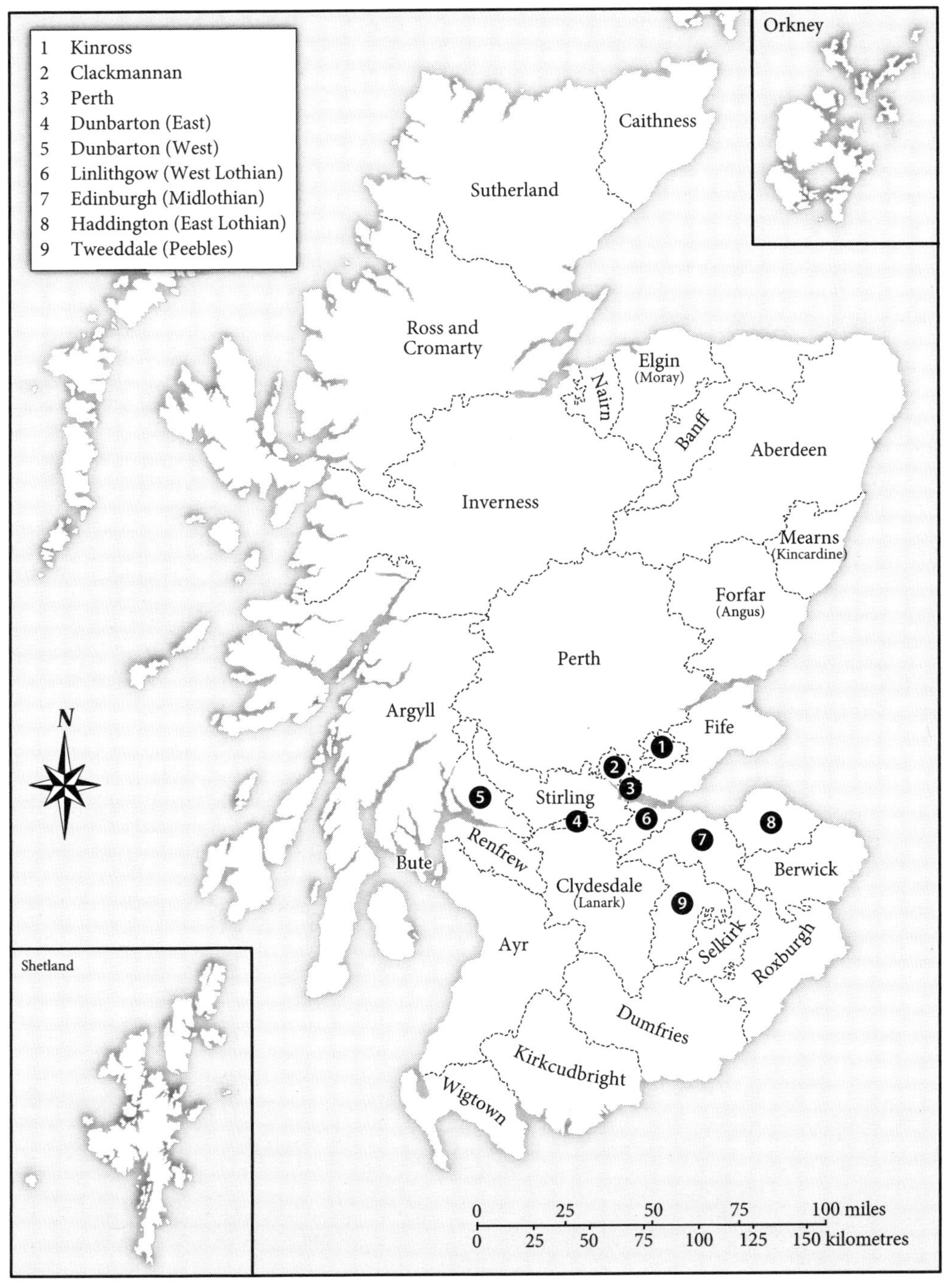

Map 2B. Scotland.

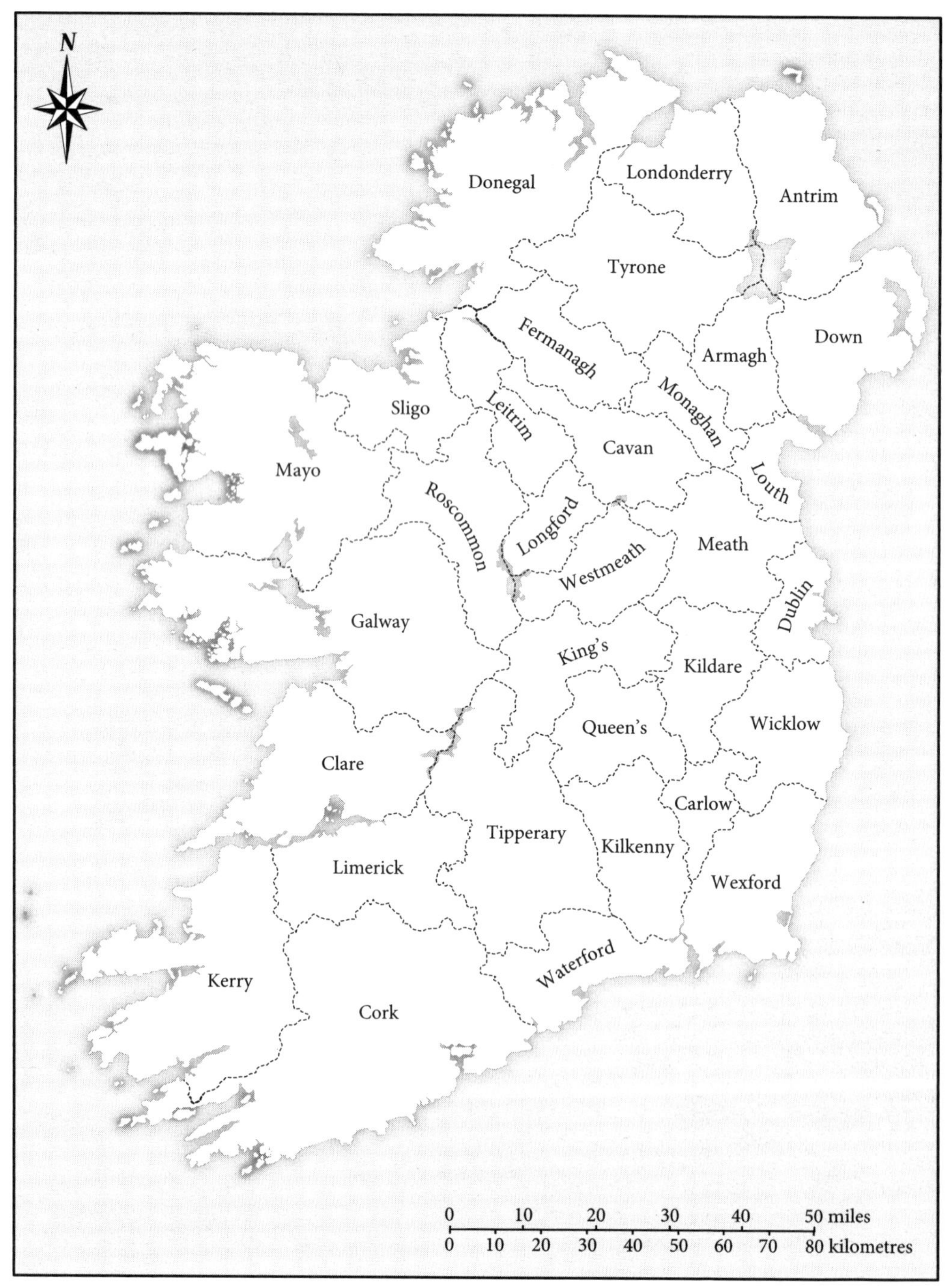

Map 2C. Ireland.

Map 3. England.

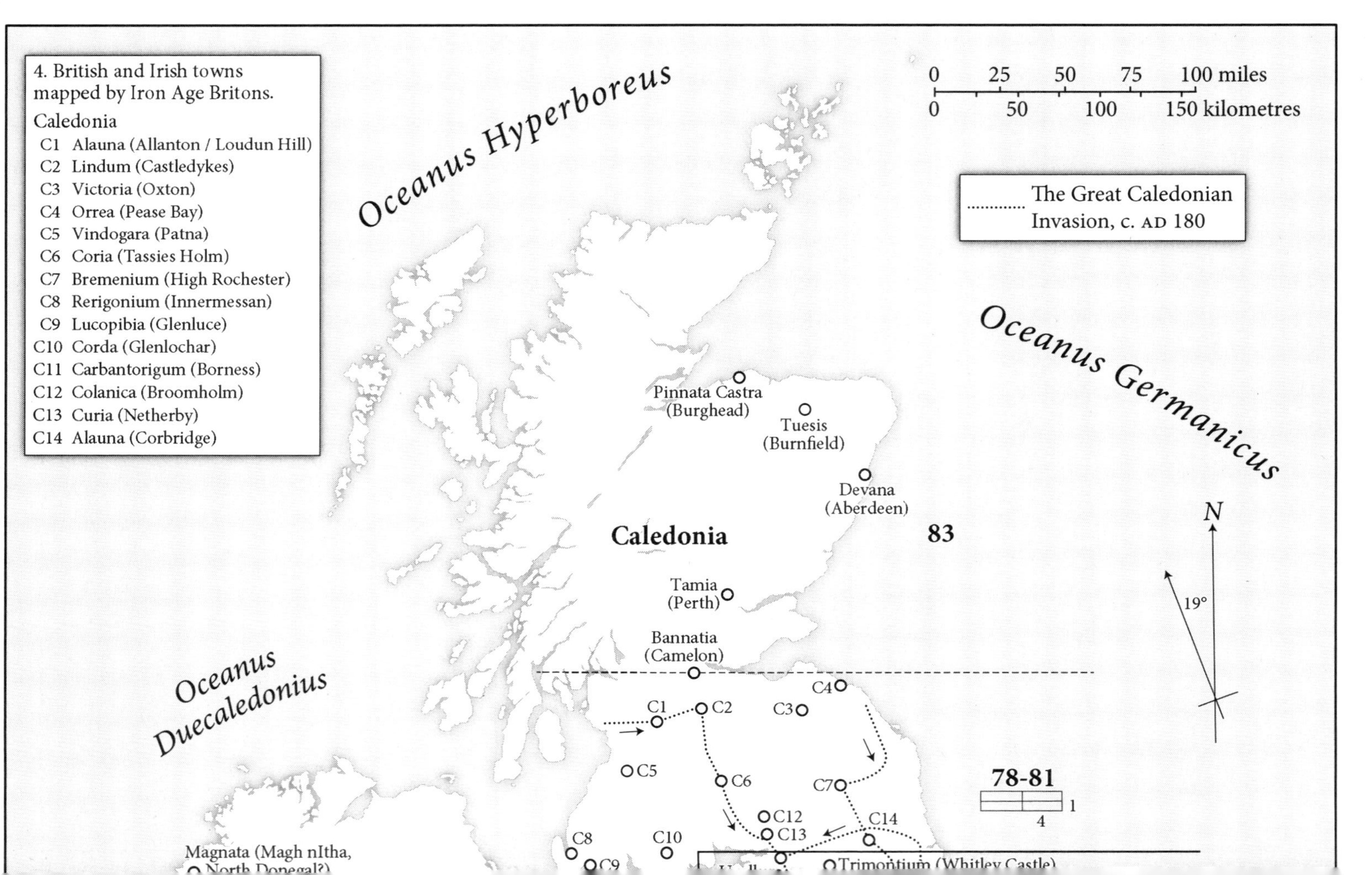

4. British and Irish towns mapped by Iron Age Britons.
Caledonia
C1 Alauna (Allanton / Loudun Hill)
C2 Lindum (Castledykes)
C3 Victoria (Oxton)
C4 Orrea (Pease Bay)
C5 Vindogara (Patna)
C6 Coria (Tassies Holm)
C7 Bremenium (High Rochester)
C8 Rerigonium (Innermessan)
C9 Lucopibia (Glenluce)
C10 Corda (Glenlochar)
C11 Carbantorigum (Borness)
C12 Colanica (Broomholm)
C13 Curia (Netherby)
C14 Alauna (Corbridge)
0 25 50 75 100 miles
0 50 100 150 kilometres
The Great Caledonian Invasion, c. AD 180
Oceanus Hyperboreus
Oceanus Germanicus
Oceanus Duecaledonius
Pinnata Castra (Burghead)
Tuesis (Burnfield)
Devana (Aberdeen)
Caledonia
83
Tamia (Perth)
Bannatia (Camelon)
N
19°
C1
C2
C3
C4
C5
C6
C7
C8
C9
C10
C12
C13
C14
78-81
1
4
Magnata (Magh nItha,

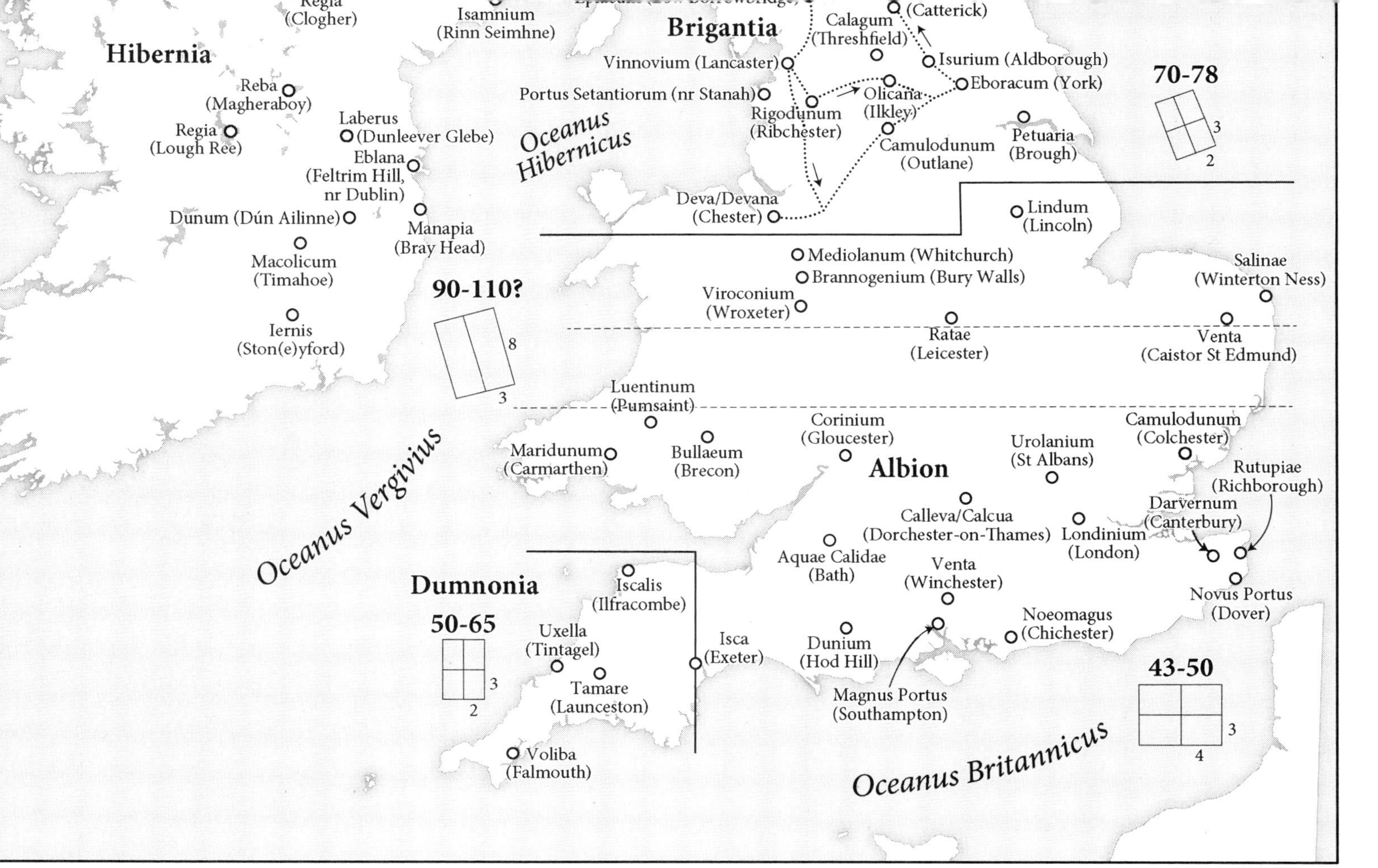

Map 4. British and Irish towns mapped by Iron Age Britons.

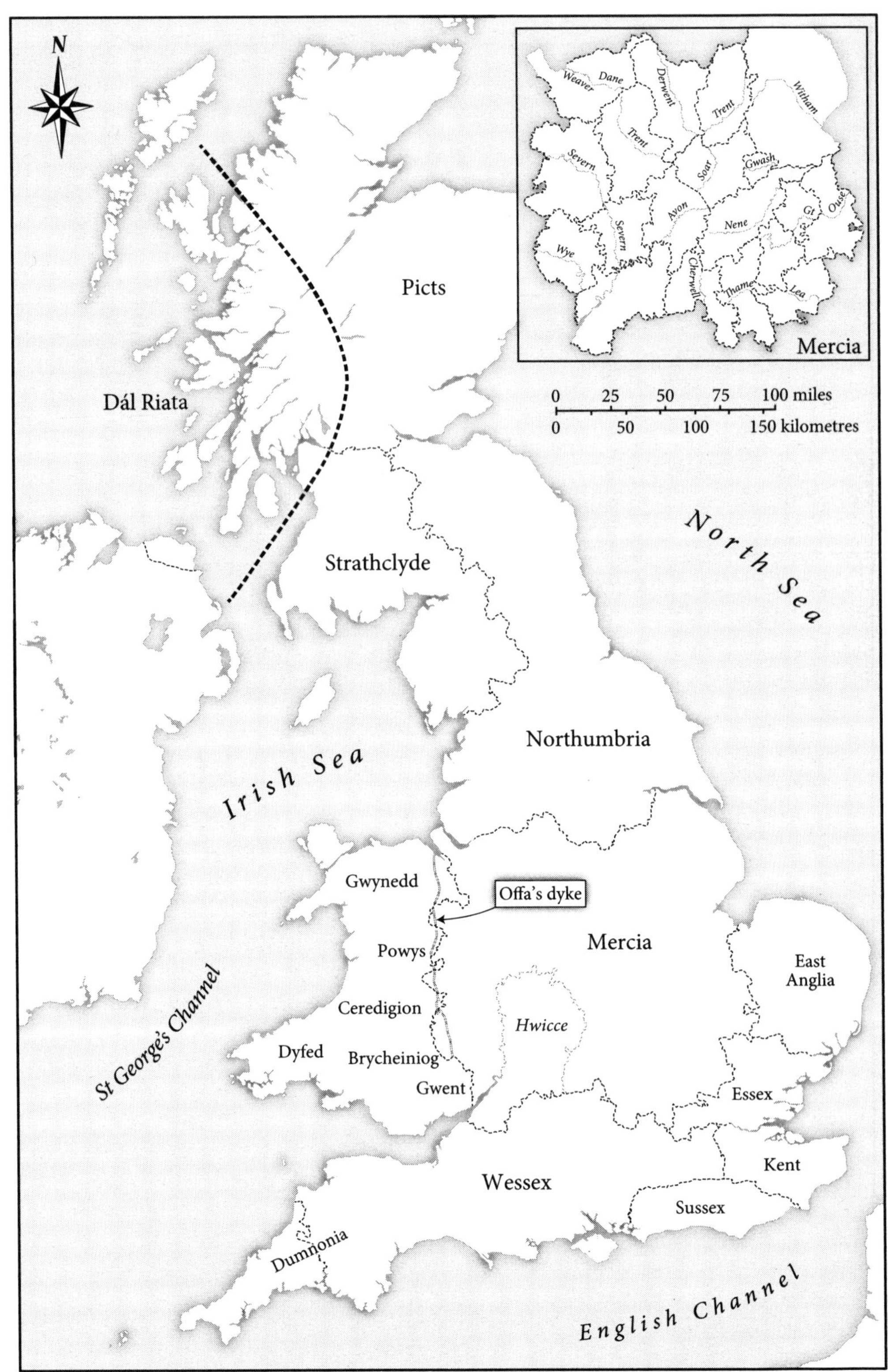

Map 5. British kingdoms, c. 780.

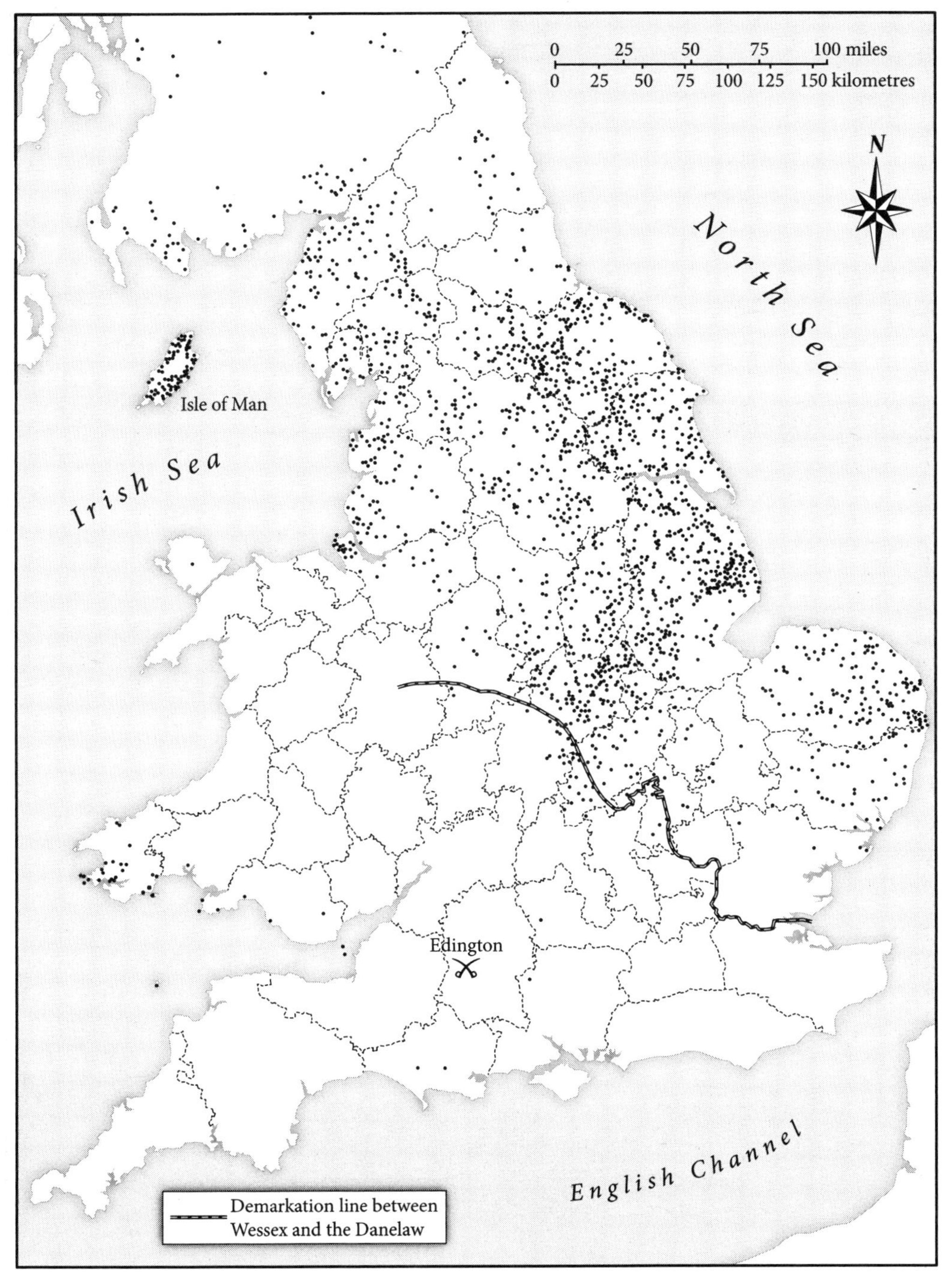

Map 6. Danish place names in Great Britain and the Isle of Man.

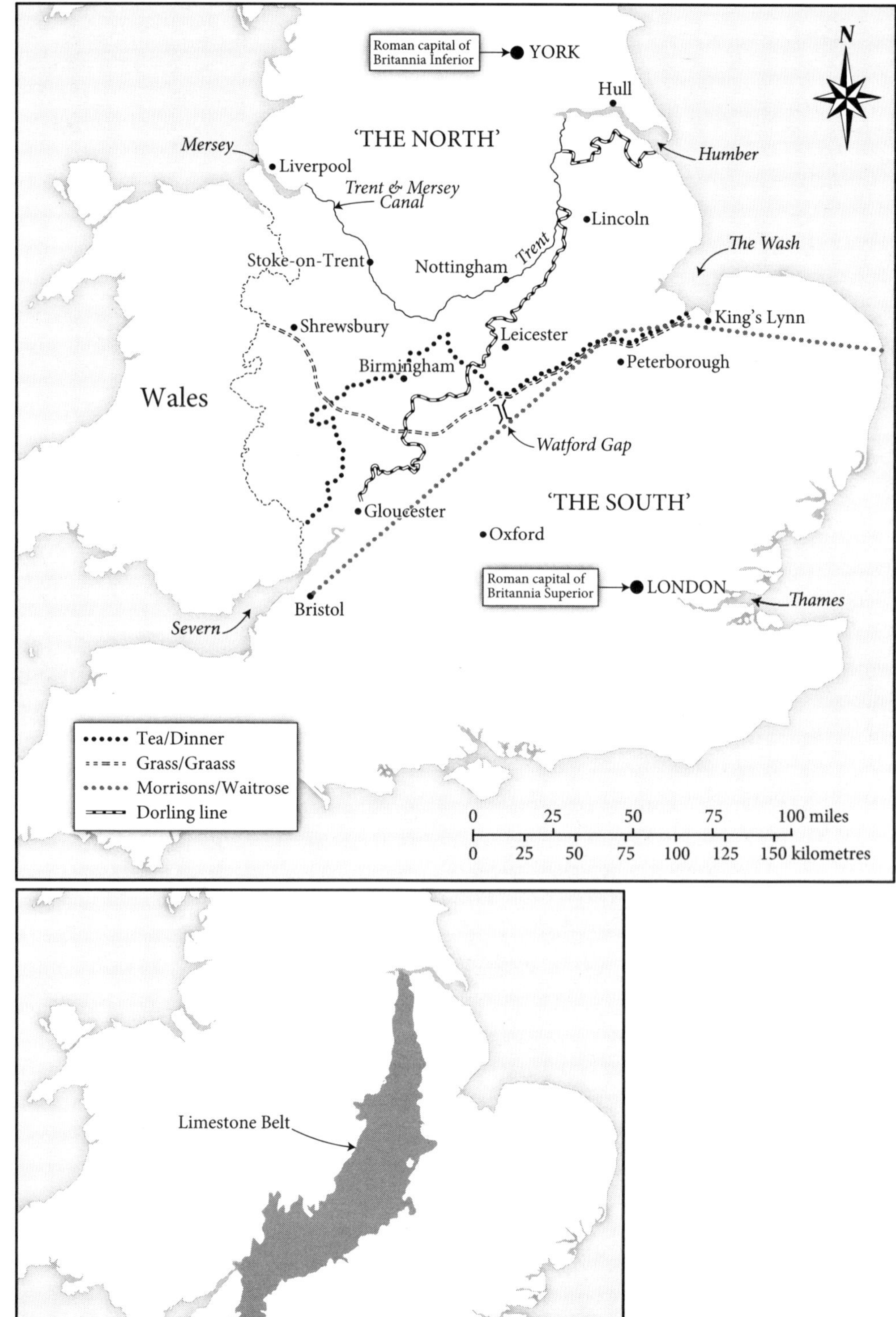

Map 7. Perceptions of a North–South divide.

Map 8. The twelve administrative subdivisions of the United Kingdom.

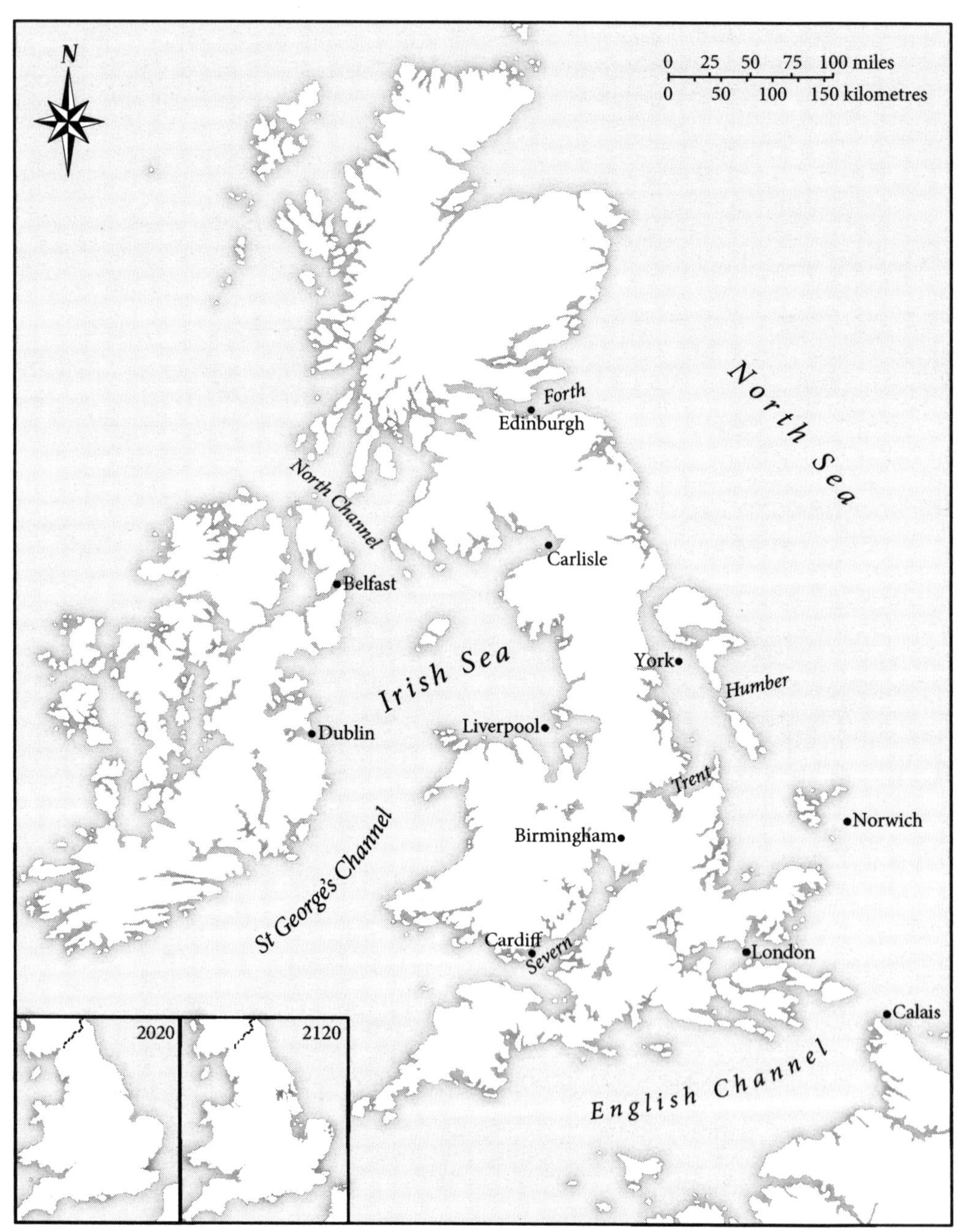

Map 9. Coastlines of the British Isles.

References

1. Off Course

2 'The only two lines': *German Invasion Plans for the British Isles 1940*, tr. A. Matthews (2007), pp. 43–4.

3 'It was a town of red brick': C. Dickens, *Hard Times* (1854), ch. 5.

4 'About ten miles from Preston': T. De Quincey, 'The English Mail-Coach', *The Collected Writings*, ed. D. Masson, XIII (1897), p. 309.

5 'I rose in horror': Ibid., p. 317.

6 'standing veri blekely': *The Itinerary of John Leland the Antiquary*, ed. T. Hearne, V (1711), p. 82.

6 a Roman road: The exact course was rediscovered in 2020–21: D. Ratledge, 'The Roman Road from Walton-le-Dale to Lancaster' (2024): http://www.twithr.co.uk/lancs-gm/M70d.htm

2. 'Crap Country'

9 'requesting reduced speed': G. P. Neele, *Railway Reminiscences* (1904), p. 508.

9 'dungeons of the soul': V. Hugo, 'Ce que dit la Bouche d'Ombre', *Les Contemplations* (1856): 'Aujourd'hui', xxvi.

10 random brain-wiring events: C. Wilson, 'Lucky You', *New Scientist*, 24 September 2022, pp. 36–40.

11 For the next eight thousand centuries: Summary and maps in F. Sturt et al., 'New Models of North West European Holocene Palaeogeography and Inundation', *Journal of Archaeological Science*, XL, 11 (2013), pp. 3963–76.

11 'Our time is three score yeare and ten': Psalm 90, v. 10.

12 village of Horton: Summaries in M. Symonds, 'Horton's Neolithic Houses',

Current Archaeology, 292 (2014); 'Kingsmead Quarry, Horton' (2014): https://www.wessexarch.co.uk/our-work/kingsmead-quarry-horton. On Neolithic farming: P. Rowley-Conwy et al., 'The Earliest Farming in Britain', in K. J. Gron et al., eds, *Farmers at the Frontier: A Pan-European Perspective on Neolithisation* (2020), pp. 401–24.

13 its 'aged oaks': J. Milton, 'L'Allegro', *Poems* (1645).

13 the 'enclosure green': J. Milton, *Paradise Lost* (1667; 1674), IV, vv. 33–6.

13 Langdale axes: E.g. S. Taylor, 'Journeys to Neolithic Langdale . . . Prehistoric Movement of Polished Stone Axes', *Lithics*, XXXVII (2016), pp. 15–32.

14 In central and eastern Sutherland: H. Fairhurst and D. Taylor, 'A Hut-Circle Settlement at Kilphedir, Sutherland', *Proceedings of the Society of Antiquaries of Scotland*, CIII (1974), pp. 65–99. Generally: J. Downes, ed., 'Settlement, Landuse and Resources', 3.3. in 'Bronze Age' (Scottish Archaeological Research Framework, 2021?): https://scarf.scot/national/scarf-bronze-age-panel-report/3-lifeways-and-lifestyles/3–3-settlement-landuse-and-resources/

3. The Size of Britain

17 'visibility cloak': https://www.heywhatsthat.com/

17 'liked to have books': J. R. R. Tolkien, *The Lord of the Rings* (1937–49), I, Prologue, p. 1.

17 '[They] said that you could see the Sea': Ibid.

17 Broadway Tower: J. Garth, *Tolkien's Worlds* (2020), p. 157.

18 Caesar was told by traders: Caesar, *De Bello Gallico*, V, 13.

19 the Venerable Bede in 731: *Historia Ecclesiastica Gentis Anglorum*, I, 1.

19 'Vif kinges þer were': *The Early South-English Legendary*, ed. C. Horstmann (1887), pp. 345–6 (St Kenelm).

19 'wild and waterless': Cassius Dio, *Roman History*, tr. E. Cary and H. B. Foster (1914–27), LXXVII, 12.

19 In 1676, a highwayman: T. B., 'The Highwayman [John] Nevison', *Notes and Queries*, 5 (1 February 1868), p. 109 (with references).

20 Mr Cooper Thornhill: W. Pick, *An Authentic Historical Racing Calendar* (1785), p. vi.

20 beácen-fýres: See W. Lambarde, 'The Beacons in Kent', *A Perambulation*

of Kent, (1596), pp. 68–70; H. T. White, 'The Beacon System in Kent', *Archaeologia Cantiana*, XLVI (1934), pp. 77–96; J. Nicholson, *Beacons of East Yorkshire* (1887).

20 'The ghastly war-flame': Thomas Babington Macaulay, 'The Armada' (1832, unfinished), *The Works of Lord Macaulay Complete*, ed. Lady H. Trevelyan, VIII (1866), pp. 587–8.

4. Sea-Fearing Nation

23 'The many currents of the sea': Tacitus, *Agricola*, X. My translation.

24 'Formerly two carucates': *A General Introduction to Domesday Book* (1817; 1971), I, 308; on vanished towns and villages, see also H. C. Darby, *Domesday England* (1977), and M. Green, *Shadowlands: A Journey Through Lost Britain* (2022).

24 At Wrangle: Darby, *Domesday England*, p. 51.

24 last heard of in 1888: E.g. A. Tutt, 'The Story of Shipden', Time and Tide Museum (2021): https://yarmouthmuseums.wordpress.com/2021/12/14/the-story-of-shipden/

25 'a little world within itself': 'A Proclamation for the Union of the Kingdoms of England and Scotland': J. Nicolson and R. Burn, *The History and Antiquities of the Counties of Westmorland and Cumberland* (1777), I, cxxii.

25 A trident-brandishing Britannia: J. Toynbee, 'Britannia on Roman Coins of the Second Century A.D.', *The Journal of Roman Studies*, XIV (1924), pp. 142–57.

25 'wholly unfit for sea': *The Diary of Samuel Pepys*, ed. R. Latham (1987; 2003), p. 637 (30 June 1666).

26 'to heare the thumping': *The Diary of Ralph Josselin*, ed. A. Macfarlane (1976), 31 July 1653.

26 'all our hearts do now ake': Pepys, p. 787 (12 June 1667).

27 a boy from 'Dirtewychy': J. Sumption, *The Age of Pilgrimage* (1975; 2003), p. 84.

27 Saxon place names: A. Cole, 'The Anglo-Saxon Traveller', *Nomina*, XVII (1994), pp. 7–18; J. E. Macdonald, *Travel and the Communications Network in Late Saxon Wessex*, thesis (U. of York, 2001), p. 149.

27 Under Henry VI: On the navy's primarily defensive function:

C. Richmond, 'English Naval Power in the Fifteenth Century', *History*, LII, 174 (1967), pp. 1–15; C. Lloyd, *The British Seaman 1200–1860: A Social Survey* (1968), p. 28.

27 Drake playing bowls: H. Kelsey, *Sir Francis Drake: The Queen's Pirate* (1998), pp. 321–2. (Earliest record: 1624.)

28 pipe-smoking: W. Oldys, *The Works of Sir Walter Ralegh* (1829), I, 73.

28 'a plashy place': T. Fuller, *The History of the Worthies of England* (1662; 1811), I, 287.

28 A dozen towns along the central axis: On inland ports and navigable rivers: J. Priestley, *Historical Account of the Navigable Rivers, Canals and Railways of Great Britain* (1831); J. F. Edwards, *The Transport System of Medieval England and Wales*, thesis (U. of Salford, 1987); J. Blair, ed., *Waterways and Canal-Building in Medieval England* (2014); R. Pedley, *The Brigantes: A Study in the Early History of the North Pennines*, thesis (U. of Durham, 1939); Rev. D. J. M. Caffyn, *River Transport, 1189–1600*, thesis (U. of Sussex, 2010); R. Selkirk, *The Piercebridge Formula* (1983); G. J. White, *The Medieval English Landscape, 1000–1540* (2012), p. 108.

29 Fleeing the wrath of Henry II: J. Morris, *The Life and Martyrdom of Saint Thomas Becket*, 2nd ed. (1885), ch. 17.

29 'wended his way by water': *The Early South-English Legendary*, ed. C. Horstmann (1887), p. 138 (v. 1117).

29 'You shall find': *A New Discovery by Sea, with a Wherry from London to Salisbury* (1623), *Works of John Taylor, the Water Poet*, ed. C. Hindley (1870) p. 24 (separate pagination).

30 'ditch of weeds and mud': *A Very Merry Wherry-Ferry Voyage* (1622), *Works of John Taylor*, p. 17.

30 'swam in the deepest places': *A New Discovery by Sea*, p. 34.

30 '. . . some women, and some children': *A Very Merry Wherry-Ferry Voyage*, p. 8.

31 significant invasions: I. Hernon, *Fortress Britain: All the Invasions and Incursions since 1066* (2013).

31 'these grisly feendly rokkes': Chaucer, *The Franklin's Tale*, *The Canterbury Tales*, vv. 868–75.

32 uniformly coloured red: L. Colley, '"This Small Island": Britain, Size and Empire', *Proceedings of the British Academy*, CXXI (2003), pp. 171–90; see pp. 171–2.

33 'We shouldn't lose any more': L. Mermin, dir., *Blair and Brown: The New Labour Revolution*, episode 2, BBC 2, 4 October 2021: 19'37"–19'56".

5. 'Barbarians Beyond the Ocean'

34 Atlantic–North Sea trading zone: See B. Cunliffe and J. Koch, eds, *Celtic from the West: Alternative Perspectives* (2010).

35 'traversed all of Britain on foot': Strabo, *Geography*, II, 4, 1.

35 'beyond the limits of the known world': Cassius Dio, *Roman History*, LX, 19.

35 'without battle or bloodshed': Suetonius, 'Divus Claudius', 17, in *De Vita Caesarum.*

35 Campus Martius: Suetonius, 'Divus Claudius', 21.

35 'Tiberius Claudius Caesar': A. A. Barrett, 'Claudius' British Victory Arch in Rome', *Britannia*, XXII (1991), pp. 1–19; see p. 12.

36 'islands in the Ocean': Eutropius, *Breviarium Historiae Romanae*, VII, 13.

36 consistent with the . . . evidence: E.g. C. E. Stevens, 'Claudius and the Orcades', *The Classical Review*, new series, I, 1 (1951), pp. 7–9.

36 diversity of the Orkneys: 'People of the British Isles': 'Population Genetics' (with maps): https://www.peopleofthebritishisles.org/population-genetics

36 sailed from Caledonia: Tacitus, *Agricola*, X and XXIV.

38 'the considerable difficulties': *German Invasion Plans for the British Isles 1940*, tr. A. Matthews (2007), pp. 63–4.

38 Caesar's Gaulish informants: Caesar, *De Bello Gallico*, V, 12.

39 'People of the British Isles': See note to p. 36.

39 The fabled founder: G. Robb, *The Ancient Paths / The Discovery of Middle Earth* (2013), ch. 1.

39 exodus of Gaulish tribes: Livy, V, 33 ff.; Polybius, II, 17; Diodorus Siculus, XIV, 113; Dionysius of Halicarnassus, XIII, 11; Pliny, XII, 2 (5); Plutarch, *Camillus*, XV–XVII; Justinus, XXIV, 4.

39 Isotopic analyses: C. Snoeck et al., 'Strontium Isotope Analyses on Cremated Human Remains from Stonehenge', *Scientific Reports*, 8 (2018); M. P. Pearson et al., 'The Original Stonehenge? A Dismantled Stone Circle in the Preseli Hills of West Wales', *Antiquity*, XCV (2021), pp. 85–103. The recumbent Altar Stone of Stonehenge was recently found to have come from north-east Scotland: A. Clarke et al., 'A

Scottish Provenance for the Altar Stone of Stonehenge', *Nature*, 632 (2024), pp. 570–77.

6. The Iron Age Atlas of the British Isles

41 'clever in basket-work': C. Dickens, *A Child's History of England*, I (1852), p. 4.

41 'Four Royal Roads': Mentioned by Henry of Huntingdon, Ranulf Higden, Geoffrey of Monmouth and Robert of Gloucester; drawn by Matthew Paris (The British Library, Cotton Nero D. I, f. 187 v; reproduced in G. Robb, *The Ancient Paths / The Discovery of Middle Earth*, p. 237.)

42 atlas comprising five distinct maps: Technical details in G. Robb, *The Debatable Land* (2018), ch. 24, notes on pp. 292–4 and maps on pp. 250–63.

43 the lost *mappa mundi*: R. Talbert and R. Unger, eds, *Cartography in Antiquity and the Middle Ages* (2008), p. 113.

43 'This body of knowledge': Caesar, *De Bello Gallico*, VI, 13–14.

44 'The ancient Britons': C. Dickens, *A Child's History*, I, pp. 4–5.

44 'The Celts were characterized': *The Oxford Illustrated History of Britain*, ed. K. Morgan (1984; 1997), p. 4.

44 'Why are we not starting . . . ?': Ibid., p. 1.

44 front-page news: A. Marr, review of *The Debatable Land*, *The Sunday Times*, 4 February 2018.

44 'greatly respected' friend: Caesar, *De Bello Gallico*, I, 20.

45 *physiologia* . . . house-guest: Cicero, *De Senectute, De Amicitia, De Divinatione*, tr. W. A. Falconer (1923); *Cicero on Divination: De Divinatione, Book 1*, ed. D. Wardle (2006), I, 41.

45 He once cried: Caesar, *De Bello Gallico*, I, 20.

45 Caratacus: Tacitus, *Annals*, XII, 37; Cassius Dio, *Roman History*, LXI, 33.

45 book on the Roman Empire: B. Johnson, *The Dream of Rome* (2006).

45 Roman road at Sharpstone Hill: T. Malim and L. Hayes, 'An Engineered Iron Age Road', *Transactions of the Shropshire Archaeological and Historical Society*, LXXXV (2010), pp. 7–80.

46 'roads and byways': Caesar, *De Bello Gallico*, V, 19.

46 'He accepted that dating results': 'Iron Age Road Found in Shropshire by Archaeologists', BBC News, 16 March 2011.

46 oriented . . . on the local summer solstice: See M. Fulford et al., *Silchester Insula IX: The 'Town Life' Project* (2010); also a temple: S. Frere and M. Fulford, 'The *Collegium Peregrinorum* at Silchester', *Britannia*, XXXIII (2002), pp. 167–75.

46 'outstandingly good': Caesar, *De Bello Gallico*, V, 21.

46 'Their buildings are exceedingly numerous': Caesar, *De Bello Gallico*, V, 12.

7. 'Yon Outrageous Romans'

50 'some renowned metropolis': J. Milton, *Paradise Lost*, III, 549–50, quoted in W. Hazlitt, *Table-Talk* (1821), II, 3: 'On Going a Journey'.

50 'the learnèd air that breathes': W. Hazlitt, ibid.

51 the 'fágan flór': J. Cooper, 'Four Oxfordshire Anglo-Saxon Charters', *Oxoniensia*, L (1985), pp. 15–23. Used by John Buchan in *The Blanket of the Dark* (1931), ch. 1: 'The Painted Floor'.

52 'Yon outrageous Romans': Tacitus, *Agricola*, XXX. My translation.

52 'the biggest war': Cassius Dio, *Roman History*, LXXIII, 8.

53 a list of twelve battles: Nennius (?), *Historia Brittonum*, ed. D. Dumville (1985), p. 50; G. Robb, *The Debatable Land*, ch. 27.

53 *Brittunculi*: Vindolanda tablet 164, AD 97–105?: https://romaninscriptionsofbritain.org/inscriptions/TabVindol164

54 'Barbarian Conspiracy': Ammianus Marcellinus, *Römische Geschichte*, ed. W. Seyfarth (1968–71), XXVII, 8 and XXVIII, 3.

54 the British elite: E. W. Black, 'Romano-British Gentlemen and Officers', *Britannia*, XXV (1994), pp. 99–110.

54 *pictae* or 'painted' vessels: Vegetius, *Epitoma rei militaris*, ed. M. Reeve (2004), XXXVII.

8. Invisible Invaders

55 either lacking or uninterpretable: E.g. R. Coates, 'Invisible Britons: the View from Linguistics', in N. Higham, ed., *Britons in Anglo-Saxon England* (2007), pp. 172–91. See especially B. Yorke, *Kings and Kingdoms of Early Anglo-Saxon England* (1990), ch. 6: 'Mercia'; D. Dumville, 'The Local Rulers of England to AD 927', in *Handbook of British Chronology*, eds E. Fryde et al., 3rd ed. (1986), pp. 1–25.

55 'fierce and impious': Gildas, *The Ruin of Britain* [*De Excidio et Conquestu Britanniae*], ed. M. Winterbottom (1978), 23.

56 famine and a 'famous plague': Gildas, 2, 20, 23 and 25.

58 'timorous chickens': Gildas, 17.

59 a great measuring: 'Lludd and Llevelys': *The Mabinogion*, tr. J. Gantz (1976), pp. 128–33.

59 Atrebatian, Catuvellaunian or Dobunnian: Coin distribution maps in A. Bevan, 'Spatial Methods for Analysing Large-Scale Artefact Inventories', *Antiquity*, LXXXVI, 332 (2012), pp. 492–506; see pp. 501–2.

59 nucleated settlements: E.g. T. Rowley, *Villages in the Landscape* (1978), pp. 18 and 101–2.

60 the Anglo-Saxon Chronicle: Main texts in *The Anglo-Saxon Chronicle: A Collaborative Edition*, various editors (from 1983).

60 'great unsolved problem': J. Blair, in *The Oxford Illustrated History of Britain*, pp. 64–5.

61 Anglo-Saxon boundary charters: Transcribed in the online Sawyer catalogue: https://esawyer.lib.cam.ac.uk/browse/sawyercat.html

61 'Then [go] north over the hill': King Æthelstan to Wulfgar, 931: Sawyer no. S416. My translation.

9. 'When Is This?

63 'the waste howling wilderness': Deuteronomy 22:10.

64 a 'house' made of willow: Jenny Martin, TV interview of Frank Gunnell, 1958: https://player.bfi.org.uk/free/film/watch-man-who-lives-up-a-tree-1958-online; also J. Phillpott, 'Tree-dwelling Bin Man Told Me Where Civil War Dead Lay', *Worcester News*, 28 March 2007.

64 'all the village train': O. Goldsmith, *The Deserted Village* (1770), vv. 17–18.

65 'The peculiar spirit of Scottish society': G. M. Trevelyan, *English Social History* (US: 1942; UK: 1944), p. 207.

66 The many 'Greens': O. Rackham, *The History of the Countryside* (1986), p. 344; R. Shirley, *Village Greens of England*, thesis (U. of Durham, 1994).

66 the Malvern 'wilderness': 'Saltus' before the Conquest: William of Malmesbury, *De Gestis Pontificum Anglorum*, ed. N. Hamilton (1870), p. 286 (Book IV).

66 the *ealdan straet*: King Edgar to Pershore Abbey: Sawyer no. 786 (972).

Analysed and mapped in D. Hooke, *Worcestershire Anglo-Saxon Charter Bounds* (1990), pp. 208–15.

67 'landscape provinces': O. Rackham, *The History of the Countryside*, p. 5 (table).

68 The 'English Alps': Celia Fiennes, *Through England on a Side Saddle in the Time of William and Mary*, ed. E. Griffiths (1888), p. 33.

68 'Herefordscir in Walia': *The Great Roll of the Pipe . . . AD 1170–1* (1893), pp. 81–3.

68 Welsh . . . could still be heard: John Aubrey, quoted by A. Fox and D. Woolf, in *The Spoken Word: Oral Culture in Britain 1500–1850* (2002), p. 15.

68 No Welsh translators: I. Morgan Watkin, 'Human Genetics in Worcestershire and the Shakespeare Country', *Heredity*, XXII (1967), pp. 349–58; see p. 351.

69 'a distinct ethnological frontier': J. Beddoe, *The Races of Britain* (1885), p. 256.

10. The Shires

71 'A man will be almost ashamed': A. Trollope, *Marion Fay* (1882), I, 142.

71 south-west region of 'rhoticity': A. Hughes and P. Trudgill, *English Accents and Dialects*, 5th ed. (2012); E. Asprey, 'Investigating Residual Rhoticity in a Non-rhotic Accent': https://www.latl.leeds.ac.uk/wp-content/uploads/sites/49/2019/05/Asprey_2007.pdf. Maps in H. Orton and E. Dieth, *Survey of English Dialects*, 4 vols (1962–71).

71 'fly over the country' . . . 'sacrifice a goat': Anthony Crosland on the Rate Support Grant, 25 March 1974: Hansard, DCCCLXXI, col. 49.

72 'Hereford looked west': Sir J. Banham (Chair), *Final Recommendations on the Future Local Government of Hereford & Worcester* (1994); Local Government Boundary Commission for England Report, no. 592 (1990).

72 choice of marriage partners: A. Fox, *A Lost Frontier Revealed: Regional Separation in the East Midlands* (2020), p. 6; M. Carter, 'Town or Urban Society?', in C. Phythian-Adams, ed., *Societies, Culture and Kinship* (1993).

73 called up by scīr: J. Baker and S. Brookes, 'Explaining Anglo-Saxon Military Efficiency: The Landscape of Mobilisation' (2016), pp. 3, 8

and 19–20: https://discovery.ucl.ac.uk/id/eprint/1471696/3/Brookes_Baker&B-MobilisationREV_OA.pdf

73 evidence of a historian-monk: *Hemingi Chartularium Ecclesiae Wigorniensis*, ed. T. Hearne (1723), p. 280 ('De Gloeceastre scire'); see also D. Hooke, *The Anglo-Saxon Landscape: the Kingdom of the Hwicce* (1985; 2009), p. 104.

74 In 1740, the rector of Kirkandrews: R. Ferguson, 'The Registers and Account Books of the Parish of Kirkandrews-upon-Esk', *Transactions of the Cumberland and Westmorland Antiquarian and Archaeological Society*, VIII (1885), pp. 280–306; see p. 297; G. Robb, *The Debatable Land*, p. 179.

74 system of shire boundaries: Summary in 'The Historic Counties Standard' (2024): https://historiccountiestrust.co.uk/Historic_Counties_Standard.pdf

75 list drawn up for King Offa: *Cartularium Saxonicum*, ed. W. de Gray Birch (1885), I, 414–16; C. Hart, 'The Tribal Hidage', *Transactions of the Royal Historical Society*, XXI (1971), pp. 133–57.

75 Worcestershire English: M. L. Samuels, 'Langland's Dialect', *Medium Ævum*, LIV, 2 (1985), pp. 232–47: especially pp. 237 (south-west Worcestershire) and 241 ('neither' is 'noyther', etc.).

75 'Thow myghtest better': *The Vision of Piers Plowman*, ed. A. Schmidt, 2nd ed. (1995): Prologue, v. 215.

76 'And as I lay': *The Vision of Piers Plowman*, Prologue, vv. 9–12 (my translation).

76 Mercian saint Guthlac: Felix, *Vita Sancti Guthlaci*, ed. B. Colgrave (1985), p. 110 (ch. 34).

76 All the Mercian shires: On the significance of Midland river basins: C. Phythian-Adams, 'Local History and National History', *Rural History*, II, 1 (1991), pp. 1–23; K. Taylor-Moore, *Borderlands: The Buckinghamshire / Northamptonshire Border, c.650–c.1350*, thesis (U. of Leicester, 2012), p. 86; C. Baker in 'The First Mercian Lands' (2020), fig. 2: https://profchrisbaker.com/2024/08/04/the-first-mercian-lands/

77 these Mercian treasures: M. Herman, *Iconography in Dialogue: Negotiating Tradition and Cultural Contact*, thesis (U. of York, 2013): e.g. pp. 61–148 and 195 ff.

78 to leave the 'old roads': E.g. M. Beresford and J. St Joseph, *Medieval England: An Aerial Survey* (1979), p. 74.

78 older than the parishes: N. Pounds, *A History of the English Parish* (2000), pp. 67 and 69.

79 'making bows and arrows': *Asser's Life of King Alfred* (893), ed. W. H. Stevenson (1904), p. 39.

79 'First as to the boundaries': Alfred and Guthrum treaty: parallel texts in *The Laws of the Earliest English Kings*, ed. F. Attenborough (1922), pp. 98–101.

80 Penda defeated the West Saxons: The Roman-road boundary may have been set in 577, when the West Saxons defeated three British kings at Dyrham, west of the Fosse Way, and took Gloucester, Cirencester and Bath.

80 These treaty lines: Two other, shorter coincidences of shire boundary and possible Roman road are shown on map 2. Like the Icknield Way north-east of Newmarket, 'the Devil's Highway' east of Silchester and north of Bagshot (Berkshire/Surrey) is probably pre-Roman. The section near Biggin Hill (Kent/Surrey) may be connected with the Battle of Otford (776) between Offa's Mercia and the Kentish Jutes.

80 petitioned King Æthelred: *Charters of Malmesbury Abbey*, ed. S. Kelly (2005), pp. 133–8; Sawyer no. 73 (681).

81 'a system of vast circumferences': Edward Thomas, 'England', in *The Last Sheaf* (1928), p. 111.

11. Conquered

82 the 'long-haired' comet: Anglo-Saxon Chronicle, 1066.

83 The poachers are now equipped: 'Wildlife is Easy Prey for Poacher Gangs', *Express & Star* (Wolverhampton), 4 December 2014.

83 'All the English': Henry of Huntingdon, *Historia Anglorum*, ed. T. Arnold (1879), pp. 208 and 210; sections 38–9 on the year 1087. My translation.

85 In 1966, the GPO: S. Bates, '900th Anniversary of the Battle of Hastings, 1966' (1993): https://www.postalmuseum.org/wp-content/uploads/2019/01/Stamp-History-1966-Hastings.pdf

86 Society of the Descendants of William: Bates, ibid., p. 3.

87 The English chronicler: *The Ecclesiastical History of Orderic Vitalis*, tr. M. Chibnall (1969; 2022), II, 185.

87 The scale of the disaster . . . Domesday Book: E.g. R. Fleming, *Domesday Book and the Law* (1998).

87 English diaspora: H. M. Thomas, 'The Significance and Fate of the

Native English Landholders of 1086', *The English Historical Review*, CXVIII, 476 (2003), pp. 303–33; see p. 320.

87 fewer than two hundred: E.g. K. Keats-Rohan, 'The Bretons and Normans of England, 1066–1154', *Nottingham Mediaeval Studies*, 36 (1992), pp. 42–78.

88 'Be the winter never so stark': D. Hooke, *The Anglo-Saxon Landscape*, p. 201: from *Aelfric's Colloquy* (c. 1005), ed. G. N. Garmonsway (1939).

88 a happy nation: [Maria Callcott], *Little Arthur's History of England* (1835), I, pp. 44 and 88–90.

88 'witenagemot': The 'meeting of the wise' may originally have referred to any assembly of royal advisers rather than to an institution: J. Maddicott, *The Origins of the English Parliament, 924–1327* (2010), ch. 1; P. Wormald, *The Making of English Law: King Alfred to the Twelfth Century* (1999), ch. 2.

89 dynasty of Urse d'Abetot: See 'Parishes: Powick', in *A History of the County of Worcester*, ed. W. Page, IV (1924).

89 'Hattest þu Urs': William of Malmesbury, *De Gestis Pontificum Anglorum*, pp. 384–5 (Book III).

90 a well-maintained network: O. Rackham, *The History of the Countryside*, p. 259.

90 *herepaths* (military roads): O. G. S. Crawford, 'Place-Names': https://www.cantab.net/users/michael.behrend/repubs/crawford_pn/pages/main.html

90 total arable acreage: J. Gillingham, in *The Oxford Illustrated History of Britain*, p. 157; or roughly the same, according to N. Higham and M. Ryan, *The Anglo-Saxon World* (2013), p. 420.

90 Cannock, modified: 'Cannock', in the Survey of English Place-Names: https://epns.nottingham.ac.uk/browse/Staffordshire/Cannock/53286fffb47fc40c190007d1-Cannock

91 The 'Lingua Romana' of Normandy: E.g. D. Trotter, 'An Analysis of Anglo-Norman Elements in English Place-names', *English Today*, XXX, 2 (2014), pp. 39–42.

12. 'High or Lowly'

92 'Thus did England': *The Metrical Chronicle of Robert of Gloucester*, ed. W. A. Wright (1887), vv. 7537–43. My translation.

93 a neurological disorder: D. Thorpe and J. Alty, 'What Type of Tremor Did the Medieval "Tremulous Hand of Worcester" Have?", *Brain*, CXXXVIII, 10 (2015), pp. 3123–7.

93 '[Due to] common ignorance': I have retranslated from *Rotuli Parliamentorum*, II, 273; also W. M. Ormrod, 'The Use of English: Language, Law, and Political Culture in Fourteenth-Century England', *Speculum*, LXXVIII, 3 (2003), pp. 750–87; see pp. 755–7.

93 'utterly expunge': M. Vale, 'Language, Politics and Society: the Uses of the Vernacular in the Later Middle Ages', *The English Historical Review*, CXX, 485 (2005), pp. 15–34; see p. 20.

93 'a destruire & anientier': *Rotuli Parliamentorum*, II, 158 (Edward III, 1346).

95 'A jester was insulting the English': *De Gestis Herewardi Saxonis (The Exploits of Hereward the Saxon)*, ed. S. H. Miller (1895), p. 34. My translation.

95 'a rustic who had no idea': *De Gestis Herewardi Saxonis*, p. 53.

95 'faithfully serves King William': *De Gestis Herewardi Saxonis*, p. 72.

96 states of subjection: R. Bremmer Jr, 'The "Gesta Herewardi": Transforming an Anglo-Saxon into an Englishman', in B. Summerfield, ed., *People and Texts: Relationships in Medieval Literature* (2007), pp. 29–42; see p. 30.

96 'I be' (or 'bin'): J. Wright, ed., *The English Dialect Dictionary*, I (1898), p. 197 ('Be'); also noted in *The Northern Star or Monthly Magazine*, III (July–December 1818), p. 111.

97 gendered pronouns: S. Wagner, in *Varieties of English 1: the British Isles*, eds B. Kortmann and C. Upton (2008), p. 424; *Dialectology Meets Typology*, ed. B. Kortmann (2004), p. 482.

97 'Your Dorset peasants': Florence Hardy, *The Early Life of Thomas Hardy* (1928; 2011), pp. 301–2.

97 explorer of the English shires: W. Viereck, 'Prince Louis-Lucien Bonaparte and English Dialectology', *Nazioarteko Dialektologia Biltzarra*, VII (1992), pp. 17–30; L.-L. Bonaparte, *On the Dialects of Eleven Southern and South-Western Counties* (1877).

97 'absolute poverty': Worcester City Council, Report of the Child Food Poverty Scrutiny Task and Finish Group (2020), p. 3: https://committee.worcester.gov.uk/documents/s50381/Child%20Poverty%20Task%20Finish%20Group%20Report%20Final.pdf

98 'All Things Bright and Beautiful': Mrs Cecil Frances Alexander, *Hymns for Little Children* (1848).

13. Servants of History

99 At least thirty per cent of England: Guy Shrubsole, *Who Owns England?* (2019), pp. 86 and 267.

100 '[They should] make sure': 'Duke of Westminster Dies', *Financial Times*, 10 August 2016.

101 Recent studies: G. Clark and N. Cummins, 'Surnames and Social Mobility in England, 1170–2012', *Human Nature*, XXV (2014), pp. 517–37; K. Foord, `The Changing British Interpretations of the Effects of the Norman Conquest Since 1066' (2018): https://battlehistorysociety.com/Documents/X05.pdf

103 'With their faces blackened': R. Gaut, *A History of Worcestershire Agriculture and Rural Evolution* (1939), p. 163; see also J. Maynard, *The Agricultural Labourer in Worcestershire*, thesis (U. of Coventry, 2005), p. 56.

105 'rude' or 'babbling': E.g. R. Bartlett, *England Under the Norman and Angevin Kings* (2000), p. 484.

105 ritual of the 'mead-cup': C. Riseley, *Ceremonial Drinking in the Viking Age* (2014), p. i.

106 'seemed to stabilize society': Ibid.

106 we wenten quite ofte: With borrowings from *The Vision of Piers Plowman*, II, 95; V, 540; etc.

14. 'A Tale Tauld bi an idjot'

108 the dank cave: Other 'Bruce's Caves' include Oweynagulman Cave on Rathlin Island, Uamh-an-Righ near Balquhidder, and Kings Cave, Drumadoon, Arran.

109 popularized in 1827: W. Scott, *Tales of a Grandfather: Scotland*, ch. 8: 'The Rise of Robert the Bruce'.

109 neither Scottish nor English: E.g. 'Scottish when they will, and English at their pleasure': Thomas Musgrave to Lord Burghley, end 1583, in J. Bain, ed., *The Border Papers . . . in Her Majesty's Public Record Office* (1894–6), I, 126.

109 pretended to have been captured: 'Patten's Account of Somerset's

Expedition', in W. Scott, *Minstrelsy of the Scottish Border*, 2nd ed. (1803), I, lxix; also Anon., *The Complaynt of Scotland* [1548] (1801), pp. 166–7.

110 'Wars of Scottish Independence': First used by Walter Scott in the 1832 introduction to *Castle Dangerous* (1831).

110 The first British de Brus: R. M. Blakely, *The Brus Family in England and Scotland, 1100–1295* (2012), pp. 10–11; M. E. Cumming Bruce, *Family Records of the Bruces and the Cumyns* (1870), pp. 227–8.

111 'tret him curteusly': J. Barbour, *The Brus* (1376), ed. W. Mackenzie (1909), p. 241.

112 pawned them to Scotland: B. Crawford, 'The Pawning of Orkney and Shetland: A Reconsideration', *The Scottish Historical Review*, XLVIII, 145, pt 1 (1969), pp. 35–53.

112 the 'true and ancient marches': Hugh de Bolbec, in W. Shirley, ed., *Royal and Other Historical Letters . . . from the Originals in the Public Record Office* (1862–6), I, pp. 186–8.

112 'delight in all mischiefs': K. Brown et al., eds, *The Records of the Parliaments of Scotland to 1707* (2007–15): Act dated 29 July 1587.

112 'All Inglichemene annde Scottesmene': 'A Remembrance of an Order for the Debatable Lannde' (1537), in R. Armstrong, *The History of Liddesdale . . . and the Debateable Land* (1883), pt 1, p. xxxvii.

113 Sectarian divisions: E.g. S. Whigham et al., 'Politics and Football Fandom in Post-"Indyref" Scotland', *British Politics*, XVI (2021), pp. 414–35; M. McBride, 'Nationalism and "Sectarianism" in Contemporary Scotland', *Ethnic and Racial Studies*, XLV, 16 (2022), pp. 335–58; see p. 343.

113 cross-border marriages. G. Robb, *The Debatable Land*, pp. 131–2, 204 and 245.

113 'scaremongering': A. Groundwater, *The Scottish Middle March, 1573–1625: Power, Kinship, Allegiance* (2010), p. 27.

114 'I got out an atlas': J. Buchan, *The Thirty-Nine Steps* (1915), ch. 2.

115 A sample east–west route: G. Robb, *Cols and Passes of the British Isles* (2016), pp. 60–63 and 164–9.

15. 'Al was hethynesse som tyme Engelond and Walis'

117 'an unusual star': Anglo-Saxon Chronicle, 1106: ms E ('the Peterborough Chronicle').

118 'William the Bastard [the Conqueror]': *Chronica de Mailros*, ed. J. Stevenson (1835), p. 55.

118 'England and Wales were entirely heathen': *The Vision of Piers Plowman*, XV, 442: 'Al was hethynesse som tyme Engelond and Walis.'

118 'did not forbid the preaching': Bede, *Historia Ecclesiastica Gentis Anglorum*, III, 21.

119 Eilmer, a monk: William of Malmesbury, *Gesta Regum Anglorum*, ed. T. Hardy, in *Patrologiae Cursus Completus*, ed. J. P. Migne, CLXXIX (1899), pp. 1205–6 (II, 225). On the tale's plausibility: G. Robb, *France: An Adventure History* (2022), pp. 64 and 443.

119 'Blasing starres': R. Holinshed, *Chronicles: the Historie of England* (1587), I, 197; A. Walsham, 'Providentialism', in *The Oxford Handbook of Holinshed's Chronicles* (2012), ch. 25.

120 'no law against flying': F. Bragge, *A Full and Impartial Account of the Discovery of Sorcery and Witchcraft, Practis'd by Jane Wenham of Walkerne in Hertfordshire* (1712), pp. 14, 19 and 24; also J. B. Kingsbury, 'The Last Witch of England', *Folklore*, LXI, 3 (1950), pp. 134–45; P. J. Guskin, 'The Context of Witchcraft: The Case of Jane Wenham (1712)', *Eighteenth-Century Studies*, XV, 1 (1981), pp. 48–71.

121 At the mouth of the Tyne: *Vita Sancti Cuthberti*, ch. 3, in *Venerabilis Bedae Opera Historica Minora*, ed. J. Stevenson (1841), pp. 53–5. My translation. See also R. Hutton, *Pagan Britain* (2013), p. 317.

122 'there was hardly a murmur': J. Gillingham, in *The Oxford Illustrated History of Britain*, p. 157.

122 'Now at the dawning of the day': F. Raby, ed., *The Oxford Book of Medieval Latin Verse* (1959), pp. 53 and 362–3, tr. in 'What is a Contrafactum?', ed. B. Millett: Wessex Parallel WebTexts, http://wpwt.soton.ac.uk/notes/contraf.htm; also G. Monteiro, 'Parodies of Scripture, Prayer, and Hymn', *The Journal of American Folklore*, LXXVII, 303 (1964), pp. 45–52.

123 'As you know': *Sir Thopas*, *The Canterbury Tales*, vv. 943–6.

123 a room at the *diversorium*: *The Vision of Piers Plowman*, XII, 146–8.

123 'no place to have a baby': Luke 2:7–8; see R. Miller, ed., *The Complete Gospels: Annotated Scholars Version* (1994), p. 121 n.

123 the codename 'Piers Plowman': *The* Chronica Maiora *of Thomas Walsingham (1376–1422)*, ed. J. Clark, tr. D. Preest (2017), p. 163.

123 Langland's tinkering: On John Ball and Langland: J.-P. Genet, 'Lollards

et paysans', in *L'Hérétique au village*, ed. P. Chareyre (2011), pp. 253–67.

123 'ertheliche honeste thynges': *The Vision of Piers Plowman*, XIX, 94.

123 'a shiten shepherde and a clene sheep': General Prologue, *The Canterbury Tales*, vv. 503–4.

124 translated into English: Predominantly the Midland dialect, acceptable to the London book trade: see E. Solopova, ed., *The Wycliffite Bible: Origin, History and Interpretation* (2016), ch. 10: 'Dialect'.

124 a wide readership: J. A. Ford, *John Mirk's Festial: Orthodoxy, Lollardy and the Common People in Fourteenth-Century England* (2006), pp. 22–6.

125 Dover Straits earthquake: *Chronicon Henrici Knighton, vel Cnitthon, monachi Leycestrensis*, II, ed. J. R. Lumby (2013), p. 151; R. Musson, *The Seismicity of the British Isles to 1600* (2008), pp. 45–8.

125 Wycliffe's own explanation: *Select English Works of John Wyclif*, ed. Thomas Arnold (1869–71), III, 503.

125 'world religions': R. Hutton, *Pagan Britain*, pp. 320–21.

126 the 'Apostle of the North': C. Collingwood, *Memoirs of Bernard Gilpin, Parson of Houghton-le-Spring and Apostle of the North* (1884), p. 166; G. Robb, *The Debatable Land*, p. 63.

126 'total indifference on the subject': W. Scott, *Minstrelsy of the Scottish Border*, I, lxxxv.

16. Uplonders

129 common men and women: S. Federico, 'The Imaginary Society: Women in 1381', *Journal of British Studies*, XL, 2 (2001), pp. 159–83.

129 'rebellious villeins' . . . Domesday Book: M. Müller, 'The Aims and Organisation of a Peasant Revolt in Early Fourteenth-Century Wiltshire', *Rural History*, XIV, 1 (2003), p. 2. Petition quoted in R. B. Dobson, ed., *The Peasants' Revolt of 1381* (1970), p. 77.

130 In 1377, only nine English towns: M. Keen, *English Society in the Later Middle Ages, 1348–1500* (1990), pp. 79–88.

131 'men of divers villages' . . . 'about ten thousand': R. B. Dobson, *The Peasants' Revolt of 1381*, pp. 192, 209 and 186.

133 'extremely dangerous': J. Boys, *General View of the Agriculture of the County of Kent* (1794), p. 98.

133 'Progs oft to ford the sloughs': John Clare, 'Winter Fields', *Major Works*, eds E. Robinson and D. Powell (1984), p. 198.

133 'Here therefore they wallowed': John Bunyan, *The Pilgrim's Progress from This World to That Which is to Come*, 3rd ed. (1679), p. 12.

133 interpreters as well as guides: E.g. Daniel Defoe in the Peak (Derbyshire): *A Tour Thro' the Whole Island of Great Britain Divided into Circuits or Journies*, 3 vols (1724–7), III, 51.

133 'the common people know not': Celia Fiennes, *Through England on a Side Saddle in the Time of William and Mary*, ed. E. Griffiths (1888), p. 81.

134 'scarce 3 mile from their home': Ibid., p. 118.

134 expeditions through England: W. Cobbett, *Rural Rides in the Counties of Surrey, Kent, [etc.]*, ed. J. P. Cobbett (1853), p. 192 (at Whiteflood near Owslebury).

134 'Ingeleborrow, Pendle, and Penigent': Recorded by William Camden in 'Lancashire', *Britannia*; quoted by Defoe in *A Tour Thro' the Whole Island*, III, 88 and 222.

134 to admire 'the Reeke': C. Fiennes, *Through England on a Side Saddle*, p. 191.

134 'the highest hill in each County': Fiennes, *Through England*, p. 244.

134 Packington 'is said to contain': Edward Mogg, *Mogg's Handbook for Railway Travellers, or Real Iron-Road Book* (1840), p. 107. Among others: 'Great Packington' in *A Topographical Dictionary of England* (1848).

135 'At length they arrived': Walter Scott, *The Monastery* (1820), ch. 35.

135 'so wild a country': Arthur Young, *General View of the Agriculture of Lincolnshire*, 2nd ed. (1813), p. 254.

135 'those who live in the neighbourhood': County Reports summarised by J. Sinclair, 'Address to the Board of Agriculture' (1795), in *Essays on Miscellaneous Subjects* (1802), p. 144.

135 'an absolute nuisance': P. Foot, *General View of the Agriculture of Middlesex* (1794), p. 30.

136 names of *lieux-dits*: C. Hough, 'Name Structures and Name Survival', *Journal of the English Place-Name Society*, 48 (2016), pp. 5–27; O. Padel, 'Brittonic Place-Names in England', in *Perceptions of Place*, eds J. Carroll and D. Parsons (2013), pp. 1–41; O. Padel, 'Change and Development in English Place-Names', *Quaestio Insularis*, 15 (2014), pp. 1–21; K. Cameron, *English Place Names*, new ed. (1996), p. 237.

136 The value of 'waste': 'Sketch of an Act for the Improvement of Waste Lands; transmitted to the Board by Mr Justice Buller', appendix in *Report of the Committee Appointed by the Board of Agriculture to Take*

into Consideration the State of the Waste Lands and Common Fields of this Kingdom (1795), pp. 4–12 and 39–40; M. Williams, 'The Enclosure and Reclamation of Waste Land in England and Wales in the Eighteenth and Nineteenth Centuries', *Transactions of the Institute of British Geographers*, 51 (1970), pp. 55–69.

136 'masterless men': C. Hill, *The World Turned Upside Down* (1972; 1975), p. 39; also J. Strype, *Annals of the Reformation and Establishment of Religion*, new ed., II, pt 2 (1824), p. 141.

136 specialized in various crafts: J. Birrell, 'Peasant Craftsmen in the Medieval Forest', *The Agricultural History Review*, XVII, 2 (1969), pp. 91–107.

137 'we would then have created kings': 'The Confession of John Straw', in R. B. Dobson, *The Peasants' Revolt of 1381*, p. 366; *The* Chronica Maiora *of Thomas Walsingham*, p. 162; J. Froissart, *Chroniques*, ed. G. Raynaud (1897), X, 94–7.

138 Actual campaigning: M. Keen, *English Society in the Later Middle Ages, 1348–1500*, p. 195.

138 aristocracy would be executed: M. Hicks, *The Wars of the Roses* (2010), ch. 1 and table 2.

17. The Good Fight

141 'Where there is no vision': *The Golden Age of Probation: Mission v. Market*, ed. R. Statham, foreword by Alan Bennett (2014).

142 The stool-thrower: E.g. M.-O. Pittin-Hedon, *Women and Scotland* (2020), pp. 77–88.

144 'found that Religion': Henry VIII, *Assertio Septem Sacramentorum, or An Assertion of the Seven Sacraments, Against Martin Luther* (1521), tr. T. W. Gent (1688), 'Epistle Dedicatory', p. iii.

144 obedience to the King: R. L. Greaves, 'Concepts of Political Obedience in Late Tudor England', *Journal of British Studies*, XXII, 1 (1982), pp. 23–34; see p. 23.

144 'which is also a very good medicine': Thomas Fuller, *The Church-history of Britain from the Birth of Jesus Christ Until the Year MDCXLVIII* (1655), p. 212.

145 'wicked and seditious persons': The Act Against Recusants (1593), in H. Gee and W. Harvey, eds, *Documents Illustrative of English Church History* (1896), pp. 498–508.

146 'they carried with them at all times': H. de Balzac, *La Muse du département*, in *La Comédie Humaine*, ed. P.-G. Castex (1976–81), IV, 674.

146 'Trying to unpick our history': A. Adu, 'Rishi Sunak Refuses to Apologise for UK Slave Trade', *The Guardian*, 26 April 2023; also *Daily Mail*, 26 April 2023; Fox News, 5 May 2023.

147 her speech at Tilbury: *Precationes private. Regiae E. R.* (1563), quoted by M. Yarnell, 'The Theology of Elizabeth I: Politique or Believer?', *Southwestern Journal of Theology*, LXII, 1 (2019), pp. 13–14.

18. 'Perillous Dayes'

150 'Children were encouraged to wallow': Jerome K. Jerome, *My Life and Times* (1926), p. 15.

150 'popish tortures' . . . 'and there strangled': B. Harris, *The Protestant Tutor* (1679), pp. 131–4.

150 ships of the Spanish Armada . . . 'three fire-balls': Ibid., pp. 59, 68 and 80.

150 In the winter of 1651–2: *The Journal of George Fox*, ed. N. Penney (1911), p. 15.

151 'For he that curseth': Leviticus 20:9.

151 'his lamp shall be put out': Proverbs 20:20.

152 'the late unhappy confusions': 'The Preface', Book of Common Prayer.

152 pacts of neutrality: J. Morrill, *Revolt in the Provinces: the People of England and the Tragedies of War, 1630–1648* (2014), p. 37; also B. Manning, *Neutrals and Neutralism in the English Civil War*, thesis (U. of Oxford, 1957).

152 'oddly stable substratum': J. Blair, in *The Oxford Illustrated History of Britain*, pp. 64–5.

153 vigilante 'Clubmen' . . . Glamorgan: J. Morrill, *Revolt in the Provinces*, pp. 133–4.

19. 'The Field Has Eyes, the Wood Has Ears'

156 'provide good sources of cover': *German Invasion Plans for the British Isles 1940*, p. 51.

156 underground network: 'Royal Observer Corps Post', Worcestershire

and Worcester City HER, ref. WSM28691 (accessed 2025); also 'Powick ROC Post', in Subterranea Britannica: https://www.subbrit.org.uk/sites/powick-roc-post/

157 'Civil War battles': A. Marshall, *Intelligence and Espionage in the Reign of Charles II* (2009), p. 18. Improvements were perceptible by 1651: J. E. K. Ellis, *Military Intelligence Operations During the First English Civil War*, thesis (U. of Southampton, 2010), pp. 218–19.

157 leaving Worcester: R. Woof, 'The Personal Expenses of Charles II in the City of Worcester', *Transactions of the Royal Historical Society*, I (1872), pp. 34–53; see pp. 38–9.

157 The plan . . . to reach Scotland: Summary account, texts and illustrations in A. Fea, *The Flight of the King* (1897; 1908) and 'a companion volume', *After Worcester Fight* (1904). Also *A True Narrative and Relation of His Majesty's Miraculous Escape from Worcester on the 3rd of September 1651, Till his Arrival at Paris* (1660); *A Summary of Occurrences relating to the Miraculous preservation of our late Sovereign Lord, King Charles II after the defeat of his Army at Worcester in the year 1651* (1688). Pepys's account and others in A. Fea, *After Worcester Fight*, pp. 1–44 (separate pagination), and in *Memoirs of the Court of Charles the Second*, by Count Grammont, ed. W. Scott (1846).

159 'going up and down': A. Fea, *After Worcester Fight*, p. 18 (Pepys).

159 'get either to Swansey': Ibid., p. 11.

159 'in some lurking-hole': [Abraham Jennings], *Miraculum Basilicon, or The Royal Miracle truly exhibiting the wonderful preservation of His Sacred Majesty* (1664), p. 34.

159 'I told [the smith]': A. Fea, *After Worcester Fight*, p. 21 (Pepys).

160 after the Battle of Hexham: Route details: C. Barrett, *Battles and Battlefields of England* (1896), pp. 176–7 (with maps); D. Grummit, *Henry VI* (2015), p. 213; 'Warkworth's Chronicle', *A Chronicle of the First Thirteen Years of the Reign of King Edward the Fourth* (1839), p. 5.

160 'feeld hath eyen and the wode hath eres': *The Knight's Tale, The Canterbury Tales*, v. 1522.

160 'tuned' his voice . . . 'lobbing' gait: *A True Narrative and Relation*, in A. Fea, *The Flight of the King*, p. 189.

160 walnut leaves: *A Summary of Occurrences*, p. 215.

161 'His Majesty asketh': *Miraculum Basilicon*, p. 36.

161 'I begged Mrs [*sic*] Lane': A. Fea, *After Worcester Fight*, p. 22 (Pepys).

162 'and there we staid': Ibid., p. 36.

162 'its sweet, retired bay': Jane Austen, *Persuasion* (1817), ch. 11.

162 shod somewhere to the north: E.g. [Anne Wyndham], *Claustrum Regale Reseratum, or The Kinges Concealment at Trent* (1667), p. 37; also G. Fleming, *Horse Shoes and Horse Shoeing: Their Origin, History, Uses, and Abuses* (1869), ch. 10.

163 Newsbooks reported him: E.g. *The Weekly Intelligencer of the Common-Wealth*, 30 September–7 October 1651, pp. 307–8; L. Liapi, in *News in Early Modern Europe*, eds S. F. Davies and P. Fletcher (2014), p. 101; J. Smith, 'The Commonwealth Cavalier', *Studies in Philology*, CXIV, 3 (2017), pp. 609–40.

164 'If I thought it was the king': 'Mr Ellesdon's Relation of the King's Escape from Lyme', in A. Fea, *After Worcester Fight*, p. 228.

164 'plaine country fellowe': J. Smith, 'The Commonwealth Cavalier', *Studies in Philology*, CXIV, 3 (2017), pp. 609–40; see p. 617.

165 'I beseech God': *Miraculum Basilicon*, pp. 56–7.

165 an atlas of the principal roads: J. Ogilby, *The Traveller's Guide: Or, A Most Exact Description of the Roads of England* (1699): 'undertaken at the express command of King Charles II' (Preface).

20. Megalopolis

167 'A suction so powerful': 'The Nation of London' (1853), in *The Works of Thomas De Quincey*, XIX: *Autobiographical Sketches*, ed. D. S. Roberts (2003), p. 109.

168 'Possessed of a centripetal force': *Newton's Principia: the Mathematical Principles of Natural Philosophy*, tr. A. Motte (1846), p. 530–31.

168 Three times as many people: Population figures in E. Alvarez-Palau et al., 'A New Historic Urban Dataset for England and Wales' (2022): https://sites.socsci.uci.edu/~dbogart/historicurbandatasetnov162022.pdf

168 'hellish and dismal cloud': J. Evelyn, *Fumifugium, or The Inconveniencie of the Aer and Smoak of London Dissipated* (1661), p. 5.

169 'my money and boy': *The Diary of Samuel Pepys*, ed. R. Latham (1987, 2003), p. 555 (16 November 1665).

170 'My Lord Bruncker': Ibid.

170 the 'larum wach': Pepys, p. 503 (14 July 1665).

171 'But Lord, to see how much': Pepys, p. 490 (13 May 1665).
171 'from my fasting': Ibid.
171 'within two minutes': Pepys, p. 525 (13 September 1665).
171 'the objects of sense perception': *The Principia: Mathematical Principles of Natural Philosophy*, tr. B. Cohen and A. Whitman (1999), p. 54.
172 London's 'vast extent': S. de Sorbière, *Relation d'un voyage en Angleterre* (1664; 1666), pp. 25–6.
172 'I could not make a driver understand me': C. de Saussure, *A Foreign View of England in the Reigns of George I and George II*, ed. Mme Van Muyden (1902), pp. 37–8.
173 'attempted the discovery of London': J. Stow, *The Survey of London* (1598; 1956), dedication.
173 'I myself in my youth': Ibid., p. 115.
173 Whitechapel Mount: D. Flintham, 'Whitechapel Mount and the London Hospital', 1999: https://www.mernick.org.uk/thhol/whimount.html
174 'the most insipid': Pepys, p. 226 (29 September 1662).
174 'innumerable interconnections': C. Baudelaire, preface to *Le Spleen de Paris* (1869).
174 'In Westcheape': J. Stow, *The Survey of London*, p. 195.
175 'So home, and there find': Pepys, p. 255 (28 January 1663).
176 'For example, in Coleman Street': D. Defoe, *A Journal of the Plague Year* [1665] (1772), p. 63.
176 'Going to Whitehall': Pepys, p. 989 (17 February 1669).
177 'Let no young wriggle-eyed damosel': Thomas Middleton (?), *The Testament of Laurence Lucifer (being a part of The Black Book, 1604)*, in *Key Writings on Subcultures, 1535–1727*, I, ed. A. Judges (2002), p. 297.
178 '[I] had her upper part of her body': Pepys, p. 991 (23 February 1669).

21. From the Neck Down

180 '[Mr Salter held]': Evelyn Waugh, *Scoop* (1938), ch. 2.
181 Flemish relative: J. D. Tuckett, *A History of the Past and Present State of the Labouring Population* (1846), I, 379.
181 'These people are so much attached': Jethro Tull, *Horse-hoeing Husbandry*, 3rd ed. (1751), p. 4 (editors' preface).
181 'few Swedish turnips': W. Cobbett, *Rural Rides*, p. 79.

182 anti-manuring campaign: J. Tull, *Horse-Hoeing Husbandry*, 1st ed. (1731), pp. ix and 158.

182 'A gentleman well acquainted with the theory': T. Smollett, *The Expedition of Humphry Clinker* (1771), eds T. Preston and O. Brack (1990), p. 237.

183 the 'prejudices against improvement': Wa. Blith, a lover of Ingenuity, *The English Improver Improved . . . Discovering the Improvableness of all Lands* (rev. ed., 1652; 1st: 1649), unpaginated preface, 'To the Right Honorable the Lord Generall Cromwell' et al. On 'improvement': P. Slack, *The Invention of Improvement: Information and Material Progress in Seventeenth-Century England* (2014).

183 illegal to attach a plough: T. Kelch, 'A Short History of (Mostly) Western Animal Law', pt 1, *Animal Law*, XIX (2012), pp. 23–62; see pp. 60–61: Parliament of Ireland, 1635 [under Charles I].

183 'The lake was moved': E. Waugh, *Scoop*, ch. 2.

184 the 'greatest hindrance': W. Blith, *The English Improver Improved*, pp. 51–2.

184 'morning draught': Pepys, p. 5 (12 January 1660). Other examples of inebriation and unfitness for work: pp. 80, 152, 166, 168.

184 'If sunne be at westward': This and following quotations from Thomas Tusser, *Five Hundred Pointes of Good Husbandrie*, eds W. Payne and S. J. Herrtage (1878), pp. 30, 18 and 172.

185 'grosse stupidity': *Aubrey's Brief Lives*, ed. O. Dick (1950), p. xlii.

185 '[It] struck me that': Elizabeth Gaskell, *Mr Harrison's Confessions* (1851), ch. 6.

185 'Clay soil it will be': To Eliza Fox, 26 April 1850, in *The Letters of Mrs Gaskell*, eds J. Chapple and A. Pollard (1997), p. 111.

185 'To take no notice': *Aubrey's Brief Lives*, p. xlii.

186 in *flushed* ground: O. Rackham, *Woodlands* (2006), pp. 8 and 83–4.

186 shallow not deep: Ibid., pp. 9, 32–3 and (on the age of hedges), p. 194.

186 earthworms eat corn: Gilbert White, *The Natural History of Selborne* (1788–9), ed. R. Mabey (1987), p. 196.

186 hedgehogs suck milk: *The Diary of Ralph Josselin*, 27 September 1660 and note.

186 the badger 'hath the legs . . . ': *Pseudodoxia Epidemica* (1646), in *The Works of Thomas Browne*, ed. S. Wilkin, I (1894), p. 245.

186 'goatsucker': G. White, *The Natural History of Selborne*, p. 217.

22. A New Earth

189 'with all [the] minutiae of care': [Arthur Young], *General View of the Agriculture of Lincolnshire*, 2nd ed. (1808), p. 19.

189 'inclosure came': John Clare, *Major Works*, ed. E. Robinson and D. Powell (1984), p. 486.

190 'fields, houses, towns': Thomas More, *Utopia* (1516), tr. P. Turner (1965), p. 46. Echoed in William Camden's notes on Northamptonshire, in *Britain, or, a Chorographicall Description of the most flourishing Kingdomes, England, Scotland, and Ireland* (1577; first English edition, 1610).

191 'narrow and somewhat crooked': P. Boscher, *Administration and Diplomacy: the Anglo-Scottish Border, 1550–1560*, thesis (U. of Durham, 1985), p. 202, quoting British Library, Mss. Cotton Caligula B, V, ff. 50–58.

191 took to be common land: See G. Clark and A. Clark, 'Common Rights to Land in England, 1475–1839', *The Journal of Economic History*, LXI, 4 (2001), pp. 1009–36. ('Common waste . . . constituted a mere four percent of land . . . Private property was thus the norm in England by 1600.')

191 riots . . . organized by lords or gentry: R. Manning, 'Patterns of Violence in Early Tudor Enclosure Riots', *Albion*, VI, 2 (1974), pp. 120–33.

191 urban rather than rural: C. Liddy, 'Urban Enclosure Riots: Risings of the Commons in English Towns, 1480–1525', *Past & Present*, 226 (2015), pp. 41–77.

192 'the openness . . . has to be seen': F. Pryor, *The Making of the British Landscape* (2010), pp. 299 and 302.

192 'the axe of the spoiler': J. Clare, *Major Works*, p. 260 ('Remembrances').

192 'O samely naked leas': J. Clare, *The Village Minstrel and Other Poems* (1821), I, 58 (canto 110).

193 'a cow-pasture': *John Clare By Himself*, eds E. Robinson and D. Powell (1996), p. 91.

193 before the hedges had grown up: Pointed out by W. G. Hoskins, *The Making of the English Landscape* (1955; 2005), pp. 158 and 163. Clare and the Laxton map are the only reliable detailed contemporary sources: J. Wordie, 'The Chronology of English Enclosure, 1500–1914', *The Economic History Review*, 2nd series, XXXVI, 4 (1983), pp. 483–505.

194 'It makes one smell as if smoaked': Celia Fiennes, *Through England on*

a Side Saddle in the Time of William and Mary, ed. E. Griffiths (1888), p. 219.

194 'Hardly a house [stood] out': D. Defoe, *A Tour Thro' the Whole Island of Great Britain Divided into Circuits or Journies*, 3 vols (1724–7), III, 99.

194 'a thorough searching of the Bowels': W. Blith, a lover of Ingenuity, *The English Improver Improved . . . Discovering the Improvableness of all Lands* (rev. ed., 1652; 1st: 1649), unpaginated preface, 'To the Right Honorable the Lord Generall Cromwell' et al.

195 'harmony between King, Lords and Commons': Voltaire, *Letters Concerning the English Nation* (1733), p. 59.

195 their private treasure chest: E.g. W. J. Ashworth, *Customs and Excise: Trade, Production and Consumption in England 1640–1845* (2003), ch. 1.

195 'Posterity may be surprised': Voltaire, *Letters*, p. 69. (Retranslated from the French.)

196 land tax: See J. Beckett, 'Land Tax or Excise: the Levying of Taxation in Seventeenth- and Eighteenth-Century England', *The English Historical Review*, C, 395 (1985), pp. 285–308.

197 'the cleanest and beautifullest': D. Defoe, *A Tour Thro' the Whole Island*, III, 84.

197 undescribed animal species: Gilbert White, *The Natural History of Selborne* (1788–9), ed. R. Mabey (1987), pp. 32, 36, 72, 111, 142 and 178.

197 'Saw three fellows': *John Clare By Himself*, p. 233. See also V. Hatley, 'The Poet and the Railway Surveyors', *Northamptonshire Past and Present*, V, 2 (1974), pp. 101–6.

23. The Home Empire

198 His catch-all patent: A contrary view in G. Selgin and J. Turner, 'Strong Steam, Weak Patents', *The Journal of Law and Economics*, LIV, 4 (2011), pp. 841–61.

198 running backwards: P. Hosken, 'Going Up Camborne Hill Coming Down', *Industrial Archaeology News*, 120 (2002), pp. 4–5 (not to be confused with Beacon Hill).

199 Later versions of the song: B. Carey, 'Cornish Folk Songs' (2012): https://brycchancarey.com/index.htm

199 'not so much a fringe': T. Brinley, *The Industrial Revolution and the Atlantic Economy* (1993), p. 86.

200 the pantomime horse: R. Tombs, *The English and Their History* (2014), p. 330.

200 The insulting Act of Union: 'An Act for Laws and Justice to be Ministered in Wales in Like Form as it is in this Realm', *The Statutes at Large, of England and of Great-Britain*, III (1811), p. 243.

200 colonization . . . of the Highlands and Islands: See J. Goodare, *The Government of Scotland, 1560–1625* (2004), ch. 10.

200 'sending Scots to fight Scots': V. Henshaw, *Scotland and the British Army*, thesis (U. of Birmingham, 2011), p. 62.

201 remained under-represented: Figures in J. Hoppit, ed., *Parliaments, Nations and Identities in Britain and Ireland, 1660–1850* (2003), p. 5, table 1.3: 'Size of the Electorates in the British Isles, 1831–33'.

202 he thought they looked like naked giantesses: Stephen Spender, 'The Pylons', *Poems* (1933).

203 'Some future faunist': Gilbert White, *The Natural History of Selborne* (1788–9), ed. R. Mabey (1987), p. 99.

203 daughter of an Irish mill worker: See A. Beatty, 'The Two Irish Wives of Friedrich Engels', *Socialist History*, 60 (2021), pp. 5–22.

203 the 'wild Milesian': F. Engels, *Die Lage der arbeitenden Klasse in England* (1845); tr. *The Condition of the Working Class in England* (1887; 1973), p. 116 (quoting Thomas Carlyle). My translations.

203 'With the Irish': Ibid., p. 273.

205 'the dominant occupation': M. Daly, *Sixties Ireland: Reshaping the Economy, State and Society, 1957–1973* (2016), p. 87 and, generally, ch. 4: 'Coping with Change 2: Agriculture and Rural Ireland'.

205 education beyond primary school: T. O'Donoghue and T. O'Doherty, *Irish Speakers and Schooling in the Gaeltacht, 1900 to the Present* (2019), p. 97.

206 Arthur Colahan's song: D. Ó Cearbhaill, 'The Colahans – A Remarkable Galway Family: Snadh na Sean', *Journal of the Galway Archaeological and Historical Society*, LIV (2002), pp. 121–40.

206 'was exposed to mustard gas': Ibid., p. 131.

206 The Rawalpindi experiments: R. Langworth, 'Winston Churchill and the Use of Chemical Warfare', The Churchill Project (2015): https://winstonchurchill.hillsdale.edu/churchill-and-chemical-warfare/

206 'recalcitrant natives': Churchill, letter to Sir Hugh Trenchard, 29 August 1920, in ibid., n. 6.

207 The trade figures: See B. Thomas, 'Feeding England During the Industrial Revolution', *Agricultural History*, LVI, 1 (1982), pp. 328–42; N. Crafts, 'British Industrialization in an International Context', *The Journal of Interdisciplinary History*, XIX, 3 (1989), pp. 415–28.

207 exports . . . actually increased: C. Kinealy, *A Death-dealing Famine: The Great Hunger in Ireland* (1997), pp. 77–9.

207 reports of French students: J. Chartres, 'How the Explosion Finally Came in Ulster', *The Times*, 14 August 1969.

208 Ireland's . . . tourist industry: P. Heneghan, 'The Tourist Industry in Ireland, 1960 to 1975', *Studies: An Irish Quarterly Review*, LXV (1976), 259, pp. 225–34.

208 Irish Tourist Board: M. O'Sullivan, Professor of History, in 1949, quoted in D. Ó Cearbhaill, 'The Colahans', p. 131.

24. Speed

209 'As we sailed ahead': Herman Melville, *Redburn: His First Voyage* (1849), p. 164.

209 'felt dusty particles': Ibid., p. 167.

210 'not the slightest resemblance': Ibid., p. 193.

210 the 'unhappiness': Ibid., p. 198.

210 first integrated canal system: For a summary of what remains: K. Falconer, *Canal and River Navigations National Overview* (2017): https://historicengland.org.uk/research/results/reports/7242/CanalandRiverNavigationsNationalOverview

210 'Not a negro was to be seen': H. Melville, *Redburn*, p. 255.

211 Africans and people of African descent: A black population rather than a 'community': R. Costello, 'The Making of a Liverpool Community: An Elusive Narrative', in *Britain's Black Past*, ed. G. Gerzina (2020), ch. 6.

211 'In New York': H. Melville, *Redburn*, p. 255.

211 reminiscent of the Welsh: H. Paton, 'Influence of Liverpool Welsh on Lenition in Liverpool English' (2013): http://cecils.btk.ppke.hu/wp-content/uploads/2013/02/Paton_Influence-of-the-Liverpool_REVISED_v5_fin_corr1.pdf, pp. 184–5.

212 a 'wide sweep of view': H. Melville, *Redburn*, p. 264.

212 the nascent chemical industry: On Merseyside: J. Tucker, 'Dangerous

Exposures: Visualizing Work and Waste in the Victorian Chemical Trades', *International Labor and Working-Class History*, 95 (2019), pp. 130–65; see p. 136.

213 'employed in the making of sickles': W. Cobbett, *Rural Rides*, p. 558.

213 'But this is all very proper': Ibid., p. 557.

213 scarcity of orchards and gardens: Ibid., p. 633.

213 Scouse was indistinguishable: P. Honeybone, 'New-dialect Formation in Nineteenth Century Liverpool: A Brief History of Scouse': http://www.lel.ed.ac.uk/homes/patrick/livengkoi.pdf, p. 21; also K. Watson and L. Clark, 'The Origins of Liverpool English', in *Listening to the Past*, ed. R. Hickey (2017), ch. 6.

213 Geordie, the English of Tyneside: R. Hermeston, *Linguistic Identity in Nineteenth-Century Tyneside Dialect Songs*, thesis (U. of Leeds, 2009), pp. 230–31.

213 pronounced 'Baernegum': U. Clark, 'The English West Midlands: Phonology', *A Handbook of Varieties of English*, eds B. Kortmann and E. W. Schneider, 2 vols (2004), I, 147.

213 standard West Midland: P. A. Johnston, in *Studies in the History of the English Language*, eds M. Adams et al. (2015), p. 192.

214 'the ease and rapidity': G. Head, *A Home Tour Through the Manufacturing Districts of England in the Summer of 1835* (1836), p. 415.

214 'So quick were our movements': Ibid., p. 417.

215 'swift-boats' . . . 'fly-boats': R. Philp, *The Progress of Carriages, Roads and Water Conveyances* (1858), p. 198.

215 the weekly rent: W. Neild, 'Comparative Statement of the Income and Expenditure of Certain Families of the Working Classes in Manchester and Dukinfield', *Journal of the Statistical Society of London*, IV (1841), pp. 320–34.

215 A Manchester cotton broker: Samuel Sidney, *Rides on Railways* (1851), p. 152.

215 at Parkside Station: 'Dreadful Accident to Mr. Huskisson', *The Times*, 17 September 1830, p. 3; 'The Fatal Accident to Mr. Huskisson', *Manchester Guardian*, 18 September 1830, p. 3.

216 'Beware of yielding': Dionysius Lardner, *Treatise on the New Art of Transport* (1850), pp. 189–90.

216 Countess of Zetland: Ibid., p. 182; also *Report of the Commissioners of Railways, 1848, II*, (1849), appendix 29 (December 1847), pp. 73–8.

216 'for the attention of railway directors': *Bradshaw's Monthly Railway and Steam Navigation Guide* (February 1844), preliminary pages.

217 both living and dead: Mrs B. (Isabella) Holmes, *The London Burial Grounds: Notes on Their History from the Earliest Times to the Present Day* (1896), pp. 102, 150 and 168.

217 'an awful waiting look': C. Kingsley in 1848, in C. Kingsley, *His Letters and Memories of His Life* (1908), p. 71.

217 'the student in human character': E. and W. Osborne, *Osborne's London and Birmingham Railway Guide* (1840), p. 180.

217 a bamboozling innovation: As 'explained' in 'The Guide to Bradshaw', *Punch*, 19 August 1865.

217 'It was his horrible fate': C. Dickens, 'A Narrative of Extraordinary Suffering', *Household Words*, 12 July 1851, pp. 361–3.

218 seven and a half thousand stations: Calculated from H. Oliver and J. Bockett, *Hand-book and Appendix of the Stations, Sidings, Collieries, &c. on the Railways in the United Kingdom* (1871).

218 'Now then! Show your ticket': Lewis Carroll, *Through the Looking-Glass, and What Alice Found There* (1872), pp. 48–52.

218 'A railway train moving': D. Lardner, *Treatise*, p. 182.

218 'some huge steam night-bird': T. Carlyle to J. Carlyle, 13 September 1839, in J. A. Froude, *Thomas Carlyle: A History of His Life in London* (1885), I, 167.

218 'the flapping of mighty wings': G. Head, *A Home Tour*, p. 312 (on the Stockton and Darlington railway).

218 'continuous burring noise': E. and W. Osborne, *Osborne's London and Birmingham Railway Guide*, p. 80.

219 'squish-squash': E. Lear, *Journals of a Landscape Painter in Albania, &c.* (1851), p. 115.

219 'perfectly and wonderfully true': Quoted in D. Olson and R. Sinclair, 'The Origin of "Rain, Steam and Speed" by J. M. W. Turner', *The British Art Journal*, XIX, 1 (2018), pp. 42–7; see p. 43.

219 His prose poem: M. Spencer, 'A Fresh Look at Rimbaud's "Métropolitain"', *The Modern Language Review*, LXIII, 4 (1968), pp. 849–53; see p. 850.

219 'Off again [from Blackfriars]': F. T. Jane, 'The Romance of Modern London', III: 'Round the Underground on an Engine', *The English Illustrated Magazine*, X (1893), pp. 787–92; see p. 788. Reproduced with Jane's illustrations at https://basilicafields.wordpress.com/round-the-underground-on-an-engine-fred-t-jane/

220 crooked plank cabin: 'Manchester: Chat Moss', *The Lancet*, 3866 (2 October 1897), p. 885. On Chat Moss: R. Pike, *Railway Adventures and Anecdotes* (1884), pp. 35–55.
220 'very insecure': House of Commons, *Report from the Select Committee on Conveyance of Mails by Railways* (25 July 1854), p. 52.
220 'systematically stopped': G. P. Neele, *Railway Reminiscences* (1904), p. 42.
220 'the greatest robbery': *Report from the Select Committee on Conveyance of Mails*, p. 71.
221 'feelings of delight': E. and W. Osborne, *Osborne's London and Birmingham Railway Guide*, p. 133.
221 'the grime and misery': F. Engels, *The Conditions of the Working Class*, pp. 77–8.
221 'Directly under the railway bridge': Ibid., p. 82.

25. Muddling Through

223 Border Union Railway: Waverley Route Heritage Association, 'Building the Waverley Route' (2020): https://waverleyrouteha.wordpress.com/2020/05/09/building-the-waverley-route-the-story-of-the-whitrope-contract-1859–62/
223 'the hardest of all the routes': E. Foxwell, 'English Express Trains: Their Average Speed [etc.]', *Journal of the Statistical Society of London*, XLVI, 3 (1883), pp. 517–74; see p. 563.
223 'many women but few wives': J. Francis, *A History of the English Railway* (1851), II, 71–2.
223 'pouring in masses': Ibid., II, pp. 68–9.
223 'workshop of the world': Disraeli in the House of Commons, 15 May 1846: Hansard, LXXXVI, col. 667; Thomas Evans, *Christian Policy, the Salvation of the Empire* [. . .] *this only real and Desirable Remedy, which would elevate these realms to a Pitch of Greatness, hitherto unattained by any Nation that ever Existed*, 2nd ed. (1816), p. 18.
224 'vitiated' sons: J. Francis, *A History*, II, pp. 73–4.
224 John Donnelly: *The Carlisle Journal*, 26 July 1861.
224 the deaths of navvies: D. Brooke, 'The Railway Navvy – a Reassessment', *Construction History*, V (1989), pp. 35–45; see p. 35.
225 'Peterloo' was the name: R. Pike, *Railway Adventures*, pp. 47–55. Several accounts in H. Jennings, *Pandaemonium* (1985; 1987), pp. 146–55.

225 'All such suspicions': *The Times*, 19 August 1819, p. 2.
226 'the utmost decorum prevailed': 'Dorchester Unionists. Meeting of the Trades' Unions', *The Times*, 22 April 1834, p. 6.
226 'strife-makers': George Loveless, *The Church Shown Up* (1838), p. 5.
227 Only twenty thousand: A plausible estimate in 'Kennington-Common', *The Times*, 11 April 1848, p. 6.
228 meeting in Merthyr: 'The Chartists in Merthyr', *The Cardiff and Merthyr Guardian*, 22 April 1848.
228 'Victoria Rex [*sic*]': 'The Chartist Petition – Messrs O'Connor and Cripps', House of Commons, 13 April 1848: Hansard, XCVIII, col. 285.
228 Cuffay's fellow Chartists: 'The Story of William Cuffay, Black Chartist', from P. Fryer, *Staying Power: the History of Black People in Britain* (2010): https://libcom.org/article/story-william-cuffay-black-chartist
228 'would lead to family dissensions': D. Jones, 'Women and Chartism', *History*, LXVIII, 222 (1983), pp. 1–21. Also P. Scott, 'Female Chartism and the Press': https://www.chartistancestors.co.uk/female-chartism-and-the-press/

26. Black Country

230 widening fans of coal smoke: R. Phillips, *A Morning's Walk from London to Kew* (1817), p. 131.
230 From the heights of Abberley Common: W. G. Hoskins, *Chilterns to Black Country* (1951), p. 23.
230 'more barbarous': D. Horovitz, 'The Black Country', *Journal of the English Place-Name Society*, XLIII (2011), pp. 25–34; see p. 27.
230 'like a smouldering carpet': J. B. Priestley, *English Journey* (1934; 1994), p. 111.
231 'rare regional names': A. Everitt, 'County and Town: Patterns of Regional Evolution in England', *Transactions of the Royal Historical Society*, XXIX (1979), pp. 79–108; see p. 81.
231 a giant scrapyard: The term is applied to the Black Country by T. Rowley in *The English Landscape in the Twentieth Century* (2006), p. 5.
233 'He heard the bones of her arms': John Brown, *A Memoir of Robert Blincoe, an orphan boy; sent from the workhouse of St. Pancras, London, at seven years of age, to endure the Horrors of a Cotton-Mill, through his infancy and youth, with a minute detail of his sufferings* (1832), p. 26; also P. Park, *Between a Rock*

and a Hard Place: The Poor Law Commission's Migration Scheme, 1835–37, thesis (U. of Central Lancashire, 2008).

233 'quietening mixture': E. Lomax, 'The Uses and Abuses of Opiates in Nineteenth-Century England', *Bulletin of the History of Medicine*, XLVII, 2 (1973), pp. 167–76. Alcoholic remedies for infant colic were not banned until 1982 in the US and 1992 in the UK: I. Blumenthal, 'The Gripe Water Story', *Journal of the Royal Society of Medicine*, XCIII (2000), pp. 172–4.

234 'Is it possible to imagine . . . ?': F. Engels, *Die Lage der arbeitenden Klasse in England* (1845); tr. *The Condition of the Working Class in England* (1887; 1973), p. 163. My translation.

234 'working system': Factories Inquiries Commission, *Supplementary Report of His Majesty's Commissioners*, pt II (1834), p. 352 (John and George Gartside, Holmfirth Mills, Wooldale).

234 'generally arise through carelessness': Ibid., p. 269 (Scholes, Varley and Co., Holme, Marsden).

234 'legislate for the whole world': Ibid., p. 135 (Hinchcliff and Horncastle, Cartworth).

234 'Parents are so anxious': Ibid., p. 133 (G. & J. H. Farrar, Low Mill, Holmfirth, Cartworth).

235 The 1842 report: Commissioners for Inquiring into the Employment and Condition of Children in Mines and Manufactories, *The Condition and Treatment of the Children Employed in the Mines and Collieries of the United Kingdom* (1842).

235 'a place of comparative comfort': *Report from His Majesty's Commissioners for Inquiring into the Administration and Practical Operation of the Poor Laws* (1834), pp. 240–41.

236 'To the English, I am "shoking"': Victor Hugo, *Moi, l'Amour, la Femme*, in *Oeuvres Complètes* (1985–90), XIV, 269–70.

236 'treated like men': J. Francis, *A History of the English Railway* (1851), II, 86.

27. Classrooms

239 'dame schools': D. Wardle, *English Popular Education, 1780–1975* (1976), p. 62.

239 'A horse knows his own stable': W. Mavor, *The English Spelling-Book*, new ed. (1870), p. 75.

239 '[keeping] the teaching profession': D. Wardle, *English Popular Education*, pp. 62–3.
240 'English grammar, composition': C. Dickens, *The Old Curiosity Shop* (1840–41), ch. 8.
240 Parisian and Protestant: R. Mair, *The Educator's Guide, or Handy-book for Principals of Schools, Parents, Guardians, Governesses and Tutors* (1866), pp. 76–7.
241 'monitorial' system: D. Wardle, *English Popular Education*, pp. 32 and 86–7.
241 'did not recognise me': A. Trollope, *An Autobiography* (1883), I, 16.
241 'My master whipt me very well': James Boswell, *The Life of Samuel Johnson* (1791), I, 14.
241 'the Victorians liked to weep': J. B. Priestley, *English Journey*, p. 399.
242 The Revised Code of 1862: In Matthew Arnold, *Reports on Elementary Schools 1852–1882*, ed. F. S. Marvin (1908); also 'Education in the UK': https://www.education-uk.org/documents/cce/revised-code.html
242 paroxysms of whooping cough: Scott Nasmyth Stokes, *General Report for the Year 1866 on the Roman Catholic Schools Inspected by him in the North-western Division of England*, pp. 286–97, in *Report of the Committee of Council on Education* (1867); see p. 292.
242 save the register: S. J. Curtis, *History of Education in Great Britain* (1948; 1971), p. 267.
242 School inspectors: See M. Arnold, *Reports on Elementary Schools.*
243 'cowed and sullen': James Kay-Shuttleworth, *Four Periods of Public Education* (1862), p. 584.
244 'lower classes ought to be educated': Robert Lowe (Chancellor of the Exchequer, 1868–73), in a pamphlet (1867): D. Wardle, *English Popular Education*, p. 25.
247 Arnold's 'manly piety': Thomas Hughes, *Tom Brown's School Days* (1857), II, ch. 1.
247 'triste lupus': Ibid., I, ch. 8.
248 'back-sword': Ibid., I, ch. 2.

28. Playing Fields

250 that 'silent endurance': Thomas Hughes, *Tom Brown's School Days*, I, ch. 4.

251 One newspaper headline: *Daily Star*, 25 January 2024.
251 'in country curacies': T. Hughes, *Tom Brown's School Days*, II, ch. 1.
251 'with hand-grenade and sabre': Ibid., I, ch. 1.
251 'We seem, as it were': J. Seeley, *The Expansion of England: Two Courses of Lectures* (1883; 1914), p. 10.
251 'Twas here that the battle of Waterloo was won': Montalembert, *De l'avenir politique de l'Angleterre*, new ed. (1856), p. 159; first in *Le Correspondant* in 1855.
252 'Disasters have been prepared': M. Arnold, 'An Eton Boy', *The Fortnightly Review*, CLXXXVI (1 June 1882), pp. 683–97; see p. 685.
252 'very clumsy cricket': G. K. Chesterton, 'Patriotism and Sport', in *All Things Considered* (1915).
252 'ignorant, pretentious and blundering': H. G. Wells, *Experiment in Autobiography* (1934), VI, 4.
252 'subordinates I had bullied': George Orwell, *The Road to Wigan Pier* (1937), in *Orwell's England*, ed. P. Davison (2001), p. 158 (ch. 9).
252 'languid incompetence': J. Seeley, *The Expansion*, p. 229.
253 'alien race and religion': Ibid., p. 13.
253 'a great country': T. R. Metcalf, *Ideologies of the Raj* (1995), p. 59. See also B. Disraeli, *Sybil, or the Two Nations* (1845), I, ch. 6.
253 'Then [I] saw the Duke of Argyll': Queen Victoria's Journal, 21 June 1872.
253 unpromising progeny: See L. Nayder, 'Catherine Dickens and Her Colonial Sons', *Dickens Studies Annual*, XXXVII (2006), pp. 81–93.
254 'If we are to hold our position': W. E. Forster, first reading of Elementary Education Bill, 17 February 1870: Hansard, CXCIX, cols 465–6.
254 'public opinion does not know': J. Seeley, *The Expansion*, p. 220.
255 'Jiang Zemin': T. Blair, *A Journey: My Political Life* (2011), p. 126.
255 'In South Africa': Robert Baden-Powell, *Scouting for Boys* (1908), p. 312.
256 'hysterical . . . stolid, pipe-smoking . . . ': Ibid., p. 338.
256 stamp collecting: Ibid., pp. 206–7.
256 'like a squealing rabbit': Ibid., p. 10.
256 'anachronism of war': Ibid., p. 338.
256 'lady missionaries and nurses': Ibid., p. 13.
256 first Scout rally: S. Mills, 'Scouting for Girls? Gender and the Scout Movement in Britain', *Gender, Place and Culture*, XVIII, 4 (2011), pp. 537–56; see p. 545.

256 'a state of very undesirable excitement': Violet Markham in *The Spectator*, 4 December 1909, p. 942.

257 '200 not out': *The Siege of Mafeking: A Diary Kept by Trooper William Robertson Fuller*, 29 April 1900 (quoting Baden-Powell): http://www.usscouts.org/usscouts/history/siegediary.asp

257 'No man in our day': *The Times*, 19 May 1900, p. 11.

257 'In every town and village': *Daily Mail*, 17 May 1900, p. 6.

257 faithful dog, Bob: Ibid., p. 3.

257 advertised within: *Daily Mail*, 18 May 1900.

258 'public feeling': On the creation of 'public opinion': P. Krebs, *Gender, Race and the Writing of Empire: Public Discourse and the Boer War* (1999), p. 6; also F. Van Holthoon, 'Public Opinion in Europe During the Boer War', *Publications de l'École Française de Rome*, LIV, 1 (1981), pp. 397–407.

258 'temporary spasm of jingoism': P. Krebs, *Gender*, p. 7.

258 scorched earth' policy: E.g. Emily Hobhouse, *The Brunt of the War and Where it Fell* (1902), p. 3, quoted in J. Scott, *British Concentration Camps of the Second South African War (The Transvaal, 1900–1902)*, thesis (Florida State U., 2007), p. 46.

258 'war against women and children': E. Hobhouse, *The Brunt of the War*; 'The Outlook. "War upon Women"', *Daily Mail*, 24 June 1901, p. 4.

259 'Never such innocence again . . . ': P. Larkin, 'MCMXIV', *The Whitsun Weddings* (1964).

260 'The losses in human life': 'The German Invasion', *The Times*, 3 August 1914, p. 7.

260 'It is nothing but killing': *Crewe Chronicle*, 10 October 1914, in K. Good, *England Goes to War, 1914–1915*, thesis (U. of Liverpool, 2002), p. 115.

260 the Boer War was 'a picnic': *Echoes of the Great War: the Diary of the Reverend Andrew Clark*, ed. J. Munson (1985), p. 33, cited in K. Good, *England Goes to War*, p. 115.

260 an 'absence of gaiety': In C. Pennell, *A Kingdom United: Popular Responses to the Outbreak of the First World War in Britain and Ireland* (2012), ch. 1, n. 113.

260 'people of all ages': C. Pennell, *A Kingdom*, ch. 1, n. 109.

260 not 'the slightest sign': Ibid., ch. 1, n. 133.

260 'Boys of Britain!': E.g. in W. Cecil Price, 'The Practical Utility of the Boy Scouts During the War', *The Nineteenth Century and After*, LXXVI (1914), pp. 691–701; see p. 698.

261 to Calais or Dieppe: Ms. letter of 24 August 1914, in 'Scouts on Home Front 1914–1918': https://www.scouts.org.uk/about-us/our-history/our-online-exhibitions/scouting-in-the-first-world-war/scouting-on-home-front-1914–1918/

261 'Your forefathers worked hard': R. Baden-Powell, *Scouting for Boys*, pp. 314–15.

262 'A bumping pitch': H. Newbolt, 'Vitaï Lampada', *Clifton Chapel and Other School Poems* (1908).

262 'O living pictures of the dead': H. Newbolt, 'The War Films', *The Times*, 14 October 1916, p. 7.

29. Semi-Detached

265 'a glorious day': *The Collected Poems of Edward Thomas*, ed. R. G. Thomas (1981), pp. 135–6.

265 In that morning's *Times*: 25 June 1914, pp. 5 and 7.

265 shown on the timetable: B. Derrick, '"Adlestrop", by Edward Thomas' (2012): https://blog.nationalarchives.gov.uk/adlestrop-by-edward-thomas/

266 'that which is entirely true': C. Baudelaire, 'Puisque réalisme il y a' (c. 1855), in *Oeuvres Complètes*, ed. C. Pichois (1975–6), II, 59.

266 In the graveyard: Fred Turner, killed in action in France, 19 July 1917, and his brother Maurice, who died at Brighton Military Hospital.

266 'When in officer's uniform': M. Hentel, *Temporary Gentlemen: the Masculinity of Lower-Middle-Class Temporary British Officers in the First World War*, thesis (U. of Western Ontario, 2017), p. 6; also L. Root, '"Temporary Gentlemen" on the Western Front: Class Consciousness and the British Army Officer, 1914–1918', *The Osprey Journal of Ideas and Inquiry*, V (2006).

267 'It is conclusively proved': To the Minister of Munitions, in B. Waites, 'The Effect of the First World War on Class and Status in England, 1910–20', *Journal of Contemporary History*, XI, 1 (1976), pp. 27–48; see p. 36.

267 'pianos, furniture': Ibid., p. 35.

267 shorthand typists . . . Land Girls: C. Hibbert, *The English: A Social History* (1987), pp. 692–3.

267 Women in factory teams: E.g. R. E. H., 'Women Footballers', *Daily Mail*, 29 November 1918, p. 4.

268 'people of indeterminate social class': George Orwell, 'England Your England', in *Orwell's England*, p. 273 (pt 6).

268 'the extensive [employed] middle class': *German Invasion Plans for the British Isles 1940*, tr. A. Matthews (2007), p. 47.

268 'Between the mother': T. Hardy, *Tess of the d'Urbervilles* (1891), I, ch. 3.

269 'that upper-servant tenant class': H. G. Wells, *Experiment in Autobiography* (1934), II, 4.

269 'furniture shops that catered for democracy': Ibid., II, 1.

269 Crystal Palace Exhibition . . . the Lord's Prayer . . . : E.g. *The World's Fair, or Children's Prize Gift Book of the Great Exhibition* (1851), p. 6; 'The Great Exhibition', *The Civil Engineer and Architect's Journal*, XIV (1851), p. 84.

269 '[Will] they come sober?': Henry Mayhew and George Cruikshank, *1851, or The Adventures of Mr. and Mrs. Sandboys and Family, who came up to London to enjoy themselves, and to see the Great Exhibition* (1851), p. 160.

270 'Wherever you can rest': J. Ruskin, 'The Uses of Ornament', *The Seven Lamps of Architecture* (1849), ch. 4, § 19.

270 'make or break a friendship': Mrs (Jane Ellen) Panton, *Homes of Taste: Economical Hints* (1890), p. 21.

270 'more like a gentleman': Daisy Ashford, *The Young Visiters, or Mr Salteena's Plan* (1919), p. 35.

270 'compartments' in the Crystal Palace: Ibid., p. 36.

270 'The toilit set': Ibid., p. 49.

270 Lever Brothers: J. Wilson et al., *Building Co-operation: a Business History of the Co-operative Group, 1863–2013* (2013), p. 116.

271 'Oh Hurrah shouted Ethel': D. Ashford, *The Young Visiters*, pp. 72–3.

271 'Mr Pooter' of *Punch*: Instalments collected in G. and W. Grossmith, *The Diary of a Nobody* (1892).

271 'Three times he said: "Thank Heaven"': Jerome K. Jerome, *Three Men on the Bummel* (1900), ch. xiv.

272 'Great Britain [will] hold out': TNA, CAB 23/9 War Cabinet 539, 13 March 1919, cited by L. Seabrooke in 'Legitimacy Gaps and Everyday Institutional Change in Interwar British Economy', International Center for Business and Politics, working paper no. 14 (2005), p. 19.

272 One-third of all the houses: T. Rowley, *The English Landscape*, p. 195.

272 semi-detached physiognomy: On semi-detached housing, Metroland

and snobbery: T. Rowley, *The English Landscape*, pp. 199–220; *Metro-land* (1924), ed. O. Green (2004); P. B. Lofthouse, *The Development of the English Semi-detached House: 1750–1950*, thesis (U. of York, 2012).

272 a quarter of farms: Rowley, *The English Landscape*, p. 226 (from the Scott Report of 1942).

273 'the Drage way': L. Wright, *The Social Life of Words: A Historical Approach* (2023), p. 124.

274 'And bright within each kitchenette': J. Betjeman, 'The Outer Suburbs', *Mount Zion, or In Touch With the Infinite* (1931).

274 the Euston Road area: E.g. H. G. Wells, *Experiment in Autobiography*, V, 6.

275 'industry is not depressed but dead' : *The Times*, 20–22, 24 and 26–28 March 1934; raised in Parliament by J. Dickie, National Liberal MP for Consett: *The Times*, 23 March 1934, p. 7.

275 'long sad roads': J. B. Priestley, *English Journey*, p. 244.

275 'Special Areas': A. Page, 'State Intervention in the Inter-War Period: the Special Areas Acts, 1934–37', *British Journal of Law and Society*, III, 2 (1976), pp. 175–203.

275 also labelled 'deprived'. E.g. D. Linehan, 'Regional Survey and the Economic Geographies of Britain 1930–1939', *Transactions of the Institute of British Geographers*, XXVIII, 1 (2003), pp. 96–122.

275 'out-migrate': 'Out-migration' was also 'Industrial Transference': ibid., p. 111.

275 *The Listener* magazine: 'Envisioning Industrial Migration', *The Listener*, 30 October 1935, in D. Linehan, 'Regional Survey', p. 101.

276 'an immense waste of social capital': Capt. D. E. Wallace, 'Durham and Tyneside', in Ministry of Labour, *Reports of Investigations into the Industrial Conditions in Certain Depressed Areas* (1934), p. 107.

276 migrant Welsh . . . Cutteslowe Walls: A. Exell, 'Morris Motors in the 1930s. Part II: Politics and Trade Unionism', *History Workshop*, 7 (1979), pp. 45–65; see p. 54.

30. The Eastern Front

278 the *Athenia*: Newspaper reports and documents in B. Watson, 'Loss of *Athenia* and the First Five Days' and 'The Aftermath' (2024): https://www.benjidog.co.uk/Athenia/index.php

278 'The important thing': M. Caulfield, *Tomorrow Never Came: The Story of the S.S. Athenia* (1959), p. 50.

279 'a silver-haired veteran': According to T. Sanger, *Without Warning* (2017): 'Sunday morning, September 3'.

280 a 'mental ward': Edinburgh Castle Provisional Plan, Sheet 4: Military Hospital (drawn 1931, published 1939): https://maps.nls.uk/view/223555746

280 German aircrew shot down: Details and pictures in https://threadinburgh.scot/2023/07/14/the-thread-about-a-day-of-firsts-when-the-world-war-2-air-war-over-britain-started-over-the-firth-of-forth/

280 Gaumont newsreel: 'After the Air Raid Over Scotland', 23 October 1939: https://www.britishpathe.com/asset/166099/, 0'40" – 0'44.

281 'Es ging die Riesentochter': Friedrich Rückert, 'Die Riesen und die Zwerge', *Werke*, I (1897), pp. 299–300.

283 biggest moose shot in Alaska: 'Lord Elphinstone's Big Bag', *The New York Times*, 12 November 1903.

283 'We are the final judges': 'The Conscientious Objector', 2 March 1943: Hansard, CXXVI, col. 369.

283 'It seems to me to be a pity': Ibid.

284 'a northern coastal town': D. Bilton and M. Mann, *Hull at War, 1939–45: the Air Raids* (2019), p. 12.

284 the most heavily bombed: Figures in ibid.; also M. Ulyatt et al., *There is a War on You Know: Life in the Sculcoates Area of Hull through the Eyes of Children During the Second World War* (2011); Hull History Centre, 'Discovering Second World War Records' (2021): https://www.hullhistorycentre.org.uk/research/research-guides/PDF/discovering-second-world-war-records-at-the-hull-history-centre.pdf

284 'In Cleveland Street': D. Bilton and M. Mann, *Hull at War*, p. 10.

284 'I learned to plough': G. J. Robb, ms. letter to Rev. Malcolm Ramsay, Pitlochry, 3 August 1999.

286 The submarine commander: E. Davidson, *The Trial of the Germans: An Account of the Twenty-Two Defendants Before the International Military Tribunal at Nuremberg* (1997), p. 381.

286 'the queue system': J. K. Jerome, *My Life and Times*, p. 56.

31. This Happy Breed

288 relaxed their colour bar: F. Houghton, '"Alien Seamen" or "Imperial Family"? Race, Belonging and British Sailors of Colour in the Royal Navy, 1939–47', *The English Historical Review*, CXXXVII, 588 (2022), pp. 1429–61.

289 'One of those phrases': L. Mayblin, 'Imagining Asylum, Governing Asylum Seekers', *Migration Studies*, VII (2019), 1, pp. 1–20; also L. Mayblin, 'On the Frontline: A Long and Welcoming Tradition?', *Discover Society*, 1 May 2018: https://archive.discoversociety.org/2018/05/01/on-the-frontline-a-long-and-welcoming-tradition/

289 Polish Resettlement Act: E. Kaczmarska, 'The Displacement of Poles and Their Subsequent Resettlement', National Archives, 17 June 2020: https://blog.nationalarchives.gov.uk/the-displacement-of-poles-and-their-subsequent-resettlement-in-the-united-kingdom-1939–1949/

289 in 1938, the Home Secretary: L. Mayblin, 'On the Frontline'. Samuel Hoare's remarks are quoted in 'Anti-Semitic Danger: Hint of "Evil Movement"', *The Times*, 22 November 1938, p. 9.

289 'Undesirable Chinese seamen': D. Hancox, 'The Secret Deportations: How Britain Betrayed the Chinese Men who Served the Country in the War', *The Guardian*, 25 May 2021.

290 '100 Chinese seamen': Ibid.

291 'evasive and non-committal': *The Times*, 17 June 1968, p. 8.

291 'If we had said "yes"': *The Times*, 9 March 1968, p. 8.

291 the Southall garage: *The Times*, 3 July 1968, p. 4.

291 a speech in Birmingham: 'Enoch Powell's "Rivers of Blood" Speech' (20 April 1968): full text in https://anth1001.wordpress.com/wp-content/uploads/2014/04/enoch-powell_speech.pdf

291 'a rocket' of a speech: Powell to Clement Jones of the *Wolverhampton Express and Star*, reported by his son, Nicholas Jones, in 'Enoch Powell: A Personal Insight', *The Political Quarterly*, LXXXIX, 3 (2018), pp. 358–61.

292 accused the 'elitist' BBC: O. Esteves, 'Stigmatising the BBC in Letters of Support to Enoch Powell (1968)', *Mémoire(s), identité(s), marginalité(s) dans le monde occidental contemporain*, 27 (2022).

292 Watching television: A Marwick, *British Society Since 1945* (1990), p. 246 (viewing figures).

292 the most popular leisure activity: G. Edwards, *A History of Sport on Commercial Television, 1955–1992* (2023), p. 117.

292 a young woman from Jamaica: E. Jones, 'Barbara Blake-Hannah: How Britain's First Black Female TV Reporter Was Forced Off Our Screens', *The Guardian*, 7 January 2021.

292 In South London: Hanif Kureishi, 'Knock, Knock, it's Enoch', *The Guardian*, 12 December 2014.

292 The new Race Relations Bill: Race Relations Act [25 October] 1968, I, 1 (1); I, 7 (2); and 8 (2): https://www.legislation.gov.uk/ukpga/1968/71/enacted

293 By 1980, less than one-eighth: Brierley Consultancy, *UK Church Statistics No 3* (2018).

293 American accents: 'Supermarionettes Big Export Earners for Britain: Rocketry in a Children's World', *The Times*, 14 February 1966, p. 5.

294 'Mankind': Dorothy A. Bennett, *New Golden Encyclopedia* (1964), p. 95.

295 '. . . the old Brit'n too diplomatic': S. Selvon, *The Lonely Londoners* (1956; 2006), p. 2.

295 'In America you see a sign': Ibid., p. 21.

295 'The Englishe race': *Oxford English Dictionary*, 'Race', I.1.b.

296 'a persecuted minority': 'Enoch Powell's "Rivers of Blood" Speech', p. 4.

296 constables who were there: E.g. E. Pilkington, *Beyond the Mother Country: West Indians and the Notting Hill White Riots* (1988), p. 6.

296 'You'd really like [the culprit]': *Sapphire*, dir. Basil Dearden (1959), 62–3'.

298 St Pauls district of Bristol: On the 'race riot': A. Marwick, *British Society Since 1945*, p. 221.

298 fire-gutted house: A. Andrews, 'Truth, Justice and Expertise in 1980s Britain: the Cultural Politics of the New Cross Massacre', *History Workshop Journal*, XCI, 1 (2021), pp. 182–209.

299 'an I wish I ad been dere': Linton Kwesi Johnson, 'Di Great Insohreckshan', in *Selected Poems* (2006; 2022), pt II.

299 'institutionally racist': A summary of reports and reviews in House of Commons Library, 'Metropolitan Police Investigation into the Murder of Stephen Lawrence' (2023): https://commonslibrary.parliament.uk/research-briefings/cdp-2023–0160/

299 'a really hostile environment': J. Kirkup and R. Winnett, 'Theresa May Interview', *Daily Telegraph*, 25 May 2012.

299 'We can deport first': 'Speech by Home Secretary on Second Reading of Immigration Bill', 22 October 2013: https://www.gov.uk/government/speeches/speech-by-home-secretary-on-second-reading-of-immigration-bill

300 the landing cards: A. Boyd et al., 'The Destruction of the "Windrush" Disembarkation Cards: A Lost Opportunity' (2018): https://wellcomeopenresearch.org/articles/3–112

300 Government had not invited them: H. Saroukhani, 'Unravelling the Windrush Myth', 21 June 2023: https://www.durham.ac.uk/departments/academic/english-studies/news/unravelling-the-windrush-myth-the-confidential-government-communications-that-reveal-authorities-did-not-want-caribbean-migrants-to-come-to-britain/

300 'They won't last one winter': A. Creech Jones, quoted in 'What They Said', *The Times*, 2 May 1998, p. 19.

300 'I have asked the Prime Minister': 'Forced Repatriation of Chinese Seamen from Liverpool After World War Two', 21 July 2021: Hansard, DCXCIX, col. 1104.

32. 'Exceptional Hardship'

303 'If anybody asked': J. Cooper Clarke, *I Wanna Be Yours* (2020), p. 218.

304 Peter Mandelson: 'Lord Mandelson: Lord Speaker's Corner . . . Peter Mandelson . . . speaks to Lord McFall of Alcluith about his life in politics', 5 March 2024: https://www.parliament.uk/business/lords/house-of-lords-podcast/lord-mandelson-lord-speakers-corner/

304 the institution's 'esprit de corps': W. Hazlitt, *Table-Talk* (1821), II, essay 11: 'On Corporate Bodies'.

304 'instruments of delusion': *The Works of Jeremy Bentham*, ed. J. Bowring (1893), IX, 76.

305 'the most refractory novice': W. Hazlitt, 'On Corporate Bodies'.

305 1945 general election: On the voting figures: A. Marwick, *British Society Since 1945*, pp. 7–12.

305 'Echoes would reverberate': 'Health Service Complaints: Mr. Bevan's Forecast', *The Times*, 13 March 1948, p. 3.

306 'Fairness . . . is an argument of the Left': Liz Truss, interviewed by Beth Rigby in the Empire State Building, Sky News, 20 September 2022.

306 One example cited in Parliament: By Lord Barclay: https://hansard.

parliament.uk/lords/2021–12–13/debates/64939BD6-D16D-41BE-A564–398DCEA02BA3/PoliceCrimeSentencingAndCourtsBill

306 'weaned', as Hazlitt put it: W. Hazlitt, 'On Corporate Bodies'.

308 Paralympic medallist: M. Brown, 'Ade Adepitan', *tes magazine*, 18 February 2005: https://www.tes.com/magazine/archive/ade-adepitan

308 the England footballer: S. Astaire, *Sol Campbell* (2014), p. 16.

308 'ignore the troublemakers': Ibid., p. 18.

309 Imran Khan the lawyer: I. Burrell, 'They Said I Was Dirty', *The Independent*, 28 June 1999 (on Legal Personality of the Year Award).

33. Secrets

311 only fourteen cases: Public Health Laboratory Service Communicable Disease Surveillance Centre, 'Surveillance of the Acquired Immune Deficiency Syndrome in the United Kingdom, January 1982 – July 1983', *British Medical Journal*, 287 (1983), pp. 407–8.

311 'Of course, it cannot be': J. Bronowski, *The Ascent of Man* (1973; 2011), p. 91. In the original: 'the relation of discovery that exists between man and nature'.

313 Even alluding to the Official Secrets Act: N. Davies, *The Isles: A History* (1999; 2000), p. 790.

313 The Queen may have been told privately: Blunt's confession was made public and the Queen was formally told in 1979: C. Davies, 'MI5 files suggest Queen was not briefed', *The Guardian*, 14 January 2025.

315 Arthur Spencer: R. Sandison, *A Century of Psychiatry, Psychotherapy and Group Analysis* (2001), pp. 30–31; M. Gallagher, 'Situating Sandison and Spencer' (Worcester Medical Museums, 2020): https://medicalmuseum.org.uk/newsletters/2020/9/24/situating-sandison-and-spencer-the-social-revolution-at-powick-as-prelude-to-the-pharmacological-turn-guest-blog-by-dr-mark-gallagher; M. Spencer, 'Dr Arthur Morgan Spencer', Royal Society of Medicine, Virtual Wall of Honour: https://www.rsm.ac.uk/media/5479236/virtual-wall-of-honour-panel-19–20.pdf

316 'World in Action' documentary: Granada Television, May 1968, Charlie Nairn (producer), Vanya Kewley (investigator), Richard Martin (reporter): https://www.asylumprojects.org/index.php?title=Powick_Hospital

319 '[Fotherington-Tomas] is goalie': G. Willans and R. Searle, *Down with Skool!* (1953), ch. 1.

321 'My mum used to send them to me': Reviews of Croome Court exhibition: *Daily Telegraph*, 15 December 2018; *The Guardian*, 15 March 2019; *The Tablet*, 24 November 2018.

321 'I got this penny': Ibid.

321 'the Karate Nun': IICSA Inquiry (Independent Inquiry into Child Sexual Abuse) – Birmingham Investigation, 12 November 2018: https://webarchive.nationalarchives.gov.uk/ukgwa/20221215004711/https://www.iicsa.org.uk/key-documents/7584/view/public-hearing-transcript-12-november-2018.pdf; see p. 101, l. 8.

321 his 'star man': Ibid., 13 November 2018, p. 84, l. 4.

322 'reputational damage': Ibid., 12 November 2018, p. 73, l. 21 and p. 90, l. 3.

322 redacted from council reports: A. Clwyd, 'Insurance Companies: Child Abuse Inquiries', 16 July 2015: Hansard, DXCVIII, col. 1191. E.g. T. Kelsey, 'Abuse Claims: "Disruptive" Boy was Being Raped by Older Pupils', *The Independent*, 7 August 1994.

322 'jam-jar glasses': Ibid., 13 November 2018, p. 45, l. 17.

322 'without admission of liability': 'Church Settles Tolkien Abuse Claim', BBC News, 20 July 2003.

323 'It's very difficult to judge': IICSA, *The Roman Catholic Church, Case Study: Archdiocese of Birmingham Investigation Report* (June 2019), p. 36, no. 40; 'Cardinal Nichols at the Independent Inquiry into Child Sexual Abuse', 20 June 2019: https://marklambert.blogspot.com/2019/06/cardinal-nichols-at-independent-inquiry.html

323 one-tenth of the British population: From the National Crime Agency's National Strategic Assessment, 2023 (one in six girls and one in twenty boys sexually abused).

34. Accidental Journey

325 Elizabethan ballad: M. Drayton, 'To The Cambro-Britans and their Harpe, his Ballad of Agincourt', in *Poems* (1619), p. 305.

325 'Your travel customer': 'International COVID Pass Verifier app user guide' (12 May 2022): https://transform.england.nhs.uk/covid-19-response/nhs-covid-pass-verifier-app/international-covid-pass-verifier-app-user-guide/#Booster

326 Milton Abbas: E.g. T. Rowley, *Villages in the Landscape*, p. 136.

328 lied to Parliament: E.g. P. Oborne, *The Assault on Truth: Boris Johnson, Donald Trump and the Emergence of a New Moral Barbarism* (2021).

328 most likely to have voted to leave: M. Goodwin and O. Heath, 'Brexit Vote Explained: Poverty, Low Skills and Lack of Opportunities', 31 August 2016 (based on research by the Joseph Rowntree Foundation): https://www.jrf.org.uk/political-mindsets/brexit-vote-explained-poverty-low-skills-and-lack-of-opportunities

328 'deprived neighbourhoods': Ministry of Housing, Communities and Local Government, The English Indices of Deprivation 2019: see map 1 in https://assets.publishing.service.gov.uk/media/5d8e26f6ed915d5570c6cc55/IoD2019_Statistical_Release.pdf

329 'there was never any lockdown': J. J. Charlesworth on Twitter (X), 14 October 2020.

329 the 'welcome packs': *Daily Mail*, 20 July 2014; *The Independent*, *The Telegraph*, 21 July 2014; *The Times*, 22 July 2014; etc.

329 'the mooste meschief': *The Vision of Piers Plowman*, Prologue, v. 215.

330 The expenses scandal . . . floating duck island: E.g. 'News Coverage of the British Parliamentary Expenses Scandal', in P. Bull and M. Waddle, *The Psychology of Political Communication: Politicians Under the Microscope* (2023).

330 Elon Musk: K. Chan, 'Musk's X is the biggest purveyor of disinformation, EU official says', Associated Press, 26 September 2023: https://apnews.com/article/disinformation-musk-x-twitter-european-union-9f7823726f812bb357ee4225b884354f

330 a rogues gallery: C. Bryant, *Code of Conduct* (2023; 2024), pp. 26–7 ('MPs sanctioned in the 2019 parliament').

330 Christopher Atkinson: M. Knights, '"Old Corruption" Revived? Lessons from the Past', 30 June 2021: https://www.historyandpolicy.org/policy-papers/papers/old-corruption-revived-lessons-from-the-past

330 two former prime ministers: M. Jackson, 'Ex-PM John Major: Government Handling of Paterson Case Shameful', BBC News, 6 November 2021: https://www.bbc.co.uk/news/uk-59188972 ('the Johnson administration was "politically corrupt"'); S. Bright, 'Gordon Brown: Government Most Corrupt in "at least a century"', *Byline Times*, 6 December 2022: https://bylinetimes.com/2022/12/06/gordon-brown-government-most-corrupt-in-at-least-a-century/

331 a 'playbook' leaked: D. West, 'DHSC "Playbook" Orders Trusts to

Describe Big Building Projects as "New Hospitals"', *HSJ*, 26 August 2021.

331 'attacks on the legitimacy of Parliament itself': House of Commons Committee of Privileges, *Matter Referred on 21 April 2022: Co-ordinated Campaign of Interference in the Work of the Privileges Committee*, 29 June 2023, p. 6 (no. 16).

332 powerful sonic weapons: 'Why it's Not the Royal Navy's Job to Stop Migrant Boats', *Navy Lookout*, 18 August 2023: https://www.navylookout.com/why-its-not-the-royal-navys-job-to-stop-migrant-boats/

332 'sixty million pounds': D. Sabbagh, 'Boris Johnson Under Fire Over Remarks About Child Abuse Inquiries', *The Guardian*, 13 March 2019; also *Belfast Telegraph*, 13 March 2019; etc.

332 'the green crap': 'A senior Tory source' quoted on 21 November 2013 in *The Sun*, p. 1, and *Daily Mail*, p. 2; also A. Sparrow, 'Did David Cameron Tell Aides to "Get rid of all the green crap"?', *The Guardian*, 21 November 2013.

333 'France, UK in Diplomatic Stink', France24, 26 August 2022 (from Reuters).

333 'You are a philosopher': J. Boswell, *The Life of Samuel Johnson*, II, 235.

334 'crayfish souls': V. Hugo, *Les Misérables* (1862), I, IV, 2.

335 The city of Bradford: See S. Maconie, *The Full English* (2023), p. 160.

335 'null and void of all validity': Bull of Pope Innocent III: British Library, Cotton MS Cleopatra E I, ff. 155–6.

336 'neither worried nor unworried': Based on data from the Opinions and Lifestyle Survey collected between 14 September and 9 October 2022: https://www.ons.gov.uk/peoplepopulationandcommunity/wellbeing/articles/worriesaboutclimatechangegreatbritain/septembertooctober2022

337 'We are using up our resources': *Papers and Correspondence of William Stanley Jevons*, ed. R. Collison (1972), cited in A. Briggs, *Victorian Things*, rev. ed. (1990), p. 303.

General Index

Geographical Index

The shire names in parentheses are those of the historic counties.

Acknowledgements

The first intrepid readers of this book were, in chronological order: Margaret and Alison Robb, Natasha Fairweather and Melanie Jackson, my editors, Andrea Henry and Starling Lawrence, the infallible Nicholas Blake and the incomparable Camilla Elworthy. I am grateful to them all, as I am to Mary Mount, Lindsay Nash, Lewis Russell and Stuart Wilson at Picador, to Nneoma Amadiobi at Norton and Ivy Pottinger-Glass at Rogers, Coleridge & White. Dear friends past, present and within, named or unnamed, are or were, in order of acquaintance: Simon Phillips, Gerald Sgroi, S. D. Edwards, Paul Webb, Steve Blackburn, David Fawbert, Fiona Webb, Henry Johnson, John Harris, Jim Hiddleston, Stephen Roberts and Gill Coleridge.

Graham Robb was born in Manchester in 1958 and is a former fellow of Exeter College, Oxford. He has published widely on French literature and history. His book *The Discovery of France* won both the Duff Cooper and Royal Society of Literature Ondaatje Prizes. For *Parisians* the City of Paris awarded him the Grande Médaille de la Ville de Paris. He lives on the English–Scottish border.

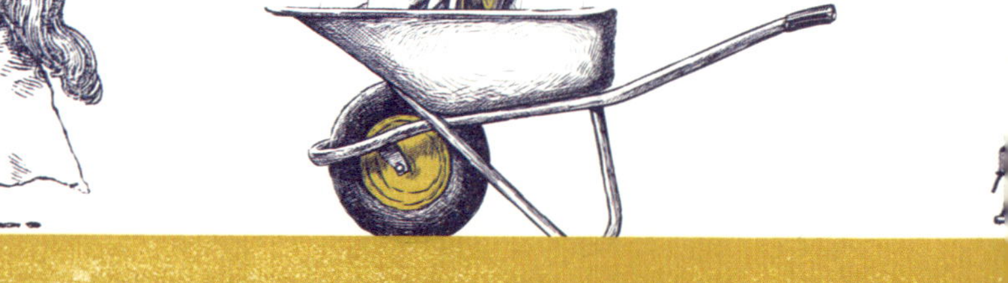